Cyber Gold:
A Guidebook on How to Start Your Own Home Based Internet Business, Build an E-Commerce Website, & Strategies for Complete Search Engine Optimization
2nd Edition

★★★★★ A Great Contribution - Read this book first, August 25, 2007
By Dr. Edward B Nuhfer "Ed in Camarillo"

It is difficult to watch television or even to drive around in one's hometown without finding an advertisement enticing the reader to get rich through using her or his computer. Most such efforts are about making the scam artists rich at the expense of the gullible. The victims targeted are motivated people, especially those living in small towns with sparse opportunities. Despite scammers' traps, the Internet truly enables one to remain in such a small town and expand opportunities to make a decent livelihood well beyond those available locally. The authors offer genuine opportunity. They have credibility because they have created their own opportunity in just such a town with sparse resources. Instead of a get-rich quick scheme, these authors offer a very reflective approach through a book that conveys honestly that there is much to know and that maintaining a successful E-commerce business is hard work. However, if seeking a book written to lead the reader by the hand to success, this is the one to buy. Authors address both PC and Macintosh equally--a rarity in most reference books, and you don't need the latest-greatest computer to do anything they tell you to do. Cyber Gold... is well written and well illustrated. If the reader has difficulty understanding the text, there's a picture; if picture and text fail to convey meaning, there's an example. This is a surprisingly fine reference for a person who is a consumer at E-commerce sites too. Knowing how to tell a secure site from an insecure or scam site by its URL is certainly good information for a consumer. Another audience could simply be those who build their own web sites, even if these are not E-Commerce sites. I've purchased books on building web sites such as DreamWeaver for Dummies, and the skills and knowledge are not nearly so clearly presented there as in this resource. This book doesn't present the information in the stuffy style of most references. Instead, the reader feels like he/she is just having a chat with the authors and learning the information through a prose that is genuinely friendly. The publisher of the "...for Dummies" series should hire the authors of Cyber Gold... to rewrite some of their texts. As soon as I cracked open this book, I went to the chapter on meta-tags and immediately improved my own web pages. Not only can readers get a good book, but also it appears from the Amazon pages that readers can take a course from the authors through an accredited university. This is a class act skillfully executed. If the authors put their course online, it will be huge--they may have to attend to that more than the business that they created. Although copyrights are addressed, trademarks are not. I would like to see the procedure for obtaining trademarks added to a future edition.

(Amazon.com Editorial Review)

Cyber Gold:
A Guidebook on How to Start Your Own Home Based Internet Business, Build an E-Commerce Website, & Strategies for Complete Search Engine Optimization
2nd Edition

Pam Mosbrucker & Tobin Alder

Word Partners Ink
http://www.wordpartnersink.com

Copyright © 2008 Word Partners Ink. All Rights Reserved.

"Cyber Gold: A Guidebook on How to Start Your Own Home Based Internet Business, Build an E-Commerce Website, & Strategies for Complete Search Engine Optimization," 2nd Edition written by Pam Mosbrucker and Tobin Alder, Word Partners Ink. Cover design, book layout, and editing by Word Partners Ink.

No part of this publication may be reproduced, stored in a retrieval system, or transmitted, in any form or by any means (electronic, mechanical, photocopy, recording, or otherwise) without prior written permission from Word Partners Ink, except by a reviewer, who may quote brief passages in a review. This publication is designed to provide accurate and authoritative information with regard to the subject matter covered. It is offered with the understanding that Word Partners Ink is not engaged in rendering legal, accounting, or other such advice. Given the changing nature of the subject matter and the internet, information provided in this manual may become out of date.

ISBN: 978-0-615-18107-3

Dedications.

This book is dedicated to all aspiring entrepreneurs and
those willing to never give up on their dreams and the pursuit of happiness.

We'd like to thank Dr. Ed Nuhfer for believing in us, his guidance, and
for leading us to the opportunity that allowed us to begin teaching
this as a course for students everywhere.

We'd also like to thank Stacey Cochran for having us on his show and giving us
an incredible opportunity. And for taking "Cyber Gold," applying its methods,
and proving to the world that our strategies are sound and that they work.
Thank you.

ACKNOWLEDGMENTS:

This guide is crammed with the business names and products of many online presences including Tripod, PayPal, Rip Off Report, and numerous others.

Though we are not directly affiliated with all of them, we chose to recommend and discuss their products and services in this guide because we have found them to be the best in what we needed to accomplish in our business ventures. Tripod, especially, deserves our greatest gratitude; for being the only webpage creation tool on the internet that allows near-complete freedom and an ease of use unparalleled by similar sites and programs.

Table of Contents.

Notes on the Second Edition……………………………………………………..9

Forward……..…………………………………………………………….....10

Intro……………..………………………………………..……………….....14

Part One: Beginning Your Business…………………………………….**17**

In This Part………….…………………………………………..………….18

Chapter One: Getting Started……………………………………….....19

Chapter Two: Steps To Success…………………………………….....42

Chapter Three: Your Business Identity……………………………………..63

Part Two: Building Your Website……………………………………….**77**

In This Part…………………………………………………………….…78

Chapter Four: Beginning Your Site…………………………………….....79

Chapter Five: Building Your Site Shell……………………………….…..102

Chapter Six: Advanced Building & Editing……………………………….....136

Chapter Seven: Getting Around Your Account………………………….....164

Part Three: Optimizing, Selling, & HTML……………………………**183**

In This Part…………………………………..…………………….….184

Chapter Eight: Required Site Elements………………………………….185

Chapter Nine: Niche Marketing, Drop Shipping, & PayPal……………...…213
Niche Marketing…………………………………………………….....213
Drop Shipping………………………………………………………...217
Adding Inventory To Your Site…………………………………………...224

Table of Contents.

Chapter Nine Cont.
PayPal……………………………………………………………………………236

Chapter Ten: Meta Tags (Keywords) Explained……………………………258
Finding Your Keywords……………………………………………………...262
How To Optimize Your Site……………………………………………………272

Chapter Eleven: Search Engines Explained……………………………...288

Chapter Twelve: HTML Primer……………………………………………304

Extras…………………………………………………………………………323

In This Part………………………………………………………………….324
How to Upgrade your Computer: RAM & Video Card……………………325
Final Checklist………………………………………………………………...338
E-Commerce Resources……………………………………………………...339

Word University Course Information…………………………………...342
Testimonials……………………………………………………………………345
Course Certificate……………………………………………………………..347

Appendix.……………………………………………………………………349
Web Addresses………………………………………………………………..349
File Types……………………………………………………………………...351
Checklists/Mistakes…………………………………………………………..352
How to Exercises……………………………………………………………...353

Index…………………………………………………………………………354

About the Authors………………………………………………………...367

Notes on the Second Edition

The first edition was published in May 2007 and was as current as we could make it at the time of its printing. In the last few months of 2007, computers have advanced, websites have changed their entire site structures and corporate images (like PayPal did in November), and even search engine optimization strategies have shifted, incorporating new and exciting methods as well as changing common tactics.

We've been working hard to get every update available into this printing and have included some of our own strategies that we've developed over the last several months as well. This wasn't just a simple re-edit and re-release. It's a complete overhaul of "Cyber Gold," from the first word to the last.

Also, because we teach "Cyber Gold" as the textbook for our course at Idaho State University, and as an online course as well (you can use the certificate at the end of this book to sign up), we've included things in this edition that our students questioned about or wanted more information on. Tidbits, exceptional resources, and checklists are all included. Trust us when we say you're getting some gems here.

Because the interest has been so great, we've also created an online course that you can access at http://www.smallbusinessonlinecollege.org .

There, you'll find everything from a downloadable business plan to our picks for drop shipper directories (meaning ones we *actually* use) and much, much more.

We wish you not only the best of luck, but also success on the internet.

Sincerely,

Pam Mosbrucker & Tobin Alder
Word Partners Ink

January 2008

Forward.

Hello, my name is Tobin Alder and I would like to say a few words beginning with congratulating you on your wise choice to purchase **Cyber Gold!** With this new information you will certainly be spared a few bruises and scraped knees. I know the amount of information may be a little intimidating for some, while others will be excited that there is so much.

In any case, this guide is simple to follow and organized into three parts, making it easy to implement while being respectful of your time. You can literally take this manual and put your business into motion today! Plus, each part is well organized and, in the future, may be studied individually.

Unlike my brilliant co-author, I grew up in the 80's when VCR's came about. I can still remember my dad and step-grandfather discussing the new VCR and its operation. I could operate one quite well and never gave it much thought (it seemed natural to me. Just put the tape in and push "play"...what was so hard with that?). However, the thing I remember now, and can relate to, is that my step-grandfather didn't even *care* that he didn't know.

Nowadays, I see that same attitude in the adults of my generation. They don't know how computers work and they really don't care. It's not all their fault; I was the same way. Oh sure, I could check my email and surf a little, but to actually use a computer and create a business and manipulate data...well, that was something else. After all, I've survived without one, and hadn't needed one, and besides, I didn't know how computers worked and I really didn't *care*.

Big mistake!

You may not realize it, but that "little box" of plastic, buzzing electrons, and ones and zeros is pure magic! A *real* money-machine that, when programmed effectively, will create an automated cash flow—straight into <u>your</u> bank account!

-Or-

Effectively reach **billions** with valuable information any instant of any day!

Amazing! Truly, amazing.

Now, I must warn you, (those of my generation), that your attitude towards the little "plastic" beast will be of some importance. Computers each have a personality of their own. Those of us who have ever used Microsoft Word, or any other documenting media, have found this out the hard way (like when Word mysteriously crashes and you've lost two hours of heavenly inspiration, or the sentence that you're typing suddenly and inexplicably jumps two paragraphs above).

In other words, I've come to understand that computers are living entities and have their little whims from time to time. Just be patient with your machine and soon you'll be creating and surfing around the net like a real pro.

Secondly, your business isn't going to take off overnight. I'm talking about once you have your site built, (here I'm talking directly to those headed towards e-commerce), and your entire product line ready, the day you turn it "on" (publish completed site to the net), it won't happen overnight. I hope it does, and I'm not saying that it's impossible, but just that it takes a little time for the search engines to establish your website in their search results (however, your customers can access your site address, i.e., www.whatever.com immediately, making a direct mail campaign very profitable).

Thinking it would happen overnight was one of my early pre-assumptions because everything is instantaneous with the internet and customer potential is virtually unlimited. Nonetheless, this assumption followed me to a point where I had to make an important decision concerning my future.

The choice: An Alaskan summer experiencing the state's awesome splendor by helicopter and providing aircraft maintenance—a great adventure to be sure! Or, stay home and help run our first e-commerce site and work as the snowcat mechanic for the local ski mountain (I am a licensed pilot and FAA A&P aircraft mechanic. And yes, as it happened, the helicopter maintenance job paid more than double comparatively).

Due to my early pre-assumption, I was certain our first "baby" would just take off once we published to the web, keeping us all busy. I had to decide between the two that week and decided to stay, unfortunately "burning a bridge" for future Alaskan adventures.

Regardless, I didn't want to just leave and place all the effort and responsibility on my partner right when everything was ready to go…Well, I made my choice, without <u>any</u> regret, but could have worked the Alaskan summer and have been ok.

Now, looking back, Alaska or no Alaska, I wouldn't trade anything for the experience of that first sale! What a feeling! Creating something from just an idea—and see it manifest and actually work! Incredible!

We had no doubt of course that it would work, but still, when "it" actually happens, it's a proud and inspiring moment. With **Cyber Gold** you'll experience it too!

People, the world has changed. It is now an e-commerce world. With the information in this guide, you can strategically place yourself within this 3.8 *trillion* dollar market!

So be excited! You now have a great "surfboard" to catch this "wave" with—and the waves to come! Don't let this opportunity to change your life go by! Don't place this book on the shelf— read it! I promise, you'll thank me later! You will have such an advantage over "brick and mortar" stores: Extremely low start up and overhead costs, minimal equipment, and distribution power over millions of dollars worth of merchandise you never have to store! Brilliant!

With this material, your building process to producing sales *will be a hundred times easier* for you than it was for us. All you have to do is follow the simple plan, step by step, and build. From City Hall and obtaining business licensing to site registry and product resources, **Cyber Gold** covers it all!

Part One covers beginning your business and getting proper licensing. **Part Two** covers everything you need to know about building your website. **Part Three** covers site optimization, finding and adding inventory, and HTML tips and basics.

Even with the step by step formula, we understand that there may still be questions during your building process. If so, please feel free to visit our Help Forum on http://www.wordpartnersink.com. Remember, you're not alone.

We're here and we're real and most importantly, we've been right were you are now.

In closing, I would like to take this opportunity and thank my brilliant business partner and computer wizard, Pam, for her truly amazing tenacity, positive attitude, and hard work; without whom **Cyber Gold** would not have been published so quickly – if at all (Pam took on the responsibility of putting all this knowledge and information into an organized, readable format). Thank you.

Lastly, remember to work at it a little every day. Like James Brown sings, "if you give out, don't give up; if you give up, don't give out." In other words, keep the ball rolling and soon it will roll all on its own. So, get yourself a comfortable chair, a quality coffee maker, and grind your own. You're about to embark on an exciting, empowering, and most fulfilling adventure!

Blessings and success,

Tobin C. Alder
Word Partners Ink

Fall 2006

Note:

For our 2nd Edition readers, I would like to add something: It's a year later and as you know, the internet is constantly changing and the success of our first book has led us to respond with a 2nd Edition—it has all the valuable knowledge as before, just with this past year's worth of updated information such as computing power and the latest SEO and website strategies, all coupled with our new online course.

We've had an exciting year of newspaper and TV interviews, public speaking, and teaching for our local university's continuing education department. Our greatest joy has been seeing our students take our advice and use it with real results—and they have—time and time again.

With no ego, I can say (at the time of this printing) that you are holding the finest book available on the subject at hand. And yes, kudos to Pam once again, you're the best!

May all we have learned be passed on to you for the success and enrichment of your life for it has surely enriched our lives by witnessing the success of our students.

All the best,

T.C. Alder
Word Partners Ink
January 2008

Change takes effort, effort takes discipline, discipline takes desire, desire takes vision.

--Tobin Alder

Intro.

An estimated 3.8 trillion (yes, *trillion*) dollars will be spent on products purchased over the internet this year alone. And that immeasurable number grows exponentially every year. Eager to get a piece of this ever-growing pie, we decided to start our own ecommerce website, without knowledge of how to get started, or which steps we should be taking when.

As a result, we made mistakes. Some small, some huge.

Actually, most of our problems occurred from a basic lack of knowledge and a general confusion over what to do next. But this won't happen to you! We're here to share those mistakes and concerns so that you don't have to make them too.

You'll probably still make your own mistakes, of course, but your mistakes will only help you grow as a business owner. Mistakes usually bring about a good sort of change. They're just part of the process. But our mistakes were made because we jumped in without knowing what we were after, how to get there, or even what we needed to *know* to get started properly.

We promise to give you at least that much.

MAKING MONEY.

Making money fast is not an easy task, and expecting to make money fast without hard work is foolish. But it isn't impossible.

Many people are under the assumption that the "entrepreneurs" on the commercials and in the mass-flyers and emails are getting rich overnight with virtually no work involved. Despite the obvious contradiction in that, it doesn't take a skilled professional, or a get-rich scheme to start a successful internet business.

In fact, most of the multi-millionaires were just getting started themselves—most without a college degree or any experience using the internet.

So, this guide is to encourage you to do something for your life, something that you'll have total control over, and only profit from in the end—from start to finish.

THE STATISTICS.

In early 2006, the number of internet users topped more than one billion. Not million. *Billion*. How many people is one billion people? If you count at one number per second (not taking any breaks, ever), it would take you more than *thirty-one* years to finally reach one billion.

The Census Bureau has been crunching the numbers and they estimate that the second billion will be reached before 2016, the number growing at an annual rate of approximately 18 percent.

Want to know how world wide the internet truly is? Only 23% of all internet users reside in North America, putting 24% in Europe and 36% in Asia. Before 2016 (even though the US drops enough cash to account for more than a third of all ecommerce), North Americans will only account for 15% of all internet users.

If you've been paying attention to these statistics, you'll have realized that the largest market for ecommerce lies *outside* the United States. What does that mean for you and your website?

Simply offer international shipping on all orders and poof, international ecommerce!

THE INTERNET, YOU & SUCCESS.

The internet as we know it didn't even exist just five years ago, and it certainly didn't have the power and promise for small businesses that it does now ten years ago. That's why it's so important to get in now, while things are looking good for websites.

With the internet, the only true limitation is yourself. How much are you willing to learn? How much time are you willing to dedicate?

How much do you want to *change* your life?

We're going to let you in on a little secret. The internet is like a big pond. Only two percent of the fish in the pond really even know how to swim. The others are only there because they knew they needed to be in the pond, but they didn't give it any more thought than that.

To put this stretched out metaphor simply, nearly every website on the internet (okay, 98% of them) have no idea what they are doing and have only ranked as well as they have because no one else knows what they are doing either.

The internet is just like anything else. To succeed, to do well, you have to put in the time and effort, and you have to learn the rules to use them and make them work for you. You have to know the rules (in anything) to break them.

All of this probably sounds crazy.

You're just starting out, and you may not even really understand the internet ranking system yet. Or the power of positive PR. Or that PR stands for Page Rank and has nothing to do with your rank in the search engines. But not to fear.

We're here to teach you how to build a fantastic website, all on your own. We'll teach you what to do and what not to do. We'll teach you how to do things right the first time.

And we'll even teach you a few tips and tricks that will put you in the pond and have you swimming with the top 2%. Because you deserve to be there.

Starting your own website is, after all, about success. Your success.

So, hunker down, caffeinate, and prepare to educate yourself. After which, you will be able to tell your friends and family that you now know how to create a website, and you could even go so far as to tell them that you're a *web designer*.

Oh, and above all else, be proud of yourself for taking this step and deciding to learn something new that will only benefit you in the future. You've just changed your life for the better.

Congrats, fellow web designer, and good luck!

Part One: Beginning Your Business.

An investment in knowledge always pays the best interest.

--Benjamin Franklin

In this part...

Beginning your business is not as difficult as it may sound, especially if you're armed with a bit of information to get you started on the right path. We spent much of the past three years, or so, just trying to figure out which steps must be completed next for our business to flourish.

Luckily, all you have to do is follow our step by step layout and you'll have few difficulties getting the basics of your business down.

In Part One you'll learn:

Chapter One: Getting Started
- Everything you need to know about buying a computer, 20-23
- Safety on the internet, and why we use Internet Explorer, 24-30
- How to save a picture to your computer, 32-38
- How to care for your computer, 38-41

Chapter Two: Steps To Success
- Ten steps to success, 43-52
- Eight mistakes to avoid, 52-60
- The least you need to know about scams, 60-62

Chapter Three: Your Business Identity
- How to create a business identity and name, 63-70
- How to choose colors for your website, 70-72
- How to create a logo for your business, 72-74
- How to create a business plan, 75

Chapter One
Getting Started.

This chapter is the basic "what you need to know to get started" sort of deal. We know that people with a variety of experience levels will read this guide, and to all of you, we hope the best and hope that you find what you're looking for.

For those of you who already have a good computer and decent access to the internet, though, you can probably just skip ahead to Chapter Two (providing you already use Internet Explorer and have turned off the tabs) because we'd hate to bore you when we know this guide has great pearls for even the experienced web designer.

If you do not yet have a computer, or are not confident in your computer abilities, read ahead, dear friend, and congratulate yourself for taking the time and effort to learn something new.

OUR FOOLISH ASSUMPTIONS.

We aren't stupid. We know that many of you know how to use the internet, probably already have a computer, and may only need a little help tweaking your site for the long run. Perhaps some of you are even doing well on the internet and just want to know a bit more about running a successful internet business. But some of you, probably most of you, need help with the basics. You've come to the right place.

We're going to teach you how to start an internet business from *start to finish*.

That means that we want to get you set up with the right computer, we want you to know how to use it, and we want to introduce you fully, and with complete understanding, to the world of internet ecommerce.

We're going to teach you how to build your own site. We'll teach you how to get your inventory onto your site properly, and we'll even teach you what you need to know about search engine marketing and how to do it all without hiring an SEO (search engine optimization) expert.

So, for those of you who know what you're doing, hang in there. We still have some real gems to offer because we've been there, we've made the mistakes, and we've learned and profited from them. And we know that you wouldn't be reading this right now if you didn't hope to find some inspiration, some truth, or at least some missing piece about proper keyword targeting.

Keep an open mind, and you'll find what you're looking for.

And, for those of you who picked up this guide because you want to learn how to build your own site, absorb it all without fear.

Right now your choice to take charge of your life will involve some hard work because you're learning new things. Any feelings of being lost or confused will be put to rest as we demystify everything and leave you with the knowledge and skills to build your own website and start your own successful internet business *without* being dependent on expensive experts.

WHY YOU <u>MUST</u> HAVE A COMPUTER.

You *cannot* have an internet business without a good computer. You *can* learn the internet using a computer at the library, and you can probably even start a decent website, but unless you have the means in your own home to build on, you'll never get your business off the ground. Trust us.

So, get a good computer. It doesn't have to cost a fortune, and it doesn't even really have to have DSL, but you must have a good machine to do business on the internet, especially if you're hoping for any sort of success.

HOW TO GET THE RIGHT COMPUTER[1].

We put together a little guide to help you pick out the right computer for your business. First of all, we know that some of you are fans of the Mac (Apple) computer. That's fine, but some of the programs that we use and many of the things that we talk about may not work the same on a Mac.

---

[1] If you already have a computer and would instead like to install RAM or a new video card, view the section entitled "How to Upgrade Your Computer" on pages 325-337.

For your sanity, and success on the internet—because it's undeniable that Windows has a monopoly on the internet—just get an IBM.

You'll be shocked by the price point difference, and truly, unless you plan on creating your own citywide newspaper, you'll never find use for most of the programs that run on a Mac.

Plus, with Windows you can play thousands of games!

Now, there is really only one major choice to make when purchasing a computer: Do you want to spend $600 or less, or $600 or more?

When shopping for a computer, you must have the right knowledge in your arsenal to make sure you get the right machine. That basically means that you need to know a bit about memory.

MEMORY

There are two different types of memory: **storage** and **active**.

Most computers now come with at least an 80 GB hard drive, or storage space. This means that you can store up to 80 GB of programs and files on your computer.

Actually, unless you load tons and tons of programs and download thousands of photos or music files, you'll probably never use all 80 GB. Most computers now are also "up-sold" with 120 to 320 GB hard drives. You'll probably never use that much memory, either. So don't worry much about it. As long as you get around 80 to 100 GB of memory, you'll be set up for a long time.

The type of memory that concerns you is the **RAM** (random access memory), the active memory, often referred to as SD-RAM, or some variant. This number needs to be understood by you because it will give you an idea of how *fast* your machine is going to be. Below are RAM speeds currently available (unless you work for NASA) at the time of this printing.

512 RAM now is the basic starting point for any decent machine. If the computer has less than this—move on, or be prepared to upgrade immediately because it won't be able to run many programs at all. If you have 512 RAM, you'll be able to run most things, and be able to have a few open programs at once with minimal drag.

1GB RAM will do most anything required and is the smallest amount of RAM that you *must* get if you plan on buying a laptop. Most desktops will be okay with 512, but a laptop will seem sluggish and you'll find yourself disappointed with the speed. 1GB RAM will allow you to run quite a few programs at once, and you'll probably feel comfortable with the speed.

2 GB or more will make your computer seem like it's alive. You'll be able to run numerous programs at once and the ones that used to run fairly fast will now seem lightning fast. You'll actually be able to watch videos and play games without drama and skipping. The newest computers, the ones coming out now (Fall 2007), with Windows Vista, will have at least 2 GB to be able to handle the new and improved version of Windows. If you get Vista, make sure to get at least 2 GB just so you won't encounter any stability or performance issues.

So, the least you need to know about buying a computer is how much RAM comes with it. 512 will set you up to do basic things, 1GB will make your life easier, and 2 GB will make computing super fast and set you up for a time without needing to upgrade.

Oh, and if your new computer doesn't come with **Windows XP version 2**, or the new **Vista**, move on. Windows XP is required for most of the new printers and digital cameras and is the only operating system that will keep you current (if you don't want to buy a new machine in a year).

You can get a very nice desktop for about $700 bucks at any local retailer or online (like at Dell or HP). A nice laptop will set you back $900 or more.

Everything portrayed in the list below is up to date and current for desktops and may be used to build your website and business. Keep in mind that computers change. All you're getting is more memory or a bigger hard drive.

Business is business and it doesn't change—it only gets more efficient.

$700 OR LESS

A computer in this category generally has:
Intel Core 2 Duo Processor at 2.0 GHz / 800 MHz FSB
Windows XP Home, Version 2 (Windows XP Professional, or Vista)
Up to 2 GB RAM
80 GB Hard Drive
DVD-RW Combo Drive (to burn and play movies and CD's)
20 inch flat panel monitor

$700 OR MORE

A computer in this category has everything in the above category, but with more bells and whistles.

You'll get:
Intel Core 2 Duo Processor at 3.8 GHz / 800 MHz FSB
Up to 4 GB RAM
320 GB Hard Drive
DVD-RW Combo Drive (to burn and play movies and CD's)
20 inch flat panel widescreen monitor

Some of you might prefer a laptop to a desktop computer. That's fine, but expect to pay about $300 more for the same things you would get in a desktop simply because of its portability and battery needs.

Plan to negotiate a bit if you can, and get more RAM or processor speed with a smaller hard drive for the same price (some of the retailers will let you do this, like Dell.com). That way, your machine will be as fast as it can be for the least amount of money and you won't be spending extra on hard drive space that you'll literally never use.

A great computer can usually cost less than $700 bucks (we've seen some with the same options for less than $500—you need to shop around, we're just giving you estimates). It's not like it was even five years ago when computers were selling in the thousands. If you buy a computer for more than a couple thousand dollars these days, it will be the highest end laptop on the market and probably come with so much memory and speed that even the hardest hard-core gamer would find it difficult to use it to capacity (but they would certainly try).

So, get what you think you can afford. We began all of our sites on a little Pentium II with 2.8 GHz and only 256 MB of RAM that cost us $385 (plus shipping) on Dell.com. While we found many reasons to upgrade, none of them had to do with running our business online, and none of them really had to do with necessity.

GETTING ON THE INTERNET.

We understand that some of you may not have DSL available in your area, and to you we offer our heartfelt apologies and deepest sympathies. But to those of you who have access to DSL, if you think that by staying with dial up, you're saving hundreds of dollars a year, you're really only prolonging your agony.

You see, while DSL may cost a couple dollars more a month, it saves an unlimited amount of time and sanity. Trust us, waiting for a hundred photos to load in the picture gallery on dial up is almost a fate worse than death.

Just take the plunge and get DSL, you'll be thanking us later.

SAFETY ON THE INTERNET.

Since you use Windows, your internet browser is probably Internet Explorer (and if it isn't it needs to be for building your website). But before you do anything on the internet, get the free updates:

http://windowsupdate.microsoft.com
http://www.microsoft.com/windows/ie/downloads/default.mspx

By the way, never install anything for your computer that claims it can improve your internet or operating system performance unless it is from Microsoft themselves. There are programs out there that can be harmful to your computer, and once they are installed, will ruin things forever.

While downloads and updates are part of owning a computer, you must first protect yourself, and inform yourself on what your machine needs, and what may be harmful to it.

So, before you download, check things out. If you know the program creator, like Maxis (for games) or Norton (for virus protection), or Adobe (for reading pdf files), then you're safe downloading things from them.

But if you find a website offering free downloads of the latest Windows something or other, and it isn't Windows or Microsoft, you're better off without it. Trust us.

SECURITY FEATURES.

Security on the internet can be tricky to understand at first, especially when you don't know what to look for.

Never enter your personal information into a form without first understanding how Internet Explorer's security features work.

We buy online all the time, and we aren't afraid to enter our credit card information into an online form because we know when it is *secure*. If the form isn't secure, we move on without giving up our information.

Oh, and just spend the bucks to get quality virus protection. We recommend Defender Pro above all the rest because they are cheap (like $19 bucks) and they have proven much less of a hassle than any of the others.

FIRST, A FEW THINGS:

Your browser security settings are your first line of defense in stopping the theft or unwanted viewing of your personal information.

The most popular browsers: Internet Explorer, Netscape, and FireFox offer you the ability to receive an alert or notification when any of the following occur:

- Changing between secure and nonsecure webpages
- Receiving invalid site identification for the site you are about to view
- Sending something over a nonsecure webpage

It's easy to change these settings to fit your purposes.

Simply open up your web browser. Every browser is a bit different, but for all browsers, click on **Tools**, then select **Internet Options**. It will bring up a window:

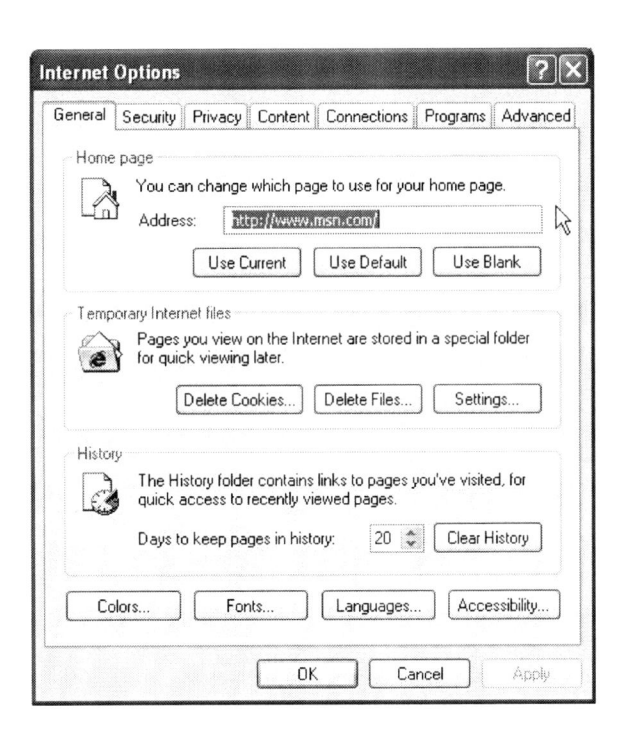

You can go over all of your internet settings on this screen, the most important being the **Security** and **Privacy** tabs. The default settings will get you by, but as you learn more about browsing, you'll find that some settings may annoy you and you'll want to change them.

For example, we deal with many secure sites and it gets tedious clicking the "okay" box that pops up every time we go between secure pages and nonsecure pages. By now, we know the difference, or we'll check to be sure.

When we are uncertain about a site's security, we look for the little **closed lock** icon that appears in the bottom right corner of the browser screen (if you have Internet Explorer 6 or below).

See the little golden lock on the Status Bar? It is next to the little globe and the word "Internet." The red negative sign lets you read about the site's identification, but usually isn't something you'll even worry about.

If the closed lock doesn't appear when you move to a secure page, then that page is *not* secure, even if it might say that it is. However, if the Status Bar isn't present at all at the bottom of your screen, then that's an altogether different matter.

We used to have the Status Bar disappear occasionally with our new laptop. If this is happening to you, click on **View** at the top of your browser and make sure **Status Bar** has a check next to it.

INTERNET EXPLORER 7

We recently updated our system with the new Internet Explorer, Internet Explorer 7, which is a bit different than the Internet Explorer 6 that most everyone has. The main thing to know here when understanding your security is that the gold lock has moved. Now, it will appear at the top of the screen next to the address bar, like so:

In the picture above, note the gold lock next to the refresh button (the green arrows) and the cancel button (the red x). This is the way the new Internet

Explorer is set up, so depending on which version you have, make sure you know where to find the little gold security lock to protect yourself.

Actually, make sure that you always see the little lock and it is in the "closed" position if you plan to enter any personal information into a form and you'll be safe. That's what the lock means, that your information is being sent over a secure, encrypted website. Knowing this means that every credit card transaction you make online will be a safe one.

However, not all pages in a site will have that lock unless *every* page needs to be secure. For example, Tripod has secure pages where you enter personal information, but their other pages don't need to be secure because you won't be entering any *sensitive* information on them.

Why?

Having that lock appear on the Status Bar means that the secure site you are visiting has paid some serious cash to protect you, and they have paid some big bucks for *every* page that gets the lock. It also means that they'll have a

https://

instead of the usual…

http://

on the pages that display the lock on the Status Bar. Check for this too.

PayPal is a great example of this because the real PayPal URL is actually: https://www.paypal.com/

If you click on a link to PayPal and the https:// doesn't appear, then you will know that you've made it one of the scam sites that attempt to trick you into giving up your personal information because they *look* like PayPal.

This happens with tons of banks, and really, any website that has a known brand name like PayPal and has a safe reputation with its clients.

Also, for your own safety, never click on a link in your email that claims to be PayPal and will take you to PayPal, **unless that email addresses you by name *and* username**. The same goes with online banking sites and other sites that you know must be secure.

Basically, never click on a link from your email, even if you suspect it might be genuine because 99.9% of the time it will be a scammer trying to steal your information. PayPal will only send you an email if you've made a transaction or personally made changes to your online account, as a receipt. Same with most banks. That's it.

The spammers will collect any and all information they can so that they can sell it to other spammers. This is how identities get stolen.

Be aggressive, and informed, about your online safety and you'll never have a problem with the scammers.

WHY YOU MUST USE INTERNET EXPLORER.

In general, we prefer FireFox, **except** when dealing with Tripod or eBay. In everything else, FireFox seems faster to us and gives us the least amount of problems. However, Netscape and FireFox have a *very* difficult text editor which replaces Tripod's "what you see is what you get (WYSIWYG)" text editor that you'd find in Internet Explorer.

For this reason alone, we suggest building your site with Internet Explorer, even if you use Netscape or FireFox (or any other browser for that matter) to surf the internet with.

Trust us, your life will be *much* easier, and all confusion when it comes to adding text on your site will be completely eliminated!

We often do quite a bit of business on eBay as well as building on Tripod, so we've noticed this text editor issue there too. Basically, FireFox and Netscape make you input HTML in a way that makes it entirely too cumbersome to deal with.

Now, we have a *great* deal of experience with HTML…and even *we* can't enter text in eBay or Tripod using FireFox without screaming.

So, for the easiest possible site building and for your sanity alone, please use Internet Explorer to build your website.

THE TAB FEATURE VERSUS OPENING NEW WINDOWS.

When you use the newer version of Internet Explorer (and FireFox and Netscape), you'll be given "tabs" to use instead of just opening a new window. If you don't know much about computers, this may sound insane, but it's really a very simple concept, don't worry.

Basically, the tab bar is found at the top of your screen and can hold many opened websites within one browser window. It looks something like this:

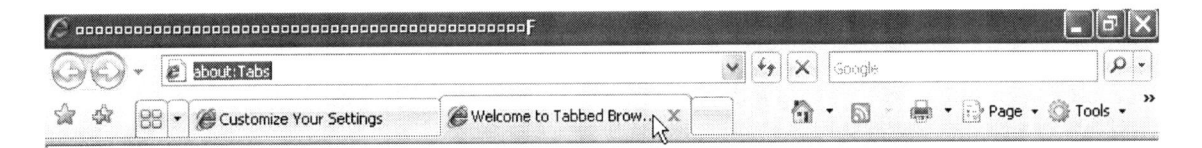

The older versions of browsers only let you open new websites in new windows that would settle themselves in the tray at the bottom of your screen, like so:

However, some websites don't work well with the tab system because they tend to crash, and then all data and everything you had opened is lost, especially in Internet Explorer. FireFox and Netscape don't seem to have this problem, but we don't recommend using them for Tripod at all, so that's why we need to explain…

For the least amount of problems when you build your site, do not use the tab feature to open new windows. Instead, hit CTRL + N to open a new window (like when we suggest having PayPal open at the same time). We've found that the tabs have a tendency to close randomly on their own, and if you're in the middle of entering a bunch of text or you just added a picture, all your work will be lost!

The easiest way to ensure you always work in a new window (by eliminating tabs) is to set your **Internet Options**.

In Internet Explorer, click Tools→Internet Options→General, Tabs→Settings

A pop-up will appear, and you'll need to **uncheck** the **Enable Tabbed Browsing** setting. This will keep your browser from using tabs and causing unnecessary problems. To enable your new settings, you'll need to close your browser and open it again.

It sounds complicated and may sound like a waste of the new Internet Explorer abilities, but we promise that it will make your life on the internet easier, and will definitely make building your website as uncomplicated as possible.

Recently, we've found that other websites don't work well with the tabs either, or will crash and cause all your other tabs to crash. Because we hate to lose information as much as anyone else, we're sure your stress will be limited by disabling this function.

SHORTCUTS TO MAKE YOUR LIFE EASIER.

Now that you know a few things about the computer, there are a few shortcuts that will help you along the way. They are easy to remember and will save you much time and frustration.

Keyboard shortcuts can also be handy for daily life, especially if you need something done fast, if you can't find the right toolbar, or if you just want to copy something and don't want to type it again. Oh, and you'll need them for the later stages of your website building.

And, don't despair Apple fans, we go over your keyboard shortcuts too.

So, here's how they work. Hold down the Control (Ctrl) button for Windows, or the Apple button if you're a Mac person, and then hit the corresponding letter to complete the desired action: copy, paste, print, etc.

SHORTCUTS FOR WINDOWS:

- **Ctrl + N**   Creates a new window, works in Word, and on the internet
- **Ctrl + A**   Selects all text, or all of the active screen
- **Ctrl + C**   Copies selected text (use your mouse or the Ctrl + A, then hit   Ctrl + C   to copy)
- **Ctrl + V**   Pastes copied text (use with the copy function)
- **Ctrl + X**   This will cut and copy text, so that you can paste it elsewhere
- **Ctrl + Z**   Undo, will undo your last action, so never panic when you can just undo! Works in Word, photo editing programs, and some websites like Tripod.
- **Ctrl + P**   Print, will print current document or screen

SHORTCUTS FOR APPLE:

- **Apple + N**   Creates a new window, works in Word, and on the internet
- **Apple + A**   Selects all text, or all of the active screen
- **Apple + C**   Copies selected text (use your mouse or the Ctrl + A, then hit Ctrl + C to copy)
- **Apple + V**   Pastes copied text (use with the copy function)
- **Apple + X**   This will cut and copy text, so that you can paste it elsewhere
- **Apple + Z**   Undo, will undo your last action, so never panic when you can just undo! Works in Word, photo editing programs, and some websites like Tripod.
- **Apple + P**   Print, will print current document or screen

So, to really get the full use of these shortcuts, you'll need to play around a bit. We suggest opening up a Microsoft Word document, typing up a bit of gibberish and practicing the cut and paste functions. Trust us, you'll use them!

You'll probably find most use from the cut and copy function (CTRL + X) and definitely the copy and paste (CTRL + C, then CTRL + V) function, so play around with them so you know how to use them when you get online too.
Oh, and give the undo function a couple tries so you can see how it works. When writing text in Tripod, the undo function works, as well as the copy and paste functions—which can be a *huge* save sometimes.

Also, printing on the internet can be a bit of a challenge because websites never really seem to fit into standard print borders. To print an area of text, use your mouse and **left** click, holding down as you select the area of text you wish to print.

Then, **right** click (or hit Ctrl + P) anywhere on the selected area and choose "print." Then, when the print pop-up appears, make sure to choose "print selection" and your printer will print only the selected area. Using this method, you'll never have problems printing a page again.

HOW TO SAVE A PICTURE TO YOUR COMPUTER.

When you're ready to start building your website, you're going to need to have photos for it, be it clipart or stock photos from your drop shippers, or photos that you take yourself and upload into your computer so that you can have them on your site.

So, we're going to take a moment to tell you how to do this properly (and for those of you who already know how, we apologize for the digression), because photos with improperly named file extensions won't be able to be placed on your site.

When you first save an image to your computer, make sure to save it as a:

.gif
.jpg
.jpeg
.zip

.gif, .jpg, .jpeg, and .zip are all **file extensions**.

Most often, your images will be a .jpg. If your images are animation oriented or have been edited a bit, they might be saved as a .gif.

Note that **.tiff**, and **.bmp** images are *not* compatible with Tripod. If your image is a .bmp, or a .tiff, you'll need to open your photo in your photoshop program and "save as" a .jpg or .gif.

Basically, all programs save their files with different file extensions, but photos will only have the above few (there are other kinds, but only these are compatible with the internet…and Tripod) so you don't need to memorize a whole list.

HOW SAVING A PHOTO WORKS:

Go to http://www.ebay.com and we'll walk you through the process of saving your first photo.

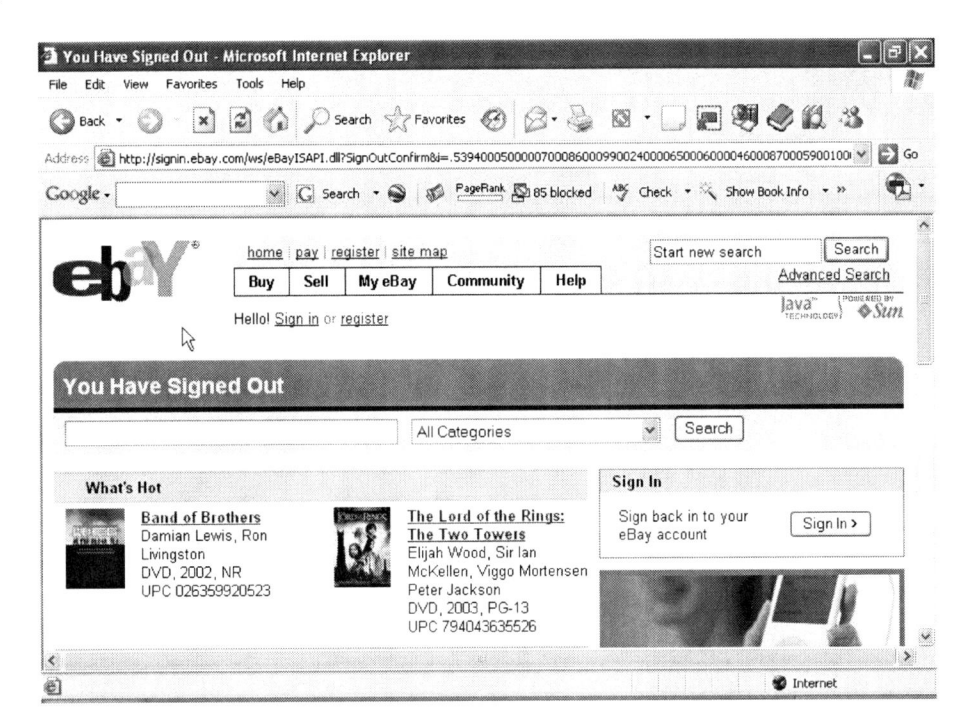

This is eBay's homepage. Their logo is in the upper left hand corner. We'll be saving their logo to our computer (logos, clipart, and photos all save the same with the same file extensions).

Now, eBay changes their homepage all the time, so if your browser window doesn't look like ours anymore, don't worry. Their logo should still be present, but if it's not, this will work with any other image you'd like to save instead.

Oh, and just a disclaimer, it's not nice to save images from other people's sites to use as your own. They might have a copyright (they probably do) or they might just not like people "stealing" their stuff.

We're only using eBay's logo for this exercise because they are so well known that they might not mind our recommending them (go eBay!).

THE PROCESS.

First, **right** click (with your mouse) on eBay's logo.

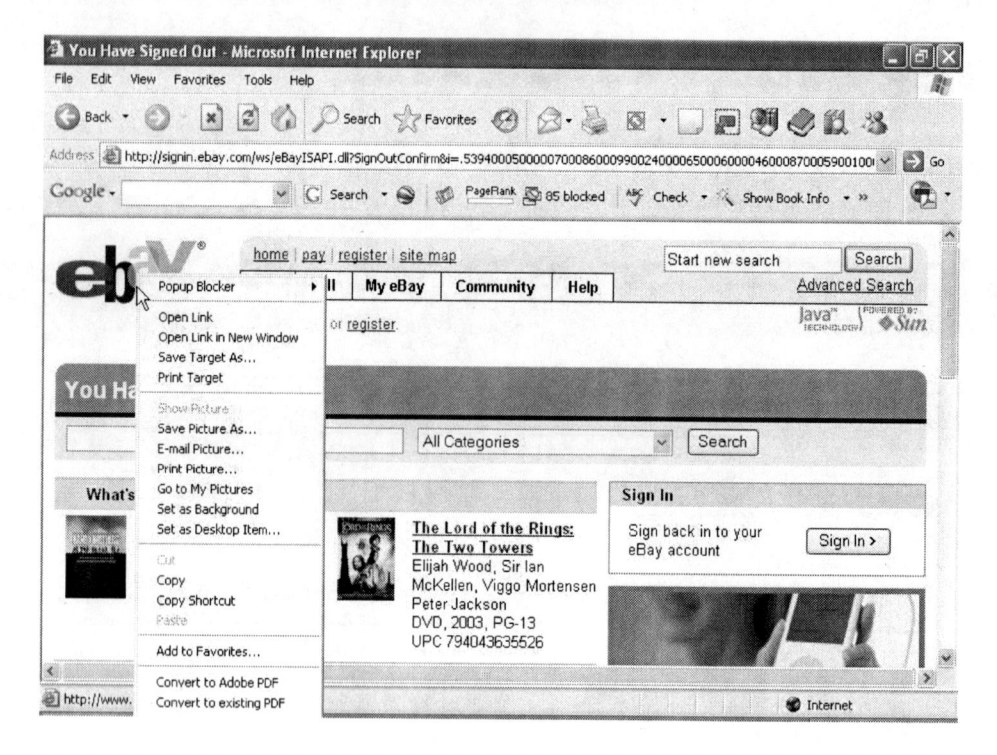

See the new little window that popped up? All the choices it has? Yours might have a few more choices or a few less (just depending on your computer's settings), but yours will have the most important ones, including "Save Picture As."

Select **Save Picture As** to continue.

A new window will pop-up, looking something like this:

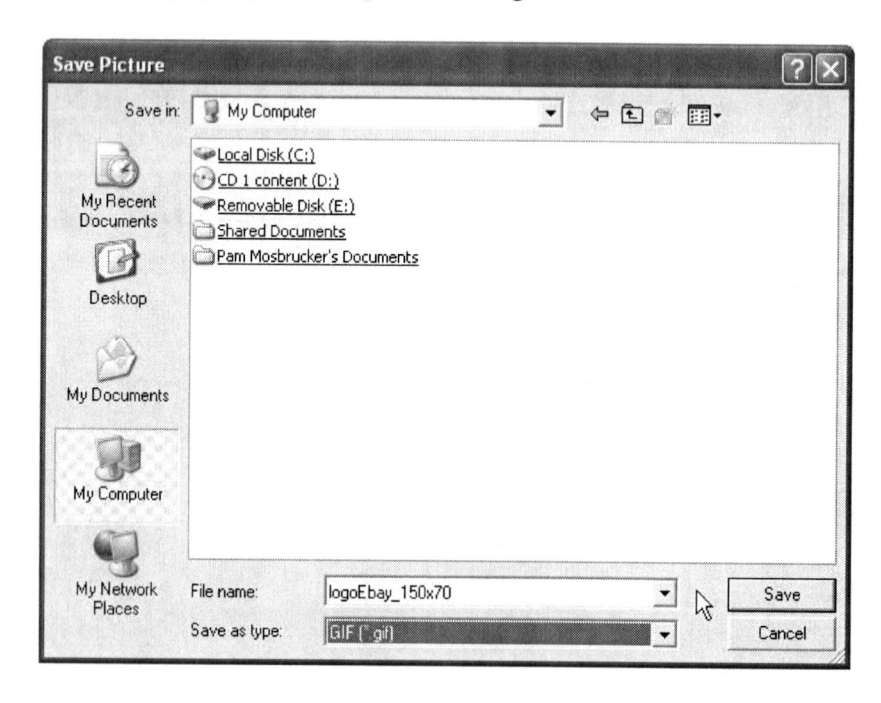

Near the top it says **Save in: My Computer**. Yours may say to "Save in" somewhere else, but that's okay, keep reading…

This means that the photo will "save in" some random place in "My Computer" (you have a "My Computer" too, it's just the name of everyone's hard drive).

You don't want the picture to save in some random place; you want to be able to find it later.

So, for now, click on **Desktop** on the left hand side of the window.

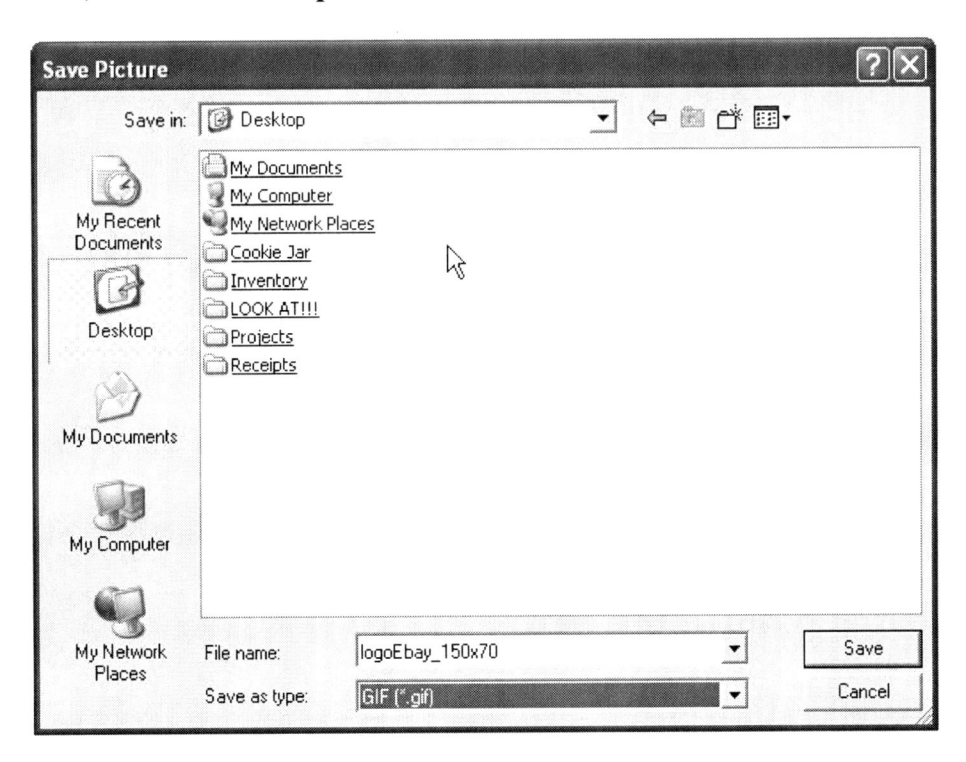

Note how the "Save in" choice has changed—it now says "Save in: Desktop"

You don't just want a bunch of pictures hanging out on your computer's desktop either, so you'll want to create a new folder for your pictures.

You can create as many folders as you like to better organize things later, but for now, just create one folder, naming it something that relates to your site or pictures.

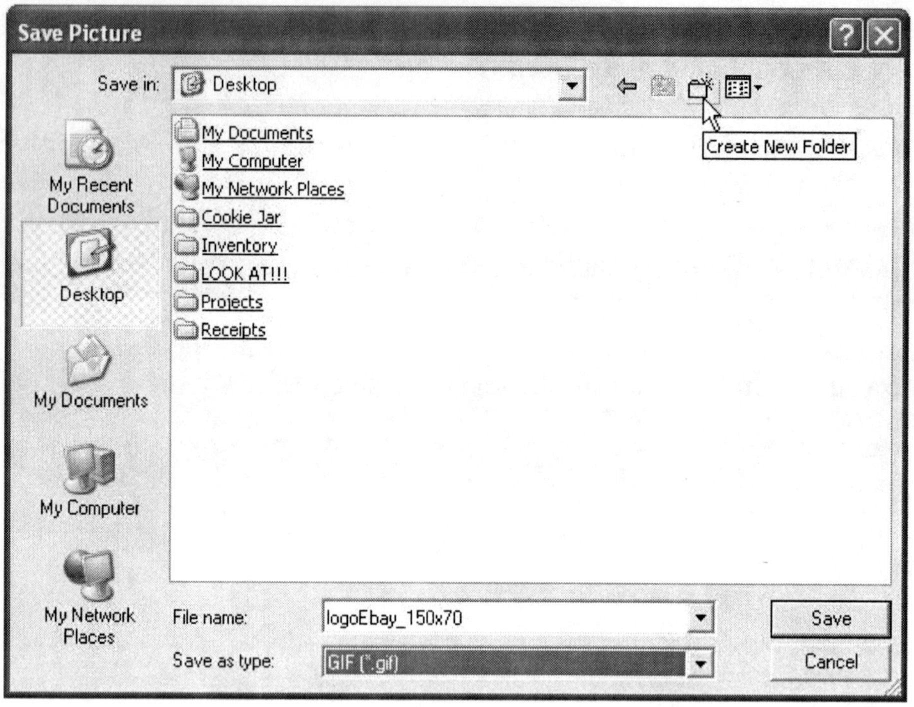

Note where our mouse is—where it says… "Create New Folder"

Select that little folder button with the spark at its corner.

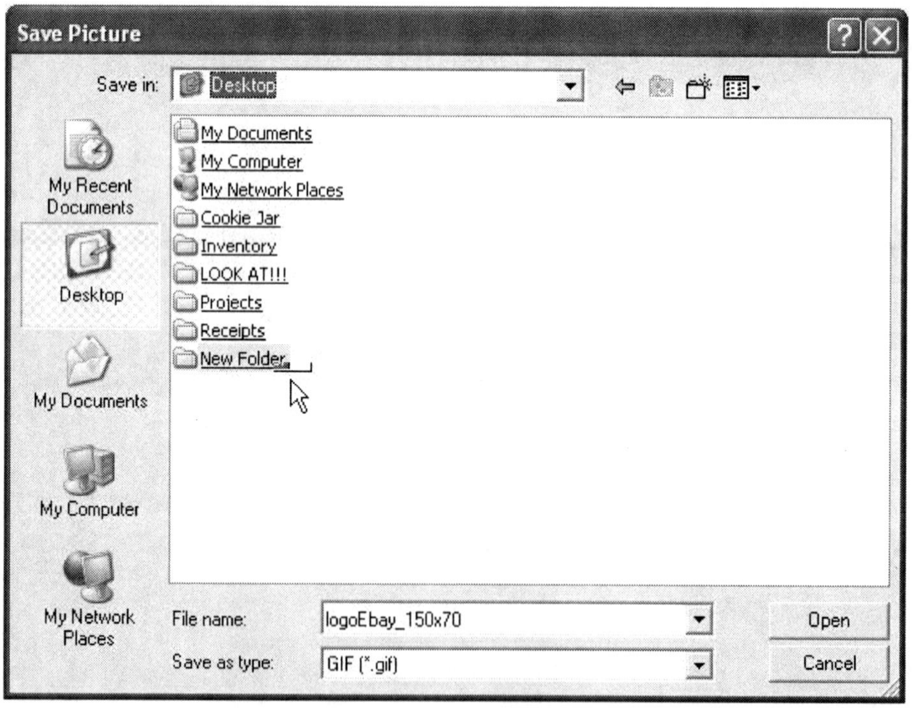

A new folder named "New Folder" will appear on your "Desktop" view. It will be highlighted in blue; so all you have to do is start typing what you'd like it to be called (we named our new folder Shop Lizards). Or, you can right click on it and select "Rename" to give it a new name.

Once you have it named, **left** click on it to open your new folder.

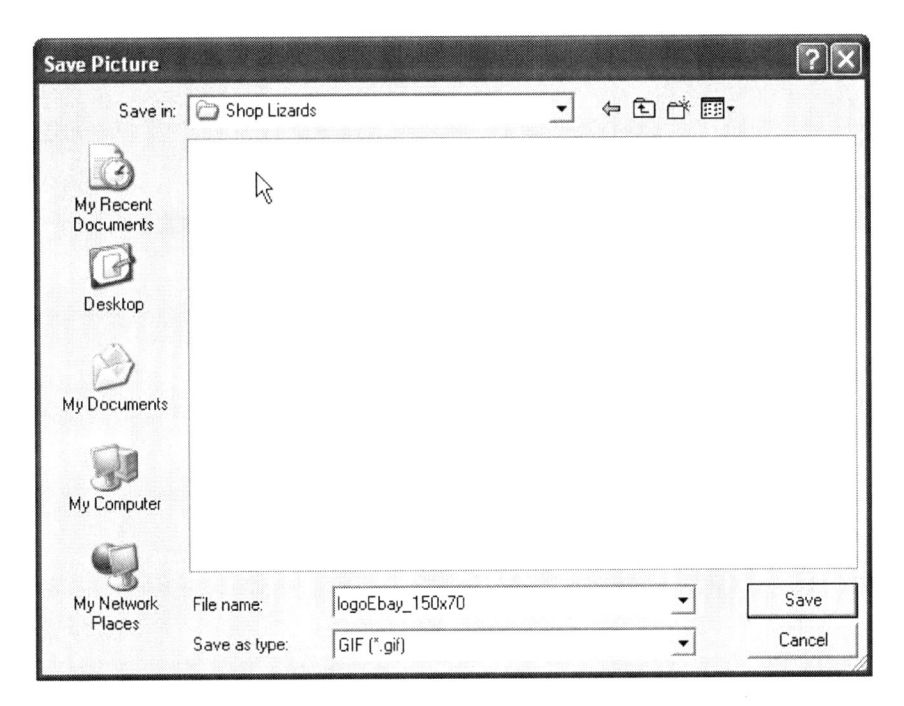

Now, it says "Save in: Shop Lizards."

That's just where we want our picture to go, so we'll change the picture name now so that we'll know what it is later. You'll be able to access everything that "Saves" to your desktop from your desktop later.

Right now, the picture's name is "logoEbay_150x70"

NOTE:

Tripod won't allow you to upload pictures with spaces in their names. So, if you want this picture to be called:

ebay logo.jpg (note the space)

you'll have to type it like this:

ebaylogo.jpg (note the removal of the space)

or like this:

ebay_logo.jpg (note the underscore used instead of a space)

Finally, select the file type, where it says: **Save as type**. We get to choose a .gif, which is the default setting, or a .bmp.

You might have a few more options, or the same ones that we do. Choose either .jpg, .jpeg, or .gif and type in the name for your picture, then hit the **Save** button. Remember that **.bmp** and **.tiff** files are not compatible with Tripod.

And that's how you save a photo to your computer!

You can now view that photo by going to your desktop and clicking on your new folder. Store all of your photos for your site in this new folder, or make more folders to better organize things.

You can always create more folders later by right-clicking on any blank space on your desktop and selecting New→New Folder.

HOW TO CARE FOR YOUR COMPUTER.

It may sound simple, but the most important thing to do to care for your computer is to scan it often for viruses and spyware. Since we're on the internet so often, we like to scan once a month, if not more frequently, just to keep things running smoothly and spyware and viruses quashed before they cause any problems.

We've actually never had a problem with any of our computers virus or spyware wise (knock on wood) because we are cautious in this and know the value of great programs. And nearly all of the programs that we recommend are **absolutely free,** with no limited trials, the only cost to you being Defender Pro—which is a measly 20 bucks. Norton and McAfee will cost double that and often cause weird issues with other programs you may be running.

You'll notice as you go through the steps below that we use several programs for seeking out and destroying spyware. We've found that each program is set up to seek out different kinds of spyware. So, to make sure we get it all (and we're often surprised when Ad-Aware finds 80, then Spybot finds another 20 and

Defender Pro Anti-Spy finds 10 more—all different!) we just use all three to be safe.

Now, we know it sounds like a lot to do, even on a monthly basis, but once you get the routine down, you just start the first program and come back to check on your computer every hour or so to deal with any prompts or to start the next program. You'll get used to the routine in no time and your computer will never have a problem with nasty viruses or spyware.

Oh, and if our instructions for use aren't complete enough for you, all of these programs have handy help functions, so you'll never be confused.

So, for best results, follow these steps:

1. AD-AWARE (takes 15-60 minutes, depending)

Can be downloaded for free at http://www.adawareresource.com . Ad-Aware will identify harmful spyware and registry keys and is perhaps the most important and useful spyware finder and destroyer on the market.

Instructions for use:

1. Check for updates when it loads by clicking Ok→Connect
2. Click Ok to download and install the file, then Finish
3. Click Start→Perform Full System Scan
4. When the scan is finished, click Next→put a check by all infected files (don't Quarantine)→click Next, Ok

2. SPYBOT SEARCH AND DESTROY (takes about 25 minutes)

Can be downloaded for free at http://www.spybot.com/en/download/index.html . Spybot will identify harmful spyware that other programs miss.

Instructions for use:

1. Click Search For Updates
2. Check the boxes next to each available update, then click Download Updates
3. Click Check for Problems
4. When bot check is complete, make sure there is a check by each infected entry and click Fix Selected Problems→Yes, Ok

3. DEFENDER PRO (takes about 1 to 3 hours, depending)

Defender Pro is not currently compatible with Windows Vista. If you use Vista, we recommend a free virus program by PC-Tools that you can find in the Appendix. For Windows XP, Defender Pro can be purchased at your local Wal-Mart for around $20 and is more computer-friendly and better at finding viruses than Norton and McAfee. Defender Pro will identify viruses, usually updates definitions on its own, and, when running in the toolbar, will usually scan the computer while you work. Note that you'll need a new Defender Pro version every year.

If you don't want to spend the bucks, PC-Tools and Avast both work comparably well (sometimes better, as with Avast) and we've been considering switching to the free versions ourselves.

Instructions for use:

1. Click Scan My Computer
2. When the scan is finished, it may either delete any viruses or prompt you for action. Make sure to delete instead of quarantine, then Finish.

4. DEFENDER PRO ANTI-SPY (takes about 30 minutes)

Comes with purchase of Defender Pro. Defender Pro Anti-Spy will identify harmful spyware that other programs miss, and usually updates definitions on its own.

Instructions for use:

1. Click Scan→Typical Scan→Next
2. When the scan is completed, click Next→make sure the infected files are checked→click Delete, Next, Finish

5. DEFRAGMENT (can take up to 2 hours)

Found on your computer under:
Start→Program Files→Accessories→System Tools→Defragment

Defragment will compact and redistribute files where they belong to free up cluttered space, making your computer run more smoothly.

Instructions for use:

1. Click Defragment

2. When finished, click Close

Now, if you're pressed for time, it's okay to leave out the Defender Pro Anti-Spy, but all the others are needed. It sounds completely redundant, but they all search for and destroy different things. The problem is that no one program out there will catch everything, so a little creativity is necessary. Luckily, they are all free, so we can't really complain.

We have yet to be destroyed by a virus (knock on wood, again), and it may seem like we're a bit overzealous here, but in this case, it's better safe than sorry. So, if you follow our simple steps, your computer will remain safe and continue to run as smoothly as the day you purchased it.

Chapter Two
Steps To Success.

Now you know the basics about computers. You should be able to access the internet, you should know a few great time-saving shortcuts, you should be able to save a photo to your hard drive, and care for your computer.

Believe it or not, you've actually accomplished the hardest part.

Building a website is just a bit more time consuming, but now that you know the basics, you'll do just fine.

DON'T LET THIS OVERWHELM YOU.

The main reason we created this guide is because we made mistakes that we feel should be shared and because we never knew if we were doing things that needed to get done in the right order.

Perhaps if we had had more guidance early on, we wouldn't have been as frustrated and burdened with problems. With that said, learn from our mistakes, because though you'll undoubtedly be making your own, your path has been cleared and we've done our best to spotlight it for you.

The reason that we go over these mistakes now, instead of in later chapters, is to give you a sort of frame to put all the information you learn into.

Half of the following steps to success and mistakes may seem insignificant now, but once you read the following chapters, they will become very clear, and you'll already know how to avoid them.

Also, since some of the things we discuss here are on the more advanced side, we thought that you had a right to know about them before you had to learn them. That way, you can be more perceptive and will be able to question things that you might not have otherwise.

So, take the following chapters with this in mind. Read and make notes as you go and if discussion of meta tags scares you, make a note of that for when Chapter 10 comes around. That way, you'll be better prepared to absorb the meta tag information (it's not hard, just detailed) because it has been in your mind for at least six chapters.

TEN STEPS TO SUCCESS.

With every venture, it's easiest to have a clearly defined goal at hand. Use ours as a guideline, and feel free to add to it if new ways emerge for you.

STEP ONE. Decide what to Sell.

A. You could Drop ship. Drop shipping is defined as finding a wholesaler or manufacturer who allows you to put their inventory onto your site, you sell the items for a nice profit, you pay them their wholesale costs, and they ship the item to your customer with your business name on the box.

We use this method because, with drop shipping, you don't have to store any inventory, you don't have to deal with shipping, and *you* decide what your profit is going to be.

We could write a whole book on drop shipping alone. So, please visit our website at http://www.wordpartnersink.com and click on Drop Ship Source Directory to find links to great resources and information that you *will* need.

B. You could sell your own products. Perhaps you make custom dolls or special fishing lures. You decide how many you can make, you put them on your site, you ship them to the customer, and you get all of the profits.

If you want to earn more, you only have to work a bit harder to do so. It's all up to you.

C. You could sell your own services, information, or even ebooks. Just like this guide you are reading, we sell it online as an ebook as well as the print edition. We had information that we felt was important to share. It took time and effort and has value, but it's really only a one-time project for a lifetime of customers.

On the other hand, maybe you wish to offer your services as a typist or window washer, build yourself a nice little site and the world is now able to find you and you'll have more business than you could have ever imagined.

D. You could review or recommend affiliates. There's a site where a woman reviews all the dating sites and writes about them, then recommends the ones she found most useful. Customers come to her site, read her reviews, and click on the dating sites. Because she's set up as an affiliate, the dating sites pay her for every click-through.

If you're interested in making money this way, join one of the major affiliate programs, like Link Share (http://www.linkshare.com) or ClickBank (http://www.clickbank.com), because they keep track of your earnings and make sure you get the payouts that you deserve for all your hard work.

You could actually manage this with little more than a basic blog. A little research and a few affiliates related to your topic…and poof! People read your blog and they click on your affiliate links, which equals click-throughs for your affiliates and commission for you.

E. You could start your own affiliate program. This is the reverse of reviewing affiliates. If you find that you want to sell something similar to what other sites are recommending, you could provide them with a link to your site, and pay them for every customer that they convert.

In this case, you'd also want to join one of the big affiliate sites, like Link Share (http://www.linkshare.com) or ClickBank (http://www.clickbank.com), to make sure that your affiliate program gets enough exposure and willing affiliates ready to promote your business.

F. You could sell ad space. This works just like it would for a newspaper. If you have information that you want to provide, you could contact businesses that have similar interests and charge them for a banner ad on your site.

Google has latched onto this idea and has opened up this market for you with their AdSense (http://www.google.com/adsense) program. Simply join their program and put the ads on your site to begin earning an income.

STEP TWO. Have a Focus.

Finding a niche market (Chapter 9) is perhaps the only thing that can make you successful fast, and there are tons of tools on the internet that can help you find one. It's tedious and time-consuming work, but it's worth it.

Once you do find a niche, use that product to your advantage. It's called a niche for a reason. Check out your competition. Look at their keywords, look at their site navigation. Find what got them to the top of the search engine, and decide that you can do better.

And then *do* it better.

More than just having a niche, you must understand what your site's purpose is. If you plan on selling cowboy boots, design your site to sell cowboy boots. Don't waste time or space with a blog about your cat and his shoelace addiction.

Do, however, dedicate your site to the sale and promotion of cowboy boots. Write up a little blog about the trends in western wear or why more people buy now that cowboys are cool…you get the idea. Whatever your focus, don't waver, unless you plan to branch out and branching out *is* your focus.

STEP THREE. Your Business Identity.

A. Decide what your business name is going to be, and make sure that it relates to what you will be selling. But spend some time on this (we'll say this a bunch of times) because Tom 6758 means nothing if you're selling cat clothing.

If you *are* selling cat clothing, try to get those keywords into your business name, so that it will be in your domain name. Chatty Cat Clothing would make a great business and domain name. It gets a few main keywords, "cat," and "clothing" into your domain name and it reflects what you want to sell.

B. You'll need a domain name, which should reflect your most profitable, targeted keywords, and not your business name. For example, if your business name is Sally Sayz, and your most targeted keyword phrase for your product is "rhinestone dog collars," buy http://www.rhinestonedogcollars.com as a guaranteed method for ranking higher in the search engines.

You can get a domain name from Tripod's site builder services for $8.95 per month (setup fee $15). You can get a domain name elsewhere, of course, and have it "transferred" to Tripod, but that costs extra and you'll be paying hosting fees through Tripod anyway once you build your website.

Before we buy our domain names we always use Network Solutions, http://www.networksolutions.com to see if our choice is available. Often, we have to try many variations of our keywords (and even look up new ones) before we find the perfect domain name. They also keep track of what you look up and show

.net and .org (among other extensions) as well, so you don't get confused. If your choice is available, head on over to Tripod and sign up with the Pro plan or above to claim it.

Now, the sooner you register your domain name the better, because someone else might take it first…and then you have to come up with a new one (after the tears and screaming stops, of course).

C. You'll also need a PO Box, with a cost of $40 a year from your local Post Office. Don't waver on this, just get a PO Box.

Why?

Because you'll be getting mail for your business, you might even get mail from your customers. This way, you can keep all of your personal mail separate from your business mail, and you can put a nice little PO Box address at the bottom of your site…instead of your home address.

D. You'll need to get a Certificate of Assumed Business Name. You can do this online, for Idahoans, http://www.idsos.state.id.us/corp/corindex.htm (everyone else, check on your state's homepage to obtain this certificate, or check to make sure that it or something similar is required)
for $25forfor a $25 fee.

E. Then you'll need to get a Home Occupation Certificate. Every state is a bit different on this, but it basically buys you the right to operate a business (be it only a website that makes a profit) from the comfort of your home. It's usually to be found in your local Planning and Development Services Office, for a $25 fee.

F. Next, you'll need a merchant account to accept payments online. PayPal is the best, http://www.paypal.com, as they have low fees (2.5% plus 30 cents per transaction). PayPal is also the cheapest and safest around, so make sure to sign up for a Business Account so you can receive all kinds of payments online.

Also, once you've been with PayPal for a while, they'll let you get a PayPal Debit MasterCard (and even a PayPal credit card), which basically allows you to spend the money in your PayPal account in the real world without first transferring it from your PayPal account to your bank account.

PayPal is also compatible with Tripod and makes listing items on your site a fairly simple operation.

G. Get an Employer Identification Number, called an EIN. This works like a social security number for your business and sets you up to pay taxes. Get it for free at http://www.irs.gov and click on:

Businesses→Small Business/Self Employed→Employer ID Numbers

As all things taxes are difficult to understand, make sure to check with your local small business administration to get the right licenses (some vary by state) and information. No one is immune to taxes, sorry.

H. Set up a business account at your bank using your new EIN number. Having a business account separate from your personal account will not only save you a major headache come tax time, but it allows you to actually use that account for the business expenses that will come your way.

Just bite the bullet and do it, you'll be infinitely grateful when the money starts rolling in and you need to track your expenses. When you do, make sure to input the business account info on PayPal so that you can transfer funds directly into that account from your online earnings.

A NOTE ON BANKS. Having a business means that you'll have a lot of expenses going out and, hopefully, more than a lot of transactions and sales coming in. Your bank needs to be able to handle this, and have reasonable (if no) fees. So, before you choose a bank, make sure that you understand their fees and that their website is easy to use. This way, you can check your account summary at any time of the day without stress.

STEP FOUR. Create a Logo.

Create a usable logo for business cards, correspondence, and your website. Once completed, to copyright your logo, you need to go the official http://www.copyright.gov/register website and click on **Visual Art Works** to download your application. They charge a small one-time fee which guarantees your copyright.

Then be sure to put the copyright information on your site to protect your images and text. It should go in the footer (very bottom) of the site and look like this:

Copyright © 2008 Shop Lizards. All Rights Reserved.

Note that you should put the copyright information at the bottom of your page (in the site footer) regardless of whether or not you register your logo.

Everything you write becomes yours, and technically you own the copyright the instant something becomes print. Protect yourself and your hard work; a simple bit of text at the bottom of your screen is so simple a method.

A good quality logo does much to enhance your business as a brand. When you see a pink bunny banging drums don't you think of Energizer? (okay, maybe that was a weird example...) When you see the big golden arches, even in China, you know that a McDonald's is nearby.

Your brand, your logo, can do the same for your business if you plan it out before hand.

NOTE: You can get a trademark or patent from the United States Patent & Trademark Office, http://www.uspto.gov/main/trademarks.htm . Review their guidelines for more information.

STEP FIVE. Inventory Management.

You'll need to create an accurate catalog of your inventory, including the pricing. Pricing can be tricky, so you need to allow enough room for profit, mistakes, shipping charges, and drop shipper fees.

We use Excel's spreadsheets (get Excel for Dummies) for inventory tracking because it allows us to see and print out our entire inventory, so that we know exactly what is selling on our site, how much we owe the drop shipper for each item, how much each item costs to ship, and how much profit we make.

Keeping track of your product is also important because one day the tax man will come knocking and he'll want to know how much you spent on a product before reselling it. If you keep accurate logs now, you'll only be in good shape in the future.

And Excel, of all programs, is very easy to learn. If you just don't like spreadsheets, write it out by hand if you have to. Either way, knowing your inventory and profit at a glance is essential.

STEP SIX. Start Building.

Take the time *now* to get all of your products online, in a uniform format, looking their best and most buyable, paying attention to what you'll learn about keywords and niche products (Chapter 9-10).

Also, make sure that your logo is in the header (the top) of all of your pages, and that your pages all have a similar color theme and design.

The building of the site will probably take up most of your time, but it's something that once done, can be easily modified and changed around in the future.

Don't worry about perfection now; just worry about getting your site up and online as soon as you can manage.

Do, however, remember that this is one of the hardest parts because it is the most time consuming, so give it the effort and consideration that it demands.

Keep in mind that making a crappy or hard-to-understand website now will only delay your success on the internet.

STEP SEVEN. Site Content.

Make sure that your content is relevant to the information or products that you are selling, and check your site navigation for ease of use. Once your products are online, check that the buy buttons work, and double and triple check your links.

Now, wait a week, then come back and check for mistakes. When everything is to your satisfaction (not necessarily perfect), publish!

But you're not done yet. Part of being a successful web designer/business owner means that you must continually update your site with new information to keep your customers coming back. A simple blog done once every few months is usually enough to do the trick, plus it will turn customers into *repeat* customers.

And a repeat customer is much easier to sell.

STEP EIGHT. Search Engines.

Spend the time to find targeted keywords, called meta tags, for each of your pages, Pay Per Click (PPC) keywords, and advertising campaigns (Chapter 10-11). This is perhaps the most important thing that you can do to ensure the success of your website.

And remember, search engines, like people, prefer to find new content on your site. If you create your site with this in mind, picking out the right keywords, and adding new content based on those keywords will help improve your performance on the internet.

STEP NINE. Making the Sale.

It might take a day or a month, but eventually you'll make your first sale. After you celebrate and jump around, you're going to have to tend to your new order. You need to have a process figured out now to deal with placing orders with drop shippers, tracking your profits, and sending out confirmation emails to customers. So take the time while you have it to figure things out now.

That way, you can celebrate when the orders arrive, and not panic when you have to deal with them.

A. You'll need to process the email, noting the customer name and item purchased in a financial ledger.

B. If you're using a drop shipper, you'll forward the email to them. Now, figure out what your profit is from the amount of the purchase by deducting drop shipper and PayPal fees (see example in Chapter 9).

If you're clever, you'll already have done this when you input everything into your spreadsheet. Then send the amount due to the dropshipper. Some drop shippers will just use your PayPal MasterCard (which is what we prefer) to do all business with. And that's handy!

This saves us the time it would normally take to forward the proper amount to each drop shipper for each customer order. The amount left over after fees is your profit.

C. Make note of your profit in your ledger, as you'll be paying tax on this amount, quarterly. Keep careful logs of your transactions and you'll be safe tax wise. The drop shipper will then send you a confirmation email that your customer's order has been sent.

You can do with this what you will, but we like to copy and paste it into a pre-made template for each customer and send it to them if a tracking number was provided, so that it looks like everything came from us.

That's why we use a drop shipper, after all, so that the customer thinks everything comes from us.

STEP TEN. Keep Learning.

Always think of ways to improve, keep up with the current search engine procedures and meta tags, and check your site often. You'll find that there are things that can be improved once you've let them sit for a while.

Furthermore, track your visitors. See what pages they look at, which get the most traffic, and which never get viewed. Then make changes to accommodate. Sign up for the free service from StatCounter (http://www.statcounter.com) to get a clear and accurate picture of how long visitors stay on your site and which pages they view the most.

Tripod offers this for free also, but we like the way StatCounter breaks it down better. Plus, we have tons of websites and have them all signed up on StatCounter under the same name so that we can view all of our website statistics at the same time without having to log in and log out for each on Tripod (again, it's a time-saving thing).

If things aren't working well, change it up. Generate better, more targeted keywords, optimize your text, start a blog, find new drop shippers…you get the idea.

If any step could be considered the most important, it would be this step. We often thought that we'd had things figured out.

At every turn, we learned something new that totally blew what we thought we knew out of the water. It's important, above all, to keep an open mind when learning and growing your business online.

You never know when you'll come across something new, or even something slightly different than you first thought, that will change the way you do business for the better.

Never stop learning and you'll find success.

It's actually the only way that we can guarantee your success. You see, your success isn't in our hands, it's in *yours*. If you think you know it all too soon, and aren't getting the sales on your site that you believe you should be, you may overlook the real reason, or the one thing that would bring more visitors to you.

Or, if things aren't moving as fast as you'd hoped and you feel like you might as well go back to your 9-5 job before you get divorced, you might miss the one thing that could have saved you.

Never stop learning, never stop reading those articles, never stop visiting the blogs on internet marketing, and never say that you've tried it all. Only commitment to learning can ensure your success online.

It's only a matter of time.

So, congratulations on taking the first step and reading this. Your future is officially in your hands.

EIGHT MISTAKES TO AVOID.

Everyone makes mistakes when they're just getting started, so be prepared to deal with those mistakes (however painful) accordingly. Keep in mind that you aren't *expecting* mistakes, but you're being vigilant to keep the worst of them from hurting you.

If you're prepared for the worst, you'll be ahead of the rest. Like when the tax man comes and you've kept those receipts an extra year, or when a drop shipper's credit card machine goes bonkers but you are protected by PayPal's guarantee from fraud. That sort of thing.

Visualize the future you want to have, but be realistic and aware of the obstacles that you may find in your path.

With that in mind, we've put together a nice little list of *our* mistakes. Some really sucked, some could've really sucked, and some, well some just happen to everyone starting out with high hopes and little knowledge.

MISTAKE ONE.

TIME. Websites simply cannot become famous overnight. No matter what Joe Millionaire in the late night infomercial has to say. He did not make $100,000 the day after he published his site.

Even a proper pay per click campaign takes a few days (three days, actually, because Yahoo and Google like to review things first), and cannot be done without a fully optimized website, which also takes a few days, depending on how fast you are. The truth is that it takes time. The good thing is that everyone has time.

You just have to decide how much time you're willing to put into something that can literally change your life. So, don't get anxious. You have time. Just let your business grow.

Why is this a mistake?

We thought that pressing the "publish" button meant that instantly the entire world could see and access our site. In theory, we were correct...now everyone can see our site. But we're only visible on the web and in the search engines because we waited.

The truth is that you can spend all the money you want paying the search engines to "include" you in their directories, but it's only a waste of time and money. When they get to you they get to you, but they won't get to you any faster just because you paid.

Actually, it takes nearly the exact same amount of time to get listed as it would if you hadn't paid a dime—and can truthfully be much faster if you follow our strategies.

If you're really anxious, you can of course play the pay per click game, but only do so if you have all of your keywords targeted and your site is optimized for the right visitors.

Otherwise, you'll just be wasting your money *and* time.

MISTAKE TWO.

TAXES. We aren't tax experts. Before you really begin your business, you need to know how to handle all of your tax requirements, because when things get busy, you just won't have the time…and by then you could get into trouble.

This is a mistake because people tend to get into online businesses without understanding that everything they make counts as an income for the IRS, especially after registering yourself an EIN.

So, find a taxes for dummies book, keep records of everything, and maybe plan to hire a tax man come tax time—at least your first year in business to make sure you get all the right deductions. Trust us, unless you're a tax expert yourself, you'll appreciate the help. And it's a well spent hundred bucks because the tax man will sit with you and go over a financial plan for your business.

MISTAKE THREE.

INVENTORY. Unfortunately, not all drop shippers can be trusted. Their pricing changes (sometimes often) and shipping rates may fluctuate. So, stay on top of your inventory, pricing, and shipping charges.

This problem may only arise when you sign up with a drop shipper, then let them sit for a while before putting their inventory on your site. We've done this, which is why it's mistake number three.

When we finally had time, we signed up with close to a hundred drop shippers at once, getting ourselves all excited that we could have that much inventory at our fingertips. Well, obviously it takes a little time to list a ton of inventory on a site.

When we finally got our act together, some of those drop shippers had gone out of business, some had raised their prices enough to leave almost no room for profit, and some just never responded to their emails anymore.

When you find a drop shipper, spend some *serious* time on their site getting to know their inventory and policies. If you can, order a product from them to see how fast they can ship and process things. At the very least, call them and talk to a real person about their policies and products. If their customer service sucks, then you might get screwed. But if you talk to them and are pleased with what you find, then you know (without any concerns) that you've found a good drop shipper.

Let's digress a bit…one drop shipper (who will remain unnamed because we are above such things, but they are *definitely* on Rip Off Report) had a great inventory and promised a three day processing time, with priority mail shipping. Sounded great. Well, when Christmas came around, we decided to use our wholesaler discount and ordered some of their products for ourselves.

Nearly two and a half months later we received an email that the product had been shipped from the warehouse. At this point we were so mad about the poor customer service and missing purchase that we began to do some digging on the scam-alert site, www.ripoffreport.com.

To our great surprise, we found more than a *hundred* complaints about them.

Luckily, we never sold any of their products on our site or we'd probably be in court right now…

We finally got the items a few weeks later, but we learned our lesson. From now on, we check every drop shipper on Rip Off Report, we check their policies, and we call them to make sure someone actually exists on the other end. If at all possible, we even order products to check them out for ourselves.

It just *has* to be done.

If you want to have a great business, you have to have a great inventory, and you must have quality drop shippers to supply it for you, and quality customer service in case things go awry. If you don't check things out, you'll get into trouble, big trouble, like we almost did.

MISTAKE FOUR.

PRICING. Make sure you put enough profit in every item to have room for any possible oversights. Generally, you'll price 60-100% over the wholesale price to make a good profit, and still have room in the item for sales and markdowns (or free shipping).

Actually, 100-250% over wholesale is accepted (see Chapter 9), so use your judgment based on researching your competitors to see what they sell things for.

We won't use a drop shipper unless we can price at least 100% over the wholesale price. Usually, this has to do with the competition. If that drop shipper only offers a 30% discount, then they are probably already selling to the public and that makes them just another middleman that we have to go through.

You want to be the *only* middleman in the process.

The other reason we won't use a drop shipper without much profit in their items is because we always offer free shipping. Our customers like free shipping and we think it gives us a little something extra over our competition, but it also means that we make less profit until our volume of sales picks up.

Basically, we have to make enough profit in each item to keep the business going, so when we get inventory from a drop shipper, the first thing we go over is how much profit is in each item. If the profit margin is too slim, we simply find another drop shipper.

We do have sound reasoning behind this other than what seems like greed.

If the profit is too slim, bad things can happen. We had a drop shipper who only had about $2 room in each item, since we offered free shipping, we just couldn't make it work because the shipping for some of the items cost nearly nine bucks. So, if we used that drop shipper, we'd have to charge shipping (and expensive shipping, at that) for those items. Or charge our customers more than retail for something they could just pick up at Wal-Mart for probably half the price.

Another time, we had a drop shipper who gave us about a 25% discount. We thought that was okay until they raised their drop shipper fees, and switched to a different shipping carrier. So our 25% went down to about 7% overnight. On some items it was almost a *negative* percentage. We would have been paying our customers to buy from us.

Talk about bad business!

MISTAKE FIVE.

AFFILIATES. A fantastic way to make easy money on the internet is to add a few affiliates to your site. They pay big if you do the marketing right, and it can be fun to do the work once and let it roll in the cash for you.

But having too many affiliates on your site may get you ranked in the search engines as a link farm. A link farm is described as a site that is dedicated to the blatant self-promotion of other non-related sites dedicated to blatant self-promotion.

There are ways around the whole link farm thing, as in everything, but spammers know that too and that makes the rules, be they broken by you or them, harmful to all.

Surely you've seen the new sites that have been cropping up for every search. They sound really good, so you click them, only to find out that they are just a site of links to other sites which mostly just serve as links to other sites. Whole sites dedicated to links of other sites. The clever thing is that these "link farms" know the rules. They know that Google gets angry at having more than three affiliates per page, and that all the affiliates on each page have to be related. So that's how they structure their site.

But that's all there is to their site. They have six pages, with three affiliates on each page. Technically, you could do the exact same thing and make money for a while riding this rule until Google figures things out. Actually, many of the link farms do just that. They'll make up a quick site, make money for a few weeks, then get banned and have to make another.

But...they make money, right, you ask.

Not exactly. These affiliate sites only get ranked quickly by running expensive pay per click campaigns. This means that they have to bid on and pay for each keyword, and each visitor finds them by clicking on that keyword.

Affiliates pay the most for conversions from the highest priced keywords, of course, and so the link farms have to bid on the expensive keywords to get the clicks that they need just to maintain their pay per click campaigns. Sometimes they'll have to spend $1000 a week just to make $100 in conversions. The more they spend, the more they'll make, but it's a dangerous gamble.

By the time Google bans them, they're lucky to have made a dime, if they haven't lost everything.

If you really want to make a go of the affiliates route, you'll have to use your mind more than your pocket book. The best way to use them is to have your own content (like a blog) and let them supplement your text. Write about fishing lures and include a reference and link to a fishing lures affiliate. That way, you'll get the affiliate, you'll get the traffic eventually because of your quality content, and you'll never have to spend money that you may never get back.

MISTAKE SIX.

META TAGS. Meta tags (keywords) are perhaps the most important thing that you can add to your site to immediately increase your traffic. In fact, if you don't have meta tags then you're in trouble.

Meta tags go hand in hand with quality content, though. You can't have a page of sports memorabilia and put real estate keywords in your meta tags. You must understand how important quality content and keywords are to the success of your site.

This mistake actually has much to do with mistake number one: time, because meta tags take time to work properly. Any SEO (search engine optimization) company worth their salt will tell you that you must have the foundations of the site in place for a certain amount of time (say three months) before search engines will pick up on your changes and rank you accordingly.

This is a mistake because, and it pains us to say this, you may still make this mistake thinking you have it all figured out.

You need to do your research on all of your meta tags, keywords, and page content. You need to understand exactly who you want to *visit* your site, and who it is that will actually *buy* from you.

There is a *huge* difference between a visitor and a buyer. Don't worry, we'll provide you with all the tools to accomplish this research in Chapter 9.

Unfortunately, all products are different and we can't tell you who your buyer is going to be, but if you do your research before you even get the product on your site, you can save yourself a little stress and a lot of time by having things right the first time.

MISTAKE SEVEN.

SEO CONTENT. Search Engine Optimization (SEO) content is essential for the success of any website. This basically means that the text, or content, on your website is *directly* related to your keywords.
If you sell fishing lures, the text on that page of your site *must* discuss fishing lures.

Whole businesses have sprung up (okay, us too) about doing SEO right because though it seems simple in theory, it can be difficult and hard to implement.

HERE'S A GEM: You need a lot of content for every keyword. Actually, you need about 300 words for every keyword, sprinkling in that keyword about 8% of the time.

Any more, and your readers will probably think you're crazy, but any less and Google thinks that you have no idea what you're talking about because you didn't mention your keyword enough. It's a difficult line to walk.

And if your page has more than one keyword, it just gets more complicated. Since you have to have about 300 words per keyword, having three keywords on a page means that your page needs more than 900 words, with 24% reflecting all three keywords equally, 8% per keyword.

The easiest way to manage this is to just limit yourself to one keyword per page, but some items won't allow that. For example, leather jackets. You could use: leather jackets, leather coats, women's leather jackets…etc. The list goes on and on, and we haven't even mentioned any brand names or varying kinds of leather.

So, we'll pick out three of the top keywords for a product and write up our 900 words to include all three, often sprinkling in variations, just in case, though the variations will only be mentioned in passing.

The fact is that you must do your research in this of all things to find success on the internet. Without proper SEO content, you'll be left to use the only method available to you: pay per click marketing, and it costs money, perhaps more money than you have to spend.

We can tell you the truth in this without risking our business because it's hard to do. And, if you get it right the first time, then perhaps you've found a new calling. If you get it wrong, you're not alone.

At the very least, we told you the truth, and hopefully we made your task a bit less difficult.

MISTAKE EIGHT.

NICHE MARKETS. Essentially, niche markets are needed for immediate success on the internet. You can, of course, become successful without them, but it won't be immediate, and it won't be easy.

Not having a niche means that you have to be more creative in your marketing efforts and be willing to spend more money and time doing so.

A niche can be defined as a "market" with less than a million sites dedicated to it. Less than five hundred thousand is a real niche, and less than a hundred thousand is like finding a very rare diamond in your yard.

Now, finding a niche is more difficult than it sounds. You first have to understand what people are searching for, and then branch off a niche from there (niches are fully explained in Chapter 9).

We recommend spending the time to find a niche market because it will make your life on the internet *so* much easier. Having a niche product and selling something that isn't readily stocked on the shelves of Wal-Mart means that you don't have to *compete* with Wal-Mart, after all.

WATCHING OUT FOR SCAMS.

There are so many scammers on the internet that you really have to watch out for yourself. They come in emails, in websites, and in late night infomercials. They sound and look like your grandparents and you actually feel proud of them for making more than a million last year.

If they did it, then surely you can too.

No. They did *not* do it.

Probably 98% of the time they are paid actors for a website that really has had no success stories.

Basically, you cannot get rich overnight, even if the guy in the mailer did. No one will help you make millions, without a cost.

With that said, scammers are also the most avoidable and most annoyingly persistent problem that you'll probably experience.

Follow these steps to stay safe:

STEP ONE.

Trust your judgment. Nothing is free, without *some* catch. No one will make you an overnight millionaire. You can make yourself a millionaire, of course, but it's not that easy and it actually takes time, dedication, learning, and hard work. And besides, it wouldn't be any fun or rewarding if it wasn't.

Trust your gut instinct, and question why someone would offer some miracle product to you for **JUST $197!!!!**

Why would they? Does Donald Trump offer a get rich quick real estate course for just $197? No.

Why?

Because though he is a very rich man, it wasn't easy. It's easier for him now because he knows the rules, he's done the work, and he's learned from his mistakes. Instead, Trump writes his experiences down and sells his knowledge in books published and accepted in the real world. There's nothing quick or easy about his philosophies, only a strong business sense and hard work.

If you're really willing to put in the time and learning required, you can become a millionaire, because you *worked* for it. Not because you bought some sales pitch.

STEP TWO.

Ask questions. Read the fine print, or lack thereof. Ask yourself why they would help make you rich. What's in it for them? Are they really going to send you an all-inclusive special report that tells you exactly what to do to get rich in one day?

Probably not.

If you really think you found a gem, call them or email them and ask. Say, "I was looking into your program and wanted to know what state your business is registered under" (or something equally qualifying). It's a fair question and every customer has a right to know. The fake ones will freak, the real ones will tell you. But keep in mind that some of the "real businesses" can also be scam artists. They'll send their high-pressure salesmen after you, or they'll call you often and with startling persistence. If you suddenly feel like you're being backed into a corner to sell your home for the down payment because the salesman is screaming at you that your life will never change, hang up immediately.

Any good business will be there for you. Good businesses were built on great customer service and trust. They'll tell you why their service costs what it does, they'll answer any questions or concerns you might have, but they certainly won't scare you into buying anything.

STEP THREE.

Do your research. Check out Rip Off Report http://www.ripoffreport.com and type in their business or personal name. You can even search by type of business.

You'll be surprised by what shows up. You'll notice that many scammers come around once every two or so years, preying on a certain area of the country before moving on.

If you find some entries, read them thoroughly, find out why people have complained about what they have. And if you feel you have the same complaints, leave them. Rip Off Report was established to protect people from being scammed. Familiarize yourself with them to protect yourself.

The thing is that you have to feel safe about any transaction you make, be it shopping for shoes or buying into a new business venture.

It's true what they say: the customer is always right, and should always be treated with dignity and respect. If you feel pressed, inadequate, or rushed for time, move on. You know deep down that real, good businesses would never treat a customer that way.

Chapter Three
Your Business Identity.

We designed this guide to help you build your own website and ecommerce business. We want you to be able to do every aspect of the business yourself, including the web design, and we want you to feel at least semi-comfortable doing so.

This chapter is about structuring your business identity *before* the design comes in, because that's when things tend to get messy.

But we also want you to design your business image with an end product in mind. Your colors, your slogan, your logo, will all need to be present on your website, and if they don't match, or the colors are too harsh for the buyer's eye, then you've made a mistake.

Your business identity needs to be one that buyers can understand and appreciate. Your colors need to draw them in, not blind or frighten them. Your logo needs to be catchy enough that customers remember it, and will type in your domain name the next time around, instead of going back to the search engines. And this can all be accomplished with a bit of planning.

CREATING A BUSINESS IDENTITY.

Start by deciding what it is *exactly* that you want to sell. Information? Other people's services? Are you going to drop ship? Once you know what you're going to sell, you'll be able to decide how your business is going to do so.

Before you even create a logo or choose your business name, you need a few fundamentals to get you started.

The first thing you must do is look inside yourself for your core marketing message.

Oh, blah blah blah…you say.

Actually, this is the most important aspect of creating a successful business. You must know the value of the things you sell, and you must know why anyone will care.

Think about the leather jacket drop shipper you liked. Why would people buy those jackets from you, if they could just head on down to their local Wilson's at the mall? Why are yours better? What do you offer that the retailers don't?

Now, leather jackets are perhaps a bad example because they are not a niche market, but most things *aren't* niche markets. However, whether you have found a niche or not, you must be able to answer these questions:

- Why are your products better?
- Why would anyone bother to come to your site, let alone trust you enough to buy from you?
- What do you offer that will turn a visitor into a buyer?
- What do you offer that will keep a buyer coming back?

Okay, these questions are hard to answer, yes. But they are actually much simpler than you might first imagine.

We sell a variety of products, some of which can probably even be found at Wal-Mart. But we have lots of pictures, offer very detailed descriptions, and have a bunch of related information, blogs, and free online games (Java based, you can get them for your own site by searching for "free games for webmasters" on Google).

We even offer free shipping. So, the question we ask is: why would someone bother to drive all the way to Wal-Mart when they can get our stuff online, with free shipping, and a 100% satisfaction guaranteed policy instead?

Of course, many people would still rather shop at Wal-Mart because they are distrustful of online shopping. So, we tell them about PayPal at every turn, even having PayPal's "verified" logo prominently displayed on all the pages of our site.

You don't have to do all of this to get customers; you don't even have to do *any* of this to get customers.

But, you get the idea.

What can you offer your customers that your competitors aren't? Or, what can you offer them that's better than what your competitors are offering? Be it only better customer service or a blog that criticizes or reviews a product, you *must* show your customers value before they'll buy from you.

Be creative, but be honest with yourself and what you want to accomplish as a business. If you really want to compete with the big dogs, then you're in for a lot of work, a lot of tears, and a lot of wasted money.

But if you just want to offer the best customer service on the web, and you treat every customer as if they were your only customer, then you'll find that your customers have talked about you to their friends, and they talked about you to *their* friends, and their friends talked about you to *their* friends in a forum...

SOLVE A CUSTOMER'S PROBLEM.

If you had difficulty finding out something to offer your customers (other than just *super great* customer service), you are not alone. Not every business can afford to offer free shipping or a free product with purchase.

WE'RE GOING TO DO A LITTLE EXERCISE NOW...

Groan all you want, but get a pencil and a piece of scratch paper, or come back to this exercise when you have a few moments to ponder your business success. Either way, you'll be filling in the blanks to get you business message started.

This will not only make sense in the end, but it will provide you with hundreds of new possibilities for business ideas.

STEP ONE:

Think of the problems that your potential buyers face. Or any buyer on the internet. What do they hate? What do *you* hate when you shop online? Are you afraid for your safety? Do you hate filling out tons of forms before getting to the final checkout button?

Take a few moments here to pick out five distinct problems: customer challenges, their pains, their predicaments, their worries, their fears…and write down each one. Think of them as "most common" shopping complaints, if you want. They can be what you've experienced or what your friends have experienced, either way, come up with a few. Don't worry about the solutions yet, we'll get to them in step two.

The problems that you write down will probably seem unrelated to your products or services right now, but that's perfectly fine.

Take your time.

Problem   **Solution**

1. _____   _____

2. _____   _____

3. _____   _____

4. _____   _____

5. _____   _____

STEP TWO:

You probably have a few great complaints by now, right?

Look them over and seriously consider how your product or service can *solve* some of those problems. What can you do to help these people? What would you like to have done for you?

Obviously, many of these problems are completely unrelated to your current product or service, but they don't *have* to be.

FOR EXAMPLE...

Problem: people are afraid of shopping online because they fear their identity will get stolen

Solution: we use PayPal for all transactions and PayPal guarantees the protection of all customers, plus we offer a 100% Satisfaction Guaranteed Policy.

Notice how simple that solution is?

You could find a solution to any problem no matter what your services are! That's the beauty of this.

Now, security online is probably one of the biggest problems. No matter what your product or services are, if you can offer *something* that will also make people feel safe online…then you've solved one of the greatest complaints in the online world.

If you can offer something that will solve a problem for people (even a small problem), that will turn them into *repeat* customers.

You could literally come up with something for every problem and it would help people because everyone has the problems that you came up with.

And if you came up with a problem that you feel is completely unique, write it down and come up with a solution for it anyway (people will buy something if they think they have the problem because they *believe* you can help).

What emotional gratification can your customer get from you? Ohhh, cheesy yes, but oh so profound.

Say you offer lessons in golfing and you've written a little ebook that you can sell online, reaching a huge new audience.

People read your ebook, they learn to golf better, and they are *happy* because they now have a new skill that they would not have had otherwise, without your book. Then they'll come back to your site to see if you offer a newsletter with quick tips for the new golfer. They'll probably even buy your next ebook for the more advanced golfer.

There. You've made a customer happy and turned them into a repeat customer simply because you tapped into their emotions: their need to be a better golfer.

You must tap into emotions.

People find it very hard to back away from a purchase if they have an emotional reason to buy something. Emotional reasons for purchase literally run the internet ecommerce world.

Now, go back to your list of five problems and fill in a solution for each. Some problems you might not be able to solve, but you may be surprised by what you do come up with!

Again, take your time.

When you're done, you should have quite a list of things that people suffer from and things that your business (or maybe a few new business ideas struck you) can do to help them. Keep this list and let it generate new business ideas for you.

No one has become an internet billionaire with just *one* business, after all.

You may have come up with ten more things that you could do to help people. Keep them in mind, because once you have one business up and running, you'll be ready to create the next, and the next, and the next…

CHOOSING A BUSINESS NAME.

Naming your business can be the best or worst thing that can happen to a fledgling company. Many a neo9090 has appeared on the internet and none of them sold a thing.

Why?

Because no one in their right mind would type neo9090 into the search engines when they were looking for a product (unless they were searching for the neo9090 that owes back taxes or something).

Before you come up with a name, you must decide what it is that you plan to sell, be it products or services. Then you need to do a little research and find out exactly which keywords people are using to find that product or service.

This is discussed in detail in Chapter 10 because understanding keywords is essential to proper website design, but it's something that you also need to be aware of *before* you name your business.

We decided right from the beginning that we wanted to sell a bunch of things, and we would use a drop shipper to do so. Knowing that the biggest keyword for our category was "shop," we put it in our name, Shop Lizards.

In the long run, "shop" probably shouldn't have been our primary keyword, but it gets us hits for that word, so we can't complain.

The smarter route would have been to name ourselves based on what exactly we sell, though we've changed our products around so much we would have been in trouble.

But stick with this idea.

If you plan to sell rhinestone dog collars and you'll make up another site for the Porsche hood ornaments, call your first business Rhinestone Dog Collar Haven and the second, Quality Porsche Hood Ornaments, and buy the domain names http://www.rhinestonedogcollars.com and http://www.porchehoodornaments.com for each business.

See how the keyword of the product you sell, is in the business name, and more importantly, your domain name?

It might not always work for the best this way, but if you can accomplish it, do so. Cutesy names have their purpose, but your online business name needs to be keyword targeted because having your main keywords in your business name also means that your keywords will be in your domain name, and that's priceless.

SELECTING A DOMAIN NAME.

Even if you already have a business name, and it has nothing to do with the products you might be selling, you can still select a domain name that will reflect your most profitable, targeted keywords. You don't have to be stuck, here. For example, if your business name is Sally Sayz, and your most targeted keyword phrase for your product is "rhinestone dog collars," buy http://www.rhinestonedogcollars.com as a guaranteed method for ranking higher in the search engines. You can create a nice logo around Sally Sayz, even though you domain name reflects something different.

You can get a domain name from Tripod's site builder services for $8.95 per month (setup fee $15). You can get a domain name elsewhere, of course, and have it "forwarded" to Tripod, but that costs extra and you'll be paying hosting fees through Tripod anyway once you build your website.

Before we buy our domain names we always use Network Solutions, http://www.networksolutions.com to see if our choice is available. Often, we have to try many variations of our keywords (and even look up new ones) before we find the perfect domain name. They also keep track of what you look up and show .net and .org (among other extensions) as well, so you don't get confused. If your choice is available, head on over to Tripod and sign up with the Pro plan or above to claim it.

Now, the sooner you register your domain name the better, because someone else might take it first…and then you have to come up with a new one (after the tears and screaming stops, of course).

CHOOSING COLORS FOR YOUR WEBSITE.

We've all known since elementary school that some colors are better than others. They just are. Yellow is the best color for drawing the sun and blue is the best color for filling in the sky.

You could, of course, make the sky black and the sun green or something, but even if you are a fan of the alternative, some people just *won't* understand.

Or they won't care to understand.

Using colors on the internet works in the exact same way. They actually have a very profound impact on your visitors and can even negatively impact your sales.

Pleasing colors can actually boost your sales and inspire confidence in prospective buyers while irritating color choices can turn your visitors off. There are no real rules to this, just what we've noticed ourselves. So use this purely as a guideline, and if you feel the need to be alternative, just keep in mind the affects of the colors you choose.

Obviously, make sure that your color choices don't clash. No one could hate a red and bright orange website with flashing purple and yellow banners more.

Also, keep the colors down to just a few selections (photos of course don't count here). Use just the green, white, and black. Or use just the purple, blue, and white. Keep it as simple and as complimentary as possible. However, consider the mood that you want to create. Colors can inspire certain emotions that will trigger sales. **Remember, on the internet, people buy what they want—not what they need.**

Here are the major colors (alphabetically) and how we think they affect emotion:

BLACK: Neutral yet strong. When used with complimentary colors can inspire confidence and power. Use sparingly because it also implies submission, and is sometimes too dark or scary when used with certain colors (think Dracula, black and red).

BLUE: Inspires peace, confidence, and safety. It is known for its calming elements and is often used in bedrooms or bathrooms. It symbolizes loyalty, strength, reassurance and trust. It has also been shown in studies to help weight lifters lift more weight and to help people to lose weight (so don't put it on a cooking site).

BROWN: Credibility, stability, comfort and strength. Use as a neutral with other colors for best results.

GREEN: Easy on the eyes if the right shade is chosen. It feels natural, and inspires people to think of money, wealth, hope, and growth. Can inspire responsiveness and prosperity.

ORANGE: Health and vitality, youthfulness, cheerful, also stimulates the appetite (would be great for that cooking website).

PINK: Romantic, soothing, has a calming affect. An entire site of pink though, would hurt the stomach more than the eyes.

PURPLE: Dignity, sophistication, mystery. Associated with royalty and richness. The right tones work nearly the same as blue and inspire confidence and safety.

RED: Emotionally intense. Used most often in pornography because it creates such strong emotions. Too much red can freak people out, though, or hurt their eyes. Use in moderation, and use the least threatening tones.

WHITE: Innocence and purity. Neutral, goes with everything. If you have no idea what to do with color, simply have black text on a white background and decorate the header and footer with your logo colors. White makes things easy to read and understand.

YELLOW: Understanding, brightness, intelligence, springtime, organization, light, energy, and happiness. Too much yellow, though, can create caution and shakiness.

Basically, use color to your advantage, knowing that certain colors inspire more confidence for buying than others. You know how certain colors make you feel when you're online, so go with your feelings if they differ from ours. You know the sites you've been to that give you that warm fuzzy feeling of security—that's what you're shooting for. To inspire safety, confidence, and a need to buy from your visitors.

Know though, that color can also literally anger or scare your visitors away, so use all colors with caution. And work with the shades of colors rather than choosing primary red or blue for best results.

Worst case, just stick with the black text on a white background and use your logo colors at the top and bottom. It's what people are used to, and unless you get the color thing right, you'll lose more visitors than you would gain buyers.

CREATING A LOGO.

We'll just be honest with you here: you absolutely *must* have a logo if you hope to become successful on the internet.

Why?

Surfers have come to expect certain things of the websites that they look at, one of them being a respectable site image. You've probably even noticed this yourself. You'll trust sites more if they have a nice logo and nice pages to match.

Think about it. If you saw a site with the business name in text at the top and weird colors that don't seem to have a theme, would you trust them enough to buy from them? Probably not.

So, take the time and create a logo. You should have some sort of photoshop program on your computer, but if you don't, you can always buy one of the logo creation programs out there, like Logo Creator, http://www.logocreator.com, go to Kinko's to get a logo created, or even come to us and we'll design a nice logo for you.

It's that important.

From experience, your logo doesn't need to fit any certain parameters because the header of your site can be adjusted in Tripod. You can go with page width or create something fairly small. Here are a few of our examples:

Above is our Word Partners Ink (http://www.wordpartnersink.com) logo. It's 8 inches long by about 3 inches high. To make up any difference for screen size and resolution, we simply add black in the header choice of Tripod's site builder.

Above is the logo that we made for Bigwood at Thunder Springs (http://bigwoodgolfcourse.tripod.com). It didn't quite fit on the page at 8 inches long by 3 inches high, so we just added black in the header choice of Tripod's site builder.

Above is our Shop Lizards (http://www.shoplizards.com) logo (which we update to reflect every season) and it very nearly fits on the page at 10.5 inches long and 3.5 inches high. We add a bit of black around the edges in the header choice in Tripod's site builder.

Above is our Word Partners Ink University (http://www.smallbusinessonlinecollege.org) logo and it's 8.5 inches long by 3 inches high. To fill in the space behind the logo in the header, we added a green tile background image and set it to repeat.

So, as you can see, none of our logos are the same, and none of them *actually* fit onto the screen, but we can adjust what doesn't fit later in Tripod's site builder. It doesn't matter what you end up with as long as you like what you create and are proud to display it on your site.

No matter what though, you *must* have a logo if you plan to be successful on the internet.

CREATING A BUSINESS PLAN.

Every business, big or small, needs a business plan if for the only reason that it puts a realistic focus on your business and your future as a business owner. If you need a small business loan, the bank won't even talk to you unless you have a detailed business plan.

The primary purpose of your business plan is to describe *what* you will do as a business, what you *want* to do as a business, and how you plan to *grow* as a business.

Get these questions defined, and you'll have the perfect business plan, even if it is only three sentences.

If you're just starting out with a little ecommerce website, your business plan will be very simple. In fact, the hardest part about the business plan will be the time spent at the keyboard hammering it out while so many other things seem to warrant your time.

The best source of business plan information, including the planning, the templates for one, and writing suggestions, is Entrepreneur's site, http://www.entrepreneur.com. They are also crazy with free articles for new businesses.

While we've done our best to tell you everything that you need to know about starting a business in this guide, we aren't above acknowledging when other people know what they're talking about.

So, check 'em out.

We also have a free sample business plan for you to download on our website, http://www.wordpartnersink.com and click on Cyber Gold Resources.

Part Two: Building Your Website.

A journey of a thousand miles begins with a single step.

--Lao-tzu

In this part...

The most important thing to keep in mind is to be patient—doing it right takes time and effort. So, don't ever get discouraged! You *can* create a site to fit your needs, and trust us; it will be better than anything a pro could design for you, it will cost significantly less, and you'll be infinitely proud of yourself.

In this part you'll learn:

Chapter Four: Beginning Your Site
- Why we use Tripod to host websites, 79-80
- How to choose and sign up for a Tripod membership plan, 81-90
- How to select a template design and navigation, 92-100

Chapter Five: Building Your Site Shell
- How to edit your site title, 105-120
- How to use the picture gallery, 106-115
- How to use your logo as the site title, 115-120
- How to change the look of your site, design, & page background, 121-126
- How to edit your title area and title area background color, 126-129
- How to edit your top accent stripe, 129
- How to edit your site navigation: color, height, font, & alignment, 130-132
- How to edit your main area, 132-133
- How to edit your bottom area (site footer), 134-135

Chapter Six: Advanced Building & Editing
- How to use Tripod's toolbar, 138-140
- How to add text, pictures, links, & tables, 140-148
- How to utilize Tripod's site add-ons, 149-155
- How to add a new page, 155
- How to move items, copy, & delete items, 156-160
- How to preview and publish your site, 160-162
- How to use Tripod's site organizer, 162-163

Chapter Seven: Getting Around Your Account
- Everything you need to know to use your Tripod account, 164-181
- How to use subdomains and your Tripod email, 175
- How to use the Build & Edit menu, 176-177

Chapter Four
Beginning Your Site.

By now you should have a pretty good idea for a business (if not, don't panic), and you're probably ready for the rest of it: the planning of a website and the process of building.

First, we're going to tell you why we use the products and services that we do, and then we'll show you how to use them too.

By the end of this chapter, we'll have you signed up with a host (Tripod, http://www.tripod.com), have helped you to select a template for your site, and we'll have you ready to begin building your website.

HOSTING A WEBSITE.

Owning a website means two things. First, you purchase a domain name, and second, you host your site somewhere. Both can be done via the same vendor, or they can be done by two separate companies.

You could probably even build your site with another vendor, host with another, and have the domain name through another. It doesn't matter.

Sometimes we buy our domain name through Yahoo because they have that $2.99 (or even $1.99) a year deal going on, but we still have to host and build our site somewhere, so we use Tripod to achieve that part.

For some of our sites we buy the domain name and host on Tripod, it just depends, really, on how much of a hurry we are in.

We'll explain a bit about what this means. Basically, a website is just a really big folder full of stored files and photos. For everyone on the internet to see it, a "host" needs to open the folder for them, so to speak. And, the domain name gets them to the right host who opens the right folder.

Every host is different and every host has their own fees, options, and securities.

You can look around at a few for comparison if you like, but we guarantee Tripod and their services because we've been using them for years.

Actually, we'll tell the whole truth here.

Over the years, for one reason or another, we've thought about finding a new host. But it never worked out. None were as sophisticated or as reasonable and easy to use as Tripod, and we *looked*.

We use Tripod because they let you build your own site for free, they give you tons of templates to choose from and use (for free) and they even let you host your very own site for free.

Now, if you want the ads removed from your site you'll need to pay the domain name and hosting fee of $8.95 a month, but even that is the best deal on the internet, by far.

Think about it, all you have is an overhead of $8.95. No rent, no inventory in the wings, no plumbing problems, just $8.95 a month.

It's worth it and we love and trust their services.

You might be asking about the whole merchant account thing here. Just sign yourself up with a **PayPal Business Account** and you're good to go. PayPal's shopping cart is fully compatible with all of Tripod's templates, and it gives you a Premier Business Account, which means you'll have the ability to take e-checks and credit cards for your sales. We discuss PayPal and its fees fully in Chapter 9.

CHOOSING A TRIPOD MEMBERSHIP PLAN.

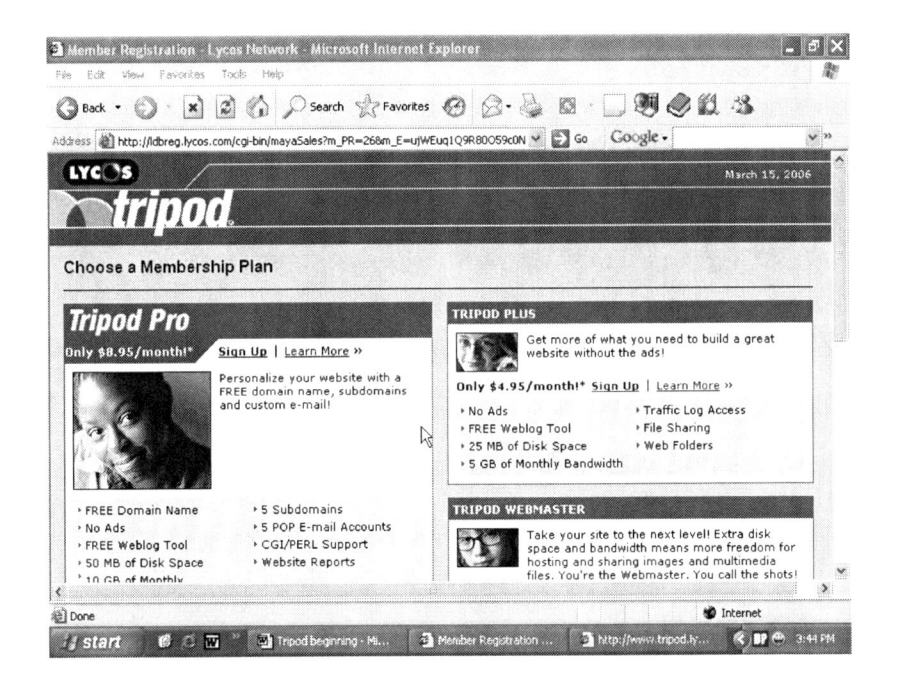

Tripod gives you quite a few options for your website design. Look through the membership plans to decide which will work best for you. This can be one of the most confusing aspects of getting started because the choices may seem daunting at first.

Almost always, you'll be fine getting the Tripod Pro plan because it buys you a domain name, tons of storage room, and tons of bandwidth.

But for those of you who like your options, below is the breakdown (note that we only added the options that actually make each plan *different* from the others).

Also, all of the plans come with the free images and templates, have easy to use building tools, are Microsoft FrontPage Enabled, and have web folders.

TRIPOD FREE
COST: ABSOLUTELY FREE

-20 MB of disk space
-1 GB of Monthly Bandwidth
-Easy to use Building Tools

-Free Images – Choose from over 10,000 images, including photos, etc

WE SAY:

Free is perhaps the best way to get building right away. You can still publish your site as often as you need and you can store quite a few pictures. The only drawback is the ads that will appear and the lack of a domain name. If you're really new to this, select the Free plan to get started, and then upgrade later once you are ready to publish your site.

Actually, we often start our sites out with the Free plan while we do site construction to avoid paying the $8.95 monthly until we're ready. It's always smarter to get your domain name as soon as possible, but that's just how we've done things.

So, if you don't feel comfortable starting right out with a monthly payment, sign up for the Free plan and get started building anyway. What do you have to lose if it's free?

TRIPOD PLUS
COST: $4.95 / MONTH

(One-time setup fee of $10.00)

- No Ads on your site
- 25 MB of Disk Space
- 5 GB of Monthly Bandwidth
- Live Customer Support
- Traffic Log Access for the past 30 days
- File Sharing
- CGI / Perl Support
- JavaScript & CGI Library

WE SAY:

Plus is a good all-around plan if you've already purchased a domain name elsewhere, at just $4.95 per month. We did this with wordpartnersink.com.

Yahoo had this deal for $2.99 a year for a domain name, so we bought it. Now, Plus does not offer a domain name with its plan, but you can forward one to your Plus account.

You need to purchase the Plus plan if you want to get rid of the ads on your site and appear reputable to your customers, but you need not pay more than the $4.95 a month if you already own a domain name.

All you have to do is set your domain name to forward. Forwarding is done in Yahoo, or wherever you purchased your domain name. For example,

we bought:

wordpartnersink.com (from Yahoo for just $2.99 a year)

we set it up to forward to:

wordpartnersink.tripod.com (which is our Tripod Plus account for $4.95 a month)

It sounds more complicated than it is, but whomever you buy a domain through will explain it very well, so don't panic if you've already bought one and will need to go through the forwarding process.

If you haven't already purchased a domain name, save yourself the trouble of forwarding and just buy the **Tripod Pro** plan. It will include a domain name and hosting fees for just $8.95, and you won't have to worry about renewing a domain name every year.

TRIPOD PRO
COST: $8.95 / MONTH

(One-time setup fee of $15.00)

- FREE Domain Name
- No Ads
- 50 MB of Disk Space
- 10 GB of Monthly Bandwidth
- Live Customer Support
- 5 Subdomains
- 5 POP e-mail accounts for your domain
- Website Stats
- CGI/Perl Support
- JavaScript & CGI Library

WE SAY:

If you don't own a domain name already, choose Pro to buy one from Tripod. This is helpful because the domain name and the cost of hosting are in the same payment, at just $8.95 a month. Pro also offers a great deal more storage and bandwidth than the Plus and Free plans.

Pro can pretty much be considered the standard plan on Tripod. It offers tons of disk space and bandwidth, plus a domain name is included in the cost. Weigh the options, but you'll probably find that Pro is the best plan to start with.

TRIPOD WEBMASTER
COST: $11.95 / MONTH

(One-time setup fee of $15.00)

- FREE Domain Name
- No Ads
- 100 MB of Disk Space
- 20 GB of Monthly Bandwidth
- Live Customer Support
- 10 Subdomains
- 10 POP e-mail accounts for your domain
- Website Stats
- CGI/Perl Support
- JavaScript & CGI Library

WE SAY:

Webmaster is for the very serious ecommerce sites that need bunches and bunches of bandwidth and file space for the $11.95 monthly charge.

If the Pro plan isn't working out because you need more space or room to grow, upgrade to the Webmaster plan.

TRIPOD DELUXE
COST: $19.95 / MONTH

(One-time setup fee of $15.00)

- FREE Domain Name
- No Ads
- 150 MB of Disk Space
- 30 GB of Monthly Bandwidth
- Live Customer Support
- 15 Subdomains
- 15 POP e-mail accounts for your domain
- Website Stats
- CGI/Perl Support
- JavaScript & CGI Library

WE SAY:

For $19.95 a month Tripod gives you nearly unlimited everything, so weigh this to your advantage and decide what will work best for your website.

TRIPOD EXTRAS.

As a Tripod member, you can always upgrade your plan with individual extras depending on your needs. Extras can be purchased at any time from the **My Account** page.

Tripod Extras are priced *per month*, and are in addition to your current plan fees. You can add or delete the extras whenever you want, so you'll never feel stuck.

ADDITIONAL BANDWIDTH

500 MB - $4.95
1.0 GB - $9.90
1.5 GB - $14.85
2.0 GB - $19.80
2.5 GB - $24.75

ADDITIONAL DISK SPACE

50 MB - $4.95
100 MB - $9.90
150 MB - $14.85
200 MB - $19.80
250 MB - $24.75

ADDITIONAL EMAILS

5 Addresses - $4.95
10 Addresses - $9.90
15 Addresses - $14.85
20 Addresses - $19.80
25 Addresses - $24.75

ADDITIONAL SUBDOMAINS

5 Subdomains - $4.95
10 Subdomains - $9.90
15 Subdomains - $14.85
20 Subdomains - $19.80
25 Subdomains - $24.75

SIGNING UP FOR A MEMBERSHIP PLAN.

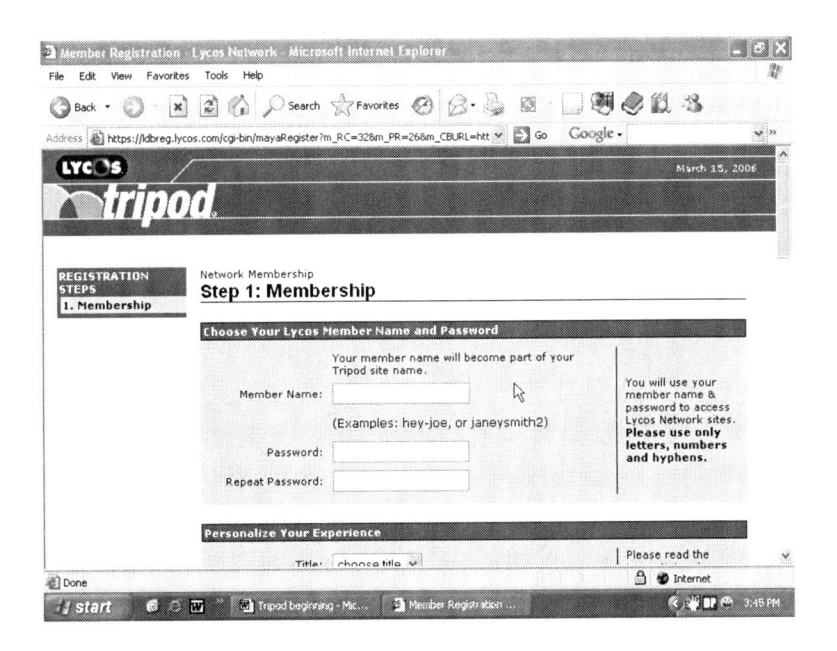

After selecting the plan for your needs, (**this walkthrough goes through the Tripod Free plan with the understanding that you'll upgrade after you build and publish your site—to do so all you have to do is log in to your account, select My Account, and click to upgrade**) you'll need to fill out a quick membership form.

Choose a member name that best reflects your business (remembering what we discussed about business names from Chapter 3).

Our business name is Shop Lizards, so shoplizards is our member name. Keep in mind that your member name will become your Free and Plus plan domain name.

For example, since shoplizards is our member name, **shoplizards.tripod.com** is our domain name with the Free and Plus plan. When we purchased the Pro plan, our domain name became **www.shoplizards.com**.

Spend time on this and choose wisely. If your business name is Tike's Trucks, do not choose Tike69 for your member name, like Tripod's weird examples suggest.

Select a password, and remember not to tell it to anyone, for your safety. Tripod (and any other reputable establishment like banks, eBay, or PayPal, will *never* ask for your password unless you are logging onto their site…keep this in mind to avoid scammers).

Just something of note on this, see the little yellow lock next to the globe and the word Internet on the Status Bar?

As you've read in Chapter 1, you'll know that the closed lock on the Status Bar means that this page within Tripod is secure, and that no one can view your information other than Tripod.

So, when you are using other pages on the internet that need to be secure, like when you enter in your credit card information, or even your email, remember to make sure that the lock is present and you'll be hacker safe.

PERSONALIZE YOUR EXPERIENCE.

Tripod also gives you the option to personalize your experience. Fill in your name and birth date, as Tripod will use this information later if you forget your password. Fill in your address now, and you won't have to fill it in on the credit card screen (but you won't need to worry about that if you're sticking with the Free plan for now). Everything is required except the Education and Occupation.

NOTE:

Tripod can only accept payment via credit card or debit card. We had a bit of trouble with this when building a site for a client, as they only used checks.

So, we had them put a hundred bucks on an American Express gift card (can be found at all Zion's Bank locations, or check with your local banks). This pays for their membership for about a year, and we got them around the check issue. So be prepared for this.

If you cannot get a gift card right now or if you don't have a credit card or debit card, you can still use Tripod's Free plan, so don't panic.

Right now, you don't have to enter in anything unless you've chosen a plan other than the Free plan. If this is the case, just fill in the required information and follow Tripod's steps.

CHOOSE YOUR ADS AND INTERESTS.

If you decide to use Tripod's Free plan, select your interests and they will be reflected in the ads on your page. For example, if you choose automotive, you'll have ads from Vehix.com and AutoTrader.com on your site.

Also, under the Tripod & Lycos Network Offers, make sure that only the ones you are interested in are checked. You may or may not want all the newsletters available. Or, you may not want any newsletters at all, so make sure to uncheck everything if that's the case.

ENTER CONFIRMATION CODE.

Fill in the numbers (and/or letters) as they appear and take the time to read Tripod's Terms and Conditions and their Privacy Policy. These will always be available to you, so if you know you'll agree, just select "I Agree" to finish with the membership registration.

FREE OFFERS.

After Tripod creates your account, you will be taken to a "Special Offers" page. Read through them carefully and make sure you check the ones you want or select the little "No Thanks" button at the bottom of the screen if you aren't interested.

If you do click "yes" for any of the offers, you'll be taken to that sponsor's page, and away from Tripod to continue with your special offer participation. If you check "yes" for a bunch of them, plan to spend some time dealing with all the new registration. Note that you don't have to participate in any of the special offers.

UPGRADING YOUR ACCOUNT.

To upgrade your Tripod account at any time (preferably when you are ready to publish your site), you'll use the orange navigation bar at the top of the main Tripod screen to select:

My Account→Membership Type→Upgrade Your Membership

You can downgrade, upgrade, or add extras to your account whenever you want. We suggest upgrading to the Pro account, $8.95 a month, when you are ready to publish your site, but you can certainly do it before you even get started, as long as you have your perfect keyword-targeted domain name in mind (see the exercise under the heading Finding Your Keywords in Chapter Ten).

When you get your site completed and ready for the world to see, you'll publish it, then we suggest upgrading at that point to the Pro or Plus plan (depending on your domain name needs, as we explained earlier) because you'll be ready for business!

TRIPOD'S WELCOME PAGE.

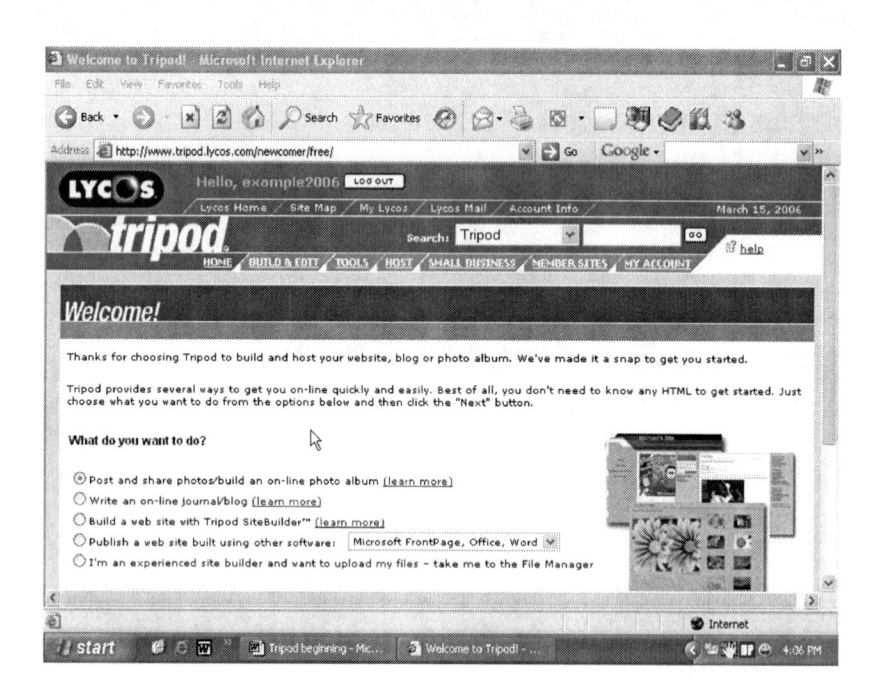

You're all done registering, so now you need to decide what you want to build. You do have a fair amount of choices here, so it depends on your needs.

This walkthrough goes over building a site using **Tripod's Site Builder**, but if you have experience with Microsoft FrontPage, Macromedia DreamWeaver, want to create a blog, or just want to make a quick photo album, you can choose them instead.

To create your own website, select the **Build a Site** option.

WHY WE USE TEMPLATES VS HTML.

We said we'd teach you how to build your own website, and to do that we won't be using much HTML. Some of you may be breathing out a sigh of relief, but some of you might be frowning in confusion.

We want you to know a *bit* of HTML, of course (and you'll learn some in Chapter 12), but building a website with HTML now is only done by the *super* cocky techies.

It's a lot of work, very easy to make mistakes in, and if the templates have already been created by someone who actually hosts the sites, and are as customizable as you need them to be (and are much better than any HTML a techie could create), why bother with the hard stuff?

Now, for some of the really customizable stuff, you will be expected to learn enough HTML to get yourself by, but we'll teach you everything you might possibly need to know, so don't stress.

And won't that be exciting the next time a family function rolls around? You…and HTML!

We'll teach you what you need to know, and we'll even teach you enough that if you wanted to branch off on your own and learn more, you certainly could (and should! Never stop learning…), and you'd understand the more complex stuff without much difficulty.

But for now, you'll be building your site using a template. The HTML part comes later, once your site is all set up and you're ready to add inventory and shopping cart buttons.

SELECTING A TEMPLATE.

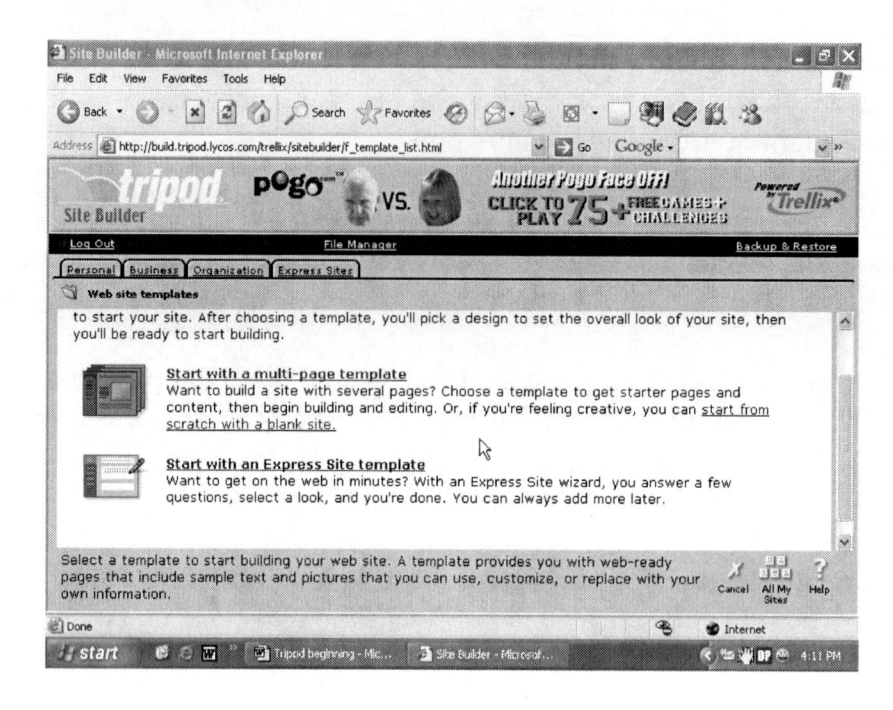

As always, Tripod attempts to make your experience as easy as possible. From this page, you can choose to "Start with a Multi-Page Template" or to "Start with an Express Site Template."

From experience, the multi-page template is the easiest to customize, while the express site is better for more simple sites. But they both offer the same options and same customizable templates.

If you choose one and don't like the options it gives, you can always come back and choose the other later.

So, for the purpose of building a more customizable website, select "start with a multi-page template." Even if you don't think that your site will be very complex, for the purpose of this guide, go ahead and select **multi-page template.**

That way, at the very least, you'll know what you can do and what Tripod is capable of doing for you.

STARTING WITH A MULTI-PAGE TEMPLATE.

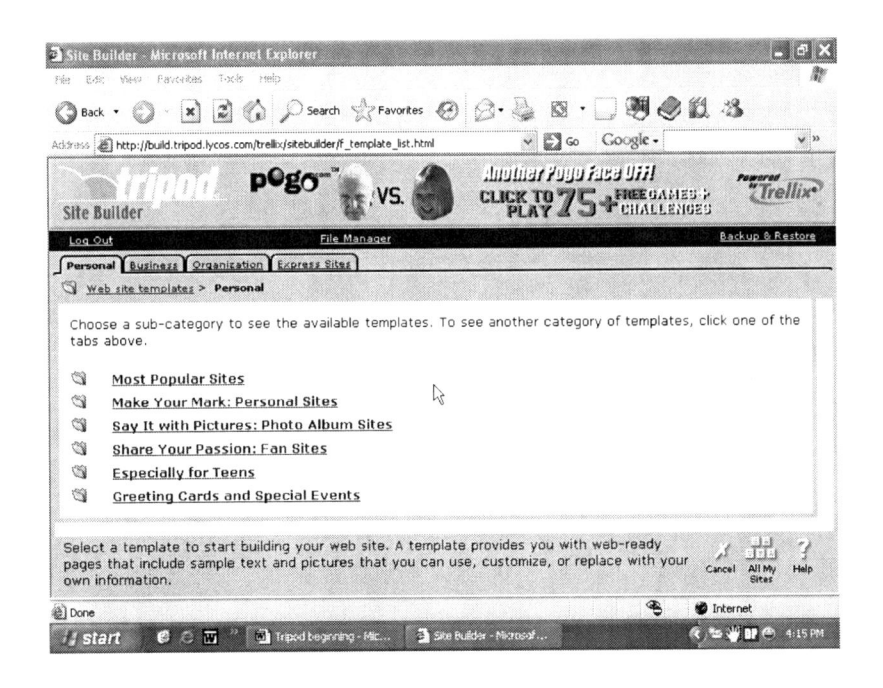

Pick a category that best suits your needs to continue. When you pick a category, another list will come up, giving you the option to choose a template.

Nothing is set in stone here, so just pick out the category that sounds the most like the site you need/want.

Since this walkthrough is based on the construction of Shop Lizards, which is an ecommerce shopping site, we'd choose the yellow "Business" tab, and then from the new list that comes up, we'd choose "Shopping and Sales."

In all actuality, your choice will have no effect on our instructions, so feel free to look through your options and make the best choice for your site.

The only real difference in templates will be the pages that your template offers, but you can add, delete, and change them later, so really, this choice is *just* to get you started.

So, a shopping site template will have a pre-created page for inventory, but you can always make one later, so don't worry about any of your choices now.

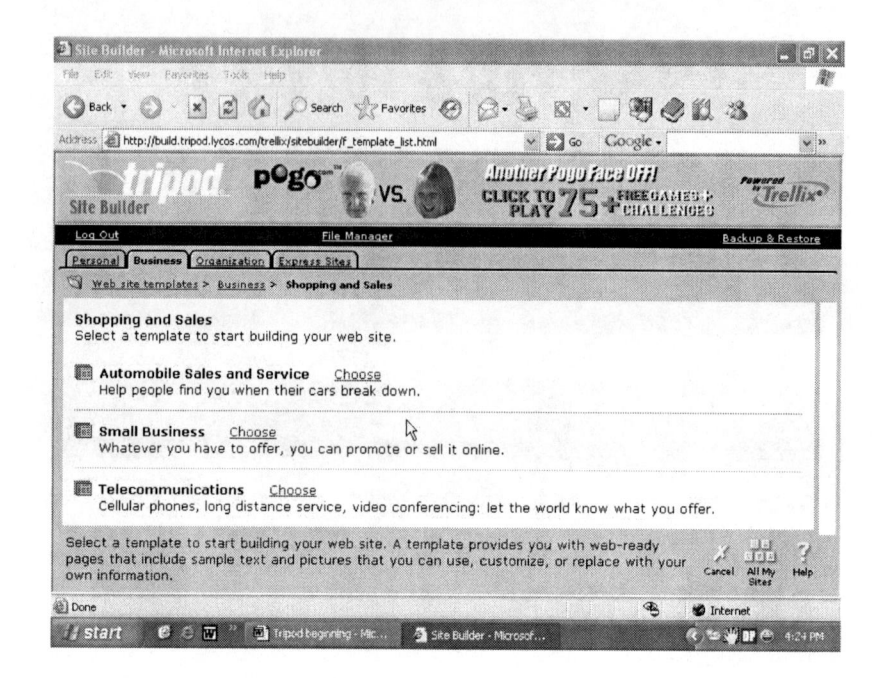

Your next page will look much like the picture above, with a complete breakdown of templates offered in your chosen category.

Again, it doesn't matter which you choose since everything can be changed later, but pick the one that you'd like to work with to continue. There's no reason to use the telecommunications one, though, if you'll be selling rhinestone dog coats.

Next, you'll be taken to this page…

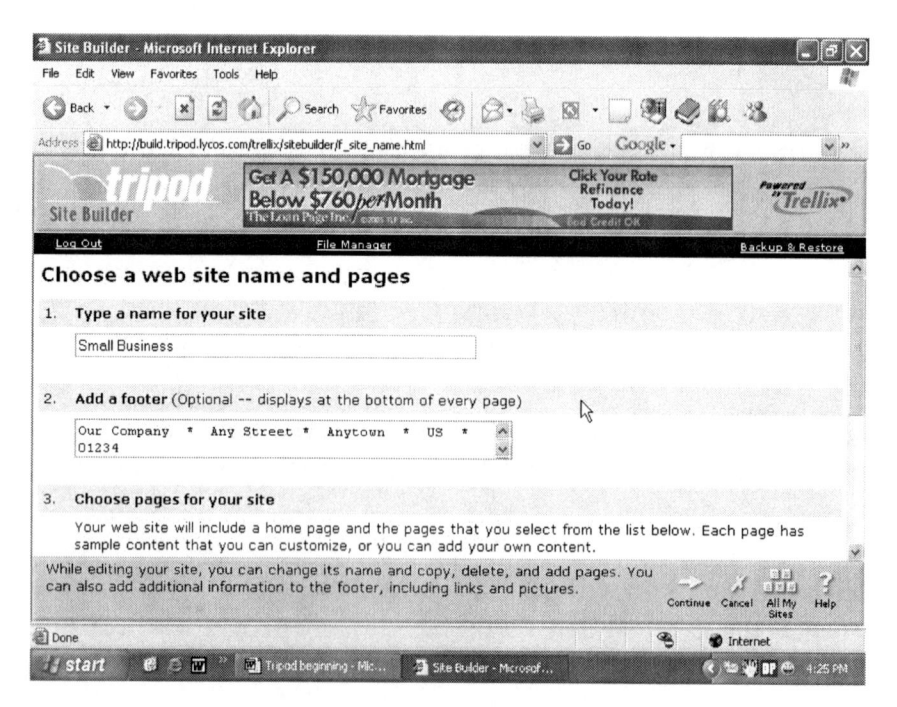

Here, you'll be given three steps.

FIRST, you'll need to input a **Site Name**. Go ahead and fill in your business name here. We'd input Shop Lizards.

SECOND, you need to fill in your **Site Footer Info**, meaning that you'll need to fill in the info that will appear exactly the same on the bottom of every page, on your footer. So here, fill in your company name, street, town, and zip code.

This is our site footer:

If you don't want this info given out, don't fill it in; and later, you'll be adding copyright info, etc to the footer, so don't stress about it being perfect now.

THIRD, scroll down the page a bit and you'll get to choose **which pages you might need**.

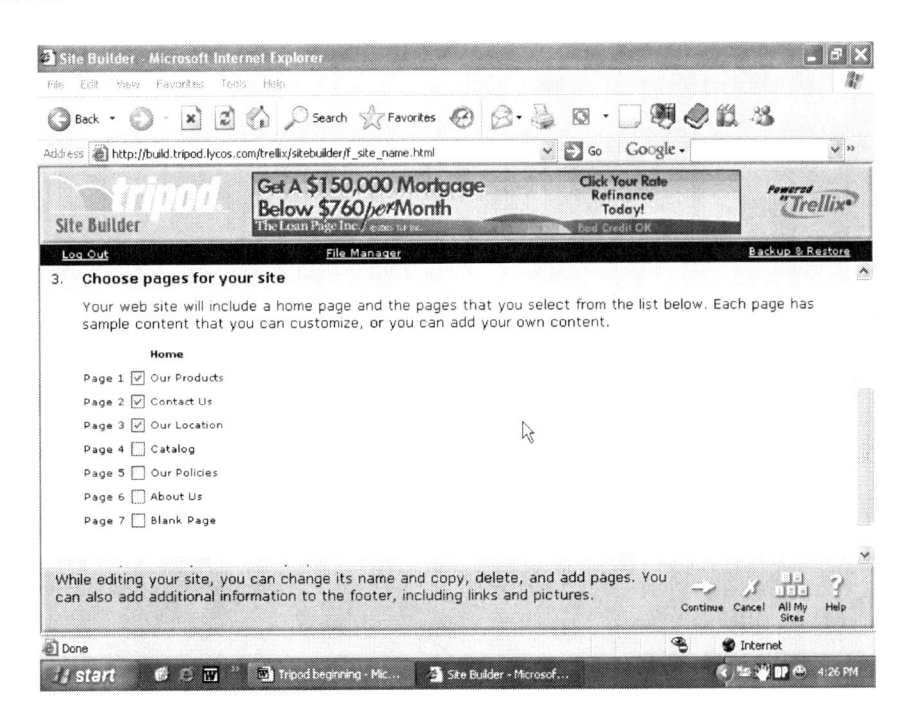

Chapter 8 goes over the pages required for a site to get ranked in the search engines, but none of them are actually listed here. Go figure. For now, put a check by a few pages, like the **Our Products**, **Catalog**, **Our Policies**, and **About Us**, to get you started. You'll change the page titles later, but this will just get you started with a nice chunk of the pages that you'll need.

Keep in mind that you can always add or delete pages later; this is just to get you started with a few template pages right now. And you can have as many pages as you want (one, one thousand, or more!), so don't worry that this list only contains seven pages.

Check the boxes next to the pages that you want, and then select the "Continue" check mark on the bottom, gray, toolbar to continue.

CHOOSE A WEBSITE DESIGN.

Now you'll come to a page where you need to choose your **Site Design**.

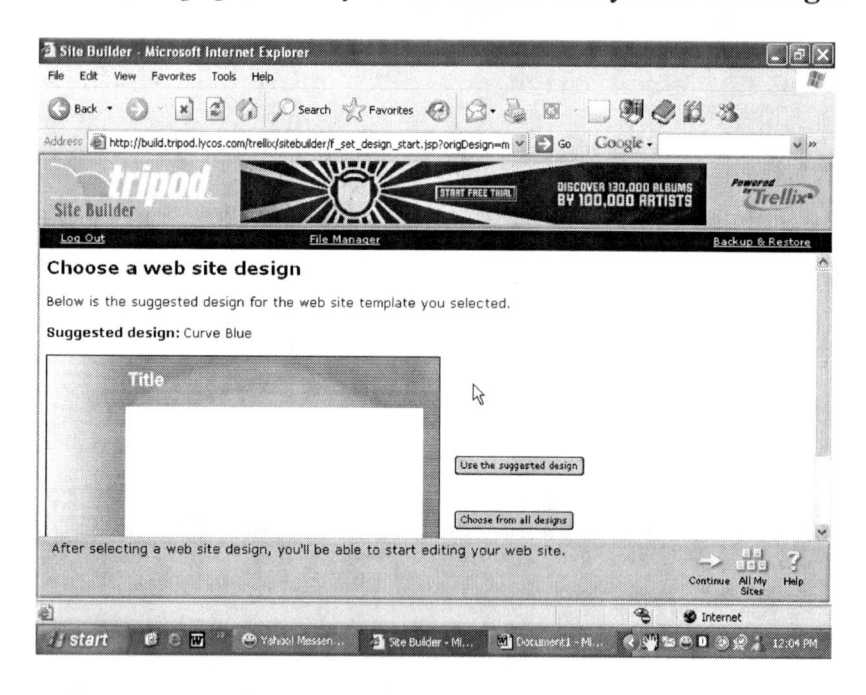

If you like the suggested site design (which you don't have to), click the "Continue" button on the gray toolbar, or the little **Use the suggested design** button.

Most likely, you'll want to see the templates gallery (and we actually insist that you do so you can select an easy to customize template), just to see your other options. So, click the **Choose from all designs** button.

CHOOSE FROM ALL TEMPLATE DESIGNS.

It's important that we explain something about using templates and still be able to call ourselves website designers.

The templates may be pre-created for us, but we *always* change them to suit our needs, or our client's needs. When we're done, you'd never be able to tell that the finished product came from a template. And, you'll soon find that just using a template means nothing compared to what you'll learn to change it to fit your business image.

That, in itself, is an art. It's just an art made easier by a pre-created template.

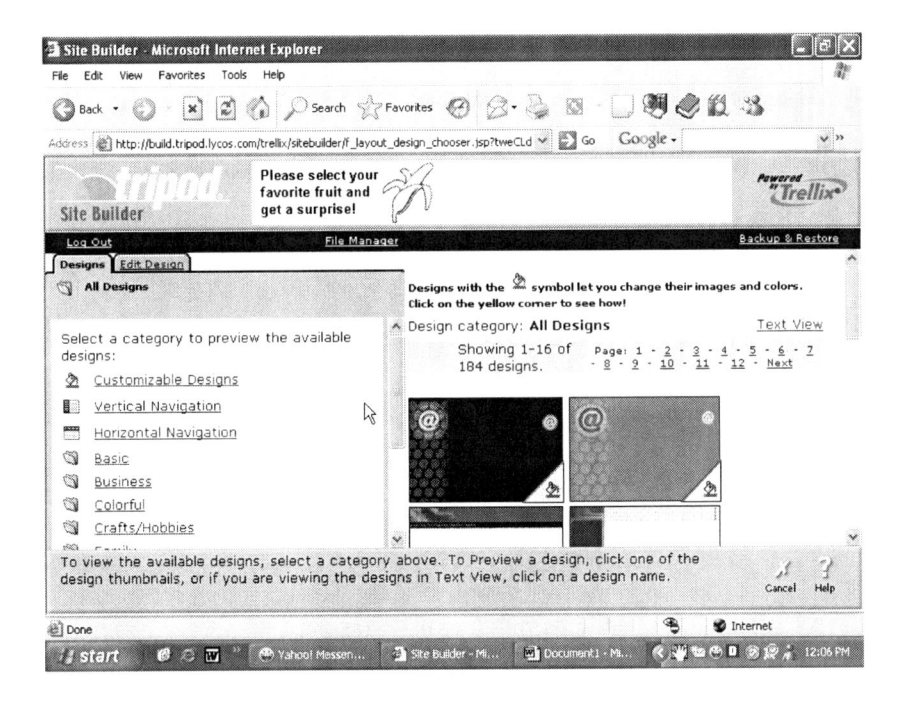

The screen shown above is split in half by your choices.

To the left, you'll see "All Designs" within a gray frame. This is a list of all of your available templates. To the right, all the templates for the category you have selected will be displayed for you to choose from.

HORIZONTAL VS. VERTICAL NAVIGATION.

Tripod separates the templates for your convenience. There are two basic kinds: horizontal navigation, and vertical navigation. The navigation bar is the "bar" that holds page selections sort of like a Table of Contents for your website.

Horizontal navigation means that your page selections will run horizontally; vertical navigation means that the page selection choices will run vertically.

Home | Play Free Games | Diecast Collectible Cars & Trucks | Diecast Collectible Aircraft

Above is Shop Lizard's navigation bar; it's horizontal navigation.

Below is the vertical navigation bar from our Word Partners Ink website. Vertical navigation looked better for this site because we have quite a few pages and it allows the pages to be seen easier if you have more than four or five you want listed on the navigation bar.

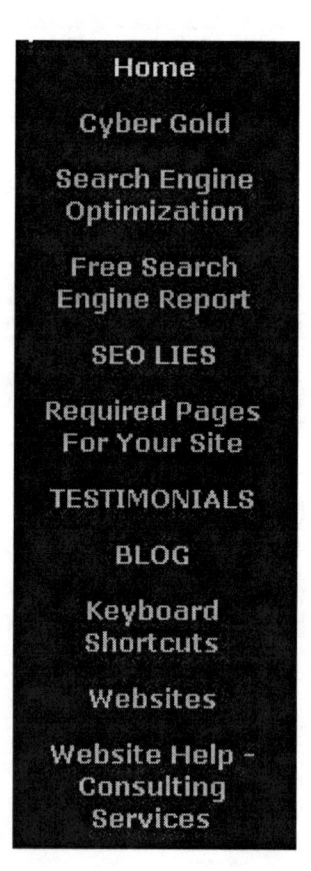

Home
Cyber Gold
Search Engine Optimization
Free Search Engine Report
SEO LIES
Required Pages For Your Site
TESTIMONIALS
BLOG
Keyboard Shortcuts
Websites
Website Help - Consulting Services

Basically, horizontal navigation tends to look better for sites that have fewer pages to display.

But experiment with this, as in all things.

It sounds simple, but some sites look terrible with one sort of navigation, while others look great. So make this consideration carefully, and if your site looks funky with one, come back and try another template with the other kind of navigation until you find one that works.

Note that templates come with *only* vertical or horizontal navigation. A template will not have both as a choice. So, if you fall in love with a horizontal navigation template and it doesn't work well for your site, you'll just have to find another or make it work.

Now, if you know which sort of navigation you'd like for your site, choose one or the other instead of going through all the other categories, as all the templates are either horizontal or vertical navigation anyway. If you don't yet care which sort of navigation your site has, go through all the templates until you find a design that suits your needs.

When you're editing a template and later find that you no longer like the horizontal navigation and want vertical, or vice versa, this is the page where you will be directed to make the change.

So, whether or not you find a template that you like right off, go through all the choices and get to know your selections.

CUSTOMIZING YOUR TEMPLATE.

Not all of Tripod's templates can be customized. This means that some templates come with colors, images, and even layouts that *cannot* be changed. You definitely want a template that can be fully customized (has a little paint can in the bottom right corner) because you'll want to create something unique that you can be proud of and that fits your company image.

To our knowledge, there are two designs can be *completely and easily* customized, one horizontal and one vertical. There are probably others, but we haven't spent more than a few hours testing each one out. However, we don't really want you to worry about finding a template that you like, here. Really the only thing you need to consider is your navigation bar and whether you want it to be horizontal or vertical. Everything else will be changed to reflect your company image, colors, and products. So, in general, we *always* pick one of the two customizable templates below just because some of the others are so completely limiting that they are more frustrating than anything else and we know for a fact that these two can be customized completely—colors, fonts, backgrounds, layouts, and all.

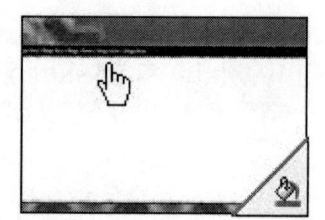

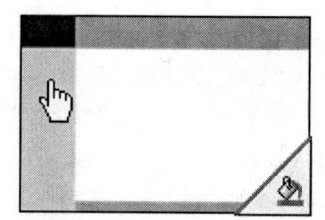

It might be hard to tell with the black and white printing, but the one on the left (the horizontal navigation) is bright pink/red with orange fire-like designs at the top and bottom and the one on the right (the vertical navigation) is gray and white with a black box in the left hand corner. If you click on "Customizable Designs," the horizontal template appears in your first page of choices in the second row, and the vertical template is in the very bottom row, on that same page.

Don't let the colors scare you, here. Shop Lizards was constructed from the horizontal navigation template and Word Partners Ink was constructed from the vertical navigation template—so the sky is the limit here with what you can do.

Keep in mind that you are beginning your site shell, you are basically selecting the pan that you'll put your crust in before you fill it in with pie. Most of this process will be taking the template and changing it completely, so you need to think of it as just a shell, and not the final design.

So, pick the one that has the navigation bar you want for your website to continue, knowing that you can come back here any time (and as often as you want) to review your options.

When the preview screen comes up, click the yellow "Continue" check mark at the bottom right of the screen to finish.

WELCOME TO YOUR HOMEPAGE.

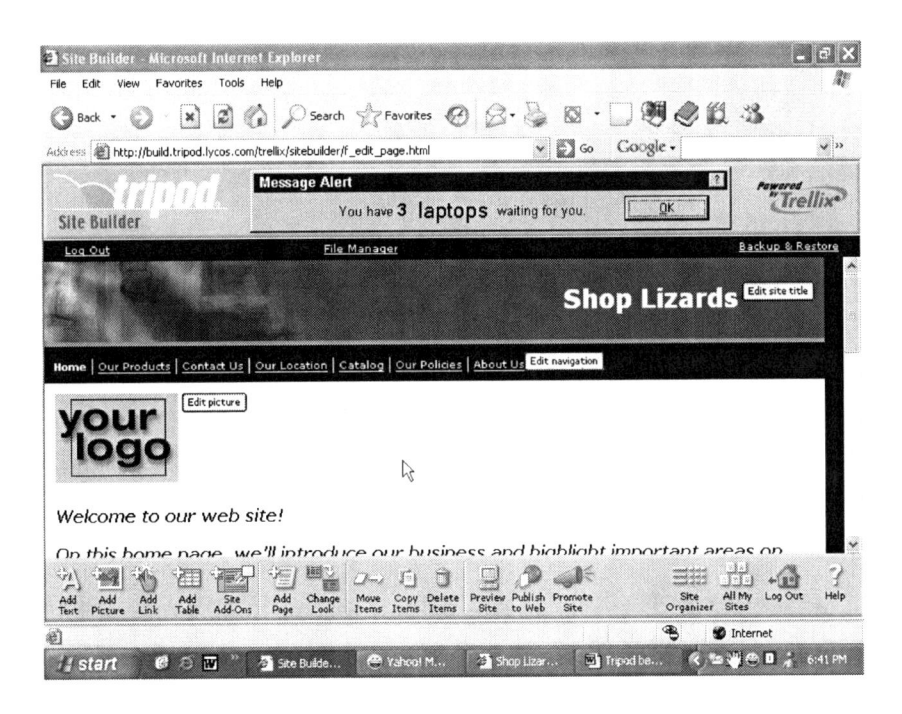

At this point, Tripod has saved all of the choices and changes that you've made, so if you need a break, you can do so now without worry. You can even close the Tripod window and shut off your computer; Tripod will remember everything.

Actually, any time that you make changes or add something new to your site, Tripod saves the changes because there is no real "save" button. This can work for the good or for the bad, but for your purposes now; think of it as a good thing.

What Tripod doesn't do for you, at this point, is make your site available to the public. But you're not ready for that yet. When your site is presentable and you want people to find it, you'll select the **Publish** button from Tripod's gray toolbar to make your site *live*.

Live means that people can type in your domain name to find you…but you won't be listed in the search engines for a while (it takes about a month no matter what you do or pay for—unless you follow the strategies we outline a bit later), so if you publish before you are really ready, you probably won't be found for some time with a search.

If you're ready to work, now comes the fun part—take a deep breath and refill that coffee mug, because it's going to be a bit of a ride.

Chapter Five
Building Your Site Shell.

You should now have a decent template that you'd like to work with. You should also have a basic idea of what you want to sell, be it products or services, and you should have a nice little logo and business name as well. If you don't have a logo or have the colors chosen for your site, we suggest taking the time to do so now.

The instructions that follow will make more sense if you do, and you'll be able to build your site without having to skip information that applies to the logo or choosing site colors during construction.

We're going to walk you through the actual site construction now, from top to bottom. By the end of this chapter, you should know what to do to get the rest of your site done, or at least have an idea of what you'd like to do and have an understanding on how to get it done without much confusion.

It's not hard, and it's not as intimidating as it sounds…just go slow and absorb what you can, finding comfort in the fact that if we don't explain things well enough, Tripod has their *own* help section, forum, and tech support.

Trust us, the more you work with Tripod, the faster and better at it you'll get. Soon, you'll laugh that we even took the time to write all of this down.

A BASIC "SHELL" FROM TOP TO BOTTOM.

You'll have noticed that selecting a template has already pre-filled a bunch of information in for you, but you won't be leaving any of it the way that it is.

You can, however, use the template's pictures and text as a guideline if you don't know what needs to go where, or if you like the way the template did things. Perhaps one of the more difficult things in web design is just having a basic understanding of what you *want* things to look like, let alone how to actually get things the way you want them. But it *will* get easier, trust us.

For now, think of your template as a basically blank slate (or "shell") that has just happened to fill in some stuff for you. Nothing is set in stone, or must be left where it is, all colors can be changed, and layouts can be tweaked. Pretty much everything can be deleted, changed, or moved. Keep this in mind.

If you're ready to build, log in to Tripod (http://www.tripod.com) and select the edit button to begin editing your site.

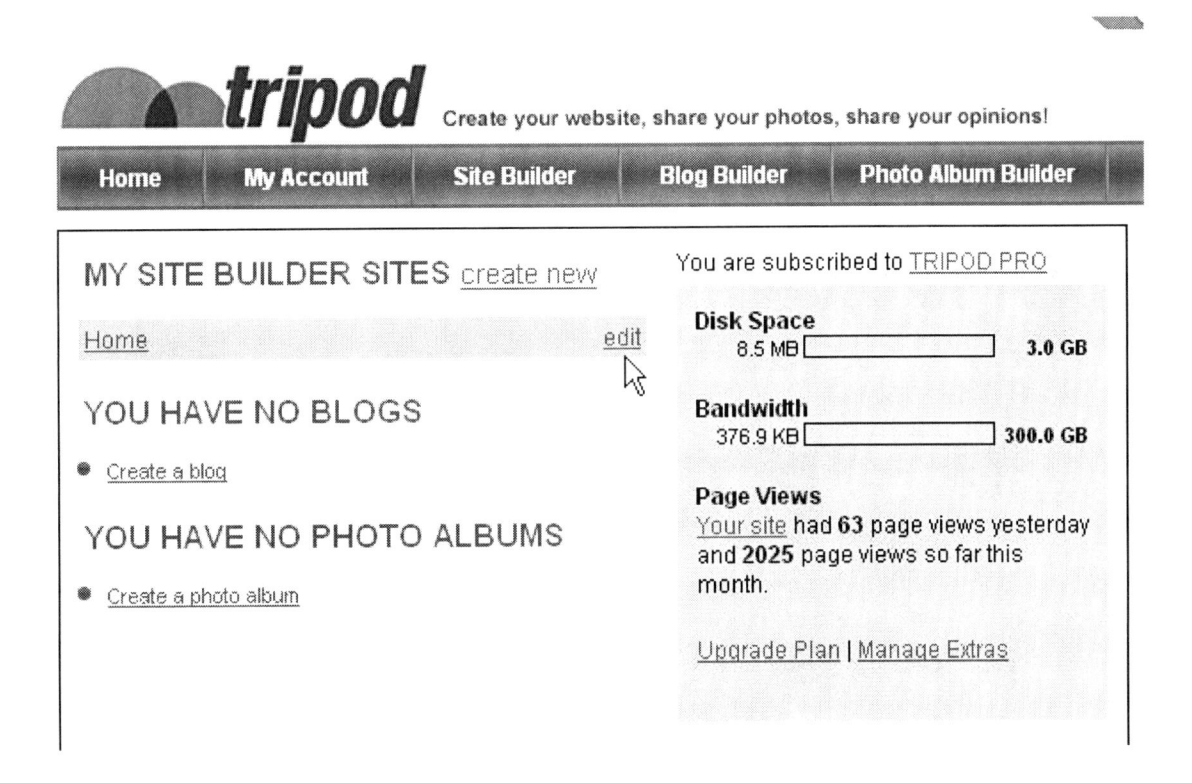

Below is the Tripod toolbar, found at the bottom of every edit screen, so get to know it well.

Tripod is always out to make things easier for you, so note the order of things. We'll go over these functions based on how they lay on your page first, from the top of your page down to the bottom.

The buttons on the toolbar are gone over in order in the next chapter, but we want to tell you how to fix and change what you already have on the page, before you need to learn about adding and deleting things. That way, at the very least, you can have a nearly finished shell of your site by the end of this chapter, and you should have a pretty good idea of what you want to do with it next.

At the very least, we want you to begin thinking about your site as a blank canvas of sorts. Your blank canvas. Anything you want for your site can probably be done, you just need to find a way to do it. And the best way to do that is to get to know Tripod's buttons. After working on Tripod for a while you'll understand what can be done and be able to imagine new and exciting things that you'll be able to put into motion on your site.

All it takes is an understanding of what you have to work with.

And, that's why we wrote this guide! It took us some serious time, too, to really understand what can be accomplished on a website. As in anything, familiarity takes time, but it brings knowledge and achievements right along with it.

READY TO BEGIN?

We'll start at the top of the page and work our way down…

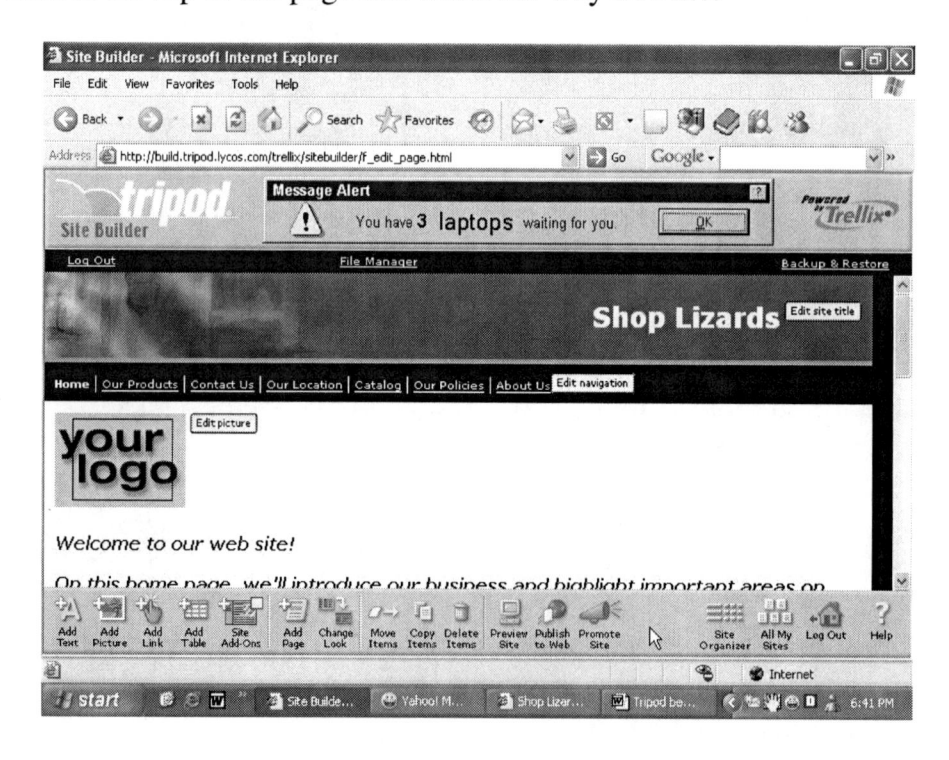

First, you'll see your site title, and a little yellow **Edit Site Title** button near it, usually to the right. Our title says "Shop Lizards" in big white lettering.

Click the **Edit Site Title** button to continue.

EDIT SITE TITLE.

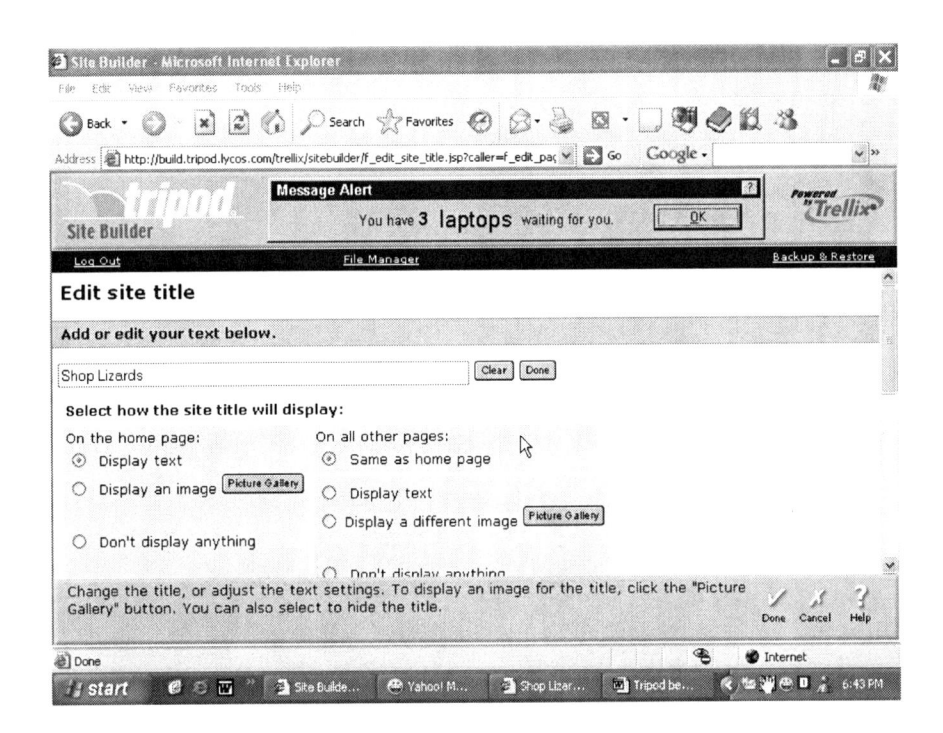

You'll be taken to the **Edit Site Title** page. From here, you can change the size, color, font, and position of your site title. This is where we'll upload our logo so that it will be displayed where the site title would be instead of the text.

This page is handy because you can select the option to also have all the other pages mimic the homepage, so make sure that it is selected because it will save you a great deal of confusion and stress.

Since this is where you'll upload your logo, select the radio button next to **Display an Image** and click the little gray **Picture Gallery** button.

GOING TO THE PICTURE GALLERY.

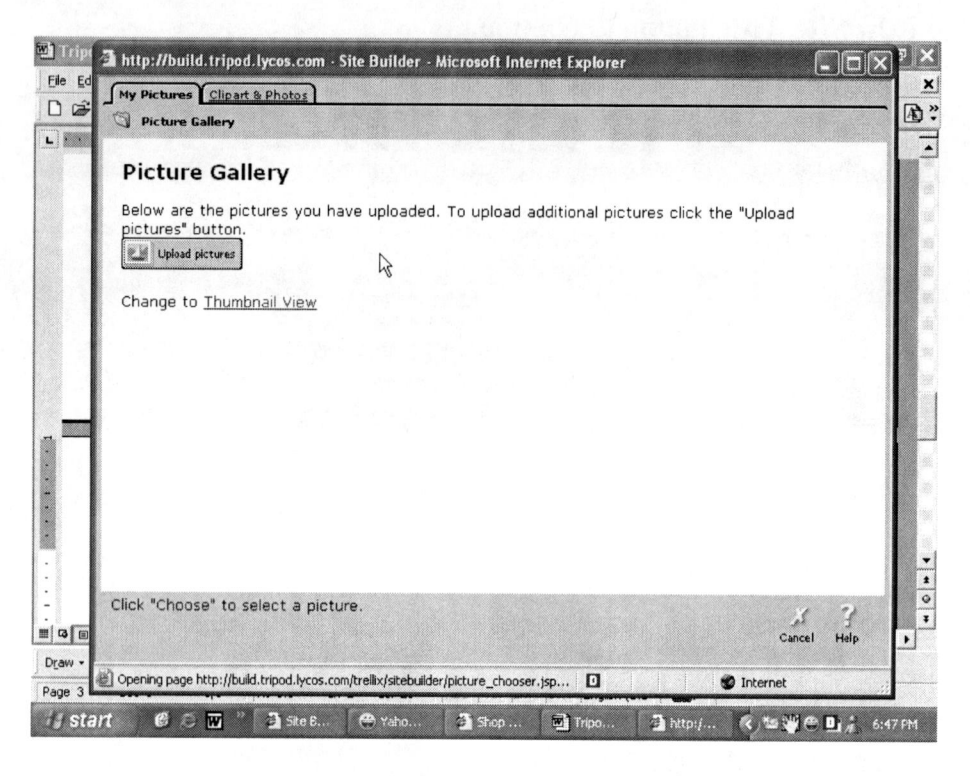

A new window will pop-up; this is your **Picture Gallery**.

Since you are just starting out, your picture gallery will be empty. You'll notice at the top of this new window that there is a gray tab labeled **My Pictures** and a yellow tab marked **Clipart and Photos**.

If you have your own images, like a logo, which most likely you will, you'll select the gray **Upload Pictures** button. For now, even if you do have an image ready, go ahead and click the **Clipart and Photos** tab so you can see Tripod's gallery.

CLIPART AND PHOTO GALLERY.

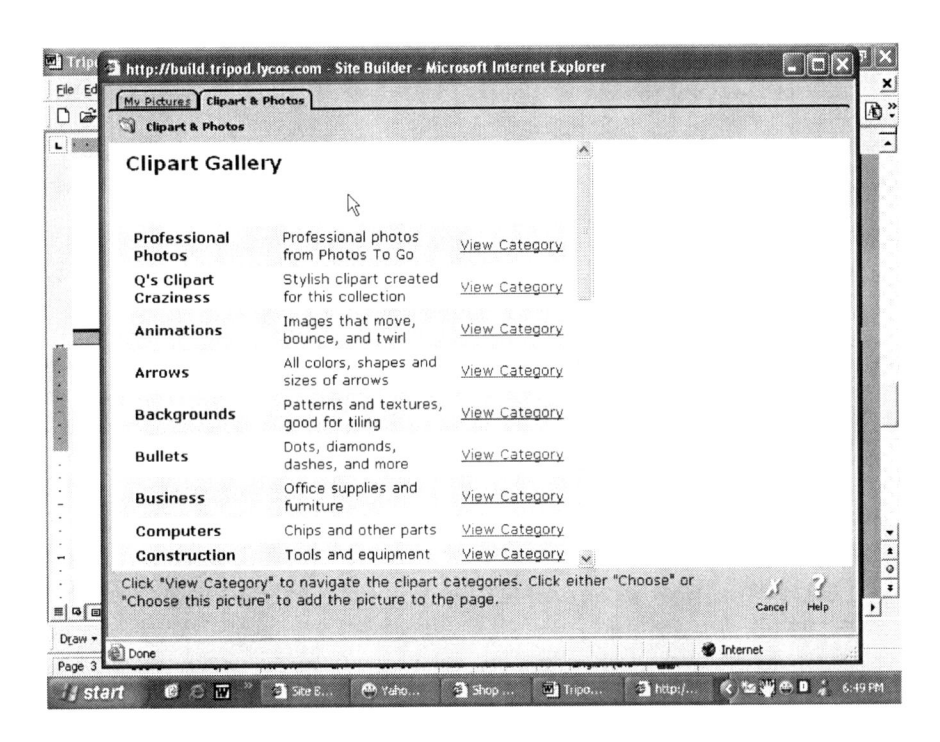

Clipart and Photos will take you to a fairly extensive gallery organized by category:

Professional Photos
Q's Clipart Craziness
Animations
Arrows
Backgrounds
Bullets
Business
Computers
Construction
ECommerce
Email
Food
Games and Toys
Horizontal Dividers
Headers
History
Mechanical
Medieval
Miscellaneous

Nature
Professional
Photos
Security
Sound and Video
Space
Sports
Template Pictures Set 1
Template Pictures Set 2
Travel

Take your time looking through the gallery, and if you find something that will fit with your site, remember where it is (like which category it's in) and come back for it later.

You can always come back to this gallery to add pictures or clipart to your site. And, this is the same gallery available to you at all times during the editing process, and everything in it is completely free—so make good use of it.

If you don't like anything you see, and since none of them should be used as your logo, click the cancel "X" at the bottom of the screen, or select the yellow **My Pictures** tab to go back to your picture gallery.

USING THE PICTURE GALLERY.

The picture gallery will keep every picture that you have ever uploaded until you delete them from Tripod. You can upload as many as you want, up to the amount available to you in your Tripod plan. We know for a fact that the Pro plan, at 50MB of disk space, can hold approximately a thousand 8x11 inch pictures, probably even more. So, upload to your heart's content.

Now, there are two different ways of viewing the gallery, in **Thumbnail View**, where you'll see little "thumbnail" images of your pictures, or the **Text View**, where you'll be able to see all of your photos in the order in which they were uploaded, in list form.

THUMBNAIL VIEW

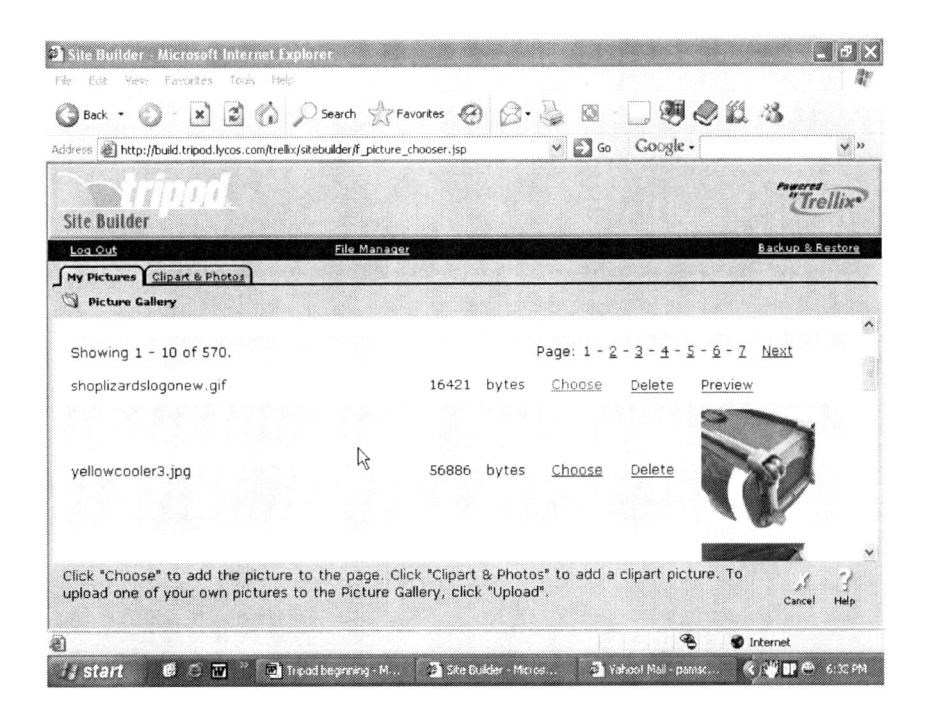

TEXT VIEW

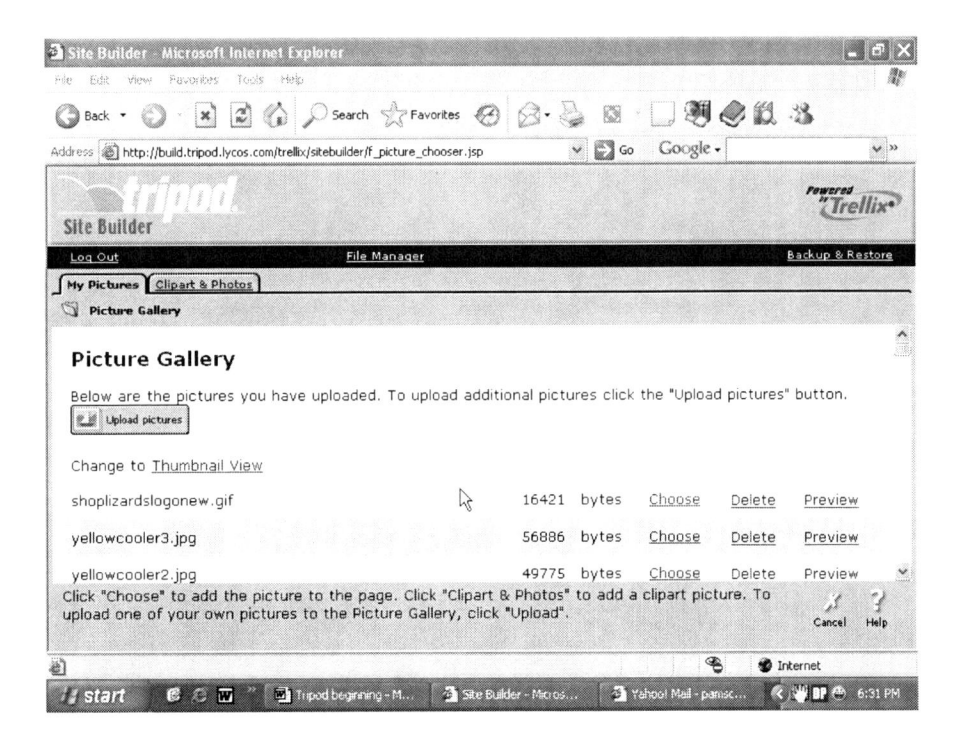

Both views have their advantages; however, the thumbnail view only lets you see ten photos at once, while the text view lets you see all the photos available in your gallery at once, except that it shows them in the *order* in which they were uploaded, and not *alphabetically*, unless you uploaded them all at once, alphabetically.

Our gallery has over five hundred pictures; so finding a picture in the thumbnail view takes an extremely long time, at just ten pictures a view. Because this is so, we always stick with the text view.

Oh and don't get frustrated if you've uploaded a ton of photos and your gallery suddenly takes a while to load.

This is normal.

The more photos in the gallery, the longer it will take for the gallery to load, so plan on waiting a bit if you'll want to put a bunch of pictures on your pages. And if you don't have DSL at this point, we offer our greatest sympathies. For the picture gallery alone, we recommend DSL—just to retain your sanity.

Since you'll be using a logo as your site title, we suggest uploading it now. This process will be the same for every photo that you upload, so take a moment when we're done to smile. It's one big thing learned out of the way.

Click the **Upload A Picture** button near the top left of the gallery.

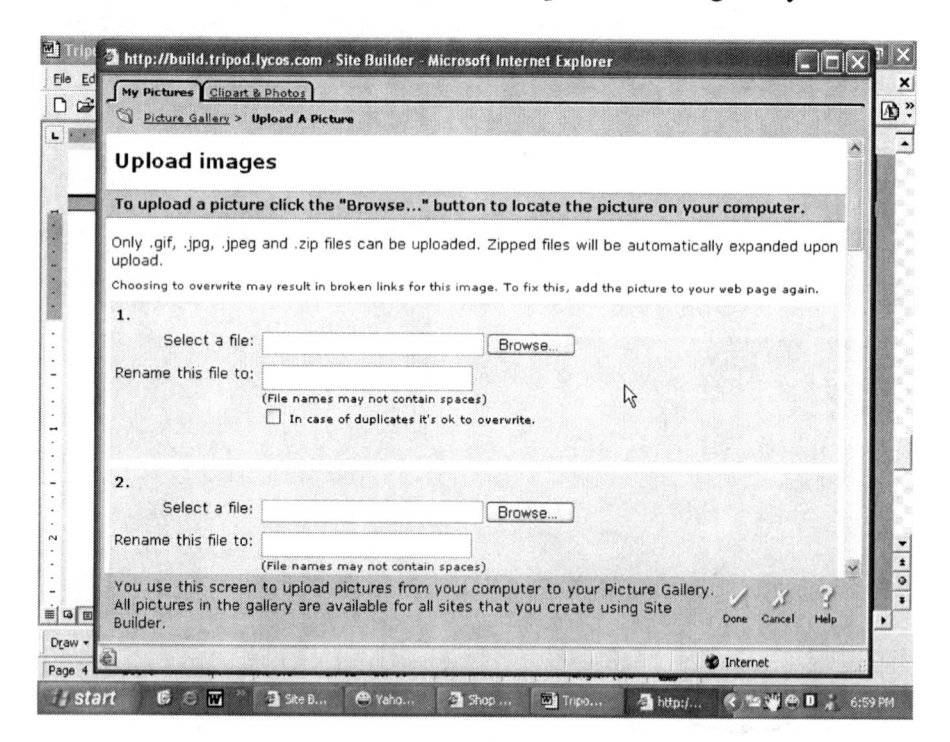

FILE EXTENSIONS REQUIRED FOR THE PHOTO GALLERY.

This is the screen where you'll upload all of your images to the Tripod server, and into your picture gallery so that they can be used on your site. Note that only certain file extensions can be uploaded.

Basically, when you first save an image to your computer, make sure to save it as a **.gif**, **.jpg**, **.jpeg**, or a **.zip**.

.gif, .jpg, .jpeg, and .zip are all **file extensions**.

If all of this is sounding a bit fuzzy to you, take a moment to review "How to Save a Picture to Your Computer" near the end of Chapter 1.

Most often, your images will be a .jpg anyway. If they are animation oriented or have been edited a bit, they might have been saved as a .gif.

Keep in mind that **.tiff**, and **.bmp** are not compatible with Tripod. If your image is a .bmp, or a .tiff, you'll need to open your photo in your photoshop program and "save as" a .jpg or .gif before uploading to your picture gallery.

Tripod lets you upload up to ten pictures at once, so if you will be loading a lot of pictures, like we did (more than five hundred) plan on spending much of your time on this screen and in the picture gallery.

UPLOADING A PHOTO.

1. Select a file: [   ] [Browse...]
   Rename this file to: [   ]
   (File names may not contain spaces)
   ☐ In case of duplicates it's ok to overwrite.

Click the **Browse** button next to "Select a file". This will open a new window giving you access to all of the files on your computer.

Go through your files and find the photo that you want to upload and select it with a left click of your mouse or click the **Open** button.

Doing so will bring you back to the **Upload Images** page and your picture name should now appear in the slot for number one.

NOTE: your image file name cannot contain spaces, so rename it now in the box Tripod provides if you didn't do so when originally saving your picture to your computer.

For example:

new globe.jpg

needs to be changed to:

newglobe.jpg

Also, Tripod will not recognize capital letters so make sure that you don't use them to distinguish between file names. And, if you upload more than one with the same name, but want the new one to overwrite the old, select the little box that says to do so under the picture that you've just uploaded.

When you've uploaded all the photos that you want (at least your logo), or up to your first ten, click the "Done" checkmark on the gray toolbar at the bottom of the screen.

You'll notice that there is also a little gray "Done" button after number ten. Either button will work, but we've noticed that sometimes the "Done" checkmark is more consistent in the information that it remembers than the little gray button.

Finicky or slow internet connections might find a problem with the little gray "Done" button, too, so just be aware of this, and, if you are noticing strange behavior, or the gallery didn't get all of your pictures loaded, use the "Done" checkmark instead.

You'll be able to do this as many times as you need to, so don't worry that this page only lets you upload ten photos.

Actually, a couple years ago, Tripod only let you upload *one* photo at a time (not ten!). So, getting a gallery of our size really took...*a very long time.*

If you aren't ready to upload any photos at this time, click the yellow cancel "X." Either the "X "or one of the "Done" buttons will bring you back to the picture gallery.

If you've uploaded photos, wait for the picture gallery to load and make sure that all of your photos appear (you'll need to give it at least a minute or two, depending on your internet connection).

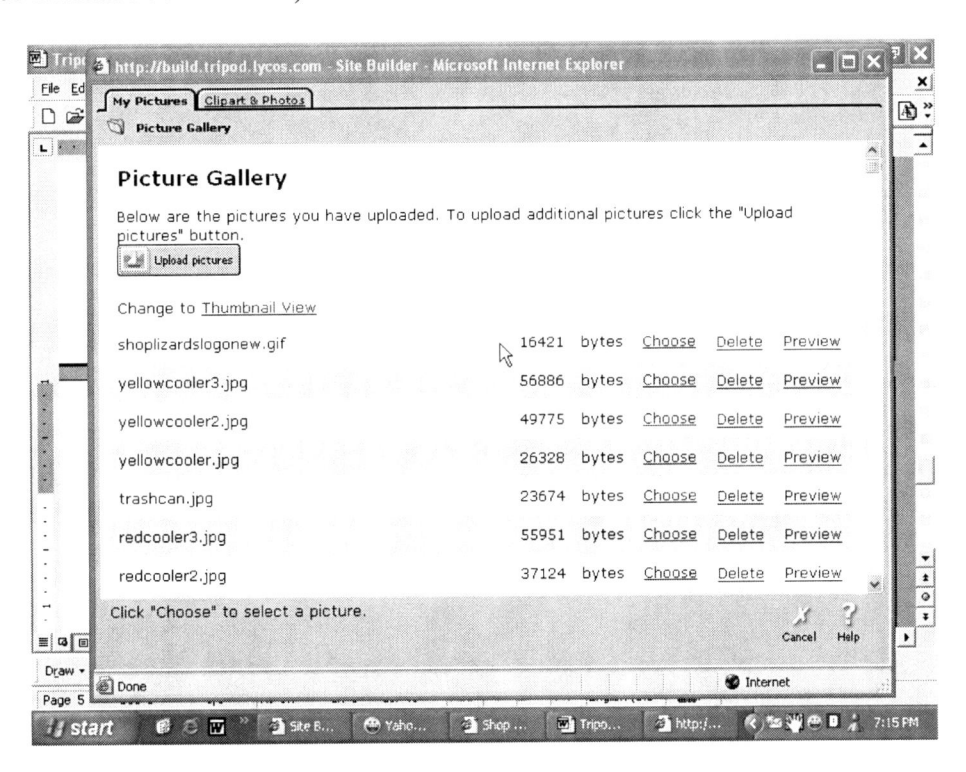

Next to each picture name, you'll notice the file size, and options for each picture:

Choose
Delete
Preview (though Preview will not appear if you are in the thumbnail view)

If you want to use a photo, you'll select "Choose."

If you want to delete a photo from your gallery, this is where it can be deleted. You can also delete photos from the **File Manager**, which is an option at the very top black toolbar on most of your Tripod pages.

It looks like this:

```
Log Out                    File Manager                    Backup & Restore
```

If you delete a photo from your gallery, make sure that you do not plan on using it *ever* again on your site, and also, make sure that it isn't currently being used on any of your pages because it will be completely removed from Tripod's server.

In general, unless you are seriously close to using all of your disk space (or your gallery takes more than ten minutes to load…seriously), you'll probably never delete a photo.

Or, if you find that the photo needs to be edited and uploaded again into the picture gallery because it didn't turn out the way that you wanted on your site, then you should delete the old picture to avoid confusion before you upload the new one.

Also, if you need to upload a picture again after you've made changes to it, Tripod will not recognize the changes unless you give the new photo a different filename, you check the little **In case of duplicates it's okay to overwrite** box, or you log out of Tripod before you upload the new photo. Sometimes, though, we've had problems with the overwrite option because Tripod doesn't always recognize the new picture if it is nearly the same as the old.

Once, we had to upload the same feather picture over ten times to get it just right on the page, and each time we renamed it to something a little different. Then, once we had it just right, we went back in and deleted all the bad copies.

We could have checked the overwrite box, but since we had to do it so many times (and sometimes Tripod didn't get the hint even when the box was checked), when we edited the photo, we just saved it as a different name each time so that we would have copies of the old (even though we really didn't need the old copies).

For your ease, just rename the new photo to something similar, newglobe.jpg, newglobe1.jpg, etc to avoid frustration, then go back in and delete the ones you didn't use later.

This may seem completely irrelevant now, but we guarantee that you'll have to do this at some point in your website creation, so we just want you to be aware of your options.

YOUR LOGO AS THE SITE TITLE.

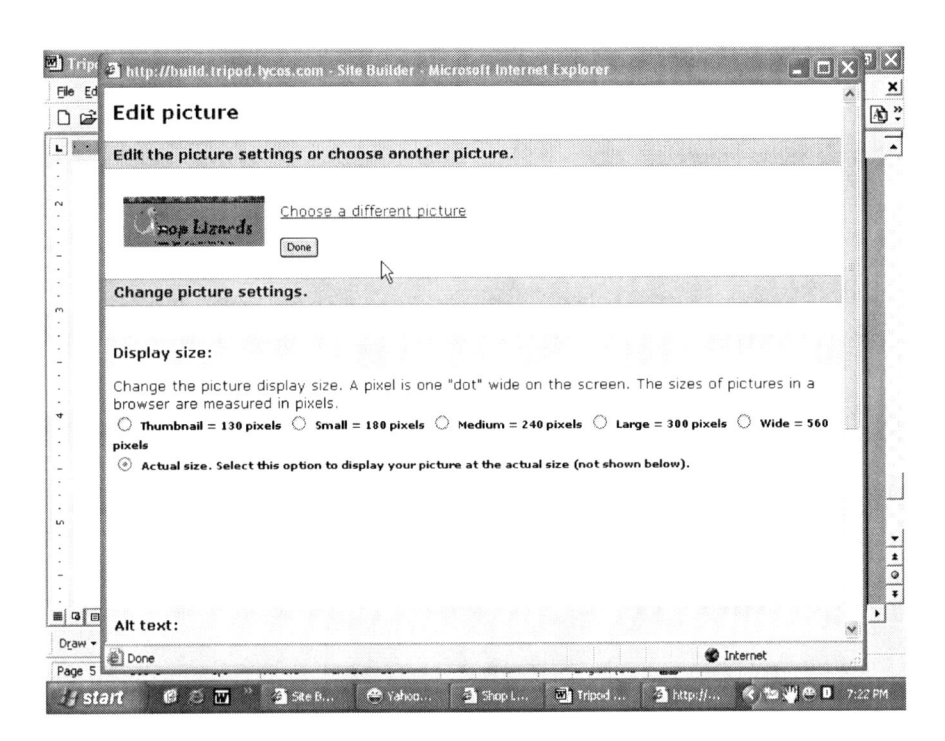

Take a moment to upload your logo to the picture gallery to use as your site title. Once you do, and you've selected **Choose** from the picture gallery screen, you'll have a lot of options for your picture, though you'll notice later that this screen is a bit different from the regular "Edit Picture" screen because that screen has even more options.

YOUR LOGO PICTURE OPTIONS:

Display Size
ALT-Text
Linking this Picture

Display size is very important and can be frustrating and tricky to master.

You can choose:

Thumbnail: 130 pixels
Small: 180 pixels
Medium: 240 pixels
Large: 300 pixels
Wide: 560 pixels
Actual Size

Clicking anything other than "Actual Size" will show a little dolphin picture in the projected size.

Before you get to this page, you need to know the basic size of your picture. If it is smaller than "Small" don't select "Medium," "Large," or "Wide" because it may distort the image too much.

This is where you need to play around with your options. If a photo is basically square, it will probably look fine in any size. Choose the size that will work for your picture now, keeping in mind that you can return immediately to change it if it turns out wonky.

If the picture is distorted, too small, or crazy looking, you'll just click on the **Edit Site Title** button to come back to the image choices. When you're working on all other pictures on your site, you'll click the yellow **Edit Picture** button that appears next to them on the main edit screen.

You can always tell what size your picture is, before you upload it to Tripod. To do so, simply hover your mouse over the picture if it is on your desktop or in a folder. Or, open your picture and click on Image Properties to get the dimensions (we'll go over this in a moment). It may say something like:

Dimensions: 2272 x 1704

That's actually quite a large photo, but it's hard to tell because the dimensions are measured in pixels, which is, incidentally, the same measurement that Tripod uses for your picture size choices.

If you really want to know how big this is (though you can kind of guess because Tripod's largest size choice is 560 pixels wide), go ahead and open the photo with your photoshop program and select the Image Properties option.

Your photoshop might be a bit different, but they all have an "Image Properties" option somewhere. When you find it, select the size choice and change it from pixels to inches.

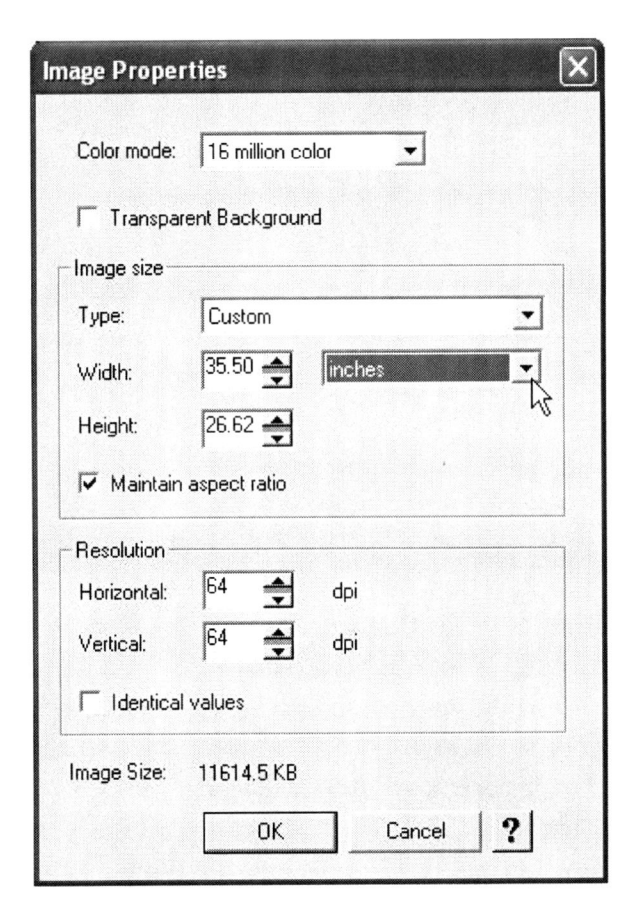

It has now converted our pixel measurement of 2272 x 1704 into 35.50 x 26.62 *inches*.

That's a huge picture!

You don't need to change your picture sizes before you upload them into Tripod if you don't want to, because you actually have tons of room to store things.

Just be aware of your file size. You can even leave it huge, upload it to Tripod, select for it to display as a thumbnail, and then have it link to itself in "actual size."

While we're on this topic, keep this in mind when it comes to emailing photos to your friends. Sending an image that is 35 inches wide by 22 inches tall will not only clog their email, but will take them quite some time to download and view.

LINKING YOUR PICTURE.

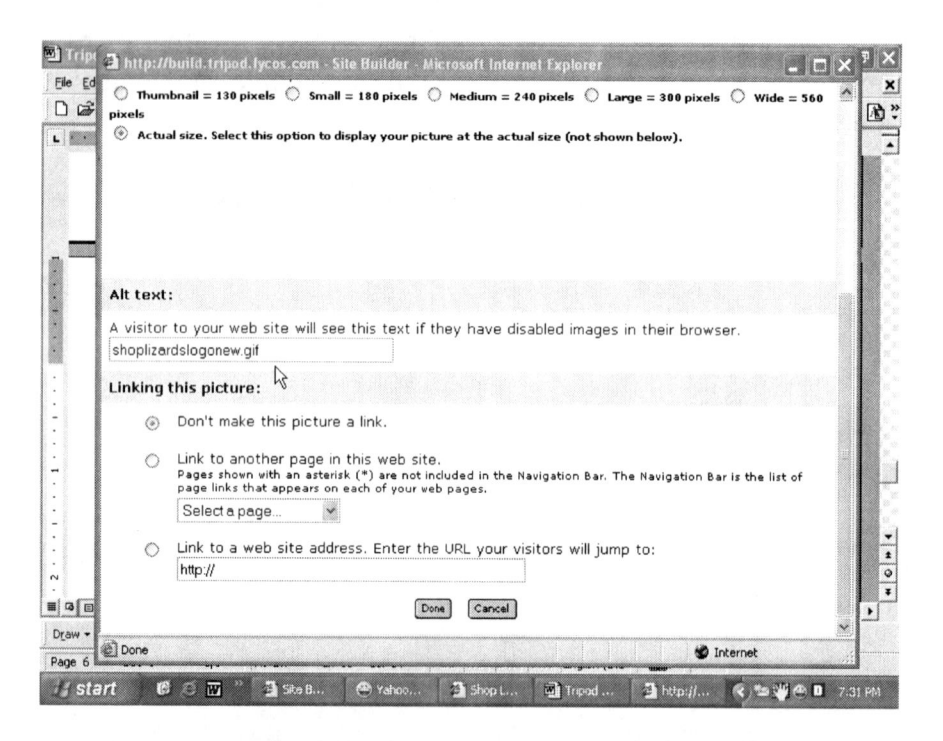

At the bottom of the regular "Edit Picture" screen, you'll get the option to **make your picture a link to itself**, (but not here) so if you want a small thumbnail on your inventory page, and want your visitors to click and see a larger or actual size photo, that's what you'd do. This is what we prefer when displaying our products because it allows for faster page loads and still gives our customers the option of viewing it in a larger size. You'll use actual size if you know the basic dimensions of your photo and know that it will look fine on the page, like a logo.

Also, linking your picture, even if only to itself in a larger size, can help you to rank better in the search engines. So, it is a habit you should get in to. Link every picture to itself in a larger size, and even link your logo back to the homepage.

The ALT text (Alt tag) is infinitely important to the search engine success of your pages. This is explained in detail later (Chapter 10), so for the moment, you'll leave this area alone. Later, you'll be coming back to all of your images to fix their ALT text. Once you get the hang of things, you'll be able to do the ALT text while uploading your picture for the first time, so things won't take nearly as long and you won't have to keep returning to pictures you've already placed on your site.

Generally, if this picture is in the site title position, you won't want to link to anything else, other than the homepage itself. If this were any other picture, though, you could link to another page within your site, called an internal link, or if you had the web address to another site, you could have the image link to that site, which is called an external link.

Get your options selected, knowing that you can return to this page later to fix or change things, and select the little gray "Done" button.

You will now be returned to the "Edit Site Title" page.

If you want the image to appear on all of your other pages as well (which you will, this is your site logo, after all), make sure that under the **On all other pages** option, you select **Same as Homepage**.

If for some reason you want to have a different header on a page, you can instead let it display text—you can change the size, the font, whether or not it is bold, italics, or underlined, and you can even pick a color from the color box—another image, or nothing at all. This just depends on your needs (we can't predict every eventuality, we just present your options), and you can always come back to change things later.

You can also align your site title to the left, to the center, or to the right. We always make sure to center it so our logo appears in the absolute center of the page, but we have played around with placement, so you should as well.

When you're done, and satisfied with your choices, select the yellow "Done" checkmark on the gray toolbar to continue.

Notice our Shop Lizards image? It is now in the site title position, but it doesn't *quite* fit on the page (there's a red and orange background behind it).

Your image will probably have the same problem, but it can be fixed by changing the background color of the page itself, instead of messing with trying to get the image to fit exactly.

That can be too difficult and frustrating even for experts.

CHANGE LOOK.

To make a simple change to the page background, click **Change Look** on the gray toolbar at the bottom of your screen. This is also the page where we'll be going over most of your site "shell."

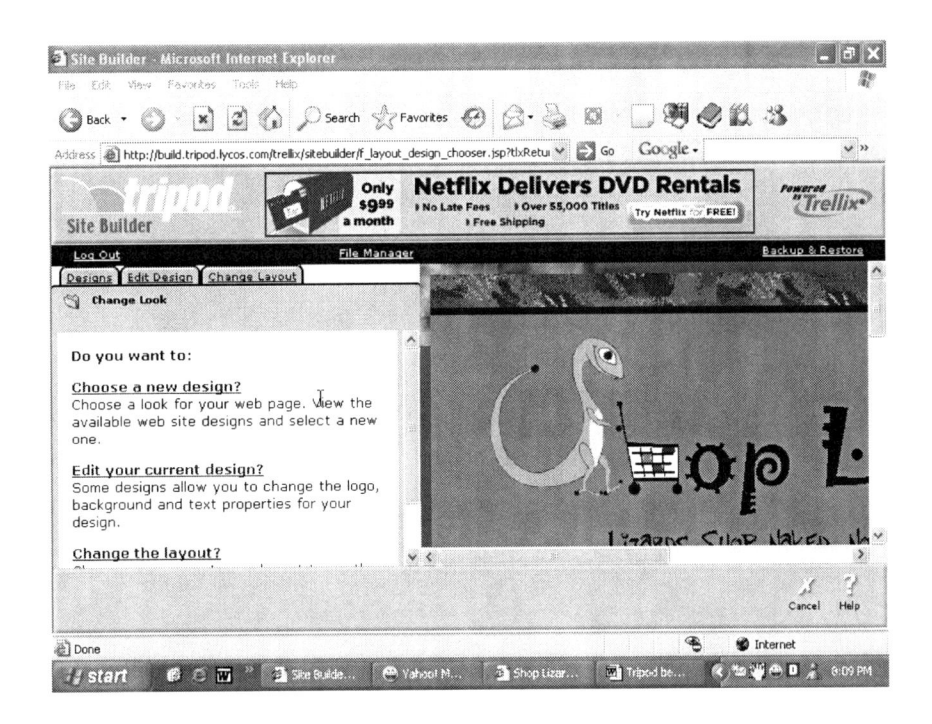

Change Look can help you change most aspects of the design, and even the layout of your site. Get to know your options now so that you know what can or cannot be easily done.

To the left of the screen that appears will be a menu of your choices, both at the top on yellow tabs, and in list form:

Choose a New Design
Edit Your Current Design
Change the Layout

Like the short description below each says:

CHOOSE A NEW DESIGN will take you back to the templates

section so that you can select a completely different design; do note that some of the changes you have already made might be changed or look different on a new design.

To avoid a headache, pick out the design you plan to stick with before making tons of changes.

EDIT YOUR CURRENT DESIGN will take you to an "Edit" page, where, depending on your design, you can make changes to the background, color of text, and pretty much anything else you might like to change on your site.

CHANGE THE LAYOUT will take you to an "Edit" screen where you can change the layout of your page, from one column, to two, etc. This option only works for the page that you are currently on and can also be accomplished in the **Site Organizer** (which we discuss a bit later).

For now, since we're just making a simple background change to make our logo appear to fit on the page better, click **Edit Your Current Design**.

EDIT YOUR CURRENT DESIGN.

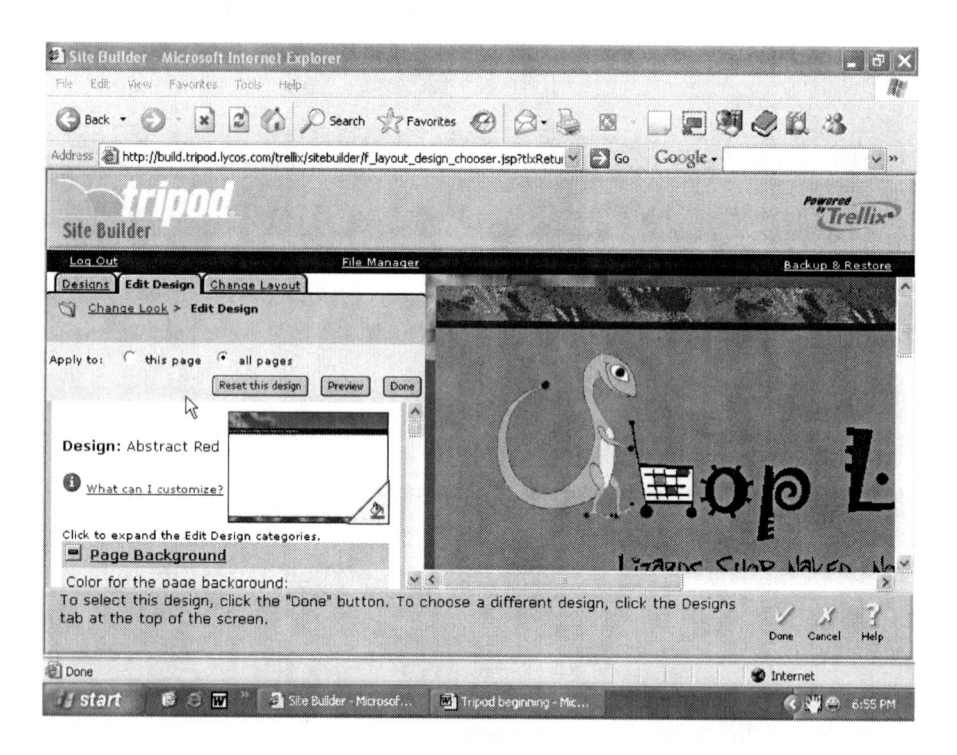

Your options for change will vary depending on your template, so when building a site, make sure that you choose a template that has enough options to work for you.

If you find when you come to this page that you can't change everything that you want to, you can either go back to "Designs" and pick out a new template, or just make do with what you can change.

Now we'll go over your site from the top to the bottom. Most of the necessary changes can be made to your "shell" here; everything else will be either added, removed, or changed later (in Chapter 6).

SEVERAL THINGS OF NOTE HERE:

You can apply your changes to:

This Page
All Pages

This is very important because if you want a different background color on one page than on another, you'll need to make sure "This Page" is selected.

Also on this menu, you'll see:

Reset this Design
Preview
Done

These buttons do just what they say they'll do.

Preview, though, can be invaluable and save you a great deal of time when you're making changes to your site. You can select the change you want, click "Preview" and your changes will appear on the right-hand side of your screen.

If you don't like your changes, you can just change them back (and click "Preview" again to make sure), or if you've made *too* many changes and don't know what to fix first, just click the little yellow cancel "X" on the right hand side of the gray toolbar, or click "Reset this Design" to return to the original template choices.

Each choice has a little negative or positive sign next to it. Clicking the positive sign will drop down that menu item so that you can see all of your options. While clicking the negative sign will minimize that item's option list.

The template we've chosen has the most options of just about all the templates, so we'll walk through each choice so that you know how they work, what to expect of a template, and give you an idea about what you'll be able to manipulate.

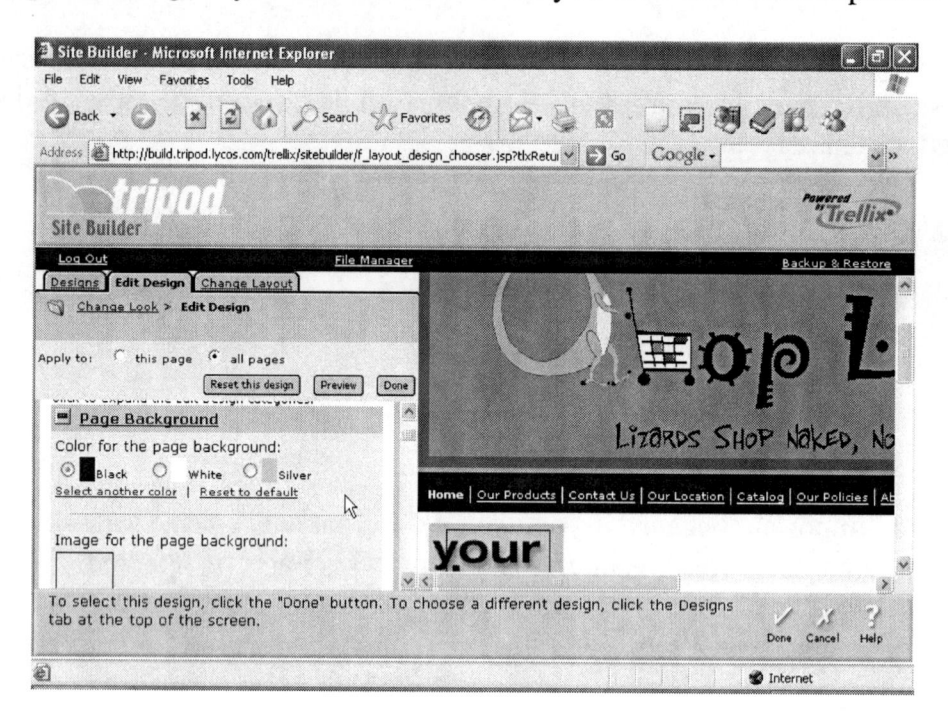

PAGE BACKGROUND.

Page Background changes the color of the page itself, behind the title area, and the main area. This is one of the choices that you'll need to use in combination with other choices to get the outcome you want.

The page background will appear as the weird color behind your logo. The black area just below that with page choices is called the navigation bar.

You can also change the page background color to something other than the suggested default black, silver, and white.

To do so, click **Select Another Color**.

A new window will pop-up:

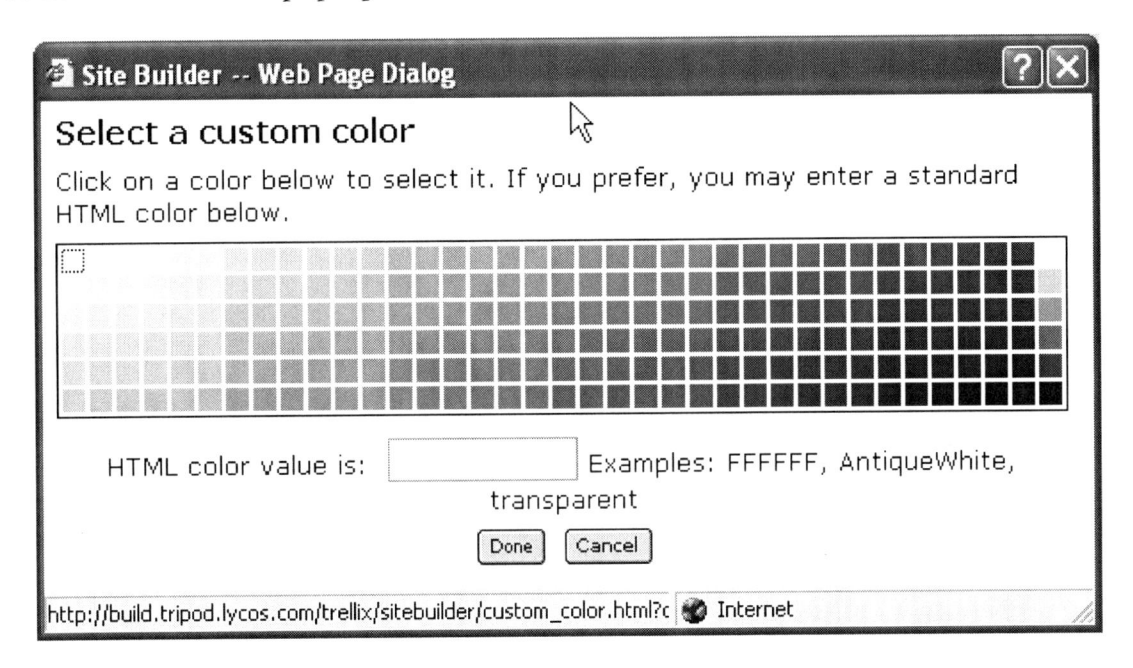

This pop-up is the entire list of colors that can be used anywhere on your site. Keep this chart in mind when matching your logo and other images on the site to your page colors.

You'll notice that every color has a **HTML Color Value**, which is a series of letters and numbers set to represent each color. Also, Tripod's color hues are the same as in most photoshop programs, so this makes things even easier. This will become very important when you play around with colors on your site because some of the colors are just similar enough that you may never find the same one again. To avoid any problems when you find a color you love, simply make a notation on a sticky note (or in a notebook) of the color hues for all the colors that you choose for your site. For example, one of our Shop Lizards' colors is CCFF66.

It sounds finicky, but trust us, you'll be glad you did.

Some of you might notice that there are also colors not being represented here. That's just the way of the internet. For your site, these are the only colors that you can use because they are the only internet-compatible ones around. Sorry.

You can also insert an image as the page background. If you do this though, you'll need to make the main area transparent so that it will show through. Again, play with your choices to get the results you want.

Nothing can be harmed in this stage of your site shell creation. Play with the choices to get an idea of what you can do—you'll be surprised by what you're able to accomplish!

When you click to insert an image, you'll be taken to the picture gallery where you'll have all of the same options that you would while normally in the picture gallery. If you need more on how this works, see the **Insert Picture** section in Chapter 6.

TITLE AREA.

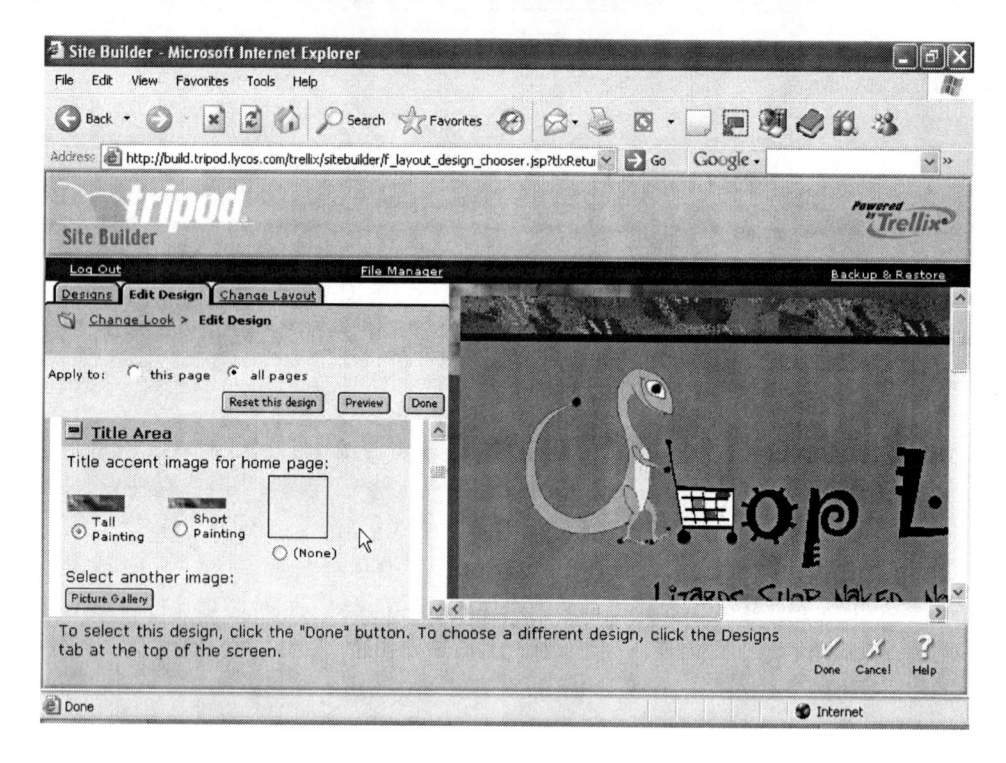

The title area usually has a slot for inserting an accent image.

Like on this template, called "Tall Painting" and "Short Painting," the accent image comes with two different sizes of the same image. The larger is the accent image on the homepage, and the smaller is the accent image on all of the other pages.

You can choose to remove the image completely (like we will), or add your own, but since you'll have your logo here, it's best to just remove the image.

As you'll probably notice, your logo is currently overtop of the accent image, because you've inserted it as the **Site Title** itself.

So, to fix this little overlap problem, select "None" to get rid of the accent image.

If you'd like to add a new accent image because you think it will enhance the look of your logo, you'll need to have some idea on how large to make it, otherwise, you can **tile** the image so that it will repeat itself across the top of the page.

Truly, this is all trial and error.

It takes some effort (and stubbornness), and you'll need to do the work in your photoshop program, and then upload the image into your picture gallery once you come to this screen.

You can do this as many times as you need to, of course, to get the picture looking the way you want. Remember to take your time to get your site looking the way you want, and understand that spending a lot of time here is not a bad thing!

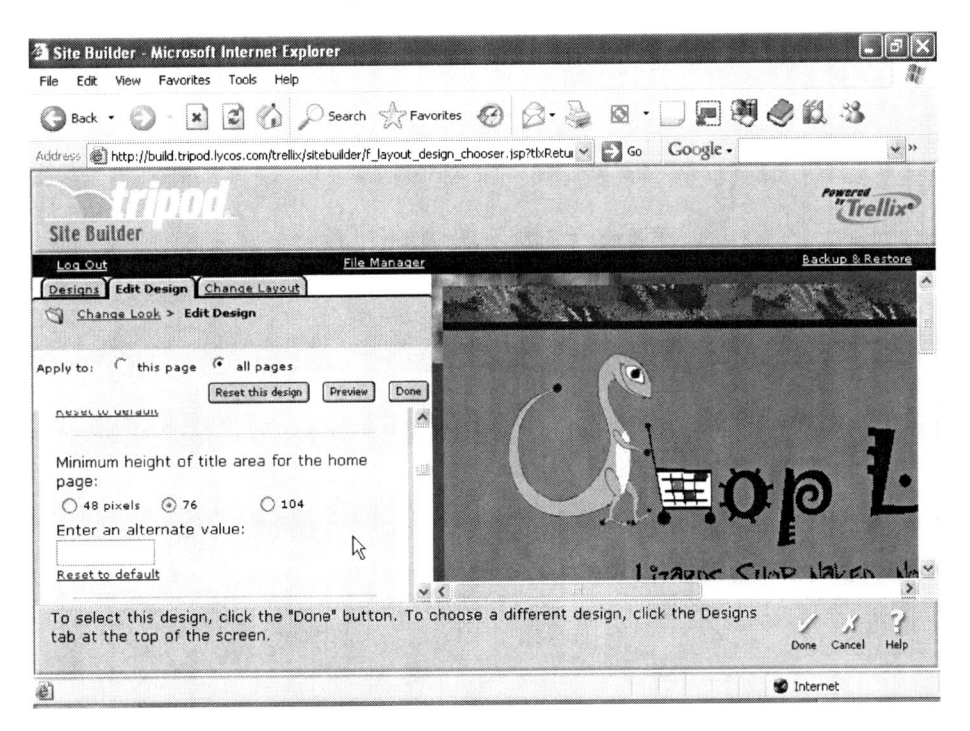

Next, you can change the **size** of the title area itself.

Now, if you've already put in a picture like we did with the logo, then you have to be careful about how much you change this number, because it doesn't reflect what you currently see. If you added your picture in the "Edit Site Title" screen, like we recommended earlier, you'll change the size of the picture by clicking the yellow "Edit Site Title" button from the main edit screen and not mess with the numbers here.

If, however, you add a picture from this screen, then you'd size it here.

From experience, pixels are hard to judge.

Our Shop Lizards image is set to roughly 222 pixels, though that number isn't reflected here. So, if we added it in the **Title Area** choice instead of the **Edit Site Title** page, then we'd play with sizes on this screen. Since it appears as the size that we wanted (even though the number isn't what we know it should be), we'll leave these choices alone.

Your next choice is for the rest of the pages, the **title accent image** and the minimum height for it, and they all work like the choices we've already gone over.

For now, we're going to change the color and behavior of our Title Area.

Currently, it has a title accent image, so we'll check the "None" option to remove it. Then we'll do the same for the title accent image for "All Other Pages."

BACKGROUND COLOR FOR THE TITLE AREA.

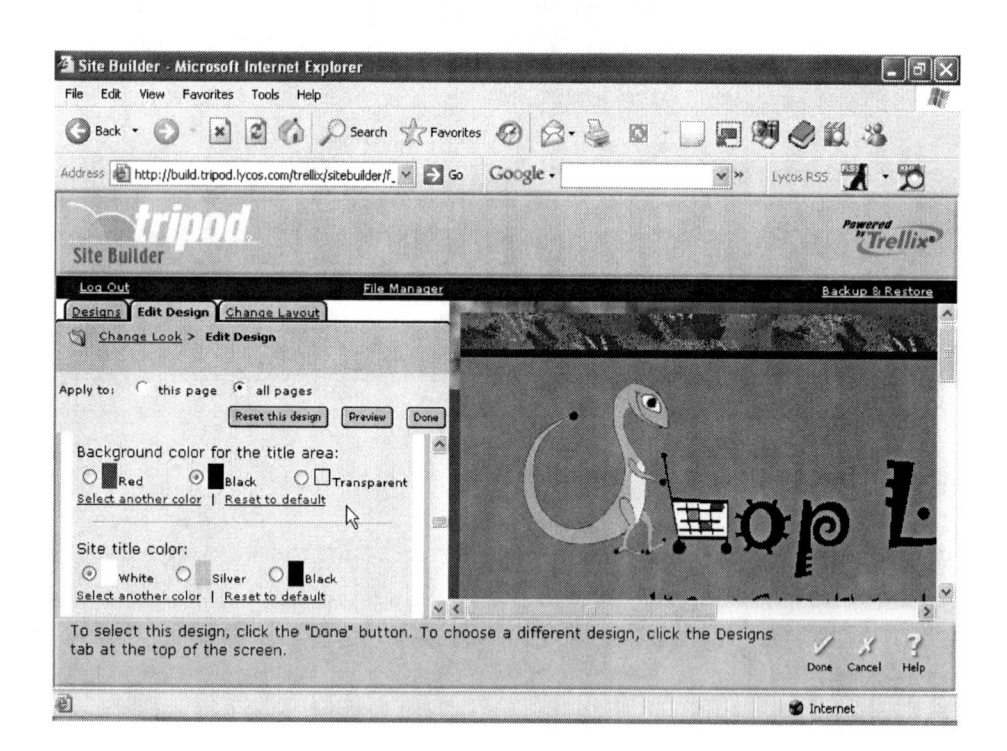

Since your image probably looks terrible on the page background of the template, you'll need to change the background color to something that compliments your logo colors. For example, our logo is mainly purple so we'll choose black because it will make a nice background for the site as a whole.

If the three options don't work for you, you can click the **Select Another Color** choice and a color selection box will pop-up. Then, you'd simply choose the color that will work best for your logo (remembering to mark the color hue down for later reference).

Keep in mind that you can click the little gray "Preview" button to see what your color choices look like in real time. Feel free to do this often (it's much faster than clicking "Done" only to have to return to this page again).

TOP ACCENT STRIPE.

Choose the color that will look best with your navigation, and choose a height for the stripe that will work for you. If you don't want an accent stripe, set the **Height** to 0 pixels.

0 equals no stripe. 8 equals a stripe that is 8 pixels tall.

If you want an even bigger stripe than the 8 pixels creates, type it into the box provided, but make sure to "Preview" your choice to see how big your stripe becomes.

NAVIGATION.

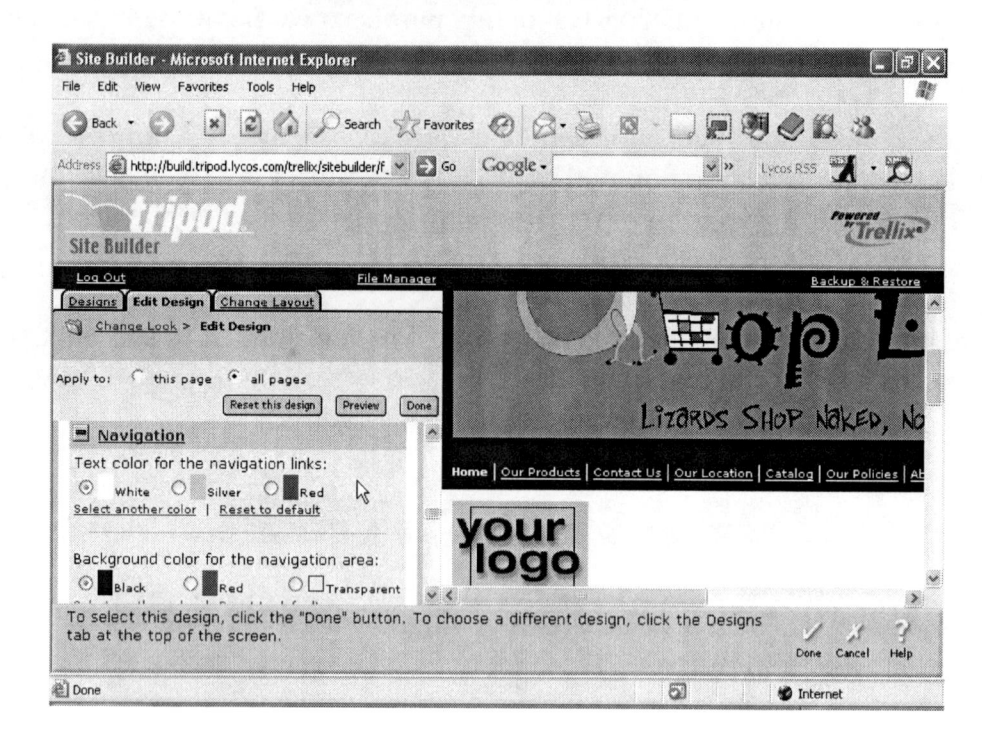

Under **Navigation**, you have these choices:

Text Color for the Navigation Links
Background Color for the Navigation Area
Height for the Navigation Area
Font for the Navigation Links
Size of the Navigation Links
Alignment of the Navigation Links

The choices work much like they sound.

Select the color that you want for the links, either by choosing one of the three given colors, or by clicking the **Select Another Color** choice. A pop-up of color choices will appear for you to select from (remember to write down the color hue for later reference).

Select the color you want and move on to the next step.

BACKGROUND COLOR FOR YOUR NAVIGATION AREA.

In the picture on the previous page, ours is still set on black with white links. This is where careful color choices come in. We played around with colors for a long time before deciding that our lizard needed to be green and our pages should have a purple background. After a bit of tweaking, our navigation area looked like this:

Home | Play Free Games | Diecast Collectible Cars & Trucks | Diecast Collectible Aircraft

We chose neon green (#00CC00) for the navigation links and black (#000000) for the navigation area. Play with your color choices to find the best match for your website.

HEIGHT FOR THE NAVIGATION AREA.

You can play around with this choice as well, but leaving it at "Best Fit" is usually your best option because the navigation area will automatically grow to be the "best fit" if you add more links on your navigation bar.

FONT & FONT SIZE.

Choose the font and font size that you like best, remembering that you can click the "Preview" button after each change to see how things appear. Whatever you choose, make sure you select the same choices for all of your other pages to keep things looking uniform. Again, you can do this by selecting "Apply to all pages" at the top.

ALIGNMENT OF THE NAVIGATION LINKS.

The default setting for the navigation links will be set at "Left," but "Center" is probably best for most sites. We tend to prefer center because it just looks better than having the navigation bar links off to one side. As always, make this choice based on the needs of your site.

MAIN AREA.

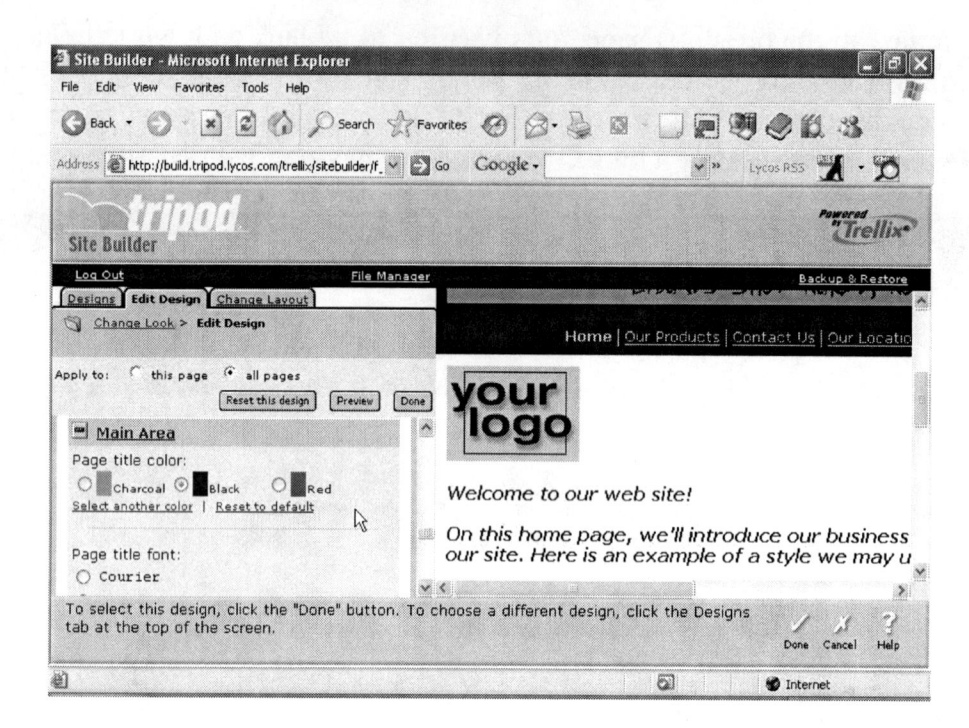

The **Main Area** is everything *below* the Navigation Bar, but *above* the Site Footer.

Your choices:

Page Title Color
Page Title Font
Page Title Size
Text Color for the Main Area
Font for the Main Area
Background Color for the Main Area
Background Image for the Main Area

Again, the choices work like they sound. Make your picks among them, using the "Preview" option to check each selection as you go along.

If you change the **Background Color for the Main Area**, make sure you make note of the color code for use on all of your other pages. Okay, we say this redundantly often because you really never know when you might need to use that same color on a page, and having the color code written down on a sticky note is much less stressful than going back through the color chart to find that same color.

Trust us.

You can have a different color on every page if you wish, but make your choices wisely and keep to a theme (remembering what we went over about colors in Chapter 3), so that your visitors don't become confused, angered, or disoriented (oh my!).

At the top of the **Edit Design** screen it says:

Apply to This Page
Apply to All Pages

If you make a color change on the homepage, it will affect *all* the other pages even if you select "Apply to This Page" because it has some kind of weird clout being the homepage.

So, if you want to make changes to the homepage, know that it will affect *all* of your other pages anyway, for reasons unknown. If you want to have different background colors for your other pages (which we've done from time to time), do the homepage color *first*, and then choose the colors for your other pages next.

Keep things easy.

That's another reason we suggest keeping a note of what page colors you use. If something somehow gets messed up, you can quickly go back in and make the changes without agonizing about what colors you had chosen before.

With Shop Lizards, we've played around with different page background colors on every page. So, we understand that you might want to play around too. In fact, we encourage it—so play around with color, but keep them complimentary and keep track of their color codes for any unseen eventuality.

BOTTOM AREA.

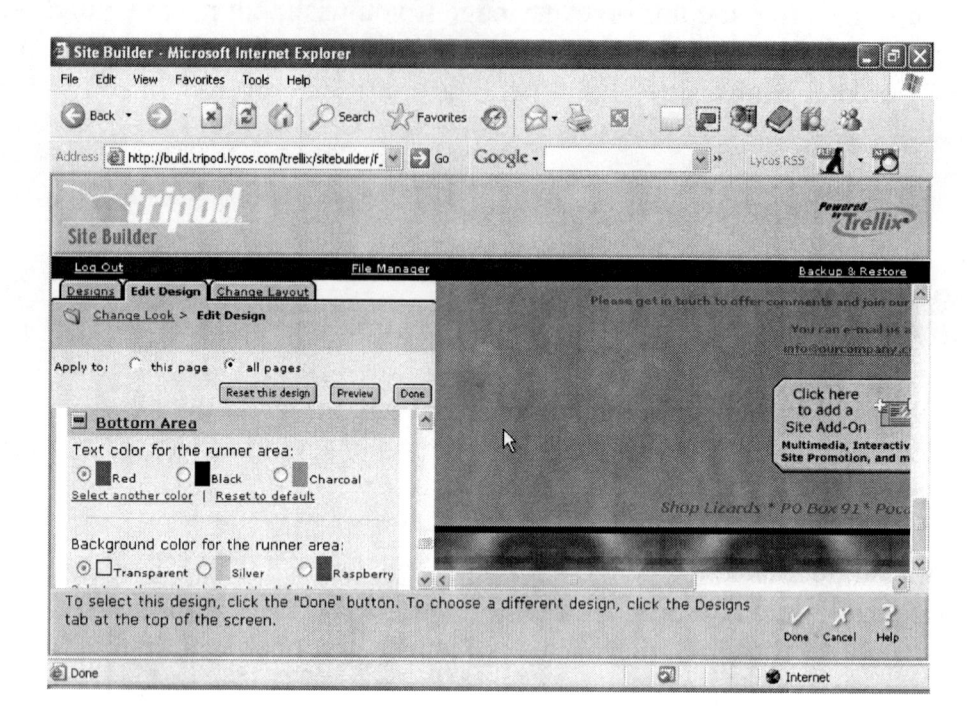

The **Bottom Area** is also known as the Site Footer, or Runner Area.

Anything on the bottom area will appear exactly the same way on all of your other pages, again, *even* if you select "Apply to This Page" because the main function of a footer is to display the same information on every page of its site.

This can be a great thing, though, because having your copyright and contact information at the bottom of every page without having to type it in a thousand times is handy.

YOUR CHOICES:

Text Color for the Runner Area
Background Color for the Runner Area
Color for the Bottom Accent Stripe
Height of the Bottom Accent Stripe
Background Image for the Bottom Area
Background Color for the Bottom Area
Height of the Bottom Area

We created our own footer picture in our photoshop program to go where the red, orange, and yellow footer image is.

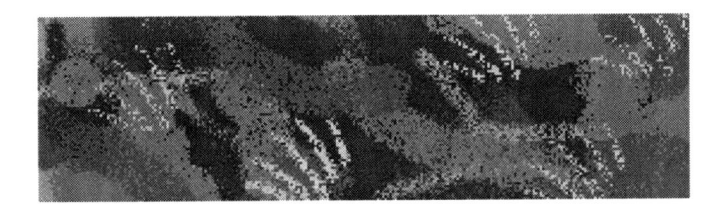

Our footer matches the site header, our logo, and can also have Alt tags inserted. Since we only created it to be about 2 inches by 1 inch high, we set it to *repeat*. You should consider creating a footer for your site that matches your logo, or you can simply remove the background image in the bottom area, and leave it blank.

The footer is nowhere near as important as the logo, and we actually don't even use a footer image on any of our other sites.

The **Runner Area** works the same way as the Title Area; so make your choices to mimic the choices that you made above. And remember, you can click the "Preview" button after every selection to see how your choices appear.

Once you're done making all of your changes, or you're done checking out everything you can change, click the yellow "Done" checkmark, or the yellow "X" if you'd prefer to cancel your changes and return to the main edit screen.

Those are your options for changing the shell of your site itself. Anything else like adding pictures, changing text, adding HTML; will be done from the main edit screen using Tripod's handy gray toolbar and will be explained fully in the next chapter.

Chapter Six
Advanced Building & Editing.

By now you should have a basic idea of what to do to edit your site shell, and perhaps you've already made many changes. But that's really all it is right now. A shell. You need to add in what you want like new text and pictures, make changes, and delete stuff that doesn't work for your site.

It's time to give your shell some stuffing—and really turn it into something you can be proud of.

GETTING AROUND TRIPOD.

Before we really get started editing, we need to remind you that everything on Tripod is saved automatically as you build. Anything you move, delete, copy, etc, will be there exactly as you put it if you close your browser and shut down your computer right after. So make your edits, and take breaks when you need to. Creating a website actually takes a lot of time, especially if you are just starting out, and especially if you have a lot of inventory.

So, don't panic, just get done what you can, when you can. Eventually, it will get finished, trust us.

Now, you need to begin thinking of your site shell as a canvas of sorts. Just recently, we added a picture to the text at the bottom of our Shop Lizards welcome letter because we wanted to use a certain font, but Tripod only lets you choose from four fonts or so because only those four are internet-compliant.

To get the signature looking the way we wanted, we had to create an image using our photoshop program, and then upload the photo and put it on the page below the text.

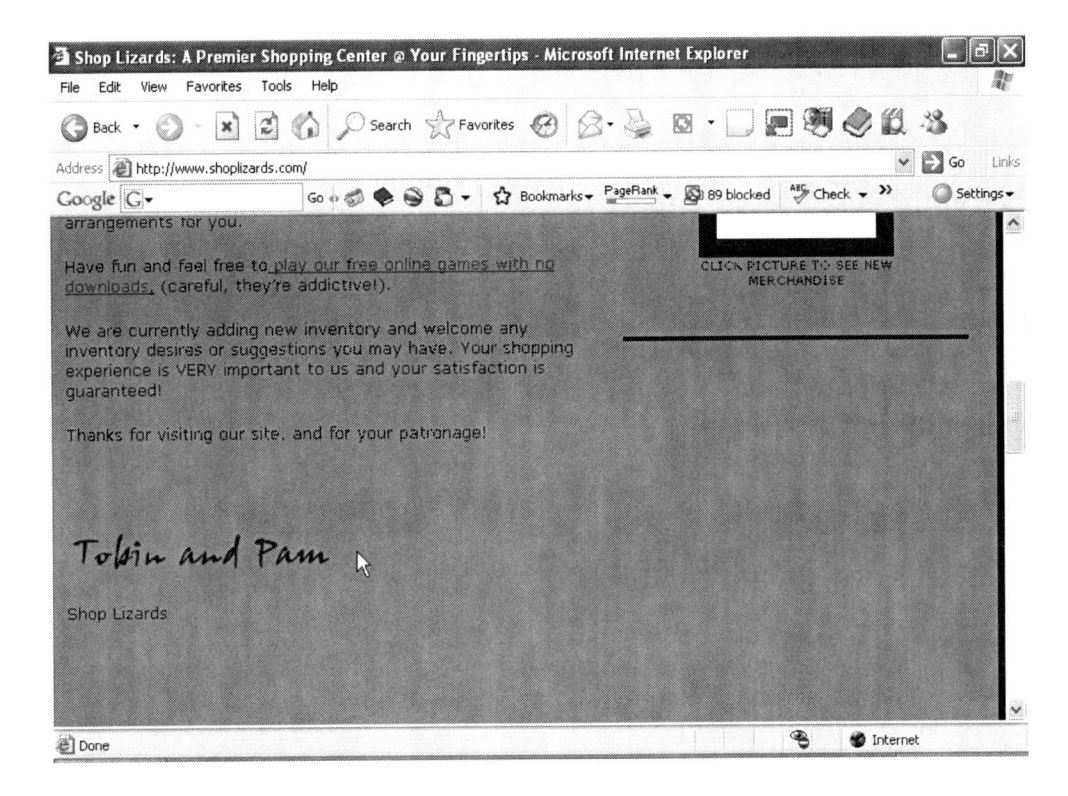

You can see in the screen shot above that we added the picture of our signature and it looks like part of the page. When we created the image, we had to know the exact color hue of our background color to get the image to look like part of the page…luckily, as we mentioned over and over in the previous chapter, we keep track of all our color hues and were able to create the image without unnecessary stress. And, color hues are the same on Tripod as in most photoshop programs so this is even easier to keep track of.

The moral of the story: we had to think **outside the box** to get the results that we wanted. It helps that we've been doing this a long time, but you can train yourself to think this way too. Actually, you need to.

You've started with a Tripod template because it's the easiest way to get a site going, but there's so much you can do to change and manipulate your template (unless you chose one that isn't customizable). Practically anything is possible.

This is about creating the website and business image that you want. Take what we say as a guideline, and learn from the way we do things, but force yourself to look at your site as a shell of what it *can* be. You can add things, remove things, and move things…so use what Tripod has given you to get the results that you want, and get the website that you've dreamed about.

Trust us. In web design, anything is possible, you just need to know the rules and options to make it happen.

TRIPOD'S BUTTONS, IN ORDER.

Now you're ready to think outside the box and edit your site!

This is your Tripod toolbar. You'll be using it for nearly everything you do, so take note of the order of things.

FIRST, WE HAVE THE "ADD" BUTTONS:

Add Text
Add Picture
Add Link
Site Add-Ons
Add Page

If you want to **add** something, (anything!) these are the buttons that you'll be using. If you want to make changes to something *already on the page*, you'll use the little yellow buttons on the main edit screen next to the item that you want to change instead.

THEN WE HAVE THE "EDIT" BUTTONS:

Change Look
Move Items
Copy Items
Delete Items

These buttons should be used to **change** things on your site, or basically, changing everything except actually *editing* a picture or text.

THEN WE HAVE THE "PROMOTION" BUTTONS:

Preview Site
Publish to Web
Promote Site

These buttons do the obvious, and you'll probably only use the "Publish" button.

AND FINALLY WE HAVE THE "SITE" BUTTONS:

Site Organizer
All My Sites
Log Out
Help

Of all the buttons, you'll probably find that you use the "Site Organizer" button more than the others.

That's just how we look at things. And, actually, once you've been using Tripod for a few days, you'll get to know where the buttons are as well as you know the buttons on your TV remote.

TAKE A DEEP BREATH AND REALLY "LOOK" AT YOUR SITE.

You'll see that next to each picture is a little yellow **Edit Picture** button, and next to each section of text is a little yellow **Edit Text** button. You'll also see **Edit Site Title**, **Edit Navigation**, and if your site has any Site Add-Ons (HTML banners, calendars, etc), **Edit Site Add-ons**.

All of these buttons are discussed below, under the corresponding Add sections, but they work exactly the same way.

NOTE: clicking any of the "Add" buttons will refresh the page with dotted lines and little gray **Add It Here** buttons. Make sure you take note of how the dotted lines are drawn because they indicate page columns, and different sections of the page, and it will make a difference in the placement of your text, picture, link, or add-on.

This sounds strange, but you'll see what we mean if you place something between the wrong lines and it turns out differently than you thought. If it does end up in the wrong column, it might turn out as a different size, shape, font, or color, but don't panic, it's very easy to move, and you'll soon understand how this works.

REMEMBER THIS:

If you want to change something already on your site, you'll need to click the corresponding yellow button on the main edit screen. However, if you want to add something new, move something, or delete something, you'll need to use the buttons at the bottom of the screen, on Tripod's toolbar.

ADD TEXT.

You can add text just about anywhere on your site. If you click the **Add Text** button on the toolbar, it will take a moment and will add dotted lines and gray **Add It Here** buttons all over your page.

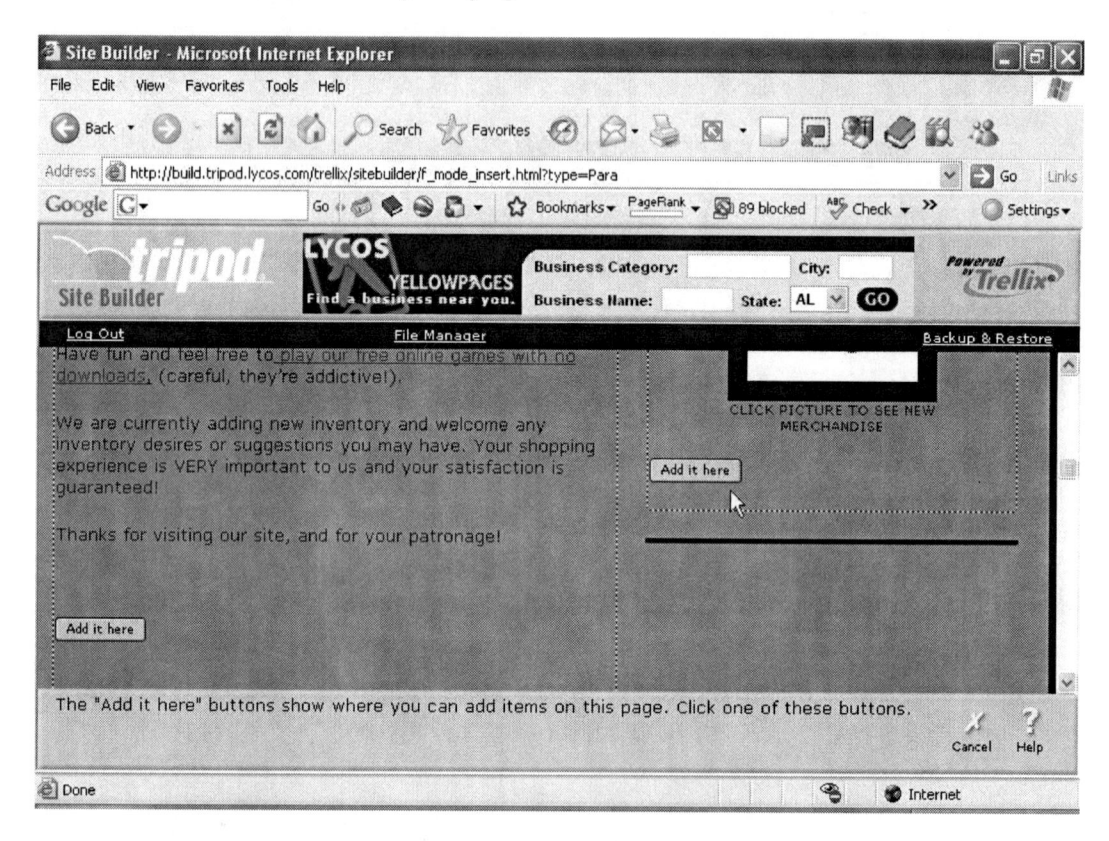

Again, note the placement of the dotted lines that appear and make sure to select the Add button that fits within the lines that you want. This will make sense once you get editing, but begin paying attention to these things now because it will save you some hassle and you won't freak out when you have to move things to get them where you wanted them in the first place.

When you're ready, select the **Add it Here** button where you'd like to add text.

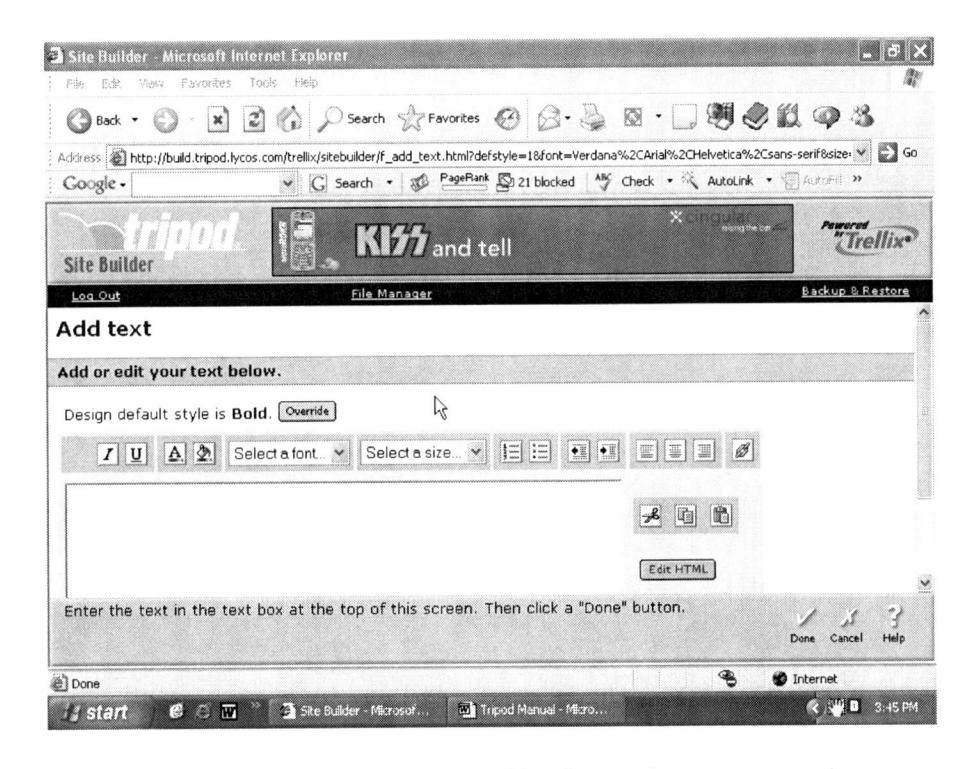

This will bring up a new window with a white box where you can input your text, and even manipulate it a bit with HTML.

You've got the basic options:

B=bold
I=italics
U=underline
A=change the text color
Little paint can= will highlight the text in your chosen color.

You can cut, paste, and copy, and even use the text as an internal text link by highlighting the text and clicking the little chain button. It will take you to an options page where you can decide if you want to link to a page from your site, link to a page from another website, or if you want to link to an email address.

We use internal links all the time to help customers navigate our site a bit easier. And actually, since we don't have our Site Map, Privacy Policy or Returns & Info page on our navigation bar (to save room), we decided to use internal text links to link to these pages from our footer.

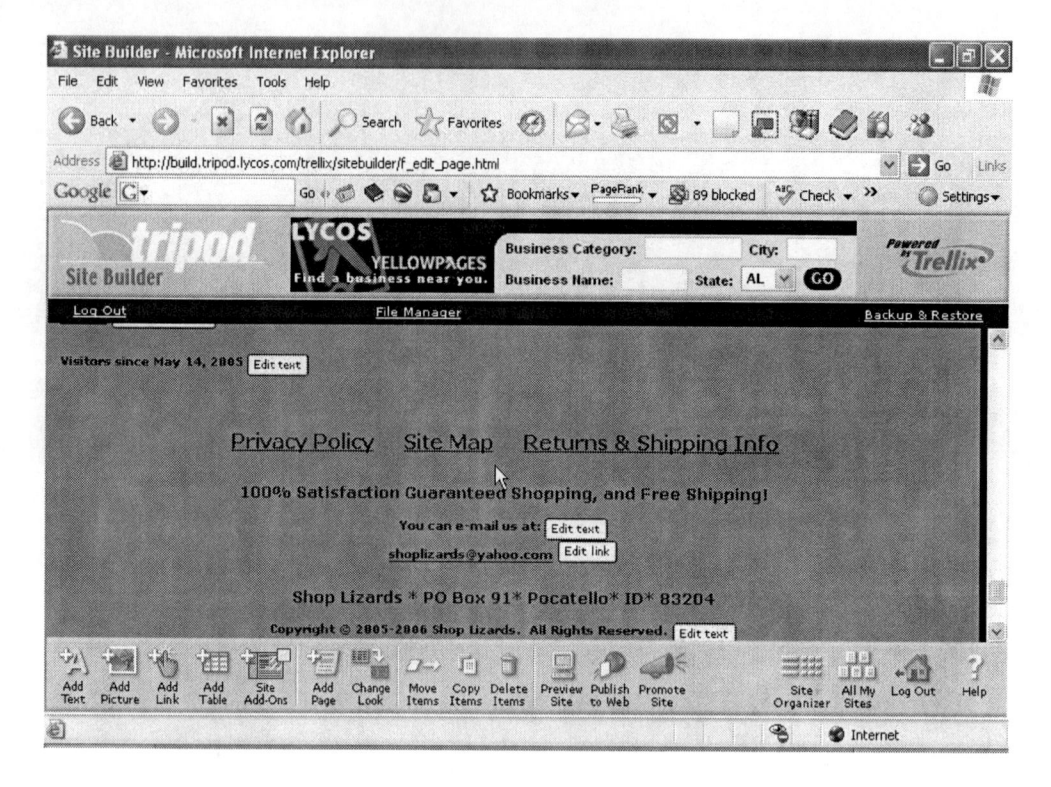

In the picture above, Privacy Policy, Site Map, and Returns & Shipping Info are all internal text links. An internal text link is basically a link *within* the text on your page. It can also refer to a link within your own site. An external text link can be done with an internal text link (inside a paragraph) but it will link to a webpage *external* from yours.

You can change the font, the size, and the placement of the text. Also, you might need to scroll a little to see the "Remove Space Above and Below the Text" option. Check the little box and it works as it sounds, removing the space above and below your text when it appears on the page.

You'll also see an **Edit HTML** button. We'll go over HTML in detail in Chapter 12, and Tripod does most of the work for you anyway with all the text options. But this button is very important because you'll use it when you need to create anchor tags.

Either way, use your mouse to highlight your text and make selections to format your text the way you'd like. Play around with your choices now, so that you know how they work and what you'll be able to do later.

When you're done, hit either one of the "Done" buttons. If you change your mind and don't want to add text, hit the "Cancel" button.

This is also the screen that you will be working with if you click **Edit Text** from the main edit screen.

Editing text and adding text works exactly the same way.

ADD PICTURE.

Adding a picture works just like adding text. If you click the **Add Picture** button, the page will refresh with a bunch of dotted lines and little gray **Add It Here** buttons. So, go ahead and decide where you want your first picture, and select an **Add It Here** button.

Now, after a moment you will be taken to the Picture Gallery. We described how this works in detail in Chapter 5 under the "Using the Picture Gallery" section. If you haven't done so, take the time to upload any pictures that you'll need and click **Choose** to select your first picture.

Now, you have a lot of choices to make in regards to formatting your picture. Tripod explains this page very well, but we'll go over the choices with you anyway.

CHANGE THE PICTURE SIZE.

Use your discretion and play around with this option. You can make a choice now, and when you see it on the page, you can hit the **Edit Picture** button and return to make more changes later. Play around with the sizes to get an idea of what you can do.

ALIGNMENT OF THE PICTURE.

This determines where the picture will be within the space that you chose—within the dotted lines that appeared when you selected the **Add Picture** button. You'll also get to decide if the picture needs space all the way around it or not. Mostly, pictures look better with space around the edges. Again, play around with the options to see which works best for you and your picture.

TITLE AND CAPTION.

There's a little dolphin picture off to the right as an example. But there are two things that you should know about your choices here.

First, if you chose anything other than actual size for your picture at the top of this page, your picture might be bigger in reality than the size it will show on the screen. If you want to let your visitors click to enlarge it, write CLICK PICTURE FOR MORE DETAIL in the caption box, or something to that effect, so that your visitors will know they can enlarge the picture just by clicking on it. We'll explain how just below. Linking your picture actually gives your image and website a bit more power in the search engines, so even if you have nothing to link to but itself in a slightly larger form, do so.

Second, under ALT text, you should change the **Picture Name** to keywords that visitors might use to find your site. So, if you sell women's leather jackets, change the ALT text to something like: women's leather, genuine suede, leather jackets, etc. You get the idea. You can get much more specific in your keywords, and in fact, the more specific the better.

ALT text works like an additional meta tag. The more keywords on your site, the better you'll rank in the search engines. We'll be going over keywords and search engine ranking strategies in Chapters 10-11, so you might want to review those chapters before entering any ALT text for your pictures.

ADD A PICTURE FRAME.

The picture frame comes in a variety of colors and they will be about as thick as they look on this screen. If none of these choices work for you, you can add a picture frame or border to your picture of different thickness in your photoshop program, and then upload the picture to the picture gallery again. So, again, this just depends on your needs.

MAKING THE PICTURE A LINK.

If you want your picture to enlarge, select the **Link to This Picture** button, and decide if you want it to open in a **new window** or in the **same window**.

Generally, make sure that your pictures open in a new window. When it pops up in the same window, a visitor might get confused because they lose your site for a moment. A new window will give them a chance to look at the photo, close the window, and return right to your site without any difficulties.

You can also have your picture **link to a page within your site**, or even **link to an external site**. So, if we were using a picture of a leather jacket on our homepage, we would have it link directly to our leather page by making the choice to do so here.

Or, if you have a favorite or informative site that might be useful, and is related to the photo, make sure that you type the web address correctly, and definitely make sure that it opens in a new window. That way your visitor never actually leaves your site, but can still use the external link.

When you've made all your choices, click one of the "Done" buttons. Or, if you decide that you don't want to add a picture, click the "Cancel" button.

This is also the screen that you will be working with if you click **Edit Picture**. The only difference is that if you want to change the picture, you'll select **Choose a Different Picture**, and it will take you to the Picture Gallery.

ADD LINK.

When you click the **Add Link** button, the page will take a moment to refresh with dotted lines and little gray **Add It Here** buttons. Decide where you want the link, and click an **Add It Here** button. A new page will pop-up and ask you what type of link you want. Make your choice, then play around with the text settings to get the link looking just like you want. You can even change the alignment of the link, and whether or not the link has any space around it.

A THING ABOUT LINKS: Generally the text that your visitors click (that you've set up as a link) to go to another page or your email address should be done with some thought behind it.

For example:

Click here to go to our Leather Page.

Vs.

Go to our Leather Page.

See the difference? In the first example, "here" is used as the link. In the second example, "Leather Page" is used as the link. With the second example, we get one of our main keywords, "leather," into the link itself, while the first example does nothing for our search engine optimization, using "here" as the link. Always get your keywords into the link.

Simple things like this have the ability to improve your ranking within the search engines. For now, though, you really only need to be aware of this; later, in Chapter 10, we'll explain the use of keywords in greater detail.

LINK TO:

TO ANOTHER WEB PAGE (URL) will create an external link

to another website. It will let you enter the text your visitors will click, the web address they'll be directed to, and whether or not you want the link to pop-up in the same window or in a new one. **As a general rule, always select the new window option.** Again, there's no reason to lose visitors just because you send them to another site.

Adjust your text settings, and click one of the "Done" buttons.

TO A MAIL MESSAGE will set up a link to your email address. Enter

the text that your visitors will click and input your email address, making sure that there are no errors. Adjust the text settings and click one of the "Done" buttons.

TO ANOTHER PAGE IN THIS SITE will make a link to any

other page in your site, including the ones not listed on the navigation bar. Enter the text your visitors will click and select a page to link to.

Pages that have a * at the end will be pages that are *not listed* on the navigation bar, but are still part of your site. For example, for our leather page we created a size chart page. It looks like: leathersize* as a choice, and the only way for visitors to find this page is by clicking the link that we created on the leather page, because it is not listed anywhere else.

You can always access these pages yourself, of course, by going to your **Site Organizer** (which we discuss in a few moments). Adjust your text settings and click one of the "Done" buttons.

ADD TABLE.

When you click the **Add Table** button, the page will take a moment to refresh with dotted lines and little gray **Add It Here** buttons. This is a really useful option if you are selling items and want a uniformed look to your product catalogs.

We used tables for every one of our shopping pages. The **Add Table** option can also be found in the **Site Add-On** section, as a **Site Add-On**.

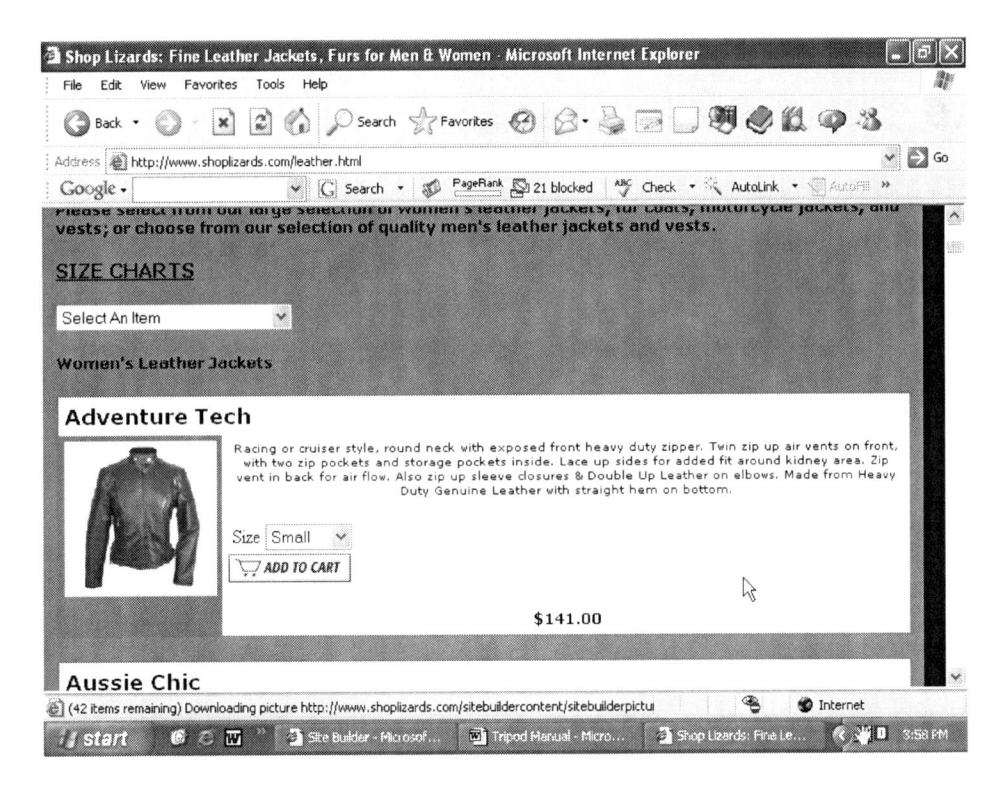

After you click an **Add It Here** button, you have quite a few decisions to make. You need to decide if you want to choose a table from the **Table Gallery,** or if you want to build your own table.

We suggest looking through the Table Gallery to get some ideas about what you *can* do, and then if they don't have what you need, you can just build your own table, which is actually a lot easier than it sounds.

CHOOSE A TABLE FROM THE TABLE GALLERY.

Choose from the available tables in the gallery to add that table to your website. You can edit the text and pictures within the table, you can add or delete elements (we'll discuss deleting items later), or you can click the **Edit Table** button.

The **Edit Table** button will take you to basically the same screen that **Build Your Own Table** uses. You can change how many rows and columns the table has, you can change all the colors, the alignment, and even the table borders. Plus, when you make changes, Tripod will show you an example of what it will look like, so you'll have a good idea.

Make your choices, knowing that you can come back and change them as many times as you'd like to get the right look, and click one of the "Done" buttons. If you change your mind about creating a table, click the "Cancel" button.

BUILD YOUR OWN TABLE.

We found that the selections in the table gallery were very customizable and easy to work with, but when we wanted just a simple two-column table, it was actually easier to make our own.

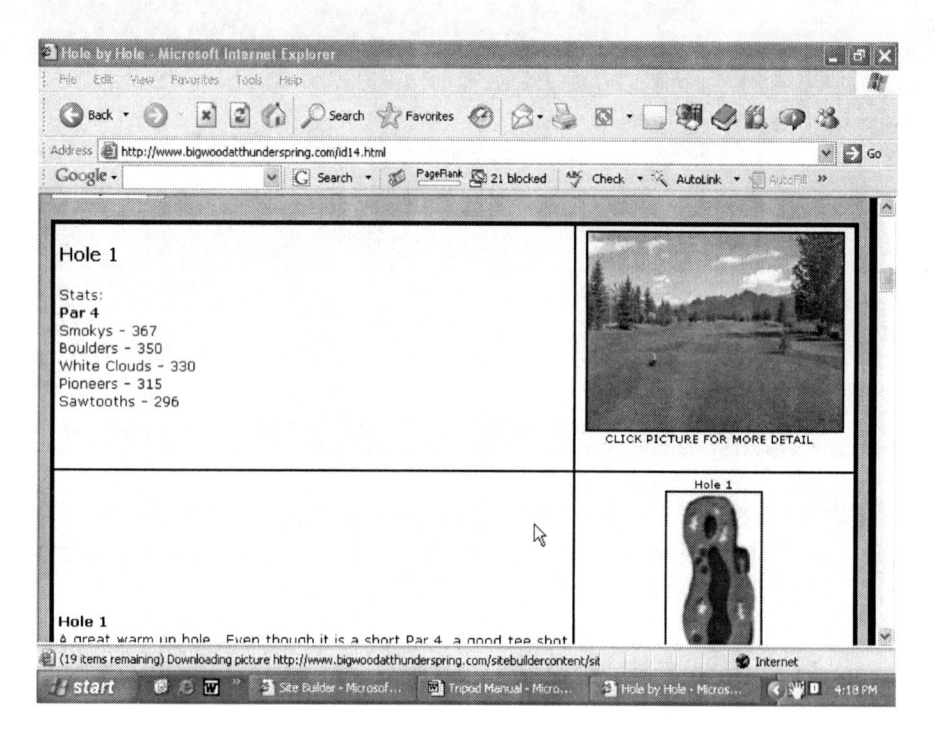

Above is an example of the table that we created for Bigwood At Thunder Spring's website, http://bigwoodgolfcourse.tripod.com.

So, if you can't find just the right table template from the gallery, creating your own is a good choice—and you can be as creative or as simple as you need once you know how things work.

If you're ready, you'll need to decide how many columns and how many rows you want, and then you'll need to decide on your colors. You can always come back and change things later. After you're done, click one of the "Done" buttons. If you change your mind, click "Cancel."

Chapter Six: Advanced Building & Editing   149

SITE ADD-ONS.

When you click the **Site Add-Ons** button, the page will take a moment to refresh with dotted lines and little gray **Add It Here** buttons. Site add-ons can be anything from adding your own HTML to setting up a newsletter sign-up form. Even if you don't want to add anything right now, you should look through the available site add-ons because some of them are really fantastic, and they might give you more ideas on what you can do with your site.

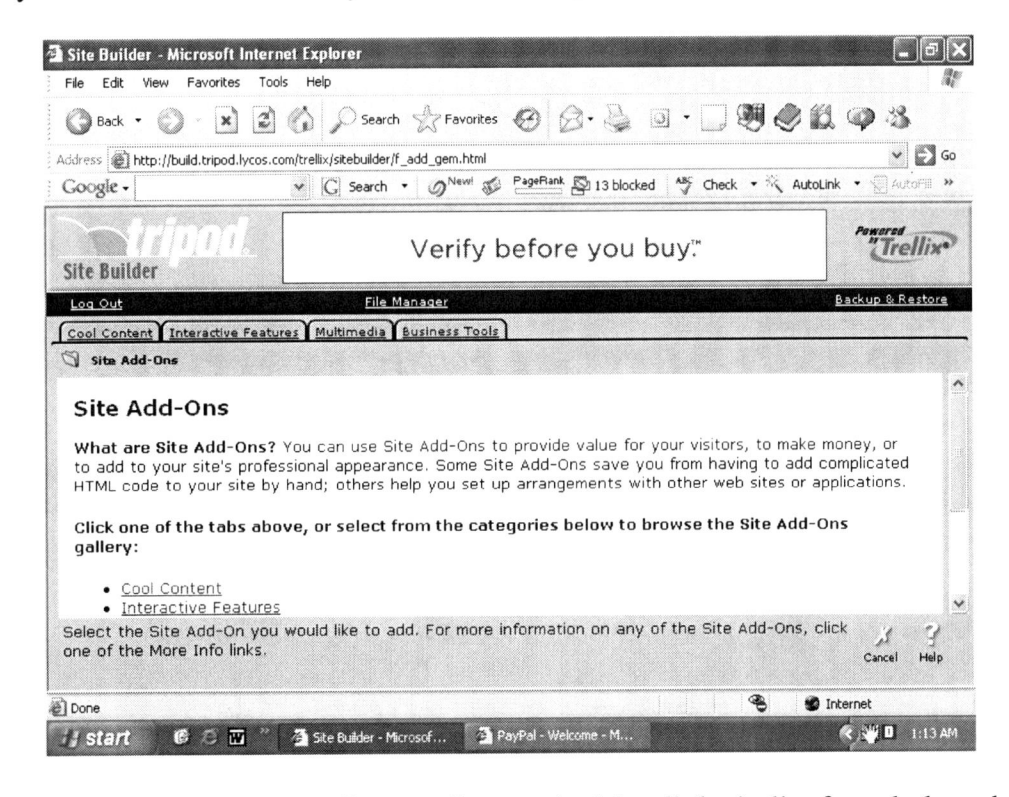

You'll be using either the yellow toolbar or the blue links in list form below the yellow toolbar to make your choices. We'll go through them with you, just so you know what Tripod offers.

All of them are very self-explanatory with clear "click and make a choice" decisions. Also, anything you add just to see how it looks on your site can always be changed or deleted later (unless you get HTML from a source outside Tripod, then bad things can happen if you don't know what you're doing—but we'll get to that later).

SITE ADD-ONS→COOL CONTENT

Under the Cool Content tab: you can add logos, a Tripod mp3 search, date and time stamp, a page counter, the table gallery (that we just went over), and animated cursors. Everything here is very self-explanatory and easy to add to your site. Play around with them a bit to see how they work on your pages.

Page counters are great for high-traffic sites because your visitors will see that you're getting a lot of hits and are more likely to come back to your site. If you aren't getting a lot of hits though, you might not want to add a counter just yet. It depends on your site's needs.

However, we actually prefer to use a page counter provided by StatCounter, http://www.statcounter.com because they offer much easier to use options for keeping track of your visitors. To use StatCounter on your site like we do, you'll add it in as HTML, which we'll be going over in a few moments.

SITE ADD-ONS→INTERACTIVE FEATURES

Under the Interactive Features tab: Amazon item listing, add your own HTML, add a guest book, recommend this site link, search, forms, Constant Contact newsletter, and add a map to your site.

Again, these are all easy to use, and we'll be going over HTML later.

If you find a good code, from a good source (of course), Add HTML to your site is the choice that you would make to add it to your page, and is not done under the Add Text section.

You'll also be adding PayPal buttons to your site if you plan to sell; so to do so, you'll be selecting Add HTML from here instead of adding text (see Chapter 9).

SITE ADD-ONS→MULTIMEDIA

Under the Multimedia tab: add sound to your site, add video, add flash media, add a file download, or add your own HTML. These can add great things to your site, but they have their limitations, so take the time to understand how they work.

If you want to **ADD SOUND**, you'll need to upload a sound file to Tripod from here, but it has to be one of these file types: .mp3, .wav, .mid, .midi, .au, .ra, or .rm.

If you want to **ADD VIDEO** to your site, you'll need to upload a video file to Tripod from here, but it has to be one of these file types: .mpeg, .mpg, .mov, .avi.

If you want to **ADD FLASH** to your site, you'll need to upload a flash file to Tripod from here, but it needs to be a flash file, or a shockwave file type.

If you want to **ADD A FILE DOWNLOAD** to your site, you can basically upload anything other than a .jsp file type. Word documents, pdf's, and most everything else can be uploaded to your site so that your visitors can download and view them. Or, pay for the file, download, and view it.

NOTE: make sure you get the right file type before you try to upload and you'll avoid a lot of stress in changing file types and re-uploading files.

SITE ADD-ONS→BUSINESS TOOLS

Under the Business Tools tab: Amazon item listing, accept online payments with PayPal, the table gallery, forms, add your own HTML, and add the Constant Contact newsletter. These are self-explanatory, except the PayPal option.

Now, from our experience, if you want to sell more than one item on your site, you'll need to have a shopping cart button. To do this the easiest way, you should just go to PayPal's site and select the options there to add buttons. We'll explain how to add PayPal to your site in Chapter 9, so for all intents and purposes, forget this option even exists.

TRIPOD RSS.

Tripod has created more site add-ons for you, but they aren't kept with the regular choices available from the toolbar under **Site Add-Ons**. To find them, you'll need to return to the Tripod homepage.

TOOLS→SITE ADD-ONS

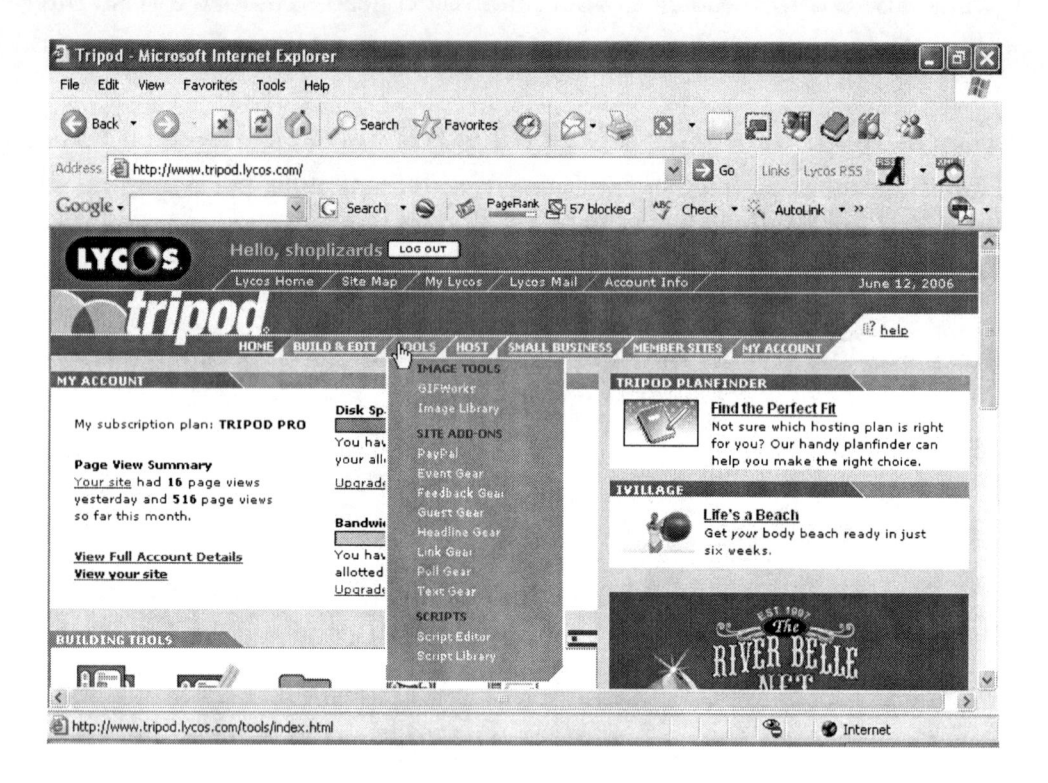

Tripod offers Event Gear, Feedback Gear, Guest Gear, Headline Gear, Link Gear, Poll Gear, and Text Gear, which are all frequently updated by Tripod and/or Tripod sponsors and can be easily added to your site.

All of the Gear is available for free (with a little "Get this Gear" ad on it). If you'd like to upgrade, Tripod makes it simple and cost effective. And it's very easy to install on your site.

Since Tripod's instructions are very explanatory, we'll leave that part alone, with one exception. When you get your Gear picked out and customized, copy the HTML code Tripod gives you, open a new window (see Chapter 9, PayPal). Log in to your account again (if you have to), go to the page where you want the Gear, and add the HTML as a Site Add-On.

We suggest doing it this way because then you can be looking at all of Tripod's gear in one window, while you add it to your pages in another, without having to keep going back and forth between a bunch of pages and logging in again and again.

When we've used Tripod's Gear, we never found the need to upgrade because the little ad ("Get this gear!") never bothered us. But if you're interested…

TRIPOD GEAR PRICING:

NOTE: All of the **Professional Gears** can only be had by Tripod's Pro members. That's the $8.95/Month plan that you signed up for if you purchased a domain name through Tripod. The below fees are *in addition* to your current plan.

The **Personal Gears** can be had by all members, though they too require the below fees if you'd like to be rid of the ads (the ads are tiny little "get this gear" links on the bottom of all gears). If you don't mind the ads and you have a Pro plan, then the gear is completely free.

The pricing for the gear plans is based solely on page views, though you can have as many of the gears on your pages as you want. Actually, you can have all of the gears on all of your pages if you like; the pricing is still the same.

Page views mean that a visitor *physically clicks* on part of your gear; for example, they click on the movie time, or they answer your poll. All plans require a one-time setup fee of $10 (but again, if you don't mind the ads, you don't pay anything).

PLAN 1: PERSONAL PLAN $5/Month
500 Ad-Free Page Views Per Month

PLAN 2: LOW ACTIVITY PLAN $15/Month
1000 Ad-Free Page Views Per Month

PLAN 3: MODERATE ACTIVITY PLAN $25/Month
10,000 Ad-Free Page Views Per Month

PLAN 4: HIGH ACTIVITY PLAN $50/Month
100,000 Ad-Free Page Views Per Month

PLAN 5: PROFESSIONAL PLAN $99/Month
2,000,000 Ad-Free Page Views Per Month

TOOLS→SITE ADD-ONS→EVENT GEAR

Event Gear is like having your date book up for people to see. It'll help you to organize plans with a large audience (all of your many visitors) and lets them know when things are happening, what to bring, etc. You can even have the movie listings up if you like.

TOOLS→SITE ADD-ONS→FEEDBACK GEAR

The **Feedback Gear** is basically a fancy version of the Form Site Add-On that we talked about earlier. So, if your form isn't working out because you get thousands, nay, millions, of forms filled out by visitors, consider this option.

TOOLS→SITE ADD-ONS→GUEST GEAR

Guest Gear is the little brother of the Feedback Gear, offering slightly different options. Again, it can be accomplished by the form Site Add-On that we discussed earlier.

TOOLS→SITE ADD-ONS→HEADLINE GEAR

The **Headline Gear** is just what we will soon be hammering into your head about "fresh content." You pick the topic that best suits your site's needs, and Tripod will update its "Wired News" when news related to your choice comes up. It keeps things fresh and gives visitors a reason to return to your site often to check for new content—which is exactly what you want.

TOOLS→SITE ADD-ONS→LINK GEAR

The **Link Gear** is a handy way to have links on your site that are monitored by Tripod to make sure they remain active. You can post your favorites (or affiliates) and even let your visitors post their own links, depending on your moderation choices.

TOOLS→SITE ADD-ONS→POLL GEAR

Poll Gear is perfect for those who like having interactive polls on their site. You can update the poll as often as you want (daily, weekly, monthly), and it will automatically display the results when visitors vote.

TOOLS→SITE ADD-ONS→TEXT GEAR

Text Gear is unique because you can enter in a bunch of text, and it will refresh with new text every time your visitor refreshes the page. You could put in cool quotes, handy sayings, etc, whatever you'd like to keep your visitors coming back to see what else you have to say.

ADD PAGE.

Clicking **Add Page** will add a new page to your site or can be used to create a new page as an external link. Choose the type of page that you want to add, enter a page title, and decide if you want the page to appear on the navigation bar. When you're done, click one of the "Done" buttons. Or, if you change your mind, click the "Cancel" button.

You might find that copying a page works better than adding a page, because sometimes it's nice to have some of the content you've already done ready to use again, instead of creating or copying it from other pages.

When you add a page, you'll start basically from scratch with that page. If you copy a page, like we do with our shopping pages (because we already created a ton of tables to show our products), all you'll need to do is change the items instead of adding everything all over again. It just depends on what you need, as they both have advantages. Again, play around with it to see which option works best for you.

COPY PAGE.

Often, we have many pages of inventory and it can become a bit of a hassle to recreate every page, table, and back to top button. It makes life a great deal easier, especially if you want a new page that will have similar information as the old to simply make a copy of a page.

Go to the **Site Organizer** to copy a page. Scroll through the list of your pages until you find the one that you'd like to copy and click the **Copy** button next to it. You'll notice that the page will be copied with exactly the same properties and title; the only difference will be the *page file extension.*

For example, our leather page is **leather.html**, and the copy is **id104.html**. You might only have a few pages on your site, so your number will be different, but that's how you can tell the copy from the original.

If you plan to make a major change on a page and are concerned about making a mistake, copy the page first, and then you can always use your original if you mess up later. Just make sure that you remove whichever you won't be using from the navigation bar by clicking **Page Properties** and un-checking the box that will list the page on the navigation bar.

Click on the **Rename** button next to your new page and give it a different name so that you don't get them mixed up. You can make as many copies as you want, and you can delete copies if you decide that you don't need them later. Don't worry, we'll go over the Site Organizer page in more detail a bit later.

To get back to the page that you were working on, find that page in the Site Organizer and click the **Edit Page** button next to it.

MOVE ITEMS.

If you put text within the wrong dotted lines, or if you just want to move something (like a picture or site add-on), click the **Move Items** button. It will take a moment and will refresh the page with a bunch of white boxes next to each item that can be moved.

Check the corresponding white box, making sure that it is the *right* white box for the item that you want moved. Sometimes the box will appear to the right or below the item, so take a moment to make sure that you check the right box(s).

You can move as many items at a time as you want, or just one, it all works the same way. However, we noticed in creating a page for one of our affiliates, that only about 100 items could be moved at any given time. Any more than that and Tripod gets a bit overwhelmed. But all things have limits!

Now, you can move items within just one page, or you can move items to another page of your site. **Keep in mind that you can only move items to pages that are listed on the navigation bar.**

Chapter Six: Advanced Building & Editing   157

If you want to move a picture around on a page, check the box next to the picture and click the "Continue" button. The page will refresh with little gray **Move it Here** buttons. Click a **Move it Here** button, and the page will refresh with the change, moving your picture to the place that you selected.

Moving an item to a different page is slightly more difficult, especially if that page is not listed on the navigation bar. So, before you click the **Move Items** button, click the **Site Organizer** button. This is your list of all your pages and their properties.

To get a page listed on the navigation bar, just to move the item, then to take it back off the navigation bar, scroll down until you find the page that you want to move the item to, then click **Page Properties**.

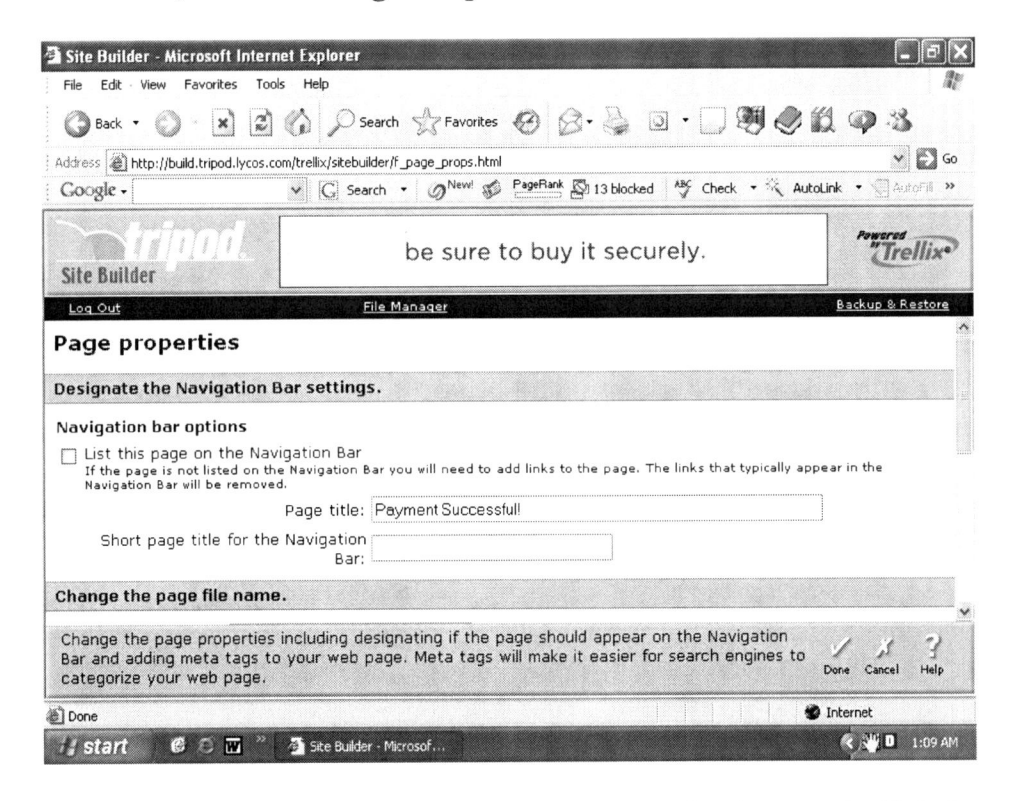

In the picture above, you can see the **Navigation Bar Options** and a little box to "List this page on the Navigation Bar."

Check the box to list your page on the navigation bar and hit the "Done" button. We'll go over the rest of this page under the **Site Organizer** section, so don't be overwhelmed, we're just moving an item for now.

Now you'll be taken back to the Site Organizer. Click the **Edit Page** link for the page that you were working on, the one with the item(s) that needs to be moved.

If you look at the navigation bar, you'll now see the new page (the page that you want to move items to) listed as well.

Click the **Move Items** button and when the page refreshes, select the white box for the item(s) that you wish to move, and click "Continue." Now select the page that you just moved onto the navigation bar, and select a little gray **Move It Here** button to move your item(s) where you want to.

When you're done, you'll need to move the page back off of the navigation bar. To do so, click the **Site Organizer** button, find the page title, select **Page Properties**, de-select the **List on the Navigation Bar** box, and click the "Done" button.

To get back, click the **Edit Page** link next to the page that you want to return to.

COPY ITEMS.

Copy Items works much the same way as moving items, except that it will *copy* a picture, text, or site add-on, table, etc, to an area on the same page, or to an area on a different page. You can copy as many items at a time as you want, or just one, it all works the same way. However, we noticed in creating a page for one of our affiliates, that only about 100 items could be copied at any given time. Any more than that and Tripod gets a bit overwhelmed.

Click the **Copy Items** button and the page will refresh with a bunch of white boxes next to each item that can be copied. Select the corresponding white box; making sure that it is the *right* white box for the item(s) that you want to copy. Sometimes the box will appear to the right or below the item, so take a moment to make sure that you check the right box(es). Check the box for the item(s) that you wish to copy and click "Continue."

Now, this will repeat all the moving item information, because it works exactly the same way, so feel free to skip ahead if you know what comes next.

If not: you can copy items within just one page, or you can copy items to another page of your site. **Keep in mind that you can only copy items to pages that are listed on the navigation bar.**

If you want to copy a picture to another place on the same page, check the box next to the picture and click the "Continue" button. The page will refresh with little gray **Copy it Here** buttons. Select where you want it to be copied, and the page will refresh with the change.

Copying an item to a different page is slightly more difficult, especially if the page is not listed on the navigation bar. Before you click the **Copy Items** button, click the **Site Organizer** button. You'll have a list of all your pages and their properties.

To get a page listed on the navigation bar, just to copy the item, then to take it back off the navigation bar, scroll down until you find the page that you want to copy the item to, then click **Page Properties**.

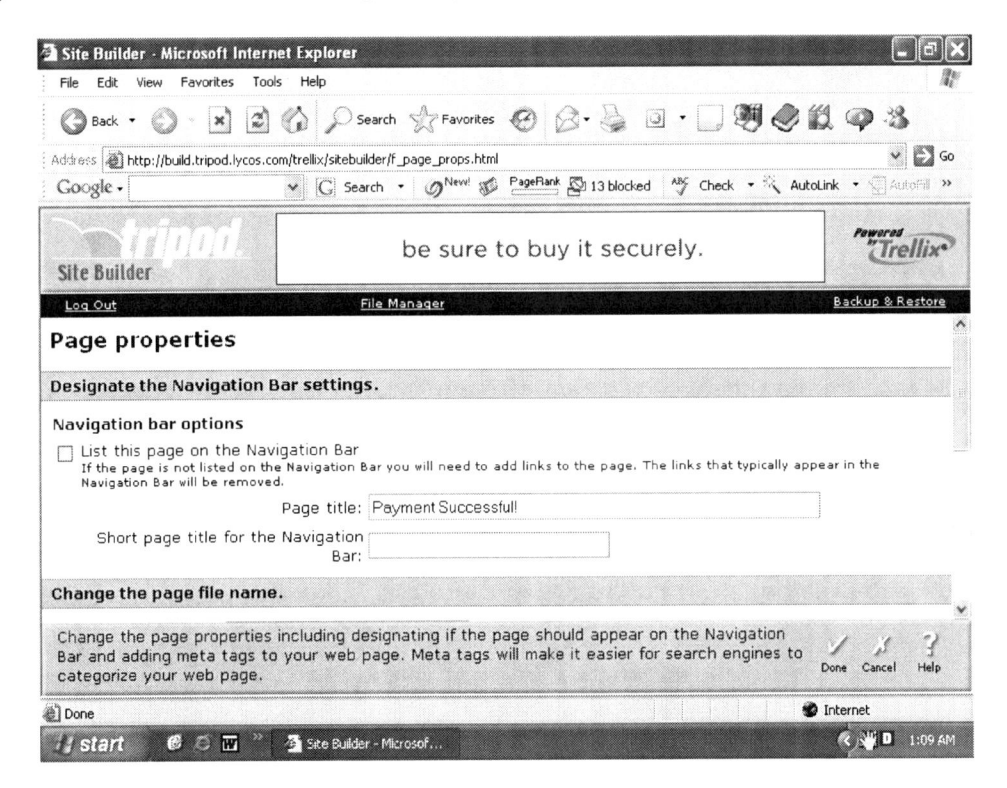

In the picture above, you can see the **Navigation Bar Options** and a little box to "List this page on the Navigation Bar."

Check the box to list your page on the navigation bar and hit the "Done" button. We'll go over the rest of this page under the **Site Organizer** section, so don't be overwhelmed, we're just copying an item right now.

Now you'll be taken back to the **Site Organizer**. Select the **Edit Page** link for the page that you were working on, the one with the item that needs to be copied. If you look at the navigation bar, you'll now see the new page listed there too.

Click the **Copy Items** button and when the page refreshes, select the corresponding white box, and click "Continue." Select the page that you just moved to the navigation bar (where you wanted to copy an item to), and select a **Copy It Here** button to copy your item(s).

When you're done, you'll need to move the page back off of the navigation bar. To do so, click the **Site Organizer** button, find the page title, select **Page Properties**, de-select the **List on the Navigation Bar** box, and click the "Done" button.

To get back, click the **Edit Page** link next to the page that you want to return to.

DELETE ITEMS.

If you need to delete something from your page, click the **Delete Items** button. After a moment the page will refresh with little white boxes next to every item that can be deleted.

Check the box next to each item that you want to delete, but make sure that the white box actually corresponds to the *right* item. Sometimes the box will be to the right of an item or right below an item, but you'll be able to tell if you look closely. It's a terrible thing to accidentally delete something you worked hard on when it takes a few seconds more to make sure you check the right box.

You can delete as many or as few items as you like, deleting ten items or just one at a time, it all works the same. Mark your boxes and hit "Done." Or, if you decide that you don't want to delete anything, click "Cancel."

PREVIEW SITE.

Clicking **Preview Site** will bring up a pop-up window with everything that you have just done, *without* publishing the site to the internet and making it live. This is just so you can get an idea of how things will look to the public, without all the little yellow edit buttons, or the big Tripod page frames and toolbar.

If you use this button, take the time to proof your site for any mistakes and check all links to make sure they work properly. But, when you're done, you'll need to publish the site to actually reflect any changes that you've made.

PUBLISH TO WEB.

Everything that you do on Tripod is automatically saved. And nothing can be undone unless you delete it. But, if you've been working for a while and the changes you made are ready for the public to see, hit the **Publish to Web** button.

The changes that you make to your site will not be available on the internet until you click this button.

When you click the **Publish to Web** button, it will take a few moments to process and publish the site, as it re-publishes all the pages, and not just the one that you were working on.

So, if you made changes on a bunch of pages, they'll all get published at this time. After Tripod has published your site, a "Congratulations" screen will appear with a bunch of options:

Promote Your Site
View Your Site
Edit Your Site
Rate Your Site Builder Experience

and at the bottom of the screen,

Edit Site
All My Sites
Site Promotion
Logout
Help

PUBLISH TO WEB→PROMOTE YOUR SITE

This will take you to a page that offers help for promoting your site. Your options:

Newsletter Management
Advertise on Switchboard.com
Announce Your Site
Simple Search Engine Submission

As you'll learn in Chapter 11, simply publishing your site gets you on the list to be crawled for inclusion in the search engines. If you find that you have some free time, though, doing the **Simple Search Engine Submission** can prove somewhat helpful in gaining your brand new site the attention of the web bots.

Nothing is guaranteed here, though; so if you don't have the time, don't bother. Optimizing your site, as we'll teach you in Chapter 10, will prove time *much* better spent.

PUBLISH TO WEB→VIEW YOUR SITE

If you click the **View Your Site** button, a pop-up window will appear with your newly published site. You can check it out to see how the changes appear live. Make sure that you take a moment to proofread *all* of your text, check all of your links, and make sure that your pictures, HTML, and add-ons appear like you wanted and nothing is looking weird.

If things didn't appear like you wanted, just go back and try again. There's no limit to the amount of times you can publish your site.

PUBLISH TO WEB→EDIT YOUR SITE

If you forgot to add something, fix something, or just want to get back to building right away, click the **Edit Your Site** button so that you can get right back to work. You can publish and edit as many times as you want. Tripod has no limits.

PUBLISH TO WEB→RATE YOUR SITE BUILDER EXPERIENCE

You can take a short survey by Tripod to rate your experience. This will also give you more options for website promotion and search engine placement; but keep in mind that nothing is guaranteed. So, if you don't have time, don't worry about this.

SITE ORGANIZER.

In the **Site Organizer**, you can manage your website by copying, deleting, and moving pages, or changing layouts and designs. It also gives you access to **Page Properties** where you can take or put pages on the navigation bar, and is where you will go to add in all of your meta tags for every page.

SITE ORGANIZER→FILE NAME

This is the page extension (file name, file extension) that we keep mentioning. For example, our Shop Lizards home page has a file name of **index.html**.

If you ever need to link to a specific page, this is how you'll reference it, by getting the correct file name. If ever a link doesn't work, a wrongly typed file name is probably to blame.

So, our home page actually looks like this: http://www.shoplizards.com/index.html

Our Diecast Cars page looks like this:

http://www.shoplizards.com/diecastcars.html

SITE ORGANIZER→PAGE PROPERTIES

Under the **Page Properties** section, you can change the Navigation Bar Options, but more importantly, you can add in and change your meta tags and descriptions. Tripod actually explains this page well, but we'll explain meta tags and how they work in the search engines starting in Chapter 10.

Know that you'll be returning here often to optimize your site.

Chapter Seven
Getting Around Your Account.

Now that you know how to edit your site, you're going to need to know a few things about getting around your Tripod account, just to make your life a little easier.

First, login to Tripod, http://www.tripod.com , using your username and password

Now, you should be signed on to Tripod's homepage. Looking at the orange navigation bar near the top of the page, you'll see:

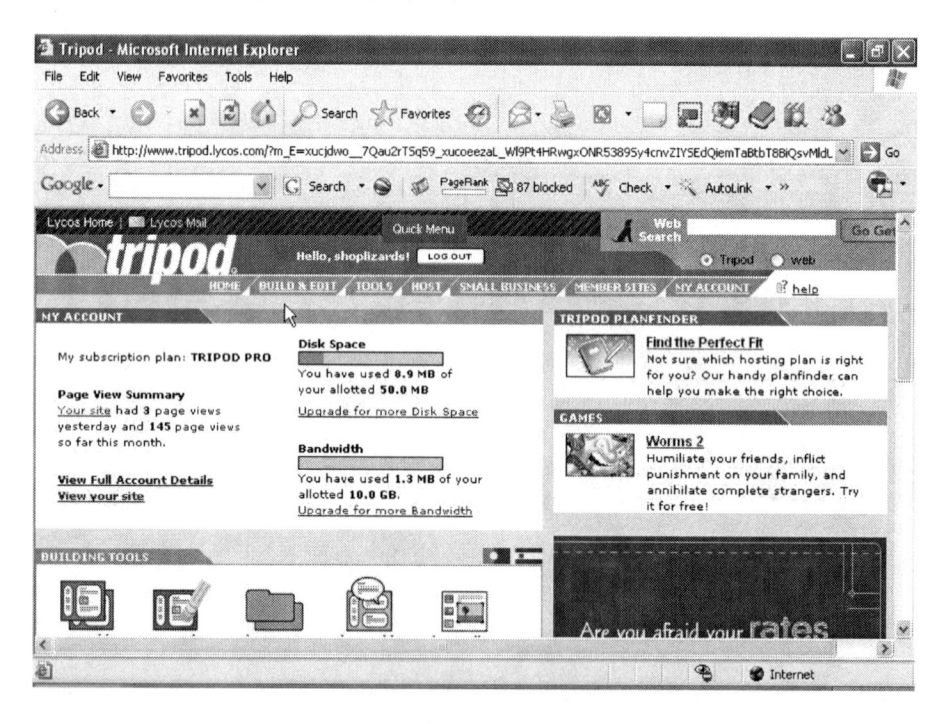

Home, Build & Edit, Tools, Host, Small Business, Member Sites, and My Account

The links are basically explanatory, but we'll go through the **My Account** section and the **Build & Edit** section in greater detail to get you started on your site as quickly as possible.

On the homepage, you'll also see a breakdown of **My Account** and **Building Tools**. This is the fastest way to get a quick glance about what's going on with your site.

Under the **My Account** breakdown, you'll see a **Page View Summary** that will show you how many visitors have been to your site, how much **Disk Space** you are using, and how much **Bandwidth** is being used.

MY ACCOUNT→BANDWIDTH

Bandwidth is defined as the amount of data that is used to transfer a webpage from the server to the person viewing the page.

For example, if the content on a page equals 1MB, and that page is viewed 100 times in one day, the total bandwidth for that page will equal 100MB. For each person to view one page per day, 1MB of Bandwidth is needed.

You can calculate this for every page, just to get a general idea of how much bandwidth is being used on a daily basis. The numbers involved can seem astronomical, so don't panic, this is just something you need to keep an eye on in the future.

The Pro plan comes with 10GB so you should be fine until you start getting major traffic to your site. But, to give you some perspective, our largest webpage is 402MB. Our typical page is about 300MB (because we have so much inventory on each page). See how large those numbers could get?

We've never seriously spent time calculating the bandwidth; instead, we just keep an eye on the little orange bar that tells us how much is being used. Tripod is anything if not redundantly helpful.

Depending on how fast your site grows; you may or may not need to upgrade the bandwidth. If you do, you can purchase additional bandwidth through Tripod in 500MB chunks. We broke down the upgrades for you in Chapter 4.

Another easy way to compute your Bandwidth is to select:

MY ACCOUNT→WEBSITE DETAILS→VIEW TRAFFIC REPORT→VIEW CUSTOM REPORT

Clicking **View Custom Report** will bring up a pop-up window with a great deal of information about your site.

All of this will be explained later under the **View Custom Report** section. But for bandwidth viewing purposes, the **General Summary** will help. At the bottom of the chart, you will see the **Total Data** transferred, or, the total amount of bandwidth being used.

So, since no one wants to calculate bandwidth manually, check out this chart to see how much you are currently using. If your site is using most of the 10GB, you might consider upgrading your bandwidth. It's just something to keep an eye on.

If you hit the bandwidth limit, no one will be able to view your site for the day (or even the month!); so upgrade when necessary to avoid any downtime.

MY ACCOUNT →DISK SPACE

Disk Space is the running total of how much space your website takes up on Tripod's server. It also counts how much file space is being used by the photos and files on your site, or the photos that have been uploaded to the photo gallery, but are not currently displayed on any of your pages.

A Tripod Pro account gives you 50MB of disk space. A basic site will use up less than 10MB. Just to give you some perspective, our Shop Lizards ecommerce website has over 500 photos uploaded onto Tripod's server, and we only use 23.7MB of disk space, which is less than half of our allotted limit.

In general, you'll probably never use up the entire 50MB, so you shouldn't be concerned.

However, just so that you know your options, if you do expand your site and get close to that 50MB of disk space, you can upgrade that part of your membership very easily. You can add disk space in 50MB increments. We broke down the upgrades for you in Chapter 4.

MY ACCOUNT →PAGE VIEWS

Page Views are broken down by how many visitors have viewed your site the previous day, and holds a running tally for the entire month. If you want more detail, to actually see which pages are being viewed, hover your mouse over the **My Account** link on the orange navigation bar and select **Website Details**.

Your other choices are **Membership Info, Website Details, Domain Info**, and **Domain E-Mail**. We'll explain these, too, next.

MY ACCOUNT →WEBSITE DETAILS

The **Website Details** page will show you all of the details about your site, much of which can already be viewed from the homepage; however, with one exception. If you scroll down the page a bit to the **Page Views** section, you'll see a little link to **View Traffic Reports**. Select this link.

VIEW TRAFFIC REPORTS.

We've said it before, but we'll say it again here since it's finally relevant. We don't really use this option from Tripod anymore because StatCounter http://www.statcounter.com has proven far superior in what it offers, and it's also free and easy to add to your site (just add it as HTML).

But we'll tell you how to use Tripod's services too, so that you can judge for yourself. On this page you can check out your site's traffic for the last thirty days. Select **View Traffic Logs**, and select a day to view, then click **View Report**.

This will bring up a pop-up window of the traffic reports for your site on the date that you chose. This is tricky to read through at first, and may seem insignificant. But if you scan through, you'll notice which pages were viewed by looking at the page file extensions, and even which pictures visitors may have clicked on.

You'll also see which "bots," or search engines, have found your site, and which pages they have indexed. The importance of this page is to see which pages are being viewed the most, and which get little traffic. You can also see this view, for the entire time your website has been online, by selecting **View Custom Reports→Request Report** (if you have the Pro plan or above).

Actually, the best way to get an idea of your website traffic is to go back to the **View Traffic Reports** page and select **View Custom Reports**, then click **View Report**.

VIEW TRAFFIC REPORT →VIEW CUSTOM REPORTS

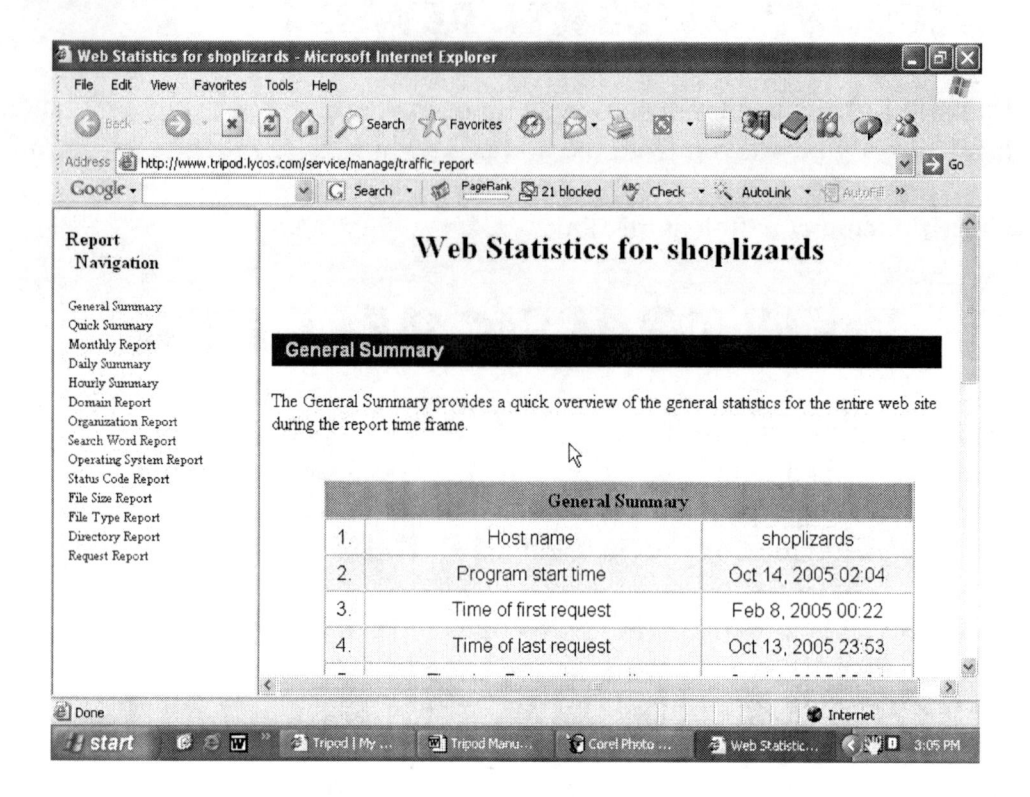

Selecting **View Custom Reports** (you'll only have this option if you have the Pro plan or above) will bring up a pop-up window with tons of options and statistics. You should view these statistics once a week or so to get an idea of your traffic, and the keywords that visitors may have used to find your site.

On the left-hand side, you'll see:

General Summary
Quick Summary
Monthly Report
Daily Summary
Hourly Summary
Domain Report
Organization Report
Search Word Report
Operating System Report
Status Code Report
File Size Report
File Type Report

Directory Report
Request Report

We'll go through each of these in detail now.

VIEW CUSTOM REPORTS→GENERAL SUMMARY

The **General Summary** page comes up automatically when the view custom reports window pops up. Here, you will find a quick overview of your site, and more specifically, how well your site is completing server requests.

Server requests are the visitors and bots that have viewed your site. Each page hit can result in several server requests as the images for each page are loaded. So, if you have a hundred photos on one page, that page might receive a hundred server requests. Also, the bottom of this chart shows the **Total Data** transferred, or, the amount of bandwidth being used.

So, if you'd like to see at a glance how much bandwidth your site is using, like we discussed before, check out this chart to find out.

VIEW CUSTOM REPORTS→QUICK SUMMARY

The **Quick Summary** page will show you the peak entries for your entire site, or the total webpage hits. You'll also see your most active day of the week.

If you're getting the most hits on Wednesday, use this information for your marketing campaign. For example, if most people are viewing your site on Wednesday between 18:00-18:59 (military time for 6-6:59pm), you should send out your emails on Wednesday night between 6 and 7pm, when they're most likely to be on your site, thinking about your business.

This summary will also show you the most requested keyword, and the most popular operating system used to view your site.

All of the information on this chart is described in greater detail on other charts, so this can simply be used as a quick overview.

VIEW CUSTOM REPORTS→MONTHLY REPORT

The **Monthly Report** identifies the activity for each month, since your site was first created. You can see which month has received the most visitors; and remember, each page hit can result in several server requests as the images for that page are loaded. So, if you have a hundred photos on one page, that page might receive a hundred server requests.

Our Shop Lizards pages have, commonly, a hundred photos each, so this report is skewed a bit for our general purposes, which is mainly why we've moved to StatCounter for hit tracking. However, the more page hits, or server requests, the better. It's also been good for us to identify the most viewed month.

You might find that Christmas shoppers are actually shopping your site in November (or even October!), to get better deals.

Use all of this information to your best advantage.

VIEW CUSTOM REPORTS→DAILY SUMMARY

The **Daily Summary** breaks down the level of activity as a total for each day of the week. This summary also compares the level of activity on weekdays and weekends as a total number of requests, since your site has been online.

This is what we were discussing before, about finding the day of the week that your site brings in the most traffic. And again, use all of this information to your best advantage when it comes to sending out marketing emails.

VIEW CUSTOM REPORTS→HOURLY SUMMARY

The **Hourly Summary** identifies the level of activity broken down by each hour, also including the level of activity during work hours and after hours as a total number of requests.

You won't be able to see your busiest day from this chart, but keeping track of your busiest hour is always interesting.

VIEW CUSTOM REPORTS→DOMAIN REPORT

The **Domain Report** will identify the top origins of visitors to your site. Use this information carefully and you may be able to define the most common geographical area for your site's visitors. The Intro goes over the importance of utilizing an international market, so always keep them in mind because they make up more than half of all ecommerce sales.

In other words, you may be able to use this information to better target your market, *and* your visitors.

VIEW CUSTOM REPORTS→ORGANIZATION REPORT

The **Organization Report** identifies the organizations (companies, ISP's, institutions, etc) whose computers have accessed your site. This is similar to the **Domain Report**, with the exception that this report will show a hierarchy of servers within an organization.

Don't worry about this chart too much, it's really just informative rather than useful.

VIEW CUSTOM REPORTS→SEARCH WORD REPORT

The **Search Word Report** *should* be your most viewed chart. Here, you'll see a summary of keywords that your visitors have typed into the search engines, and that have consequently brought them to your site.

From this, you can get a better idea about how your visitors are finding your site, and you can change your meta tags (keywords) or website content accordingly.

We'll be discussing meta tags and keyword use a little later in Chapter 10, so having a good idea about how your site is being found is handy.

VIEW CUSTOM REPORTS→OPERATING SYSTEM REPORT

The **Operating System Report** lists the operating systems (Windows, Apple) that your visitors are using to view your site. This is interesting because you'll notice that many of your views are coming from computers unlike your own.

For example, we've found that Shop Lizards is currently viewed on Mac (Apple) computers more than Windows (IBM), even though we created the site on IBM computers, without even thinking about the Mac audience.

The only difference this may make is that some computers and browsers view fonts and colors differently, but this isn't something that you really need to worry about as Tripod will only let you use the most common colors and fonts anyway; so this may never be a problem for you.

It's just interesting, and something to keep in mind about the variety of your visitors.

VIEW CUSTOM REPORTS→STATUS CODE REPORT

The **Status Code Report** lists the HTML headers returned by a server request. Most of this will not be in your control, but if you want to know more about the status codes, you can click the provided link for definitions.

This is purely informative because the status codes are not something you have anything to do with. However, if you are getting bad requests, a lot, contact Tripod and their tech guys will fix the problem.

Basically, any bad requests are a result from something that is happening on Tripod's end, and is not the fault of your site.

VIEW CUSTOM REPORTS→FILE SIZE REPORT

The **File Size Report** categorizes the size of the file being requested. This is mostly useful for optimizing page performance.

If most of your requests are breaking the 100KB mark, your site may be loading too slowly for most computers, or taking about 40 seconds per page. Usually visitors will only hang around for about ten seconds (sometimes barely even five) if they are running a DSL connection. If your pages load really slowly, consider making two pages instead of just one for that data. That way you won't lose visitors because your pages take too long to load. It's a trade-off that you need to be aware of.

But unless your pages are as long as some of our Shop Lizards pages are, you may not have to worry about this. However, if you intend to add an extensive inventory, you should keep page performance in mind.

Always keep your visitors in mind.

VIEW CUSTOM REPORTS→FILE TYPE REPORT

The **File Type Report** identifies the type of files being requested on your pages. Most of your images will be .jpg, or .jpeg, though some may be .gif files.

If you have a decent photoshop program, you should know what these are. If not, .jpg, .jpeg, and .gif are all image file extensions. This is discussed in more detail in Chapter 1.

VIEW CUSTOM REPORTS→DIRECTORY REPORT

The **Directory Report** will analyze all of the access to your site directory. Since your site was designed in Tripod, you'll only have one directory. For example, our Shop Lizards site shows that all of our activity comes from the **/shoplizards/** directory.

At the bottom of the chart it shows the total number of requests made on your site. Other summaries show this number, like the **Quick Summary**, so you may never actually use this option.

VIEW CUSTOM REPORTS→REQUEST REPORT

The **Request Report** identifies the most popular pages on your site and shows how often they were viewed. This can be confusing, at first, because this report also shows all of the picture files that have been clicked on, and they also count as requests. As we mentioned before, if your page has one hundred photos, those photos may count as one hundred server requests.

Actual webpages will be highlighted and underlined in blue. You can see this same report, though on a daily basis, if you go back to the **View Traffic Report** page and select a **Traffic Report** for a specific day, going back for thirty days.

MY ACCOUNT→MEMBERSHIP INFO

The **Membership Info** page shows a detailed account of your membership. Here, you can change your billing information, membership information, upgrade, downgrade, or cancel your membership, and change your newsletter subscription options.

We suggest that unless you no longer want a website, that you never cancel your membership. And, if you only want to upgrade bandwidth or disk space, you should consider doing it via the **Tripod Upgrades** section, which we discuss in Chapter 4 because it's the easiest way to go about things.

Also, this page will show your **Tripod Domain Name** as, for example,

http://shoplizards.tripod.com.

Our real domain name is: http://www.shoplizards.com

If you have a Pro membership and purchased a domain name, which mostly likely you have, don't panic that Tripod shows your domain name with the **.tripod.com** part.

Tripod just doesn't show the new domain name that you've purchased on this page. You can check your real domain name on the **Domain Info** page.

Also from the **Membership Info** page, you can create a **Blog** or **Album**. Keep in mind that if you do create a blog or album, it will be completely separate, and will not interfere with your current site, though it will run on the same plan. For example, if you have the Plus plan, ads will be eliminated.

But if you get creative, they can be fun. And they can be easily linked to your current site by adding a new page and selecting an external link. We actually use a blog all the time for Word Partners Ink to incorporate with our newsletter as it gives us a forum for new content and keeps our customers coming back.

MY ACCOUNT →DOMAIN INFO

The **Domain Info** page will give you access to your domain information including your current domain name, if you have any subdomains, and all of the information on your administrative contact.

If any information on your contact is wrong or missing, you can select **Edit Contact** to change things. Though, note that not all of this information is required. Actually, the only information that Tripod may ask of you, personally, is your birth date, so make sure that it is correct. If you need to change your password later, Tripod will ask your birth date for security purposes.

SUBDOMAIN FORWARDING automatically forwards domain traffic to another website. By also enabling **Domain Masking**, your domain name will appear in the browser's address bar instead of the destination site address. Your Pro subscription with Tripod will give you five domains that can be forwarded.

We don't currently have any subdomains for our Shop Lizards site, but if we added a subdomain, for leather jackets, it would look like this:

http://leather.shoplizards.com

You could then advertise for this new domain as a different store to bring more traffic to your site based on specific products or services.

If you need more than five subdomains for your site, you can purchase more through Tripod in increments of five. We broke down the upgrades for you in Chapter 4.

LOCK STATUS as "Locked" prevents your domain name from being hijacked or accidentally transferred, so do not change this. It will cause serious problems if you do.

Also on this page you can check your **Domain Email**. Or, if you want to access your domain email from your browser without logging on to Tripod first, use this link:

http://webmail.domains.lycos.com

If it hasn't already been set up for you, you can set up your domain email and have it forwarded to another email account. This is explained next.

MY ACCOUNT →DOMAIN EMAIL

The **Domain Email** page will give you access to your new email account. Tripod gives you five email forwarding addresses. If you need more you can buy them from Tripod in increments of five. We broke down the upgrades for you in Chapter 4.

We highly suggest that you set up an email account elsewhere too. We set ours up on yahoo.com, shoplizards@yahoo.com; but we also set up a few accounts to receive specific emails from customers.

For Orders, orders@shoplizards.com, and for Comments, comments@shoplizards.com .

When you set up these email accounts, you can then set them to forward to a different email address that you'll access all the time. We set ours up to forward to shoplizards@yahoo.com.

That way, we get all the email, but it comes from different email addresses so that we can track our orders and comments separately. You would then put your **@shoplizards.com** addresses on your website, and they will be the addresses that your customers will use, but can be forwarded to your yahoo.com email so you appear more professional.

We don't dislike the Tripod email system; however, it is a bit less advanced than the others available to you for free like Hotmail or Yahoo. Also, the Tripod email doesn't handle HTML or images well, and it may not protect you from viruses.

To avoid all of this, but to still have an email address with your website name, like **@shoplizards.com**, just set it to forward to another email account and you'll be safe yet efficient.

BUILD & EDIT MENU.

There's much on this menu that you'll probably be using, and you'll also find great tutorial links that explain how to use some of Tripod's builders. Also, the **Webmonkey Toolbelt** has a great HTML cheat sheet that you might find useful. We've included our own HTML primer for you in Chapter 12.

To get you started, though, you'll need to click on **Site Builder**. For your ease, this is also included on the homepage, under **Building Tools**. Either link will get you there.

BUILD & EDIT→SITE BUILDER

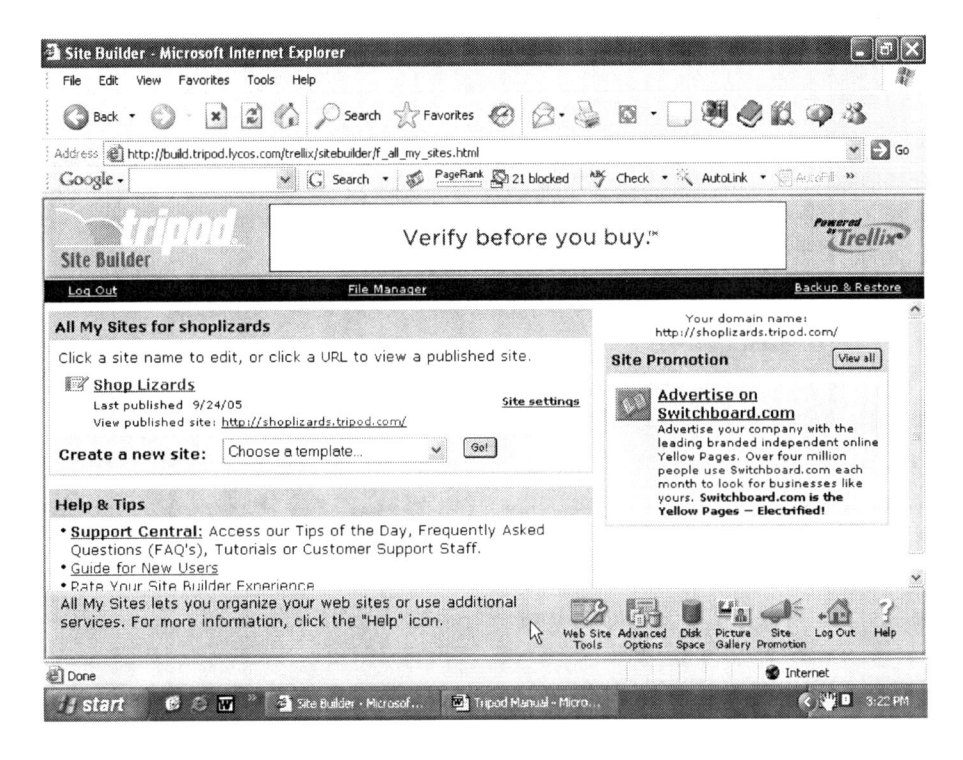

On the **Site Builder** page, you have a lot of options. At the bottom of the page on the gray toolbar you'll find:

Website Tools
Advanced Options
Disk Space
Picture Gallery
Site Promotion
Logout
Help

We'll go through each of these in detail below.

SITE BUILDER→WEBSITE TOOLS

Clicking **Website Tools** will take you to a page with two options, **Advanced Options**, and **Site Promotion**.

We'll talk about each of these separately, and since they each have their own button, you will probably never actually use the **Website Tools** button to find them, but Tripod is nothing if not redundantly helpful.

SITE BUILDER→ADVANCED OPTIONS

Advanced Options should only be used by the more advanced website builder. But we're going to make you an advanced builder, so don't panic. Just don't go clicking wildly and you'll be okay.

Keep in mind that one miss-click here and your whole site could be instantly deleted forever. But, this page does have some uses. Maybe you just want to take your site off the web for a while, or maybe you need to do a *major* update. If so, you'd click **Unpublish**.

Or, maybe you want to make major changes to the site but are really unsure if you'll want to keep them; in this case you might want to click **Copy Site**. This will make an exact copy of your site and you won't have to worry about making a major mistake and being unable to fix things.

It actually takes a while for Tripod to copy your site because it can be a very large file, but Tripod eventually makes a nice little copy for you that will be saved to your computer, and on Tripod. So, if anything goes wrong, you can always use the copy.

To be honest, though, it's hard to make a major mistake on Tripod, but we've had a few so we'll let you in on them.

A minor mistake we made happened when we wanted to change the layout of the homepage.

You can change the layout of each individual page, even the homepage, and so we decided to make it a one column instead of the standard homepage two column. Well, changing the properties of the homepage somehow messes with the page colors of all the other pages. So, we had to go back and change all the page colors back again.

It wasn't a big deal, once we realized what had happened, and it wasn't something that we would have copied the site for.

A major mistake happened later when we became obsessed with the resolution of our site. We found a code that claimed to automatically change the resolution for us. We were excited, so we put the code into the site footer of the homepage, thinking it would resize all of the pages at once. We didn't test it first.

Turns out that the code was a virus and access to every page was denied to us, because the code was in the footer. Yikes!

We cried a bit, screamed a bit, and then had to rebuild Shop Lizards from the ground up, from memory. The Shop Lizards that you see today is a different site than the one we had before—but we like it more because of the blood, sweat, and tears that went into it. Plus, we now *truly* understand the value of testing things out first.

Lesson learned. As long as you have an idea of what you're doing, and always check your code on a blank page (and not in the footer!), it's hard to make a big mistake. Of course, sometimes mistakes have value of their own. To be safe, simply copy your site at some point and you'll never have any regrets.

NOTE:

A mistake that *could* hurt you would be to use HTML from a source that you don't know or aren't sure you can trust (like we did). There's a lot of code out there on the net for free use and some of it can actually harm your site if you use it.

When you do get some code from the web (we do it all the time, you just have to be careful), simply make a copy of a page, from the **Site Organizer** (this is explained in Chapter 6), before adding the code to a page.

That way if it does do something harmful, it will have only harmed the copy of a page that you can simply delete.

SITE BUILDER→DISK SPACE

The **Disk Space** page is actually the exact same page as the **Advanced Options** page.

So, you could use either button to get to the **Advanced Options** or **Disk Space**. We discussed disk space before, so if you need more information on how to interpret this, check out:

My Account→Disk Space for more details.

SITE BUILDER→PICTURE GALLERY

If you want to upload a bunch of pictures without going into the **Site Builder**, click this button to go to the picture gallery. The **Picture Gallery** (see Chapter 6) may take a while to load, especially if you have a slower connection, or a lot of photos already uploaded. Basically, just plan on spending a lot of your time in the gallery and you won't find yourself frustrated when you do.

The great thing about Tripod, though, is that they now let you upload up to ten photos at one time, so this really cuts down on your total upload time.

When the gallery loads, you'll see all the photos currently on the server's disk space. Don't delete photos unless you know for sure that they are no longer present or needed on the site, but if you do get close to the 50MB of disk space, you can do a little housecleaning and delete the ones that you are no longer using.

SITE BUILDER→SITE PROMOTION

The **Site Promotion** section offers additional services for attracting visitors to your site. Use them at your leisure, but we'll be going over search engine placement in Chapter 11.

This section also gives you the opportunity to set up a newsletter through Tripod. **Newsletter Management** will take you to a Constant Contact page.

You can also add Constant Contact to your site later, under **Site Add-Ons**, as explained in Chapter 6. It's a quick and easy program to use and you can try it free for the first fifty subscribers, or 500 emails, depending on the offer of the month. We use it and love it more than any other newsletter program out there.

It all depends on your needs. And you can always cancel it later. If you do decide to go with a newsletter management system, you should probably choose Constant Contact over the other thousand out there on the net, simply because they are fully integrated and trusted by Tripod. It's best to go with the trusted companies.

SITE BUILDER→LOGOUT

If you are on your personal computer, you really never have to log out. This way, when you return to Tripod, you'll already be logged in and will be able to just get started.

Tripod is on a secure server, so you shouldn't worry about your information being stolen. If, however, you are editing your site on a friend's computer, or library computer, you should always logout in case another Tripod member comes to use the site.

And as always, never share your password or personal information with anyone. Also, just so that you are aware, Tripod will never send you an email or call you and ask for your password or account information. If you do get an email or phone call and it asks for *any* sort of personal information, including your password, know that it is probably a spam attempt to steal your information, and you should report it immediately.

SITE BUILDER→HELP

If you need more information, or have questions with parts of Tripod that we haven't explained fully enough, **Help** is always a good place to go.

Tripod actually has an exceptional help team, often answering questions in less than 12 hours via email. So if you need help and we didn't go over it enough, feel free to peruse Tripod's help section, or even directly request help from Tripod. They're very nice.

Part Three: Optimizing, Selling, & HTML.

The future belongs to those who believe in the beauty of their dreams.

--Eleanor Roosevelt

In this part...

It's hard knowing what to sell, how to get it onto your site (and looking good), and how to get your site in the search engines so you can start selling—so we made it easy for you.

In this part you'll learn:

Chapter Eight: Required Site Elements
- Required pages for your site, 185-195
- How to create a Privacy Policy & FAQ page, 188-193
- How to create a Site Map, optimize it, and submit it to Google, 193-210
- How to create a robots.txt file to protect your pages, 210-212

Chapter Nine: Niche Marketing, Drop Shipping, & PayPal
- How to find a niche market, 213-217
- How to find a drop shipper, set prices, and customer complaints, 217-224
- How to put your inventory on your site, step by step, 224-235
- How to add PayPal to your site, step by step, 236-257

Chapter Ten: Meta Tags (Keywords) Explained
- Intro to meta tags, 259
- How to choose the right keywords for your site, 260-272
- How to optimize your site, step by step, 272-285
- How to get ranked in 24 hours, 285-286
- SEO checklist, 286-287

Chapter Eleven: Search Engines Explained
- Intro to page content, 288
- 5 mistakes to avoid when it comes to the search engines, 288-291
- How to get the web bots to crawl your site, 291-293
- How to get the right content on your site, 293-296
- How to avoid a link farm, 298
- Search engine submission & breakdown, 299-303

Chapter Twelve: HTML Primer
- Intro to the basics of HTML, 304-321
- How to use link tags, anchor tags, back to top buttons, and drop down lists, 305-315

Chapter Eight
Required Site Elements.

Now that you know how to build your site and get around your Tripod account, we're going to teach you perhaps the most important element that you can do *right now* to get your site traffic.

REQUIRED PAGES FOR YOUR SITE.

Search engines are picky (very picky!) beasts indeed. They won't even crawl, let alone index, your site unless you have several pages that they deem as required. People are picky too, and won't give your site much credit if they can't find the information that they are looking for.

To be successful (both with search engines and with potential customers), you must have these pages:

Home page
Inventory pages (or pages that discuss your services)
Site Map
Privacy Policy
FAQ page (and/or) Returns & Shipping Information page
Payment Successful
Payment Cancelled

You might also add a Blog, a Forum, or a few articles, which would each require their own page. Basically, the more pages with more information the better. But to start, these pages will get your website running just fine.

The Payment Successful and Payment Cancelled pages are not needed to get you crawled, but they *are* needed to make a sale. They should be simple, one column page, and should basically say: "Thank you for your order; we'll send you a confirmation email with tracking information soon," or, "Your order has been cancelled and all information has been encrypted by PayPal and removed from our server."

You get the idea.

Just say something simple and to the point for each page to let the customer know what has happened with their order. And, later, in Chapter 9, you'll need these pages to make your PayPal buttons.

INFO YOU MUST HAVE ON YOUR SITE.

Some things are just expected on a site that sells something. People even expect certain things before they'll even browse around.

And, some people will only stay once they find these certain things. **So, above all else, your business is to make people feel safe enough to buy from you.**

CONTACT INFORMATION.

You *must* have your contact information on your site if you intend to do business on the internet. This can be in the form of an official **Contact Us** page or you can simply put your info in your site footer so that it appears on every page.

Either way is acceptable.

The site footer is also where you'll list your brand new PO Box information, but you don't need to put your phone number in if you don't feel comfortable doing so. You had better list your email address though, or customers won't believe you have an online business if they can't contact you with so simple a method.

Email addresses work the same (and are looked at with the same importance) as your business name. Tripod offers email addresses (bunches of them if you get the more expensive plans) but we never found their email capable of handling large attachments, and we aren't certain that they have the most up to date virus scan technology.

They might, of course, but we like Yahoo better, and we tend to stick with what we know.

It doesn't matter who you choose, but your email address had better not be stacie78654@yahoo.com if you expect to bring in the customers.

COPYRIGHT INFORMATION.

Even if you don't literally copyright your logo, you still wrote the content on the page, created the layout, and put it all together. Thus, you should put your copyright information in the site footer, if only for formalities sake.

If you do get a copyright on your logo, don't waste it by forgetting to put your copyright information on your site! Oh, and when you do put copyright information on your site; make sure to update it every year.

Ours looks like this:

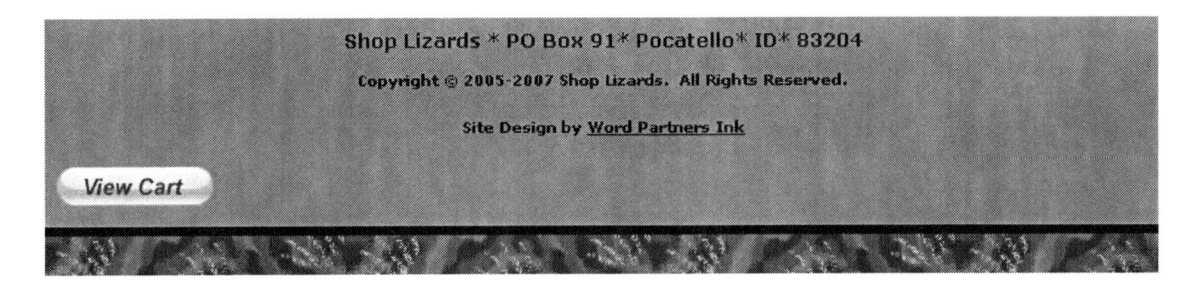

Shop Lizards * PO Box 91* Pocatello* ID* 83204
Copyright © 2005-2007 Shop Lizards. All Rights Reserved.
Site Design by Word Partners Ink

View Cart

Notice the:
Copyright © 2005-2007 Shop Lizards. All Rights Reserved.

When 2008 rolls around in a few weeks, we'll just change the 2007 to 2008, and we'll have been copyrighted from 2005-2008. If you see a copyright that only reflects 2002, what have they been up to? Have they just forgotten to update their copyright information? Or have they not been in business since 2002? Without the proper copyright information, you never know. With copyrights, it's hard to tell for sure, but it'll at least put doubt in your mind where doubt might actually be justified.

If you want to copyright your logo to add this level of confidence in your customers, you need to go the official http://www.copyright.gov/register website and click on Visual Art Works to download your application. They charge a small one time fee which guarantees your copyright.

NOTE: You can get a trademark or patent from the United States Patent & Trademark Office, http://www.uspto.gov/main/trademarks.htm . Review their guidelines for more information.

YOUR PRIVACY POLICY.

Even if you don't think you'll be a privacy risk to anyone, you *must* have a **Privacy Policy**. It can be very simple, or as complex as you want to make it.

At the very least, you must have a Privacy Policy because it alone can make the difference between a sale or no sale.

Actually, even if you don't sell anything, and even if you don't officially collect any information, you'll still need a Privacy Policy.

Why?

Because people won't know what you do or do not collect if you don't explicitly *tell* them. If you don't say, they'll just assume you collect everything and intend to sell it to a million spammers.

Yep, visitors assume the worst about you.

The web bots (search engines) are the same way. If they come to a site without a Privacy Policy, they might think something shifty is going on and list that site as spam because they are unsure whether visitors will be protected or not. Or, they may not list your site in their search results at all.

Even the search engines want people to feel (and be) protected.

Now, your Privacy Policy must be listed visibly on your site, either in the navigation bar, or in the site footer (and on your **Site Map**, of course). This is just one of those pages that the web bots expect to find and will actively search for when delving into your site.

So, get your policies figured out and get them written down and posted for the world to see. The sooner your customers feel safe, the more likely they are to stay on your site long enough to buy something.

It may sound like a task far too large to handle, so we decided it was best to just break it down for you, step by step.

Now, there are three different kinds of information that need to be addressed in your Privacy Policy. First, your **customer's financial information**: their credit card numbers; second, your **customer's contact information**; and third, your **customer's page preferences**.

Our Privacy Policy is very simple. Since we use PayPal to handle all of our monetary transactions, we don't really collect any financial information at all.

But PayPal *does* collect this information because they need to gather credit card info, etc, to accept the payments for us; thus, they have their own Privacy Policy to protect their customers regarding this information.

So, even though we don't actually *collect* a customer's financial information, we know that PayPal is collecting it so that we can ship the purchase to the customer. The customer enters this information voluntarily to place their order, of course, and it is done on PayPal's pages, but we still have access to the information.

Thus, we too need a Privacy Policy.

So, in our Privacy Policy, we need to say that we only collect customer information via PayPal to ship the item to the customer, and that all of their *financial* information is encrypted from us.

Any other information, such as the pages that they visited or the items that they purchased, is only used to improve the content of our site. And actually, we do collect this sort of information about our visitors. We know what pages they look at and for how long because we use StatCounter and Tripod's services to tell us so.

But we only use this information to make our pages better, and aren't actually targeting any specific customer by collecting their information to spam them later. So we say this in our Privacy Policy.

Your Privacy Policy might be even more simple than ours (if you don't sell anything), or it might be much more complex, depending on what information you decide to collect. And, if that's the case, there are two questions below that you need to consider and incorporate into your Privacy Policy.

Remember that there are three different kinds of customer information: **financial**, **contact**, and **preferences**, so answer each question with this in mind.

1. WHAT SPECIFIC INFORMATION DO YOU COLLECT?

    a. The email address of your visitors to keep for records or to use in your marketing efforts. This can mean: those who post messages in your forum, those who fill out survey forms, and those who contact you via email, among other reasons.

b. Name and address of your customer for shipping, and/or later marketing efforts
c. Payment information of your customer

2. WHAT IS DONE WITH THE INFORMATION THAT YOU COLLECT?

a. You use it to customize future customer experiences
b. You use it to improve the content of your pages
c. You use it to contact customers for later marketing efforts
d. You share it with other reputable organizations to help them contact consumers for marketing purposes

Decide what you will or will not collect (for future use or to discard after the customer receives their item) and write it up in several easy to read sentences.

It doesn't have to be fancy, just tell the truth about what you will or will not keep about your customers.

Go ahead and check out a few of your favorite sites to see how their Privacy Policy is structured, surf the web a bit, and check ours out if you'd like.

Whatever you do, be sure of what you write, because even the best site can fall to a lawsuit if their Privacy Policy isn't up to snuff when a customer complains. The reason they get in trouble, though, is because they either said they didn't collect certain information and the customer proves that they did, or they said they wouldn't sell customer email addresses, and they did.

That kind of thing. Just be honest, and your customers will trust you and your Privacy Policy.

Actually, since this page is so important, we've created a Privacy Policy that you can customize and copy directly onto your site. Use it, or take from it what you will. Either way, get a Privacy Policy onto your site pronto.

CUSTOM-FIT PRIVACY POLICY

NOTE: The Privacy Policy below is what we use on all of our sites, with a few variations, depending on what we are selling. Items in **<u>bold, underlined</u>** need to be removed or considered by you for insertion into your Privacy Policy, depending on the information that you collect, and of course, changing it to reflect your company information. Also, we use PayPal for all of our transactions; so if you use another merchant account, make sure to revise this Privacy Policy with your merchant account encryption information instead.

You may use the below Privacy Policy in its entirety, or make variations as you see fit. We are not lawyers, though, and may not have everything legally required for your company; so if you collect information not listed within, please add it to protect yourself.

The Privacy Policy goes from here to the line on the next page.

Your Privacy

When you buy from **Shop Lizards**, your credit card purchase is processed in real time through PayPal's secure server; visit them at http://www.paypal.com for more information.

Your order is then encrypted by Verisign before being sent to us. All credit card information is automatically deleted from PayPal's server after your business is concluded.

It is the policy of **Shop Lizards** to keep your email address and any other information we may receive about you completely private. We do not sell or share our customer information with anyone. We value your privacy as much as you. Please contact us if you need more information at **shoplizards@yahoo.com**.

PayPal

PayPal is the best secure web-processing server on the internet. Because we have a Premier Business account, you can shop and buy online from us without a membership and without worry for your security. You can just give PayPal the minimum amount of information, like your address so we can ship the item to you, and your credit card number, so they can process your order, and PayPal protects your information with secure and unbreakable encryption.

It's free for you to sign up, and if you don't want the free membership with PayPal, you never have to use them again. It couldn't be easier. And, we don't get to see any of your personal information, other than your shipping and email address, so you're fully protected.

Information We Collect

In an effort to better serve you and make our pages better cater to your needs, we collect information about which pages have been viewed, which pages were the least viewed, and which pages the search engines may have brought you to. We also keep all customer email addresses on file for sales promotions and special opportunities, but we follow the Can Spam act and allow for Opt-Out at any time.

However, we understand your need for privacy and we only use this data to better update and make additions to our pages. Your information will never be used to sell to other companies or for outside marketing campaigns. **(IF YOU DO SHARE THIS INFORMATION FOR MARKETING PURPOSES, OR WITH OTHER REPUTABLE ORGANIZATIONS TO HELP THEM CONTACT CONSUMERS…SAY SO INSTEAD)**

We want you to be happy throughout your buying experience and we will do whatever we can to make things easier for you. Just let us know how we can help.

Privacy Policy ends here.

FAQ / RETURNS & SHIPPING INFO PAGE.

The **FAQ** (frequently asked questions) page has evolved from the old Terms & Conditions page. On a FAQ, you can post all of the questions that you've gotten from customers, questions that you think you'd ask of your company if you were a customer, or just things that you want your customers to know about the way you run your business.

Even if you've never gotten a deluge of emails asking questions, write up the things that you would ask of your site. What would you want to know before you purchased something?

Do you have a Return Policy? What do you do about damaged goods? What about shipping and handling? Or rush orders?

Use this page to your advantage and write down *everything* that you think a potential customer might like to know. Otherwise, they'll just ask you (or leave your site) and you'll post the stuff later anyway.

If you don't really have any FAQ to put down (because you can't come up with anything other than return information), you might consider just having a **Returns & Shipping Info** page, with a few FAQ (if necessary) listed at the top or bottom of the page.

We actually prefer the Returns & Shipping Info page because most of our FAQ would have been returns and shipping information anyway. We could still have a FAQ page if we wanted, but we've not yet had the need or desire to do so.

Again, we prompt you to surf through a few sites and see how they structure their FAQs and Returns pages. See what they deem important for customers to know and ask yourself if any of their FAQs might apply to your site.

If so, write them up.

Your FAQ page can be as long or as short as you think it needs to be. In fact, you don't even really need one to get traffic or do well in the search engines, but it helps.

Mostly, it's a customer satisfaction thing.

If your site is all about 100% Satisfaction Guaranteed, tell your customers that. If you can't take returns, tell your customers. In this, it's best to be up front with your visitors, if only to protect yourself.

THE SITE MAP.

One way to ensure that the web bots find your interior pages without listing every single page on your navigation bar (because it can get cluttered quickly) is to list everything on your **Site Map**. The Site Map also ensures that the search engines index every page in your site that you want them to index because they have a nice little map.

Actually, the Site Map has become a required element to all sites that wish to find success in the search engines. Customers like them too because then they feel that they'll never get lost in your site because they have a "map."

So just make a Site Map.

Not doing so will *only* hurt you.

The fundamental rule of the Site Map is to literally *list* all of your pages in some sort of discernable order so that a visitor, or a web bot, who comes in on a page other than your home page, can find their way around simply by going to your Site Map.

The Site Map used to be created because navigation bars were so damn difficult to construct. But now Site Maps have become a handy little tool to get web bots to hang around and "cache" all of your pages, and creating a functional navigation bar is simply a basic requirement of a functioning website.

Caching means that the web bots collect a "picture" of your website in its current state. They do this every so often, but they may only cache a few pages at a time (for reasons unknown, they're busy little things).

Having a Site Map means that they will hang around, or at least come back, long enough to go through and cache all of your pages. And you want all of your pages cached! **Eventually, with a Site Map, all of your pages will get listed in the search engines.**

This is basically how a Site Map should look:

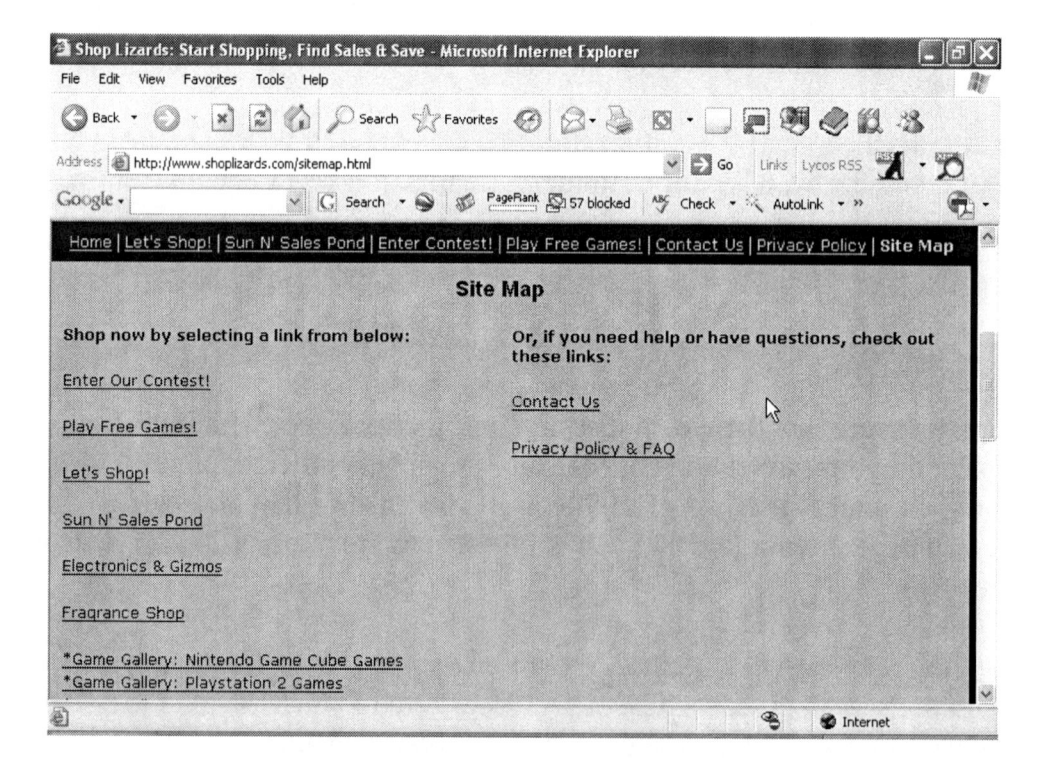

A simple two column, alphabetical listing is all that you need to make. Anything fancy is only a waste of time. And anything too fancy will just confuse your visitors and web bots. We used the two columns in the screen shot because it looked better than one long column of links, and it meant we could categorize things a bit.

As always, use your judgment, but make sure that you list every page on your Site Map that you want visitors and bots to be able to see.

If you'd like, check out a bunch of sites and see what their Site Maps look like. And you'll notice one thing: all of their pages are listed there, and in some sort of order.

Basically, every page that you want visitors to see must be listed on your Site Map. The Payment Successful page needn't (and shouldn't!) make the list, but every other page vital to your site must be listed there.

Google finds the Site Map so significant that they even created a program specifically for tracking and indexing Site Maps.

Sign up at http://www.google.com/webmasters/sitemaps to let Google know the exact moment when you update the content on your pages.

It's a little bit of work to get your Site Map generated for Google, but their instructions are easy to follow and it's worth the effort.

When you're ready to get started: we found that the easiest way is to make a text file of the Site Map and then upload it to our Tripod directory.

You'd do the upload from Tripod's **File Manager** page. Google's other options for Site Map generation are a bit more advanced than even we wanted to deal with, but creating a text file is simple enough, and it's something that you can do without difficulty too.

The steps to creating a text file are explained fully after this next section on optimizing your Site Map.

OPTIMIZING YOUR SITE MAP.

The Site Map should be the final step in the construction of your site because you'll need to have each page's title tag **optimized**.

This just means that you'll need to do a bit of keyword research to get your site ready for the search engines because you will need to name your pages something other than **id21.html**. This will make more sense after Chapter 10; so make sure to come back to this section to optimize your Site Map.

For now, just know that you'll need to make a Site Map, one for Google and one for your site, once your site is near completion if you want to be crawled by the web bots.

For the purpose of this discussion, you need to know that every page has a name, called an extension.

http://www.shoplizards.com is our homepage.

leather.html is our leather page.

leather.html is the page extension and it fits onto the web address like this:

http://www.shoplizards.com/leather.html

Every page has an extension, and if you haven't yet changed yours, you'll be able to see yours in the **Site Organizer**. Tripod uses numbers.

Tripod usually starts you out at **id1**.

So, your first page will have the extension:

id1.html

Your fiftieth page will have this extension:

id50.html (and so on)

Since this is one of the most important meta tags (read more in Chapter 10), you'll need to change the number to something keyword significant.

When you get all of your pages ready and have identified the proper meta tags (don't worry, it's much easier than it sounds right now), you'll create your Site Maps: one for your site and a text file for Google.

NOTE:

You can make a Site Map first, and then make your text file for Google, it doesn't matter the order. Just make sure that you have both. Also, the Site Map for Google is a completely separate entity from the Site Map on your site. But you'll need both to finish this process.

It's not as "instant" as it sounds, but Google takes Site Maps very seriously and will ensure that all of your important pages get indexed (sometime in the somewhat near future).

If you don't generate a Site Map for Google, all is not lost. It will just take a bit longer for your site to get fully indexed in the search engine. Longer meaning months, maybe even a year.

Keep in mind that even when you do submit a Site Map to Google, it still takes a bit of time to get fully indexed—basically Google still takes a few weeks, up to a few months or so, but they'll get to you.

Basically, the longer your site is around, the more credit Google will give you and rank you in their search engine as such. It's known as the "mythical" Google sandbox. New sites are noted and placed in the sandbox temporarily until Google judges them as fit and ready to play with the bigger kids. The exact time is unknown, but if you start your site out right (with the right keywords, content, and such), your time in the sandbox will be much shorter, especially if you've submitted a Site Map to Google.

Success of any sort on the internet takes time.

But you will now be able to track your progress and Google will let you know when your pages get indexed, or if there are problems doing so. Once you've been around for a while, Google even keeps track of the keywords that visitors used to find you. It's very neat.

But, before you get started with your text file, make sure all of your page file extensions have been optimized and you have created a regular Site Map for your site. The text file itself will come much easier, and you won't be coming back to change things once you do get optimized.

YOUR SITE MAP TEXT FILE FOR GOOGLE.

Okay, with that bit of intro out of the way…

It's easiest to create a text file with a Notepad program because creating a text file to upload into your Tripod directory is much easier than attempting Google's other options.

Now, all computers have some sort of Notepad program, found under the **Start** button.

Ours has a Notepad and a WordPad (not to be confused with Microsoft Word). They work the same, so just choose the one that you come across first. For the purpose of this instruction, though, we'll use the Notepad (no reason, we've just used it in the past).

Notepad can usually be found under **Start→Program Files→Accessories**

The best way to do this is to have Tripod's **Site Organizer** open because you can just go down the list of pages in the Site Organizer one at a time to make sure that you don't miss any; because you're going to need their *exact* page extensions.

If all of your pages are done and have been published, you can go to the live version of your site (not the site you use in Tripod's edit mode) and copy the web addresses directly from the address bar, as you click through each page.

And again, make sure you don't put in your Payment Successful or Payment Cancelled, or any other confidential pages—because you **do not** want them to get crawled. Only pages that you want visitors and bots to be able to find via search engines should be in your Site Map text file, just like the Site Map on your site.

Once you get your Notepad open, you'll be faced with a blank screen. **There are three steps that you must follow to properly upload your Site Map to Google.**

STEP 1: Create Your Site Map in Notepad.

Notepad can usually be found under **Start→Program Files→Accessories**

Basically all you need to do is to type in your website page names, using their proper page extensions (if you need a refresher on page extensions, check out Chapter 6).

```
http://www.shoplizards.com
http://www.shoplizards.com/leather.html
http://www.shoplizards.com/playstationgames.html
http://www.shoplizards.com/xboxgames.html
http://www.shoplizards.com/perfume.html
http://www.shoplizards.com/privacypolicy.html
http://www.shoplizards.com/sitemap.html
http://www.shoplizards.com/playfreegames.html
```

Example 1

See above, how we listed all of our pages? Note the page extensions. Nothing fancy. They don't even really need to be in any sort of order, ours aren't.

But notice that we also included our Site Map page, as well as our Privacy Policy page and all other important pages, including the homepage, http://www.shoplizards.com (the homepage doesn't need a file extension, though).

When you create the text file, try to make it accurately reflect your current Site Map.

NOTE:

If you make changes to the Site Map on your site later, you'll have to make the changes in your text file of the Site Map too, and then upload the new text file to Tripod, then upload it again to Google. We do this all the time as we expand our sites, and uploading a new Site Map is just part of the process. So, remember that you'll have to upload it to Tripod, and then to Google, so you don't fall behind.

Also, whenever you add a new page to your site, or change the extensions of the pages on your site, you'll need to make the changes to your Site Map text file, and then upload it to Tripod's server again, then upload again to Google.

If you don't have a Tripod Pro account, say you have a Plus or Free account, your Site Map for Google will look a bit different because your domain name is technically different.

For example, our commercial writing site, Word Partners Ink, is technically found at http://wordpartnersink.tripod.com but we use domain forwarding because we bought http://www.wordpartnersink.com from Yahoo.

Since we bought the domain through Yahoo and not Tripod, we have to forward the domain name via our Tripod Plus account. Google is a bit weird on this and doesn't look at the forward when using Site Maps; they want your *real* domain name, which has the **tripod.com** part.

So, our Word Partners Ink Site Map looks like this:

```
http://wordpartnersink.tripod.com/
http://wordpartnersink.tripod.com/commercialwritingresume.html
http://wordpartnersink.tripod.com/freelancearticles.html
http://wordpartnersink.tripod.com/ebayconsignment.html
http://wordpartnersink.tripod.com/clientprojects.html
http://wordpartnersink.tripod.com/businesscards.html
http://wordpartnersink.tripod.com/brochures.html
http://wordpartnersink.tripod.com/customwebsites.html
http://wordpartnersink.tripod.com/freelanceprices.html
http://wordpartnersink.tripod.com/blog/
http://wordpartnersink.tripod.com/shortcuts.html
http://wordpartnersink.tripod.com/privacypolicy.html
http://wordpartnersink.tripod.com/sitemap.html
```

Example 2

See the difference? Google wouldn't be able to read our Site Map text file if we used our domain name that forwards, so we must use our Tripod given domain name instead. It's just one of those technicalities.

So, make sure you get your Site Map right.

If you purchased your domain name through Tripod with the Pro plan, use the first example. If you already bought a domain name elsewhere or are using the Plus or Free plan, use the second example.

Once you get all of your site's pages on your Site Map, you'll need to save it in a specific format: **UTF-8 encoding** like so…

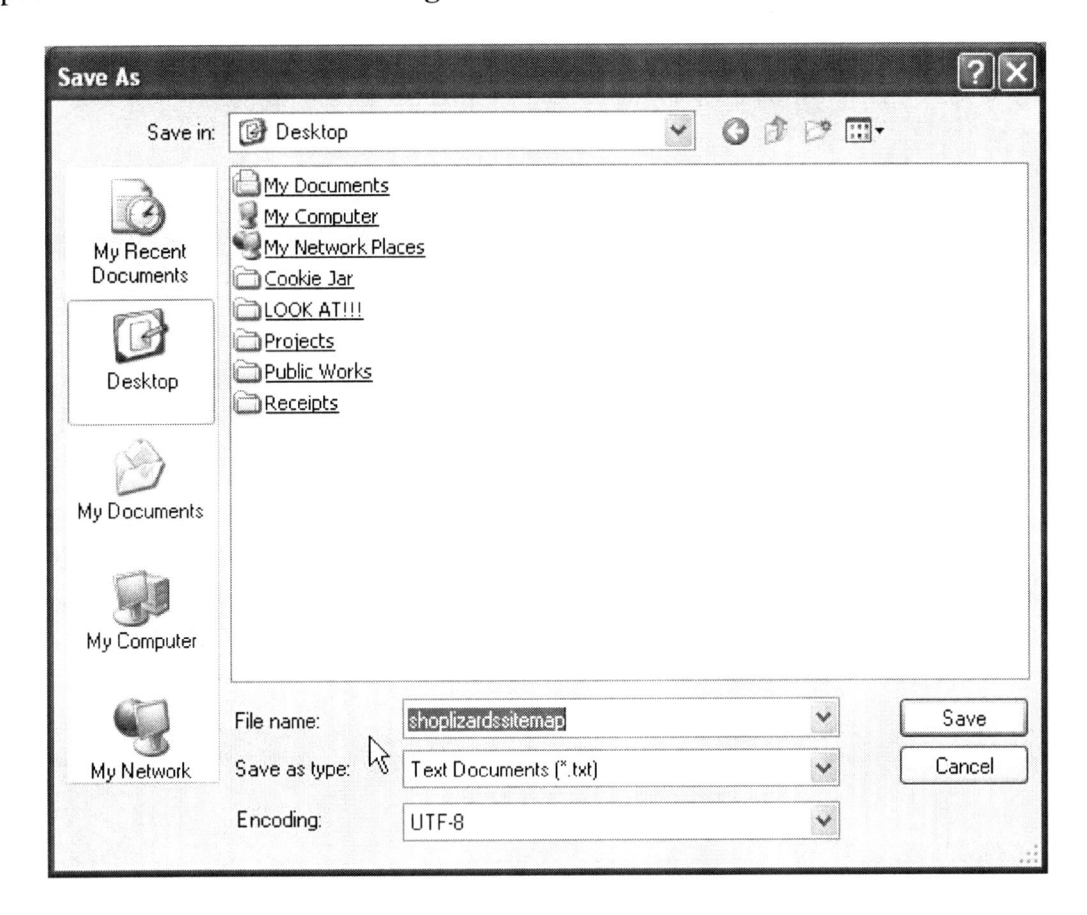

There are only several choices for encoding, but make sure you select UTF-8, and make sure to give your Site Map a name that is easily recognizable. We named ours:

shoplizardssitemap.txt

You'll also be given the option to save it someplace; in the picture above it says:

Save in: Desktop

So, make sure to change the current selected **Save in** location to something easier for you to find (the Desktop is the easiest for now and you can always move it to another folder on your desktop later).

STEP 2: Upload to Tripod's Server

It's actually quite simple to upload to Tripod's server. There will be a **File Manager** link in the black area above most of Tripod's edit pages; select it to upload your Site Map.

NOTE:

The process for uploading photos and files available for your visitors to download is done in a different location than the File Manager. If you wish to upload a file, like a Word document, for a visitor to download, it is accomplished as a **Site Add On**; photos are all uploaded from the **Photo Gallery** (explained in Chapter 6). Uploading to the Tripod server directory is altogether different, but just as easy.

Once you click on **File Manager**, you'll be taken to your File Manager screen:

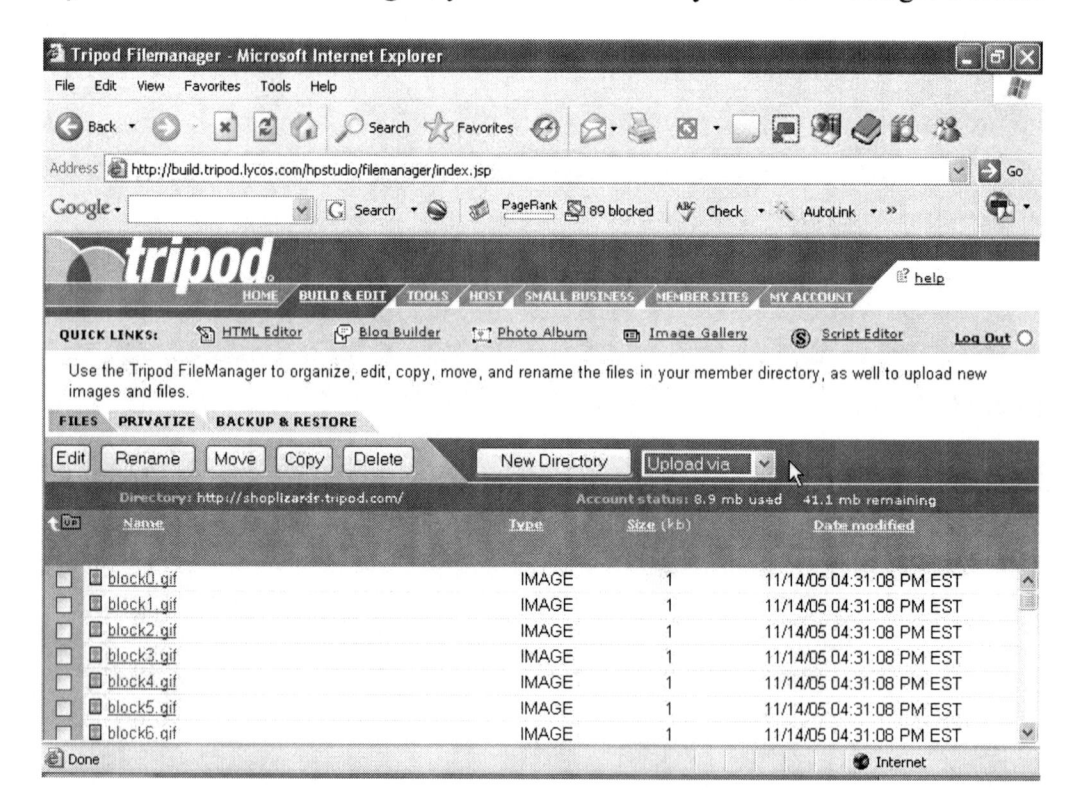

Click the **Upload Via** menu and select the **Single Files (8)** option. This will take you to a new screen:

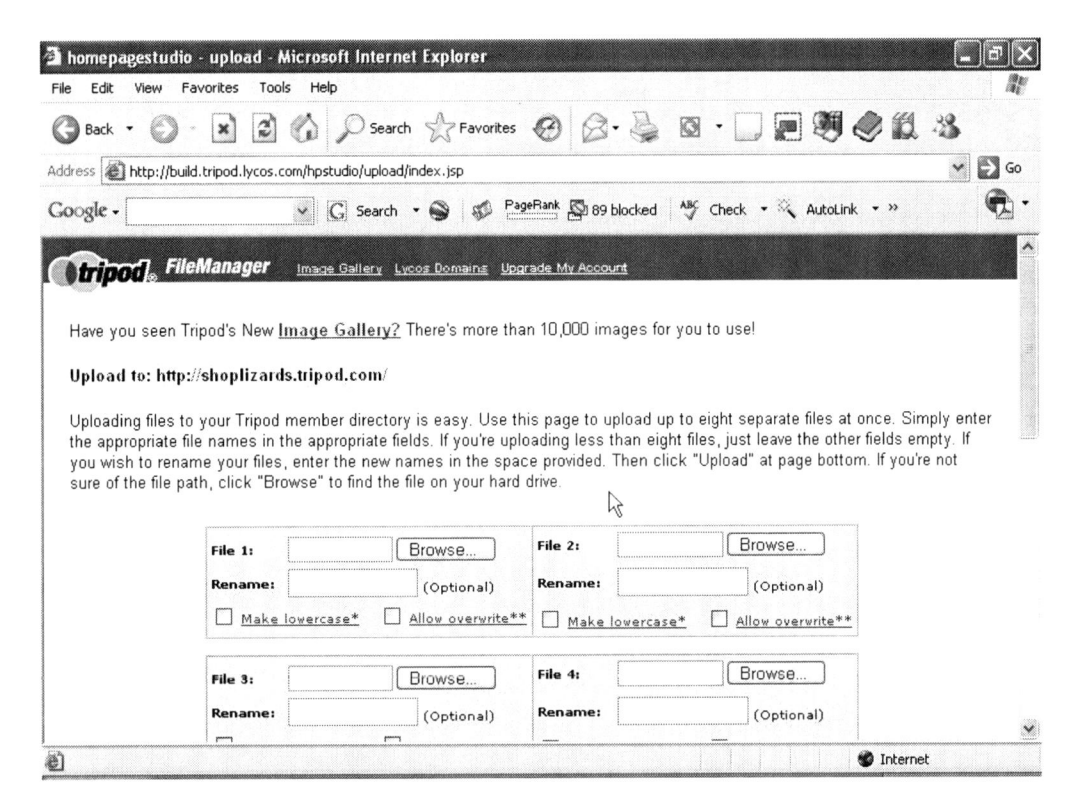

On this new screen, you have the ability to upload up to 8 files at a time, but we're just going to upload the Site Map text file for now.

Select **Browse** next to **File 1** and search through your files until you find the location where you saved your Site Map, probably on the Desktop. Select your file and you'll be brought back to this window where you'll need to scroll to the bottom and then select the **Upload** button on the left-hand side.

Tripod will take a moment to upload your file, and then will take you to a page that says your upload was successful. Select the "Close" button to return to the File Manager.

Now, you need to **Publish** your site, so select the **Build and Edit** button from the orange navigation bar at the top of your screen. Then,

Site Builder→Click the edit button for your website→Publish to Web

Then, check your results by typing your directory and file name into your address bar.

So, we'd type in:

http://www.shoplizards.com/shoplizardssitemap.txt

Remember that if you are using a Plus or Free account, you'll need to add in the **.tripod.com** part. It appears like this for our Plus account:

http://wordpartnersink.tripod.com/wordpartnersinksitemap.txt

Make sure it appears on your screen correctly and then continue to the final step.

STEP 3: Upload to Google Site Maps

You can find Google Site Maps at:

http://www.google.com/webmasters/sitemaps

You'll need to sign up for a free Google account if you don't already have one. Simply use your current email address and follow their instructions to activate your account.

Once you are logged in, you'll need to **Add** your site.

After you get your site added, by filling in the blank and hitting the **Add** button, remembering to type in the domain that you used in your Site Map, click on the **Add A Site Map** link.

ADD A SITE MAP.

You'll be given a few choices from Google:

Add General Web Site Map
Add Mobile Site Map

Select the **Add a General Web Site Map** choice.

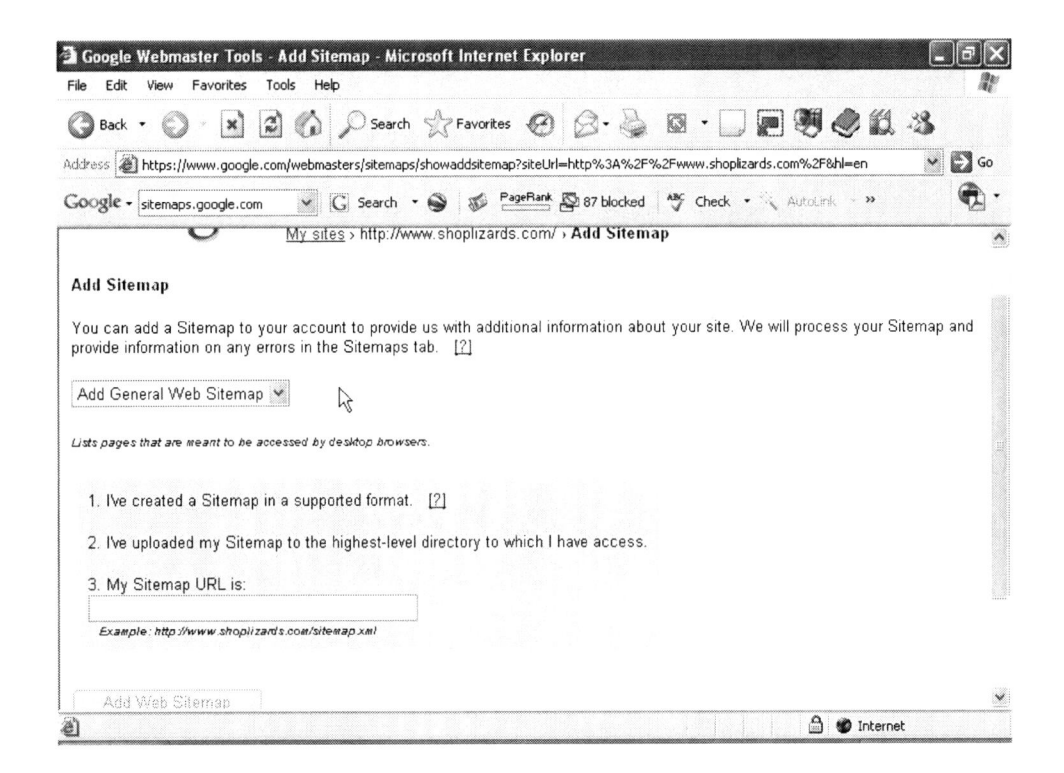

Now all you have to do is type in your new Site Map's destination URL.

Ours is:
http://www.shoplizards.com/shoplizardssitemap.txt

or,
http://wordpartnersink.tripod.com/wordpartnersinksitemap.txt

If you followed these steps exactly, your destination will be the same (just substitute your information).

Then, click the **Add Web Site Map** button. Google will refresh the page with the results of your Site Map:

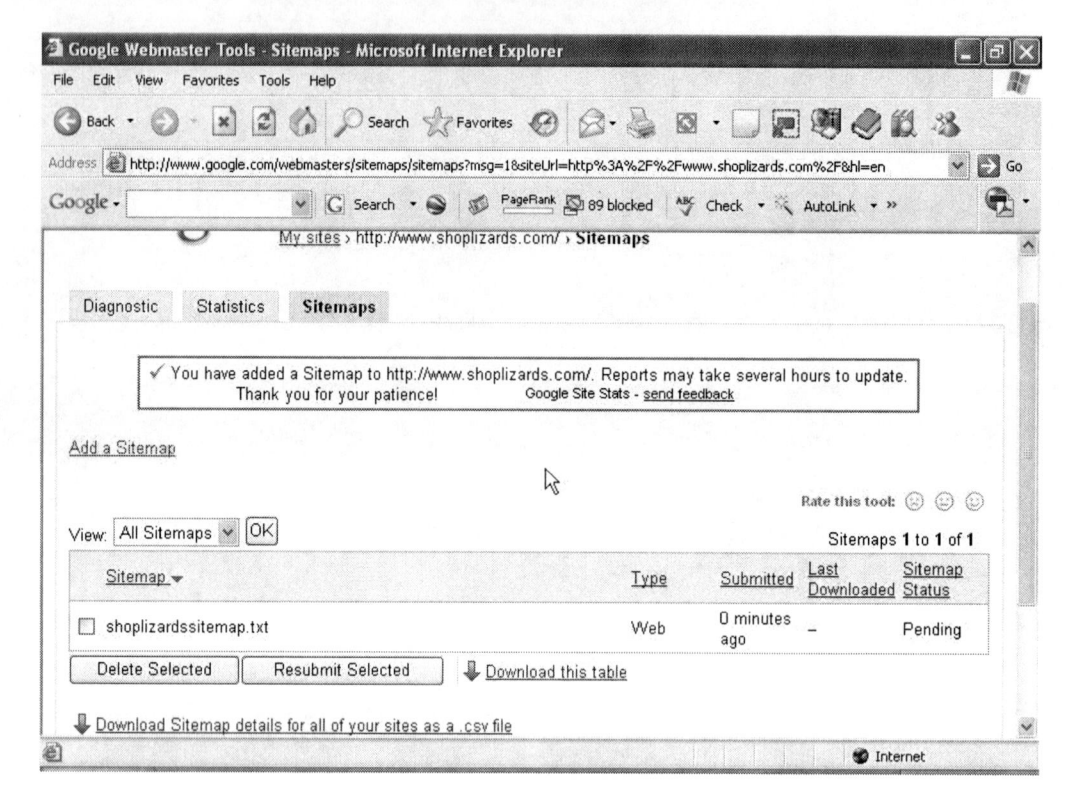

Google takes a while to review your Site Map and give it a new status, but as long as it doesn't say you have an error, you have just submitted your Site Map. This is the first step to getting yourself up there on the search engines, so well done!

Remember that if you change your site, by adding new pages, etc, you'll need to update your Site Map to reflect the changes. You'll need to first change your site's Site Map, then text file itself, then re-upload to Tripod (overwriting the existing file), and then resubmitting to Google.

Almost always, Google won't have any problems with your Site Map. If it returns an error, look at your Site Map text file very closely, making sure that every webpage is typed correctly, that no outside websites are listed on your Site Map, and that you don't have any pages you want to keep secure listed there. Then, re-upload to Tripod and Google. Usually, that's all you need to fix things.

GETTING VERIFIED BY GOOGLE.

The final step (and you only have to do it once) is to get "verified" by Google. Since you should now know how to deal with page extensions (if not, check out Chapter 6), this process will be a fairly simple.

STEP ONE: Go to your Tripod account and go to your **Site Organizer**.

Building Tools→Site Builder→Select Your Site→Site Organizer

Basically, all you need to do here is copy a random page (doesn't matter which page, just make sure it doesn't end up on your navigation bar) and enter in some quick information.

So, in the Site Organizer, choose a random page not on your navigation bar and select **Copy**, or, if you want to make a new page, select **Add Page.**

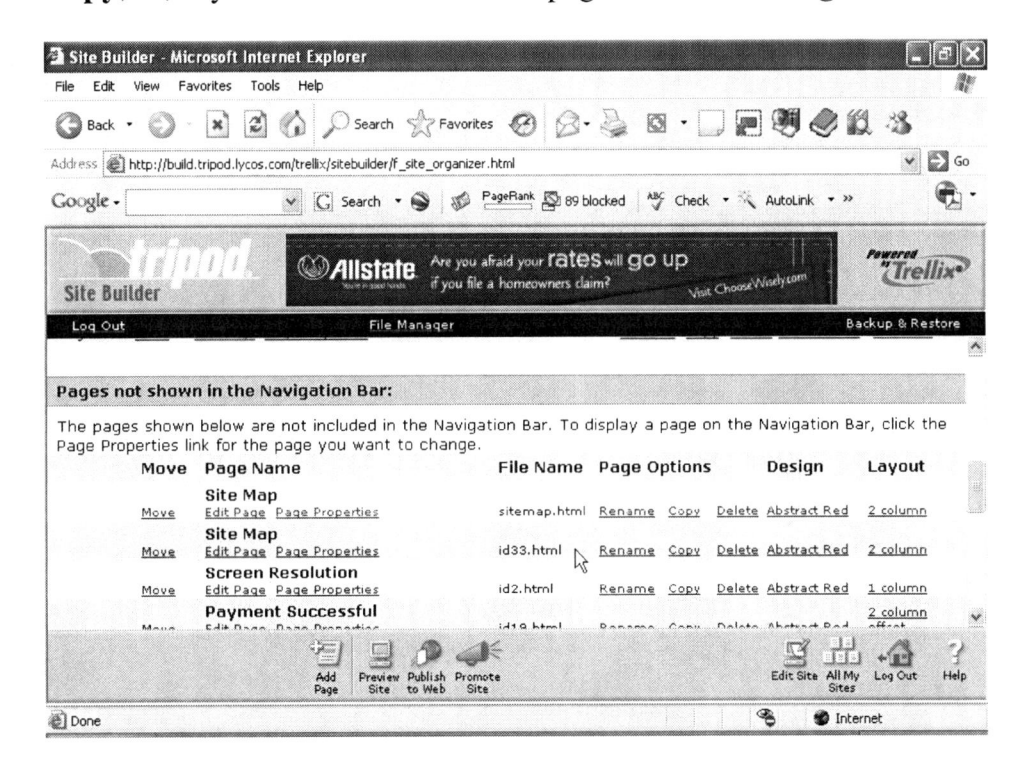

In the picture above, we copied our Site Map, the copy appears directly below the original page and has been named **id33.html** by Tripod. Your page number will be different, of course, but the number itself doesn't matter.

STEP TWO: Open a new window (CTRL + N, or Apple + N) and go to your Google Site Map account, http://www.google.com/webmasters/sitemaps

Make sure that you are logged in, and then click on the **Verify** option next to your website name. If you haven't added your website yet, use the **Add Site** box at the top of the page to do so; then the **Add Site Map** and **Verify** options will become available.

By the way, if you make more sites in the future, you can use your same Google account, and this same page, to list your Site Maps and view them all. When you get a few, it's handy not to have to log out to view the status of each.

Google currently offers two methods for verification:

Add Meta Tag
Upload HTML File

Since Tripod does all the meta work for you (you just need to input all the information), choose the **Upload HTML file** option (don't worry it's not like it sounds).

When you do, Google will refresh with the new page extension they want you to create.

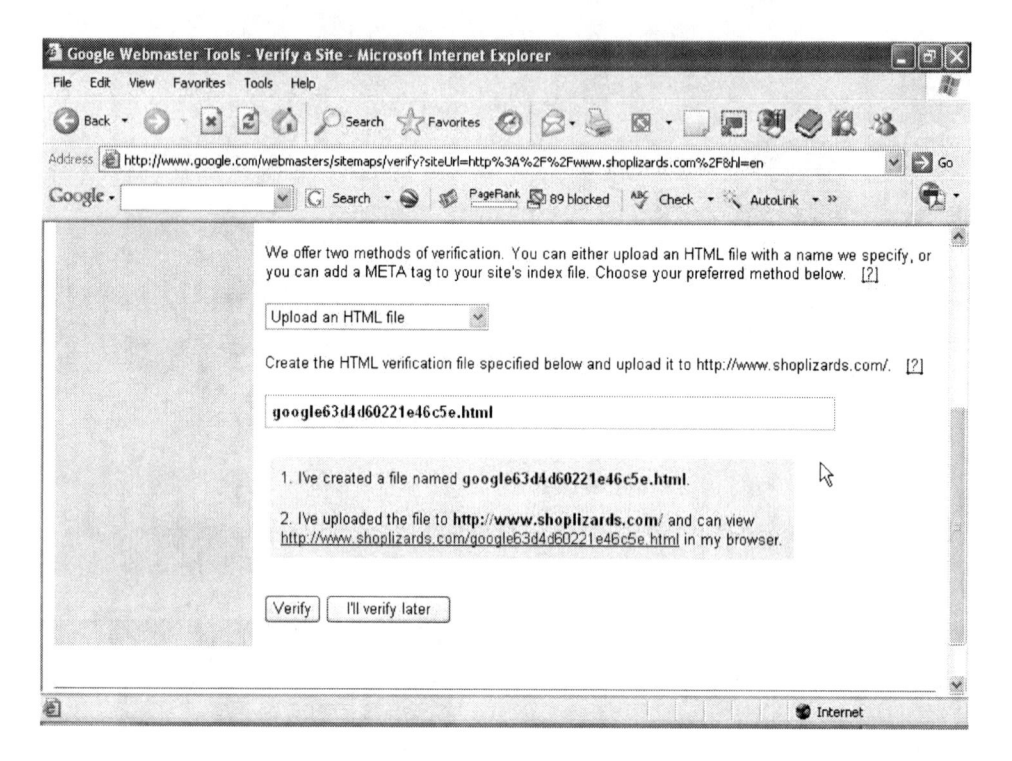

Now, you need to copy the weird number exactly, including the **google** and **.html** part, so use your mouse to highlight it and press CTRL + C to copy it. Do not close this window.

STEP THREE: Go back to your Tripod Site Organizer where you have created that new page, or that copy of a page. Click on **Page Properties**.

Chapter Eight: Required Site Elements 209

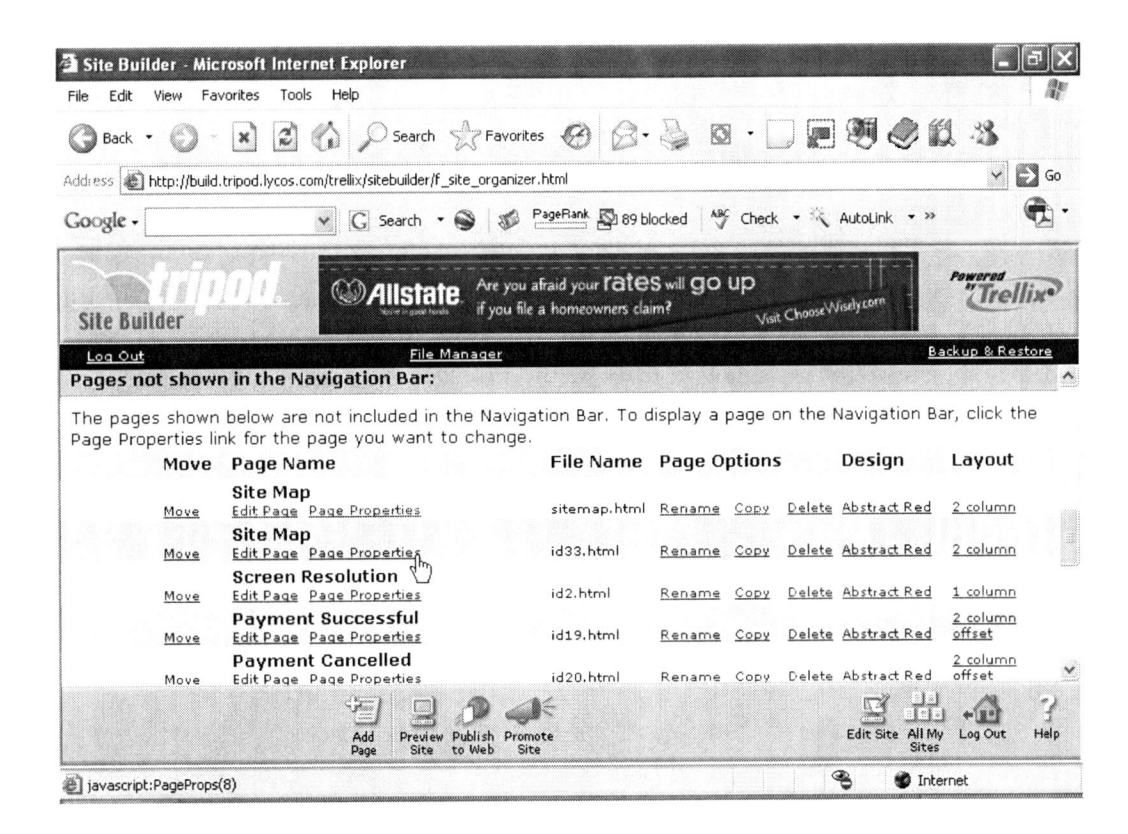

[Screenshot of Site Builder - Microsoft Internet Explorer showing the Pages not shown in the Navigation Bar interface, with a list including Site Map (sitemap.html), Site Map (id33.html), Screen Resolution (id2.html), Payment Successful (id19.html), and Payment Cancelled (id20.html).]

Page Properties is where all of your meta tag content takes place, but none of that is necessary for Google's verification page, and we'll be going over meta content later, in Chapter 10. For now, the only part that you need to concern yourself with is the **Change the Page File Name**, once you click **Page Properties**.

[Screenshot: Change the page file name. Web page file name: id33.html *Do not change the .html extension or your web page may become inaccessible.]

In the picture above, note that ours says **id33.html** (yours will display something different here, of course).

Now, highlight the file name, including the **.html** part and copy your new file name over from Google by pressing CTRL + V.

This is what it should now look like:

[Screenshot: Change the page file name. Web page file name: google63d4d60221e46c5e.html *Do not change the .html extension or your web page may become inaccessible.]

To finish, click on the yellow "Done" checkmark at the bottom of your screen. Once you are returned to the Site Organizer, you need to simply click the Publish button.

STEP FOUR: You'll need to test your work to help Google verify, so go back to your Google page, and under **Option 2**, where it says "I've uploaded the file to…" and click on the link that they provide and it should whisk you to your brand new HTML file.

If everything pops up in a new window just dandy, go ahead and close it to return to your Google page. If things went wrong, make sure you have published your site, or go back and check that you copied the Google code into your page file extension properly.

If you've published already and it still returned a Tripod error, you should try recopying and pasting the code Google gave you, making sure to include the full weird number that they provide you and the **.html** part. If you've followed the instructions, though, everything should work fine.

Now, return to your Google page, the one with the weird code on it that you copied, and click the **Verify** button. Google will take a moment, and process your verification, bringing you to a new page that says you have successfully verified your site.

This is known as the **Summary** page and once you've been online for a while, it will show some statistics about your pages. So, make sure you return to it in the future to check your status. You'll be able to find it by logging in to your Google account and clicking on the **Manage Site** link.

HOW TO CREATE A ROBOT TEXT FILE TO PROTECT YOUR PAGES.

Every website needs a robot file, if only to protect the Payment Successful and Payment Cancelled pages from being crawled. You can protect all kinds of pages, from ones you only want members to be able to see to pages you still have under construction with sensitive information on them. We sell ebooks and use the landing pages (pages customers are sent to once they made a purchase) to allow our visitors to download their product—pages that we don't want Google to be able to find.

To keep such pages from being crawled, all you have to do is make a little robot text file. And, it's even easier to do than it sounds.

First, make a list of all the pages on your site that you want to keep hidden, including their file extensions. If you have a Free or Plus site, remember that your complete website file extension includes the **.tripod.com** part. Also, keep in mind that you can have as many webpages on this list as you need, but if you decide to add more, or delete a few, later, you'll have to re-create the robot file and re-upload it to Tripod—just like you'd do with your Site Map, it's basically the same process.

For Shop Lizards, our list would look like this:
shoplizards.com/id99.html
shoplizards.com/id100.html

For Word Partners Ink,
wordpartnersink.tripod.com/id201.html
wordpartnersink.tripod.com/id209.html

Once you have a list of all the pages that need protected, open up Notepad (which we prefer to WordPad because of the encoding choices) to get started.

Notepad can usually be found under Start→Program Files→Accessories

Then, you'll specify the **User Agent** and the **Disallow** pages by typing in this:

User-Agent: *
Disallow: /wordpartnersink.tripod.com/id201.html
Disallow: /wordpartnersink.tripod.com/id209.html

The asterisk specifies that all web bots will be blocked. Each disallow is a page that you want to block them from.

Once you fill in all the pages you want to keep hidden, save your file as **ANSI Encoding** and name it:

robots.txt

making sure to save it on the Desktop or some other easily findable location.

Then, you'll need to log in to Tripod and click on **File Manager**, which can usually be found near the top of every page on the black bar. Click the **Upload Via** menu and select the **Single Files (8)** option.

You'll be taken to a new screen where you have the ability to upload up to eight files at once. For now, select **Browse** next to **File 1** and search through your files until you find where you saved the robots file. Select your file and you'll be taken back to the upload screen. Select the **Upload** button near the bottom of the page.

Tripod will take a moment to upload your file, and then will take you to a page that says your upload has been successful. Select the **Close** button to return to the **File Manager**.

Now, you need to **Publish** your site, so select the **Build and Edit** button from the orange navigation bar at the top of your screen. Then,

Site Builder→Select Your Site→Publish to Web

And that's it. Remember that if you add new pages that you want to keep hidden (or want to delete some from the list), you'll need to open your original robot text file, make the changes, re-save, then re-upload to Tripod, making sure to overwrite the old.

To make sure your file is working as expected, sign in to:

http://google.com/webmasters/tools

with your Google account (or create a new one for free). On the **Dashboard**, click the web address for the site you want to check (you may have to add your site if you haven't already by clicking **Add**). Click **Tools**, and then click **Analyze Robots.txt**

Chapter Nine.
Niche Marketing, Drop Shipping, & PayPal.

Now that you have a website, it's time for you to think about optimizing it for good search engine placement before you even add your inventory. This hinges on your ability to do two things: one, finding a good product, and two, optimizing your site with targeted keywords and quality content about your product.

In this chapter, we're going to teach you how to find a niche product, how to find a good drop shipper, and how to add the new products you find to your site with optimization in mind.

THE NICHE MARKET.

A niche market can loosely be defined as any "market" that has less than a million competitors. If you get in the thousands, you're in even better shape. But there's something that you need to understand about the niche market before you go about finding one.

A niche market will only work for you if it also has a proportionate number of people interested in it. Basically, this means that if there are five thousand sites dedicated to the cleaner for bird baths, but only 6 people a month ever search for bird bath cleaner, then you may have found a niche, but it may not be in demand.

A niche, then, needs to have a fair number of competitors, but also must have a healthy number of potential buyers.

Okay, you might say that this is impossible to find, because every internet entrepreneur in their right mind would only be selling in a niche. And this is true, to a degree.

But every product has a niche.

IT'S TIME FOR AN EXERCISE!

Don't worry; you'll appreciate this one. First, think of five unrelated things that you like.

You can use this exercise to better understand how a niche market can be found, as well as finding a niche market within a product you might want to sell. Every time we find a new product to sell or affiliate to promote, we always come back to this exercise to find our most targeted keywords as well as pinning down a niche.

We like the outdoors, reading, writing, flying, and shopping. Now, for each of the things you come up with, type them into the iwebtool,

IWEBTOOL[2]

http://www.iwebtool.com/keyword_lookup/

to see how people are actually searching for things.

We'll begin with the very general term, "outdoor," just to get some ideas of what people search for when they think of the outdoors.

---

[2] Sometimes, Iwebtool gets slow or has problems working. We've found a new, free tool that works just as well, called Keyword Discovery, http://www.keyworddiscovery.com/search.html that is just as accurate and easy to use.

iWEBTOOL Keyword Lookup

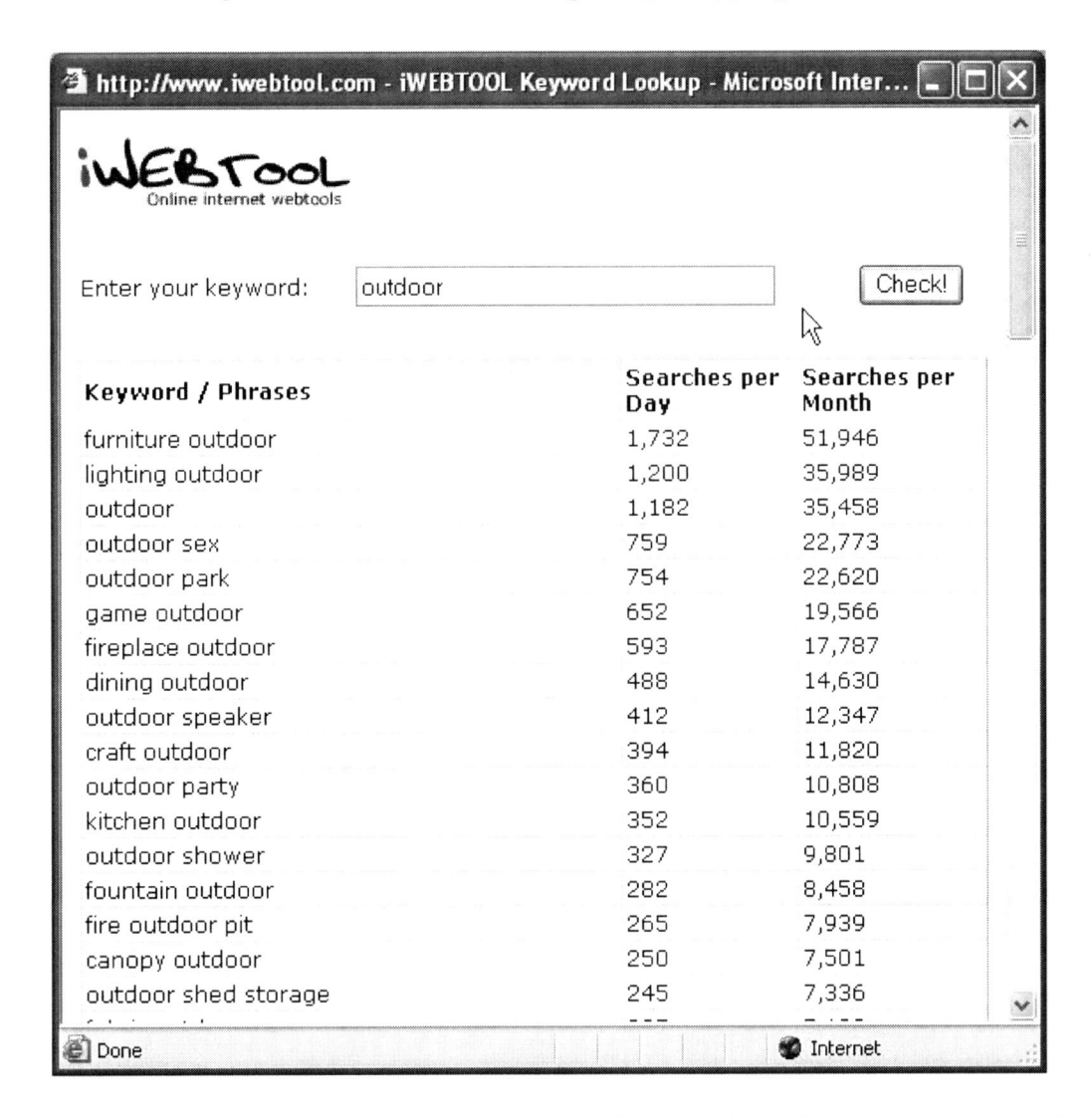

Enter your keyword: outdoor

Keyword / Phrases	Searches per Day	Searches per Month
furniture outdoor	1,732	51,946
lighting outdoor	1,200	35,989
outdoor	1,182	35,458
outdoor sex	759	22,773
outdoor park	754	22,620
game outdoor	652	19,566
fireplace outdoor	593	17,787
dining outdoor	488	14,630
outdoor speaker	412	12,347
craft outdoor	394	11,820
outdoor party	360	10,808
kitchen outdoor	352	10,559
outdoor shower	327	9,801
fountain outdoor	282	8,458
fire outdoor pit	265	7,939
canopy outdoor	250	7,501
outdoor shed storage	245	7,336

Our search for "outdoor" reveals that people like searching for quite a variety of things having to do with the outdoors, from "outdoor sex," to "outdoor shed storage" (the list continues, of course, so in your case, scroll down until you find something that interests you.

The numbers of searches are still in the high thousands, so we can guess that these are not niches, because any keyword that gets this many searches simply cannot be a real niche, but it's always fun to check. And truly, believe it or not, you'll *never* guess right.

So, to Google we go. Just so you know why we chose Google above all the rest of the search engines out there: Google is the largest (by far) of the search engines and gives us a very accurate number of competitors for a keyword.

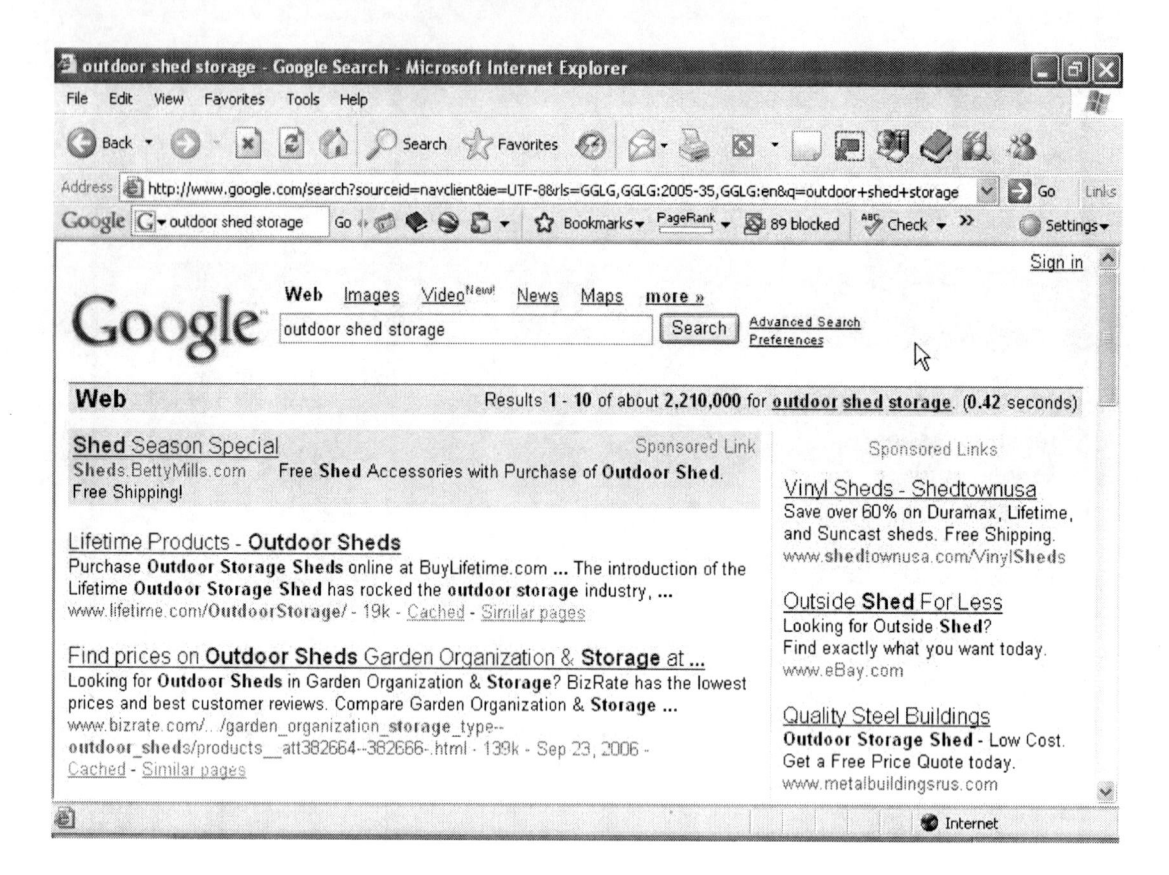

Well what a surprise! See about never knowing? A search for "outdoor shed storage," that gets 7,336 hits a month (which is HUGE!), according to iwebtool, only has 2,210,000 competing sites. Only two million! We thought that surely something as common as an outdoor shed would bring up a much larger list of competition, but two million isn't bad at all.

That's the thing about niches. **You never know until you do the research.** So, if we could find a good outdoor shed drop shipper, we might do well in this niche because with what we know about search engine optimization, we'd be on the first page in just a few months and would have no problem competing with the rest of the sites because we'd be sure to update our content all the time, and offer incentives for return customers.

This can work the same way for you.

Try all of your five things in the iwebtool, and you'll be surprised by what you can find. Check a few keywords that you like in Google, and you'll be on your way with a product that you like, that also happens to be a niche.

Keep in mind that you don't have to sell a niche to make money on the internet, but your chances of success are more than doubled. You can, however, start out selling a niche product, and then expand your site (or create another site) to sell something that is not niche at all, but that you've always wanted to sell. As long as there is demand for something (which you *must* check in iwebtool!), and you get your optimization right, you can sell anything on the web.

But, for beginners, finding a niche will make you the most money in the shortest amount of time simply because the competition is almost a non-issue.

WHAT IS DROP SHIPPING?

Drop shipping means that you decide you'd like to sell something on your site, but you don't have the funds or the warehouse space to buy and store a bunch of inventory. So, what can you do?

You can find a good drop shipper. A drop shipper is a wholesaler (or wholesale manufacturer) who has a lot of product and needs a business like yours to sell it. In fact, they need you as much as you need them because many drop shippers aren't allowed to sell their inventory to the general public.

This is where your EIN comes in (Chapter 3). You are officially a business entity that can use the services of drop shippers.

So, what exactly does this mean?

A drop shipper has a whole warehouse of inventory. You sign up with them and get their inventory list, including wholesale pricing, pictures, and product descriptions.

You review their list, use your new skills in niche marketing that we just went over, and pick out some products to place on your website.

FINDING A GOOD DROP SHIPPER.

Finding that perfect drop shipper is perhaps the hardest thing that a fledgling ecommerce company can do. Where to look, who to trust, let alone what to sell....

Start by doing your research.

What do you *want* to sell? If dealing in ceramic cats isn't your kind of fun, then don't sign up with a ceramic cat drop shipper. In fact, if you don't know what to sell, decide what you'd like to buy.

Are you into fishing? Sell fishing lures that you know to be high quality and are hard to find. Do you like rock climbing? Find a drop shipper that sells climbing gear.

But remember what you just learned about niche marketing. You can sell whatever you want, and use whichever drop shipper you want, but remember that only a niche will get you selling at the top of page one in the search engines sooner rather than later.

However, remember that you can have one niche store, along with a bunch of other non-niche stores (using as many drop shippers as you want), on your site if that's what you'd like. Hey think big!

HERE'S A GEM: We had a hard time finding quality drop shippers because all of the potential breeding grounds for them charged, and big time. We searched the web and only found shady "drop shipping guides" that promised the best drop shippers around.

This search also lead us to Rip Off Report (http://www.ripoffreport.com). Fortunately, we trusted our instincts, and Rip Off's complaints, and we didn't buy into any of the scams.

We could write a whole book on drop shipping alone. So, please visit our website at http://www.wordpartnersink.com and click on Drop Ship Source Directory to find links to great resources and information that you *will* need.

And here's a little secret, now that you have an EIN, you can sign up with drop shippers that *you* want to buy products from too. See a great leather jacket supplier, but don't really want to sell leather jackets on your site? That's okay. You still only have to pay wholesale plus shipping! What a deal!

We actually do this for Christmas presents. If a family member is into something, we find a drop shipper that deals in that sort of product and sign up with our business EIN. We pay only wholesale for something that would have cost much more in a department store. It's just one of the perks about being a business owner.

Now, we told you this anecdote in Chapter 2 but we'll tell it again because it's so important. One drop shipper (who will remain unnamed because we are above such things, but they are *definitely* on Rip Off Report) had a great inventory and promised a three day processing time, with priority mail shipping. Sounded great. Well, when Christmas came around, we decided to use our wholesaler discount and ordered some of their products for ourselves.

Nearly two and a half months later we finally received an email that the product had been shipped from the warehouse. At this point we were so mad about the poor customer service and missing purchase that we began to do some digging on the scam-alert site, Rip Off Report

To our great surprise, we found more than a *hundred* complaints about them.

Luckily, we never sold any of their products on our site or we'd probably be in court right now...

We finally got the items a few weeks later, but we learned our lesson. From now on, we check every drop shipper on Rip Off Report, we check their policies, and we call them to make sure someone actually exists on the other end. If at all possible, we even order products to check them out for ourselves.

It just *has* to be done.

If you want to have a great business, you have to have a great inventory, and you must have quality drop shippers to supply it for you, and quality customer service in case things go awry. If you don't check things out, you could get into trouble, big trouble, like we almost did.

SHIPPING & HANDLING COSTS.

Before you waste too much time getting excited about your products, calculate how much profit you can make from each, and decide if you want to charge your customers for shipping, or if you want to absorb the costs yourself.

Either way, you'll need to check with the drop shipper, *for each item*, to get the correct shipping charges. Some drop shippers use FedEx, some use UPS, some use USPS (regular mail) and yet others use DHL. Whomever they use to ship, the charges will usually vary by product or location of your customer.

We decided to offer free shipping because it is actually easier for us to absorb the costs when setting our prices than bother with the PayPal shipping calculators to charge the right amount for every item.

So, we just set our price for every item to include the cost of shipping and any drop shipper fees. If you don't want to absorb the cost of shipping for every item, then you still need to take the cost of shipping into account because if you set your price too high, and shipping is a bit steep, why would someone buy your product?

DROP SHIPPER FEES.

Some drop shippers have **drop shipping fees** which are the minimal fees that they require of you for using their services.

For example, Drop Shipper Joe charges $2.50 for every item that he'll drop ship for you. But Drop Shipper Tami charges $12 a month for an unlimited amount of drop shipping. You'll find that many drop shippers, however, don't have any fees other than the standard wholesale pricing for their items.

So, when you come across a drop shipper with fees, build it into your total costs to see if the fees are even feasible to deal with. If they aren't—find a new drop shipper.

For example, if you get a wholesale bottle of shampoo for $1, the drop shipper charges a $3 fee, and the maximum you should charge for that shampoo is $3.50 (because your customer also has to pay $2.50 in shipping), would that shampoo be the best item for you to sell; knowing that you'll only get .50 cents of profit and your customer is spending $6 for a bottle of shampoo that they could get for $4 at Walmart? Probably not.

If, however, you get an item with more room for profit in it, say, wholesale Italian shoes, that drop shipper fee of $3 will seem virtually insignificant when you can markup the shoes for over $50 of profit and still be competitive with the local retailers in price. Make sense?

SETTING YOUR PRICES.

Setting your prices is a difficult and frustrating process because there are many things to consider for every item. Drop shipper fees, shipping costs (to absorb, to not absorb), what your competition charges, how much you should markup, how much the drop shipper wants you to markup, and how much you *need* to markup.

NOTE:

The acceptable markup is 40-100% over wholesale. 50-150% is generally the standard, and many drop shippers won't even let you drop ship unless you markup the item between 100-200% over wholesale.

To be safe, we usually stick to about 100-120% over wholesale. That way we are competitive with other sites, we satisfy the drop shipper, and we make enough profit to absorb shipping costs for our customers. But as always, do what is best for your business.

Also, if you use PayPal like we do, PayPal takes 2.2% + .30 cents per transaction in fees. On an item that you sell for $20, that's .74 cents ((20 x 2.2%) + .30) = .74 that you also have to pay.

Your efforts should look something like this:

You fell in love with Drop Shipper Anna's product line of fine leather purses (even though you don't think it's a niche). You've picked out about twenty purses to add to your site.

The first, Leather Purse A, is offered to you for $40 plus a .50 cent drop shipping fee. Drop Shipper Anna ships UPS, who has a set charge of $2.20 for each purse. Drop Shipper Anna also recommends that you price at 200% over wholesale to stay competitive.

You decide to absorb the shipping cost into your pricing as an incentive to your customers since the markup is high.

LEATHER PURSE A

Drop Shipper Anna's fee: .50 cents
Wholesale Cost: $40
Shipping Cost: $2.20
Total Cost To You: $42.70 (this amount is owed to Drop Shipper Anna)

Suggested Retail Markup: 200% of $40 = $120 (you stick with the suggestion and price Leather Purse A at $120)

PayPal Transaction Fees: (2.2% + .30 cents for every transaction)
$120 - 2.2% = $2.64
$2.64 + .30 = $2.94

So…

Leather Purse A sells and the $120 is deposited into your PayPal account by your customer. PayPal takes $2.94 in fees, leaving you with $117.06. You send $42.70 to Drop Shipper Anna via PayPal along with an email including your customer's order and their name and address. Drop Shipper Anna ships the purse to your customer and you get to keep the profit of $74.36.

$120 - $2.94 - $42.70 = $74.36 (your total profit)

Oh, and remember to get all of this inputted into some sort of financial ledger (like QuickBooks), because like all business owners, you have to pay taxes on your sales. To be clear, the $74.36 will be what you pay taxes on later, and not the $120, because only $74.36 was profit.

WHEN DAMAGED GOODS HAPPEN TO GOOD CUSTOMERS.

Bad things happen, it's just a part of life. And sometimes, an item ordered on your site (no matter how great the drop shipper) will arrive broken or defective. The customer emails you, asking for a new product or a refund. But they ask nicely because you have this info in your Terms & Conditions, Returns & Shipping Info, or FAQ's page (you do, right?).

So, what do you do?

You have two options. Your first option is that you have to ask the customer to check for the instruction manual that came with the product; since you didn't manufacture or ship the thing, after all. If there is a Manufacturer's Customer Service contact there, they should try to contact them for a replacement since most new products are under Factory Warranty and the manufacturer can often replace the item faster than you could.

If that doesn't work, contact the drop shipper and tell them that the order was a defective product, ask for a Return Merchandise Authorization (RMA), and ask them to send a UPS Call Tag. The UPS Call Tag will send UPS to pick up the item and return it to the drop shipper, at no cost to you or your customer.

Then, you need to email or call your customer back, give them the RMA number, and ask them to pack the item back into the original box and write the RMA number on the outside. Tell them that UPS will be coming to pick up the box.

Depending on how your drop shipper handles such complaints, they will either send out a new product immediately or send one out when the damaged one is returned.

Now, this works all plain and good, but we guarantee 100% satisfaction with all of our customers. And, to us, this seems like too much stress to put them through.

Your second option is to do as we do. If their product arrives broken or defective and they email us, we'll immediately get in touch with the drop shipper and have the RMA and UPS Call Tag set up to collect the product. That way, we handle all of the stress in dealing with the broken item, and make sure that their new product arrives without any more hassle to them.

If they wanted a refund, we'll issue one immediately, though we'll still set up an RMA and UPS Call Tag to collect the damaged goods. Then, we'll deal with making sure the drop shipper receives the damaged product; and we'll request another if the customer was content to receive a new product.

Either way, we handle all of the steps, because, after all, the customer thinks that they're getting the product from us—they don't know about our drop shipper.

You can choose to handle this situation in any manner that you want. It all depends on what you're willing to offer your customers and how much stress you are willing to deal with yourself. But either choice is satisfactory, especially if you lay out your terms in your Returns & Info page (or FAQ page, etc).

WHEN A CUSTOMER CHANGES THEIR MIND.

Sometimes a customer will get an item and change their mind about wanting it at all, even though nothing is wrong with it. People are very picky, and internet buyers can be especially finicky. But it will happen. Someone will want a refund because they dislike their purchase.

Our return policy basically says that the customer can return an item for any reason, no questions asked. When they send us the item, we send them a refund. We send the item back to the drop shipper and, depending on the drop shipper, pay the restocking fee for returned items.

Unfortunately, we bite the bullet on this one and take the loss, but it's all part of our 100% satisfaction guaranteed policy.

You need to decide what your policy will be for customers like this. Many retailers who use drop shippers offer a refund of any purchase within ten days of the customer's receipt, minus return shipping and a 15% restocking fee. Some offer thirty days and just the restocking fee.

Again, this is completely up to your business needs and what you think you can afford. But make your decision and get it down in writing on your return policy to protect yourself.

When you sign up with drop shippers, they'll tell you all of their policies, or direct you to their website which displays all of their policies. You'll find that many drop shippers charge a 15% (or more) restocking fee and often have a limited return policy themselves. Make sure you know what all their fees are, and the details, for each drop shipper you use so that there are no surprises along the way.

NOTE:

When dealing with customer returns, you'll need to get your customer to send the product (with all of its original packaging) to the drop shipper, not to you. So, you'll need to contact the drop shipper and get an RMA. The customer will need to write the RMA on the box, and send it to the drop shipper's address that you give them.

The customer won't even know that they're sending it to your drop shipper, though, because many drop shippers keep a blind PO Box for exactly this purpose. And, your customer will need to pay for the return shipping (or you can offer to do so).

When the drop shipper receives the item, they'll inform you. You then refund your customer the product price, minus a restocking fee (you'll be charged this by the drop shipper). Finally, the drop shipper will charge you the restocking fee.

Or, you can absorb all of the fees and the return shipping—either way, get it down in writing so your customers know what they're up against should they change their mind about their purchase.

GETTING A DROP SHIPPER'S PRODUCTS ONTO YOUR SITE.

So, you go to the drop shipper's website (or order their product CD, catalog, etc), and download the product pictures and descriptions to put onto your pages. The easiest way is to right-click on all of the photos and save them to a folder on your computer (Chapter 1). Open each one in your photoshop program, making sure that the image looks okay and save it as a .jpg or .gif.

Then, go through each item and copy and paste the product descriptions into a Word file. That way, you can edit and check for spelling errors. Drop shippers are notoriously bad spellers!

Finally, create a table (you'll copy the rest instead of creating new) and upload all of your photos to your Photo Gallery. Then all you have to do is copy and paste the descriptions next to the right photos using the **Edit Text** button, add your price, and add a PayPal button.

Whew!

Since this is a bit more involved than it sounds in three paragraphs, we go over creating your inventory tables next.

CREATING YOUR INVENTORY TABLE IN TRIPOD.

Perhaps the easiest way to add inventory to your site is to use a table in Tripod, then customize it a bit to fit your needs. To save time and energy, we create one table, fill it in with our first item's information, then copy the table as many times as we need down the page.

So, we start with one table, then copy it until we have say, twenty on that page. You'll find that this is the easiest way too, but you don't have to do as we do if you'd prefer to make each table individually. Note that each item can also have its own page (that you'd link to) as well as being on an inventory page with other items.

We're only teaching it to you this way to save you time in the long run. Besides, it's something that you'd do anyway once you become more advanced.

Now, before you begin you need to do some thinking about how you'd like your inventory to *look* on your pages. We prefer a one-column page because it allows us to display our inventory with the least amount of confusion, but you can play around with two-column pages if you'd like.

You could even try a three-column layout, but in all honesty, three columns are unwieldy at best and tragically confusing at worst.

To make sure your page layout is how you'd like it to be, select the **Layout** option from the **Site Organizer** for that page and you'll be whisked to a new page where you'll be able to select the layout that you prefer, as shown below.

Page	Move	Page Name	File Name	Page Options	Design	Layout
Home		Home Edit Page Page Properties	index.html	Rename	Abstract Red	Home Page
Page 1	Move	Play Free Games Edit Page Page Properties	playfreegames.html	Rename Copy Delete	Abstract Red	2 column
Page 2	Move	Diecast Collectible Cars & Trucks Edit Page Page Properties	diecastcars.html	Rename Copy Delete	Abstract Red	1 column
Page 3	Move	Diecast Collectible Aircraft Edit Page Page Properties	modelairplanes.html	Rename Copy Delete	Abstract Red	1 column

So, before you get started, select, or copy, or create a new page for your inventory from the **Site Organizer** (Chapter 5-6), making sure it has the layout that you'd like to use.

Give your page a basic title for now so you know what it is, and then begin planning your meta tags. You can save the meta tag selections until the end, of course, because you won't be putting them in the **Page Properties** until *after* your tables have all been created.

As you'll learn in Chapter 10, meta tags need to be as targeted to your content as possible. We just want you thinking ahead because there'll be less confusion later if you have some idea of what to expect now.

GATHERING ITEM INFORMATION.

There are two ways that you can go about creating your inventory pages. First, you could collect all of your item information from your drop shippers before you begin, and then build your tables; or second, you could create your tables, and then gather your item information from your drop shippers. We prefer the first way because it seems to save more time overall. In either case, all you really need to know right now is a general idea of how many tables total (how many items you'll put on your page—one table per item) you'll be using.

However, before you copy any of your tables to create more, you need to have the first one completely done and filled in with your first item's information to minimize the total amount of work involved. So, if you choose the second option and wait to get your item information from your drop shipper, you'll just be creating one table now, and then come back and fill it in and copy the others later.

When you're ready to gather your item information, this is what you need to collect from your drop shipper:

- Inventory list with wholesale prices
- Your new prices for each item, including fees, shipping, etc
- Exact item names from drop shipper for every item
- Complete item descriptions for every item (copy from drop shipper website and paste into Word. Revise the sentences a bit if you want and check for spelling because drop shippers are notoriously bad spellers)
- Pictures for every item, saved into a folder on your desktop with easy to understand names, and saved as .jpg or .gif, then upload all of the pictures to your Picture Gallery (Chapter 5-6)
- Choices for your items (does it come in more than one color, size, etc?)

If you need some more explanation on this, go ahead and review the drop shipping section of this chapter before continuing.

So, before you even begin creating your tables, make sure you have all of this figured out and at hand.

READY?

Click the **Add Table** button on Tripod's gray toolbar. The page will then refresh with little gray **Add It Here** buttons and white dotted lines between which you can place your inventory table (if this is fuzzy, look at Chapter 6). Choose a spot on your page where you'd like to start adding your inventory, like near the top, but not in the very top (note the dotted line sections, the top section is mainly for page titles, the second section is for your page content), then **Choose from the Table Gallery**.

We have a preference, and you certainly don't have to use it too, but we'll at least show you what a typical item in our inventory looks like so you'll have a good idea about how to create and/or customize your own. Once you get the idea, you can always make changes and create your own tables however you want them to look. We just want to help you get started fast.

From the Table Gallery, this is the table that we always select:

Hampshire Daisies

Buy one bunch of daisies - get the second bunch at half price. For best results, give them plenty of sun, frequent watering, and regular fertilization.

This week only: $10.00

[Choose]

This is what this same table looks like un-edited on our one-column page:

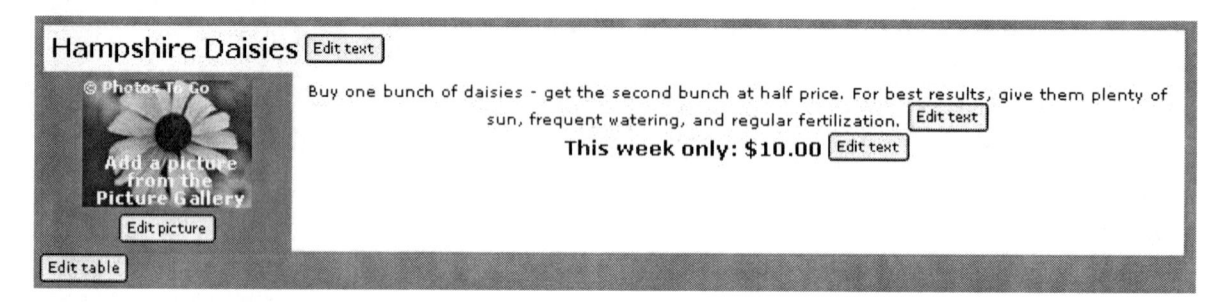

Hampshire Daisies [Edit text]

Buy one bunch of daisies - get the second bunch at half price. For best results, give them plenty of sun, frequent watering, and regular fertilization. [Edit text]

This week only: $10.00 [Edit text]

[Edit picture]
[Edit table]

And, this is what all of our tables end up looking like once we're done adding the item's information and publish:

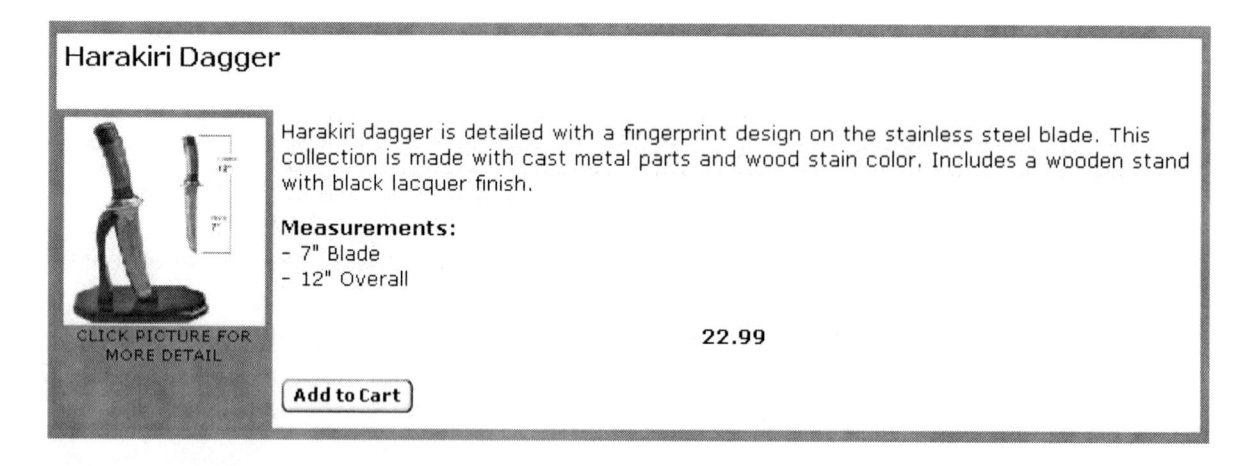

Harakiri Dagger

Harakiri dagger is detailed with a fingerprint design on the stainless steel blade. This collection is made with cast metal parts and wood stain color. Includes a wooden stand with black lacquer finish.

Measurements:
- 7" Blade
- 12" Overall

CLICK PICTURE FOR MORE DETAIL

22.99

[Add to Cart]

You can change the table frame and all the colors within, simply by selecting **Edit Table** from the main edit screen. So, as in all things, play around with your choices until you find the colors and options that best suits your inventory and site.

Note though, the order in which we present the information to our customer. In the picture above, **Harakiri Dagger** is the item name given by our drop shipper;

the description follows, with a few minor changes by us (spelling, sentence structure), then the price, and the PayPal button—this one has no options, but if it did the options would list right above the button. To the left, in the orange area, we place our pictures. All of our inventory is presented this way, so it makes things very easy for us to change and is a simple format for our customers to understand and navigate our site.

We're going to show you how to make changes to your table in this order: title, description, price, picture(s), and finally the PayPal button; because it leads well into our section on PayPal. You can mix things up if you'd like to add it in differently, but we've been doing it forever and have just found the fastest, most fluid way for us.

It's best to find your order of things so that once you get started adding new item information where the old item information was, you don't get confused and forget a step—which would be very bad.

ITEM TITLE.

The title is currently **Hampshire Daisies**, which you can see in the picture below.

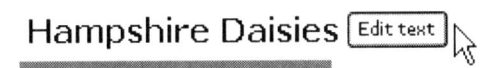

Hampshire Daisies [Edit text]

It's a very easy change, simply click the yellow **Edit Text** button next to it, but you do have a decision to make here. You can use the exact name given by your drop shipper, or you can make subtle changes to better suit your customers.

However, you'll use the exact name given by your drop shipper in your PayPal button, so make sure you keep everything straight by keeping a record of things.

For example, if our drop shipper gave us the name: **Harakiri Dagger A34TX9**, our customers might not buy it simply because the name is so weird, or they think it's a different version of the product than they wanted to buy.

So, for our title, we'd call it simply **Harakiri Dagger**. We'd then make a notation on our wholesale list next to the item with the name that we call it on the site, just so we can keep track of everything. But, if your item's given name is fine for your site, simply use it as is.

To change the title, click the **Edit Tex**t button and type in your item name, and then click a "Done" button.

ITEM DESCRIPTION.

> Buy one bunch of daisies - get the second bunch at half price. For best results, give them plenty of sun, frequent watering, and regular fertilization. [Edit text]

The item description should be taken directly from your drop shipper's website or catalog and copied into a Word document (copy and paste) so that you can go over the sentences and check the spelling.

You will probably find that the item descriptions are written weird or that there are misspellings, some of which will only be spotted with Word's help—as has been our case many, many times.

You have full authority to change your descriptions as you see fit for every item, unless the drop shipper tells you explicitly not to, which is rare.

Also, your descriptions can be as long or as short as you'd like them to be, but make sure you give your customers something of value to read about the item so that they know what they're buying.

If your drop shipper has no such information to give you, then you have to see if you can get a few sentences about the item from the manufacturer, or even be really creative and make them up yourself. Either way, you can't leave your customers hanging by giving them nothing to read about their potential purchase.

Think about it: would you buy something on a picture alone? Nope. So, give your customers something to read, even if it's only the number of batteries required.

Later, when you get into meta tags and search engine optimization, you will probably come back to these descriptions and make them more keyword-dense to gain rakings in the search engines. If you've skipped ahead to Chapter 10, or have some time before you begin building, you can always add keywords to your descriptions now, so you have less work to do later. It's work that must be done at either stage though, so plan on doing it as part of the process.

Make your changes to your descriptions in the Word document, then select the **Edit Text** button next to the Hampshire Daisies description, then copy and paste your new text directly into Tripod's Edit Text screen and select a "Done" button.

ITEM PRICE.

This week only: $10.00 [Edit text]

Once your drop shipper gives you their wholesale price list, you'll need to set your own prices for each item based on what we discussed earlier in the chapter.

We usually delete the "This week only" part from this table and edit the dollar amount area for each item. Now, if you have a sale on that item in the future, you can always put something like "This week only" in front of the price to indicate a sale. We'll often change the text color to red and make it a little bigger than usual as well.

This is an example of one of our sale items:

> Regularly $73.00
> This Week Only!
> $68.00

You can use us for inspiration, or create your own way to indicate sale items for your customers. But it's something that you'll need to consider now, before things get hectic. Whatever you do, plan what it will look like on your pages (you won't have to worry about this if you never plan to have sales).

Then, of course, you'd make sure to change the price in your PayPal button for that item as well so that your customers can get the sale price.

Since you probably aren't having a sale right this moment, you'll just insert the price for your first item into the space given, making sure to delete the "This week only" part. So, click the **Edit Text** button and type in your first item's price, then click "Done."

ITEM PICTURE.

Since there is already a picture in this table, adding your item picture couldn't be easier.

Before you get started, go ahead and upload all of your pictures into Tripod's Picture Gallery. Then, one by one, you'll click **Edit Picture** and change them for each new item. We go over pictures in Chapters 5-6, so make sure to review adding, sizing, etc before you add your first item's picture. But once you get going, it couldn't be easier; it's just a tedious process.

You can also add in your Alt tags at this point (if you've done your research), or you'll be coming back to add them in later.

Moreover, size is very important when adding pictures to your tables. We found with all of our images that they only look right when aligned vertically (horizontal pictures tend to take up a tremendous amount of room no matter the size). So, when we get pictures from drop shippers that are horizontal, we do our best to resize them in our photoshop program before uploading them to Tripod. It's weird and something of a hassle at times, but it does fit with uniformity (to have all pictures aligned the same) and it looks so much better when we're done.

Also, it's important to select **Thumbnail** as the **Display Size** for your pictures because that keeps them fairly small on the page, and your customers can view your page without too much waiting around.

Then, in the **Caption** section, if you plan to have your picture enlarge, type something like this: **CLICK PICTURE FOR MORE DETAIL**. As you'll learn in Chapter 10, images that link to something, if only to themselves in a larger version, can help you rank better in the search engines. And, every little bit helps, especially for so little effort at this stage.

In the **Title** section, you can input a few words about the picture itself, if you want, but generally, having a title looks confusing, especially with a caption. Keep in mind that the Title appears above the picture and the Caption appears right below.

Finally, because you'll probably have a larger photo that you'll want your customers to be able to view, you'll just select **Link to this Picture in Actual Size**, like shown below:

Linking this picture:

○ Don't make this picture a link.

⦿ Link to this picture, displayed in another size.
    Actual size

Show the picture in: New browser window

Linking to the picture in **Actual Size** will turn the picture into a link to the size it was when you uploaded it in Tripod's Picture Gallery. Usually, drop shippers have the largest size possible for their wholesalers, so this shouldn't be a problem for you.

If you get a fairly small image, you can still link to itself in Actual Size, or you can play around with the other sizes to link to, but keep in mind that this is something you'll be doing for *every* picture, so whatever you do, try to keep it as uniform as possible to make it easier on your customers.

ADDING MORE PICTURES.

If you have more than one picture for your items, like we do for many of our products, you'll click **Add Picture** on Tripod's gray toolbar and place the next picture below the first, as pictured on the next page. Or, you can have your item link to a new page that you create for that item and add as many pictures as you like.

This is actually the best option because it gives you an opportunity for more content, but if you have quite a few items and nothing new to add if they were to have their own pages, adding another picture into your table solves this problem.

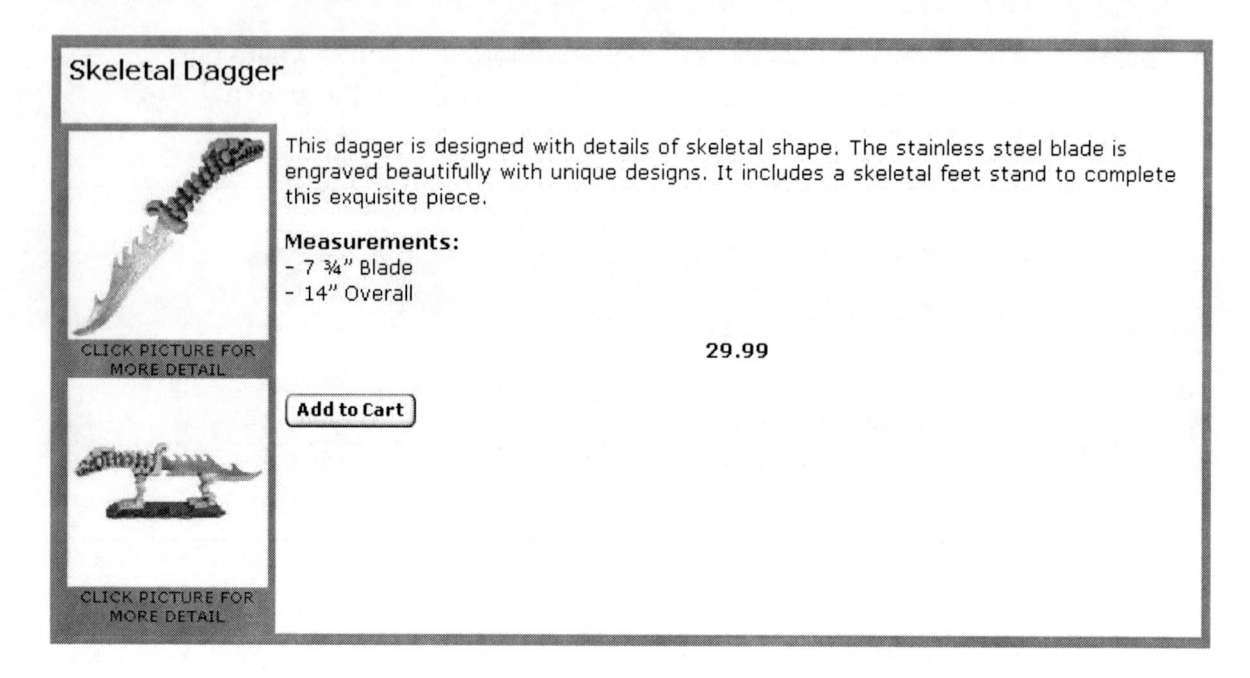

> **Skeletal Dagger**
>
> This dagger is designed with details of skeletal shape. The stainless steel blade is engraved beautifully with unique designs. It includes a skeletal feet stand to complete this exquisite piece.
>
> **Measurements:**
> - 7 ¾" Blade
> - 14" Overall
>
> 29.99
>
> [Add to Cart]

For every picture that we add, we also take a moment to type in our Alt tags as well so we don't have to go back in and do each one. So, to save yourself time, carefully craft your Alt tags (read Chapter 10 first) for every photo before adding any pictures to your site. It's all about finding the easiest, least complicated way.

You'll also have to add in a new **Caption**, and make sure the picture links as you want it to (actual size, to another page, etc).

If you need more pictures, keep adding them below the first. Keep in mind that you can move them around if you get them in the wrong order by using the **Move Items** button on the gray toolbar. Or you can delete them if you change your mind about how many pictures your item needs.

You'll also notice that for each picture you add, the table grows bigger to accommodate it. You can add in more text to fill up the blank space or leave it as it is. We usually leave it alone because it doesn't bother us, but feel free to get creative.

Keep in mind that you can put pictures (text, add-ons, etc) anywhere in this table that you want, so do not feel constricted by our way. You can also create a new page for every item, so you can keep this table small and add to your product on a new page.

This is about you and your products; we just wanted to show you how to get things done. Now that you know, you can do it however you like, so feel free to be as creative as you need to be.

COPYING YOUR TABLES.

We found in writing this guide that PayPal was so complex that it needed its own section. However, putting this section after the PayPal section didn't work for us because it seemed a bit misplaced. So, you'll actually need to create your first PayPal button on PayPal before you copy your tables in Tripod.

We apologize that this section is out of order, but it's a very important part of your table creation process and would have been easy to overlook if it came as a side note after the PayPal section.

Now, tables are actually very easy to copy because even though each table is comprised of a bunch of separate elements, you need only select *one* box to copy the whole table. Before you begin though, make sure that you have an idea of how many tables you're going to copy. You can always copy more or delete them if you copy too many, but that just means you have more steps to take, and we like to show you how to save time.

When you're ready, click **Copy Items** on Tripod's gray toolbar, then select the white box on the right hand side of your first table, as shown in the picture below.

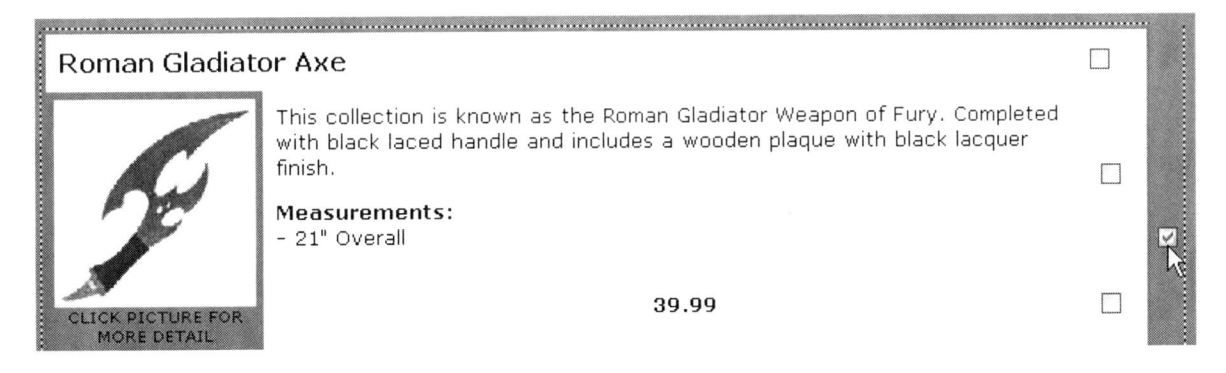

Roman Gladiator Axe

This collection is known as the Roman Gladiator Weapon of Fury. Completed with black laced handle and includes a wooden plaque with black lacquer finish.

Measurements:
- 21" Overall

39.99

CLICK PICTURE FOR MORE DETAIL

You'll copy your new table right under your first table, and then you'll copy again. Now you'll have two tables and you'll need to copy them both to make more. Say you have an inventory of 20 purses and they'll all go on the same page. That means that you'll need 20 tables, one for each purse. Instead of creating all twenty, it is much faster to copy.

So, copy the first one, then you'll have two. Copy those two, and then you'll have four. Copy those four, and you'll have eight. You get the idea. Keep copying your tables until you get enough tables on that page for all of your products.

Then, you'll go back and edit each table for each product, just going down the page until you've made changes to each one, as we've explained earlier in the chapter.

PAYPAL.

Go to http://www.paypal.com and make sure to sign up for the **Business Account** so that you can take all forms of payments online.

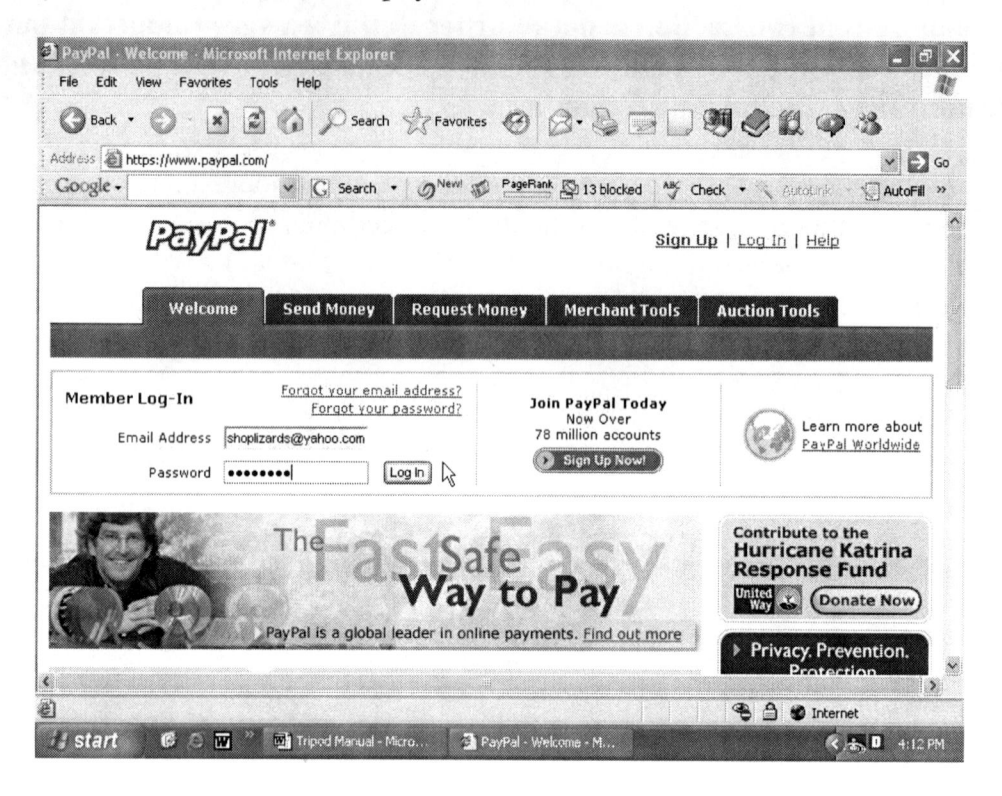

We've discussed PayPal in passing numerous times, but it's officially time for the full explanation. With a Business Account, you can accept customer payments via e-check, and credit card, online. Small fees apply when you accept payments, basically at the time of this writing, 2% plus .30 cents per payment that you receive.

PayPal is the best way to take payments online, in our opinion, because the fee is nearly negligible, there are no monthly or annual charges, and they are one of the most secure processing servers around.

When you learn more about PayPal, you'll find that you can also request money from a customer (like sending a bill), and you can transfer money right into your bank account, or even transfer it to a PayPal online "debit card" (until you get a real PayPal debit MasterCard, if you'd like) which acts like a real card that can be used to shop online or at your local retailers with the money you have available in your PayPal account.

Now, PayPal has two toolbars at the top of the screen:

My Account, Send Money, Request Money, Merchant Tools, and **Auction Tools.** The second toolbar will give you more options from the choices that you make from the first toolbar.

We're only going to go over **Merchant Tools**, but we suggest that you take the time to see how all of the other options work because you may find use for them in the future, and it's always nice to know what you can do with things.

Be aware, PayPal will never ask for your account information over the phone or in your email. We've received *tons* of fake emails from "PayPal" telling us that we just added a new email to our account, and asking us to verify the information.

You can tell the fake emails because a real one from PayPal will *always* say, Dear Shop Lizards…or something to that effect. **They *always* reference your name or username directly.** The fakes will never say your name (because they don't know it, and can't get it unless you give it to them), and that's how you can catch them. If you do get a fake, report it immediately so that PayPal can stay on top of their security. And now, PayPal has a full guide on how to protect yourself online, so make sure to read through it because in all things, it's best to know how to stay safe.

PAYMENT SUCCESSFUL & PAYMENT CANCELLED PAGES.

You'll need to make the Payment Successful and Payment Cancelled pages in Tripod before heading to PayPal to make your buttons, because they are needed to complete the button, allowing your buyer to come back to your site after they complete a payment, or after they make the choice to cancel their purchase.

Go back to Chapter 8 to get the full explanation on how to create these pages (and how to protect them with a robot file), and then get the page file extensions from your **Site Organizer** for both pages, making sure to write them down somewhere because you'll use them in just a moment. You'll need the full file extension, including your domain name.

Keep in mind that if you have a Plus account, like our Word Partners Ink site, then it will look something like this:

http://wordpartnersink.tripod.com/id998.html (because our domain name technically has the **.tripod.com** part)

Or, for Shop Lizards because it is a Pro site:

http://www.shoplizards.com/id998.html (because our domain name was purchased through Tripod)

If this is sounding a bit fuzzy, review Chapter 8, including the section on creating a Site Map, before continuing.

ADDING PAYPAL BUTTONS TO YOUR SITE.

Adding PayPal buttons to your website is sort of a two-part process. First, we're going to walk you through the process of getting your first PayPal button onto your site, and then we're going to teach you how to make copies on Tripod and simply edit future buttons so that you don't have to return to PayPal to make each one.

You could return to PayPal to create every button, of course, but PayPal times out after about five minutes, and even we don't like that kind of stress.

Before we begin, you need to write a few things down to get ready for your first item:

- **Drop Shipper Name** (unless you only have one drop shipper, then this is unnecessary)
- **Item Name** (given to you by your drop shipper)
- **Item Number** (given to you by your drop shipper)
- **Item Price** (you set the price for each item, taking everything we just went over about fees into account)
- **Exact Item Weight** (get from drop shipper)
- **Exact Shipping Fees** (ignore this if you'll be offering free shipping)

- **Payment Successful page file extension** (get from Site Organizer)
- **Payment Cancelled page file extension** (get from Site Organizer)

And, if your item has options, like size or color, you'll need a list of those options for every item that your customer must make a choice on before they buy.

For your very first PayPal button, you'll need to have both PayPal and Tripod open at the bottom of your screen (each in their own window) so that you can go between them easily. Basically, you'll input the item information on the PayPal screen and then copy and paste the code PayPal creates for you into the Add HTML screen on Tripod.

USING WINDOWS ON YOUR TRAY.

Now, we're assuming that you have knowledge of how "windows" works on your computer's window tray. If you don't, we'll go over it real quick because it will help immensely in your editing process.

Basically, every Windows computer has a tray at the bottom of the screen (unless yours is set to automatically "hide" when programs are open). When you open a program, you'll notice that it will open up a "window" on that tray. This is how you'll navigate between programs.

See how we have the Site Builder and PayPal browser windows open at the very bottom of our screen in the picture below?

You open up a new browser window by hitting CTRL + N (or Apple + N) and left-click on either window to move between them on your tray to transfer information from PayPal to Tripod.

And remember, the new Internet Explorer lets you use tabs, but tabs have a tendency to crash while working on a big site like Tripod, so don't use them (Chapter 1), instead open each new website in a new window to avoid any difficulties.

A BIT OF ADMIN BEFORE CREATING YOUR PAYPAL BUTTON

Before you create your first PayPal button, there are a few bits of administration that you need to take care of. Are you going to charge shipping? Do you need to charge for taxes? If so, these tasks must be accomplished *before* button building begins, under the My Account→Profile section of PayPal.

The Profile section has a ton of options to further customize your PayPal experience, so this is actually a good section for you to get to know.

ADDING SALES TAX

To add sales tax to your PayPal button, login in to your PayPal account and select:
My Account→Profile→Selling Preferences→Sales Tax

Here, you can set your Domestic and International rates. Also, you can define a separate sales tax rate for each of the 50 US states. PayPal's instructions are straight-forward, so fill in any tax information (and make sure to "Save") before you proceed to creating your PayPal button.

ADDING SHIPPING PREFERENCES

To add shipping preferences to your PayPal button, select:
My Account→Profile→Selling Preferences→Shipping Calculations

Here, you can set your shipping rates for your items for both Domestic and International shipping. Again, PayPal is very straight forward—simply fill in the information as prompted by clicking "Add Another Shipping Method."

If you ship based on the weight of the total order (most common choice), total order amount, or total order quantity, PayPal will calculate that amount when your customer checks out.

If you're using a drop shipper, they will specify what to charge for shipping, so fill in those rates as instructed. If you're shipping your own items, make sure to weigh them "in-box" to get the appropriate weight. PayPal even has a handy Shipping Calculator to help with these calculations that you can find under:
My Account→Profile→Selling Preferences→Shipping Calculator.

Otherwise, you can set up free shipping at this point, depending on your needs. Either way, make sure to set your shipping calculations (and make sure to "Save") before moving on to creating your PayPal button.

HOW TO MAKE YOUR FIRST PAYPAL BUTTON.

Add to Cart Button

It's a fairly easy process, but it can seem daunting at first, so we'll go step by step, so you know where you are at all times when creating your first "Add To Cart" button.

STEP ONE: We're going to go over everything involved in creating your first button on PayPal.

Select: Merchant Services→Key Features→PayPal Shopping Cart

You'll now be prompted to enter the **details** of the item that you wish to sell.

INPUT PRODUCT NAME/SERVICE.

Item Name/Service: [   ]

You'll get this name from your drop shipper, and unless they specify that you need to change the item name, you should input it here exactly as they list it in their inventory. For example, one of ours is **Off Road #21 Race Image,** so we'd type it in exactly as it was given (even if the #21 makes no sense to us).

INPUT ITEM ID/NUMBER.

Item ID/Number: [   ]
(optional)

You'll also get this from your drop shipper, and again, type it in exactly as they gave it to you. For example, the Item Number for **Off Road #21 Race Image** is **TZ920002102**, so that's what we'd type in.

If you have more than one drop shipper, like we do, then you can put that drop shipper's name here along with the item number so that you can keep track of things when PayPal sends you a customer's order via email. So, we'd type:

TZ920002102 / Nugin

into our Item ID/Number box because **Nugin** is the name of our drop shipper for this item.

INPUT ITEM PRICE.

This is where you'll input the price for your first item. PayPal says that $2,000 is the limit, but that's a pretty pricey item anyway. Remember what we went over about drop shipper fees, and make sure you take the time to price all of your items with room in them for mistakes and profit.

INPUT ITEM WEIGHT.

When PayPal updated their website this November, they realized that one of the most important things needing changing was the ability to add a **weight** for an online item, to calculate proper shipping for each order. As crazy as that sounds, very few shopping cart services have their act together on this. We went to random websites testing their shopping carts (before PayPal updated theirs) and found (we won't name names here) that you could get a $2000 gun safe that weighed more than a few hundred pounds shipped to your home for around $9 because of their shopping cart formula that stated that anything over $400 shipped for $9. They weren't running a special, it was just how things were calculated. Talk about taking a loss on something!

So, fill in your item weight as given to you by your drop shipper or weighed by yourself "in box," meaning that you weighed it as you would literally ship it—packing peanuts and all.

CHOOSE BUTTON STYLE.

PayPal Shopping Cart Buttons

Choose a add to cart button to put on your website (optional)

Your customers will use the image you select below to add items to their shopping cart before they checkout.

○ Add to Cart   ○ Add To Cart   ○ PayPal Add Item To Cart   ○ PayPal Add To Cart

○ Add To Cart

[Continue]

Above is the choices for an Add to Cart button that you can choose for your website. We like the one on the far right because it gives us that warm fuzzy feeling of safety. But you can certainly choose whichever you want. Also, if you're really creative, PayPal even lets you use an image that you made (and uploaded to Tripod's server), but it's best to stick with PayPal's choices because they are well known, look trust-worthy, and couldn't be easier to use.

SHIPPING METHOD AND SALES TAX OPTIONS.

As we mentioned at the start of this button-building process, these options need to be set before you begin creating your button (because PayPal won't let you save your progress so you would have to start over). However, if you haven't done so yet, head on over to:

My Account→Profile→Selling Preferences→Sales Tax
My Account→Profile→Selling Preferences→Shipping Calculations

to set your rates. Again, use the rates given to you by your drop shipper or rates you calculated yourself. Then, since you're going to at least enter in your Payment Successful and Payment Cancelled page information, you'll need to click **Add More Options**.

ADD OPTION FIELDS.

If you want to add options, it's quite simple to do so. We have options on quite a few of our buttons because it lets our customers choose the right size and color for their purchase. And it's very easy to input the information, and it's even surprisingly easy to make the changes when editing a button later.

Add Option Fields to Your Page (optional)

Option fields specify information about the item you're selling, such as color or size. To add option fields to your website, go to Option Field Type and select either Drop-Down menu or Text, then enter your Option Name. If you choose Drop-Down Menu, you must enter the different options for your product in the text box.
Learn more about how to use option fields on your website.

    Option Field Type: - Select Type -
    Option Name: Size   (60 character limit)
    Drop Down Menu Choices: (if applicable)
    Small
    Medium
    Large

(10-choice limit, 30 characters per choice; separate each choice using a return)

    Option Field Type: - Select Type -
    Option Name:
    Drop Down Menu Choices:

In the picture above, it shows how we create our drop-down buttons. You select **Drop Down Menu** for the **Option Field Type**, input your **Option Name**, as size, color, etc, and then list your drop-down choices, one on each line in the box provided. If you have both size and color options for an item, you'll fill in the second option field below.

Unfortunately, you can only have two options for your customers to choose from. If you really have more than two options, you can get creative with the **Customer Notes and Special Instructions** down at the bottom of this page and ask your customers in your item description to input their third choice before they complete their purchase.

CHOOSE VIEW CART BUTTON STYLE.

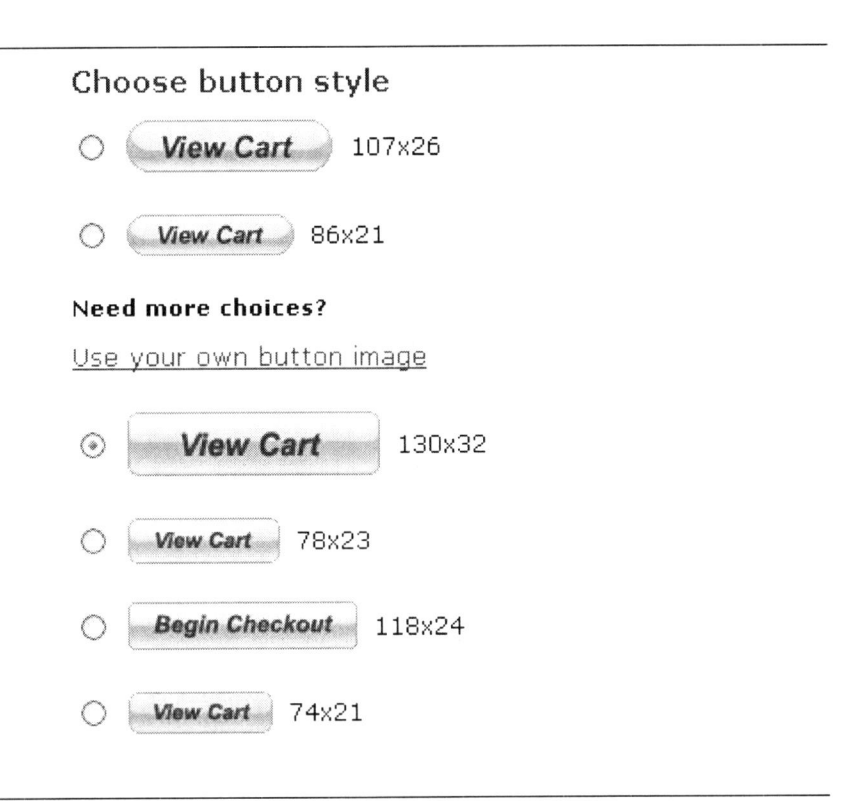

Choose button style

○ View Cart 107x26

○ View Cart 86x21

Need more choices?

Use your own button image

⊙ View Cart 130x32

○ View Cart 78x23

○ Begin Checkout 118x24

○ View Cart 74x21

The buttons basically look the same, here, the only real difference is that some are oval, some are more rectangular, and some say **Begin Checkout** instead of **View Cart**. Pick whichever you like the most. And again, you can create your own View Cart button that will match your Add to Cart button, if you are feeling creative.

CUSTOMIZE YOUR PAYMENT PAGES.

Customize Your Payment Pages (optional)
Choose a Custom Payment Page Style to match your website and give customers a seamless payment experience. Learn more.

Primary Page Style : PayPal
Custom Payment Page Style: Select one...

Unless you spend time on PayPal creating a custom page for your buyers, which you certainly can if you'd like, you will usually just leave this option alone. If you do create a custom payment page on PayPal, you'll follow PayPal's instructions to make sure everything turns out as it should.

CUSTOMIZE YOUR BUYER'S EXPERIENCE.

Customize Your Buyer's Experience (optional)

Successful Payment URL - this is where your customers will go after they complete their payment. (e.g. www.yourshop.com)

- Successful Payment URL: http:// [Edit]
- Payment Data Transfer: Off [Edit]

Cancel Payment URL - This is where your customers will go if they cancel their payment. (e.g. www.yourshop.com/cancel)

- Cancel Payment URL: http://

Make sure to put in the full web address with file extensions for the Payment Successful and Payment Cancelled pages that you made on Tripod in the boxes provided, being careful to get the page extensions exactly right. Your customers will be directed to the appropriate page when they either complete a transaction or cancel their order.

Either way, you want them to return to your site so you can tell them their purchase was successful, or try to convince them to buy from you again on your Payment Cancelled page.

SHIPPING PREFERENCES.

Shipping preferences

Would you like your buyers to provide you with their shipping address?

- ⊙ Make shipping optional.
- ○ Yes, require shipping.
- ○ No shipping needed.

If you will be shipping something (or will need to give your drop shipper the customer's shipping address so they can ship the item) make sure to **Require** the customer's shipping address.

Usually, requiring shipping is not the default option; so make sure to mark your choice. And if you are selling, for example, an ebook, you may not need the customer's shipping address because you won't be shipping anything; in this case, you can choose the **No Shipping Needed** option.

CUSTOMER NOTES AND SPECIAL INSTRUCTIONS.

Customer notes and special instructions
Do you want customers to have the option to include a note with their payment?
○ Yes ◉ No
Note Title: Optional Instructions   (30 character limit)

You can allow your customers to leave you instructions, comments, or questions in this option. We'll often let them leave **Optional Instructions** because they may have concerns that we hadn't yet addressed, or we may have asked them to fill this in before placing their order because an item had more than two drop-down menu choices and this was the only way to make sure we get the entire order correct.

Either way, it leaves customers a place for asking questions or leaving their concerns.

CHOOSE YOUR EMAIL ADDRESS.

Choose an email address to receive payment (optional)
I would like to receive payments at the following email address:
Email Address: shoplizards@yahoo.com

Make sure that your PayPal email address is correct in the box shown (it should be, though note that you can have more than one email address available on your PayPal account), and then select **Create Button Now**.

COPY THE ADD TO CART BUTTON.

Now you need to take the **Add to Cart** button code given by PayPal and copy it into your **Add HTML** screen on Tripod. To add this code to your page, click CTRL + A, then CTRL + C to copy the code from PayPal, then use your mouse to click back to Tripod's window on your tray.

Add to Cart button
The HTML code below will create your **Add to Cart** button. Click the **Select All** button to highlight the code within the box and then copy it.

"Add to Cart" button code
(Copy and paste this HTML onto your website)

```
<form target="paypal" action="https://www.paypal.com/cgi-bin/webscr" method="post">
<table><tr><td><input type="hidden" name="on0" value="Color">Color</td><td><select name="os0"><option value="Black">Black<option value="Tan">Tan<option value="Pink">Pink<option value="Blue">Blue</select>
</td></tr><tr><td><input type="hidden" name="on1" value="Size">Size</td><td><select name="os1"><option
```

Copy the code into Tripod's Add HTML screen by hitting the CTRL + V button. The code should fill in exactly as it was given to you by PayPal. And poof! You have an official button for your item.

All other buttons can be copied and edited in Tripod, so you'll never actually have to go through this again unless you build a whole new site or just happen to like the process.

So, well done webmaster!

VIEW CART BUTTON.

You're not done yet though. You'll need to add the **View Cart** button that you selected to the footer of your site so that your customers can add items to their shopping cart and view them before making a purchase. The View Cart button also happens to allow your customers to make that purchase, so it's a necessary and handy addition to your site.

Conveniently, PayPal gives you the code, just below the Add to Cart code, when you make your first button.

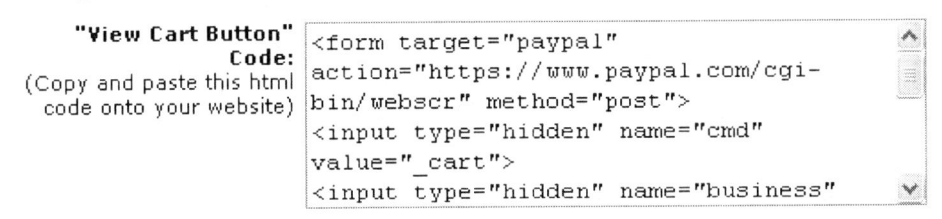

View Cart Button

The HTML code below contains your "View Cart" button. Copy the code and paste it onto your webpage. When your customers press the button, they will be taken to a webpage listing the items they will purchase from you.

"View Cart Button" Code:
(Copy and paste this html code onto your website)

```
<form target="paypal"
action="https://www.paypal.com/cgi-
bin/webscr" method="post">
<input type="hidden" name="cmd"
value="_cart">
<input type="hidden" name="business"
```

We prefer to add our View Cart button to the very bottom of our site footer, simply because it puts it easily at hand for those who scroll down to the bottom of all screens habitually. Also, it makes it very easy to find, and because it's in the footer, it copies itself automatically onto the bottom of every page.

This is what our View Cart button looks like in our Site Footer:

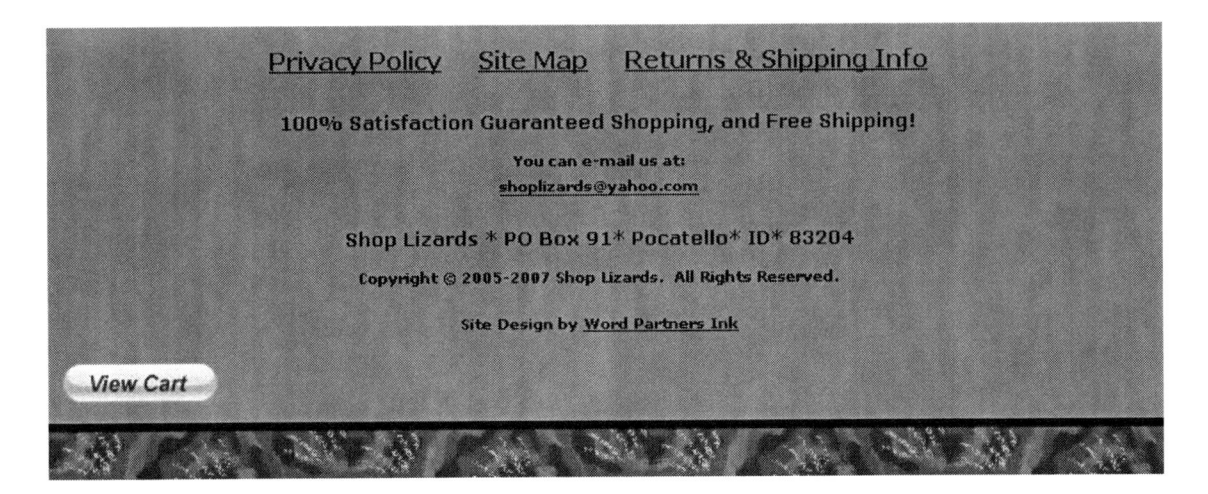

Privacy Policy   Site Map   Returns & Shipping Info

100% Satisfaction Guaranteed Shopping, and Free Shipping!

You can e-mail us at:
shoplizards@yahoo.com

Shop Lizards * PO Box 91* Pocatello* ID* 83204

Copyright © 2005-2007 Shop Lizards. All Rights Reserved.

Site Design by Word Partners Ink

View Cart

To add this code to your page, click CTRL + A, then CTRL + C to copy the code from PayPal, then go to Tripod. You'll add HTML just like we had you add HTML for the first button, so click to add a **Site Add-On**, and select a spot near the top or bottom of your page, preferably at the very bottom in your page footer, like we do as shown in the picture above.

HOW TO EDIT YOUR PAYPAL BUTTON IN TRIPOD.

We're going to show you how to edit your PayPal buttons, because it's what we do to get things done with the least amount of hassle. You don't, of course, have to start off creating your buttons this way if you are still uncomfortable with HTML, but we thought you'd at least like to know how it's done, and dealing with PayPal timing out all the time is simply unnecessary.

NOTE: If you charge for shipping or add taxes to your item on your first PayPal button, you'll still be able to copy your PayPal buttons as we are about to go over. It has been our experience that the shipping and taxes setting affects the shopping cart as a whole, and once set, would automatically do what it needs to do if your customer buys more than one item.

However, you will need to set this information, meaning fill out the whole shipping chart (or tax setting) in PayPal on your Profile page for your first button, because you won't be able to edit this information in the button HTML. If your shipping rates change later, PayPal should note the change for every button—if you make this change in your Profile section—though always check to make sure.

EDITING YOUR PAYPAL BUTTON.

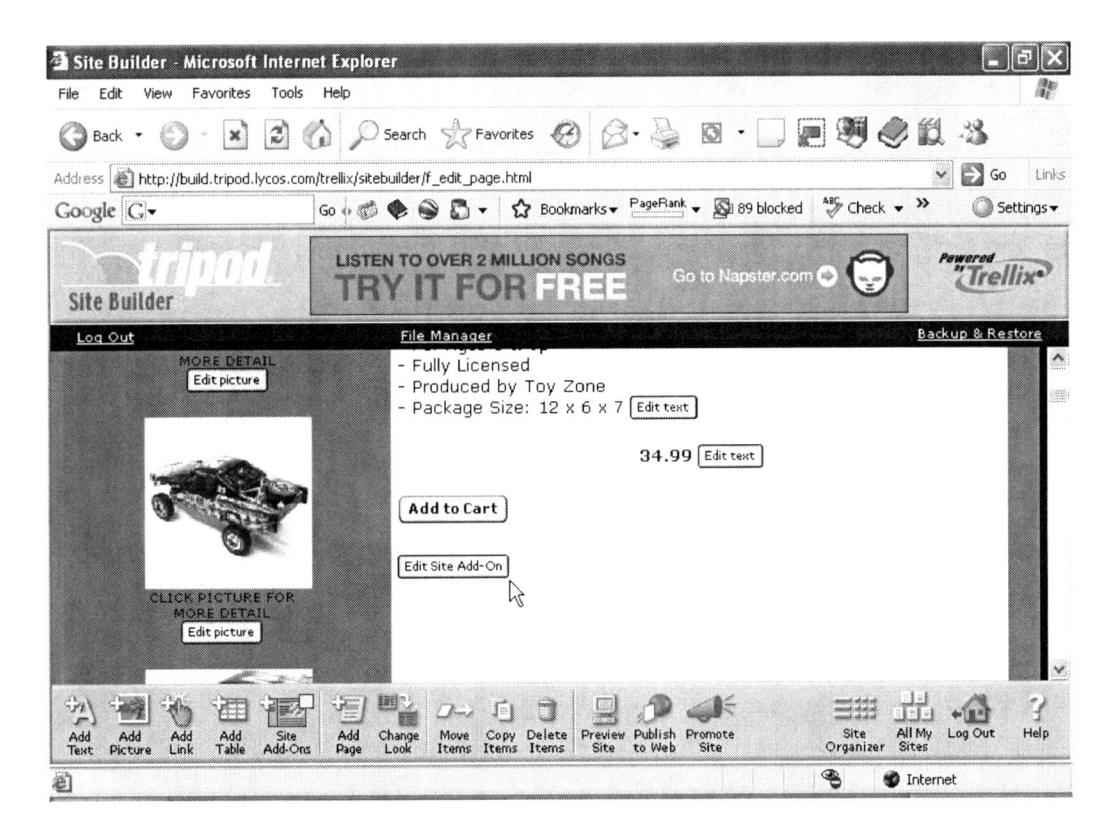

Above is an example of what a PayPal Add to Cart button looks like on our site from the main edit screen. To edit the PayPal button, click the little yellow **Edit Site Add-On** button.

You'll be taken to the **Add Your Own HTML** page. Below is the exact code copied from our PayPal button. We're going to show you what to change in **bold, underlined** text for every item.

```
<form target="paypal" action="https://www.paypal.com/cgi-bin/webscr" method="post">
<input type="image" src="https://www.paypal.com/en_US/i/btn/x-click-but22.gif" border="0" name="submit" alt="Make payments with PayPal - it's fast, free and secure!">
<img alt="" border="0" src="https://www.paypal.com/en_US/i/scr/pixel.gif" width="1" height="1">
<input type="hidden" name="add" value="1">
<input type="hidden" name="cmd" value="_cart">
<input type="hidden" name="business" value="shoplizards@yahoo.com">
<input type="hidden" name="item_name" value="OFF ROAD #21 RACE IMAGE">
<input type="hidden" name="item_number" value="TZ920002102 / NUGIN">
<input type="hidden" name="amount" value="34.99">
```

```
<input type="hidden" name="no_shipping" value="2">
<input type="hidden" name="return" value="http://www.shoplizards.com/id19.html">
<input type="hidden" name="cancel_return" value="http://www.shoplizards.com/id20.html">
<input type="hidden" name="currency_code" value="USD">
<input type="hidden" name="lc" value="US">
<input type="hidden" name="bn" value="PP-ShopCartBF">
</form>
```

As you'll see, the three things we change for every button are:

"item_name" value="**OFF ROAD #21 RACE IMAGE**"
"item_number" value="**TZ920002102 / NUGIN**"
"amount" value="**34.99**"

All of the rest of your code should remain exactly the same as any other changes could affect the button's ability to accept payments for you.

So, change the **"item_name"** value to reflect the new item name, making sure to keep all of the quotes in tact. So, we'd change:

"item_name" value="**OFF ROAD #21 RACE IMAGE**"

to reflect our new item:

"item_name" value="**Harakiri Dagger**"

Then, change the **"item_number"** value to reflect the corresponding item number. So, we'd change:

"item_number" value="**TZ920002102 / NUGIN**"

to reflect our new item:

"item_number" value="**TZLOPNMU / NUGIN**"

You'll notice that in this value we also have **Nugin**, the name of our drop shipper present. You don't actually have to do this with your button, especially if you only have one drop shipper, but we do because we have more than one drop shipper on our site and need to keep track of this information.

This helps us to match the item to the drop shipper without having to look anything up because the PayPal email will arrive with exactly what we input in all three values.

Finally, change the **"amount"** value to reflect the new item's corresponding price. So, we'd change:

"amount" value="**34.99**"

to reflect our new item:

"amount" value="**22.99**"

And, that's it! It will get easier the more you look at the code, and the more buttons you change, but that's all you have to know to change a button.

EDITING YOUR PAYPAL BUTTON IF YOU HAVE DROP-DOWN CHOICES.

This may sound a bit frightening at first, but it is really just as easy as making any of the other changes in your PayPal button HTML. Below is the exact code copied from our PayPal button. Again, we're going to show you what to change in **bold, underlined** text for every item.

```
<form target="paypal" action="https://www.paypal.com/cgi-bin/webscr" method="post">
<table><tr><td>
```
<input type="hidden" name="on0" value="Color">Color</td><td><select name="os0"><option value="Black">Black<option value="Brown">Brown<option value="Tan">Tan</select>
```
</td></tr><tr><td>
```
<input type="hidden" name="on1" value="Size">Size</td><td><select name="os1"><option value="Small">Small<option value="Medium">Medium<option value="Large">Large</select>
```
</td></tr></table><input type="image" src="https://www.paypal.com/en_US/i/btn/btn_cart_LG.gif" border="0" name="submit" alt="Make payments with PayPal - it's fast, free and secure!">
<img alt="" border="0" src="https://www.paypal.com/en_US/i/scr/pixel.gif" width="1" height="1">
```

```
<input type="hidden" name="add" value="1">
<input type="hidden" name="cmd" value="_cart">
<input type="hidden" name="business" value="shoplizards@yahoo.com">
<input type="hidden" name="item_name" value="Leather Jacket">
<input type="hidden" name="item_number" value="Ladies Leather Jacket 2524 JJ Jackets">
<input type="hidden" name="amount" value="99.95">
<input type="hidden" name="no_shipping" value="2">
<input type="hidden" name="return" value="http://www.shoplizards.com/id19.html">
<input type="hidden" name="cancel_return" value="http://www.shoplizards.com/id20tml">
<input type="hidden" name="currency_code" value="USD">
<input type="hidden" name="lc" value="US">
<input type="hidden" name="bn" value="PP-ShopCartBF">
</form>
```

In the code above, we have a leather jacket as our item for sale with two options as our drop-down choices: color and size.

The color choices look like this in the code:

```
<input type="hidden" name="on0" value="Color">Color</td><td><select name="os0"><option value="Black">Black<option value="Brown">Brown<option value="Tan">Tan</select>
```

And the size looks like this in the code:

```
<input type="hidden" name="on1" value="Size">Size</td><td><select name="os1"><option value="Small">Small<option value="Medium">Medium<option value="Large">Large</select>
```

If our next item only had color choices, we could just delete the portion that relates to the size:

```
<input type="hidden" name="on1" value="Size">Size</td><td><select name="os1"><option value="Small">Small<option value="Medium">Medium<option value="Large">Large</select>
```

and the button would function with only color as the drop-down choice, or vice versa.

If the next item had Blue, Pink, and Green as the color choices, we would change the code to reflect that by inputting those colors like we show below. To make this as easy as possible, we'll bold our changes.

<input type="hidden" name="on0" value="Color">Color</td><td><select name="os0"><option value="**Blue**">**Blue**<option value="**Pink**">**Pink**<option value="**Green**">**Green**</select>

instead of:

<input type="hidden" name="on0" value="Color">Color</td><td><select name="os0"><option value="**Black**">**Black**<option value="**Brown**">**Brown**<option value="**Tan**">**Tan**</select>

Do you see how we changed the Black to Blue, the Brown to Pink, and the Tan to Green?

It works exactly the same way with the second option. For example, say we wanted to now have a jacket with only Large and X-Large as choices. This is a bit more complicated as we'll have to remove an option; we'll bold what we change below.

<input type="hidden" name="on1" value="Size">Size</td><td><select name="os1"><option value="**Large**">**Large**<option value="**X-Large**">**X-Large**

instead of:

<input type="hidden" name="on1" value="Size">Size</td><td><select name="os1"><option value="**Small**">**Small**<option value="**Medium**">**Medium**<option value="**Large**">**Large**</select>

Note that because we only wanted two drop-down choices instead of three, we had to remove this part of the code:

<option value="Large">Large</select>

And that's it. It really gets easier once you look at the code for a while, but just keep in mind that changing your code shouldn't be a difficult chore for you. If you don't feel comfortable making these changes for every button, we suggest that you go ahead and make each button individually. Sometimes, when our options get too complicated or one item needs color and size while another needs shape and weight, we'll just make a new button for every item. If things get confusing, make a new button for your items in PayPal, if you feel okay with manipulating the HTML, do so. We only show you how to do this to make your life easier for you—so this should become an easy routine for you, not a source of displeasure and confusion.

"BUY NOW" BUTTON.

If you have just *one* item to sell on your entire site, a PayPal shopping cart might not be the way to go because one item doesn't really need a shopping cart. In this case, you'll need to create a **Buy Now** button. This button can also be used to create a link for an item to put in your email for an email campaign.

Under PayPal's Merchant Services select: Create Buttons→Buy Now

Fill in the information just like you would've for the shopping cart button, following PayPal's instructions, and make sure to get your Payment Successful and Payment Cancelled pages in as well, by clicking the **Add More Options** button.

Note that when you create the **Buy Now** button, you have to de-select the option for security settings if you want customers to be able to buy something from an email, or if you want to add more options.

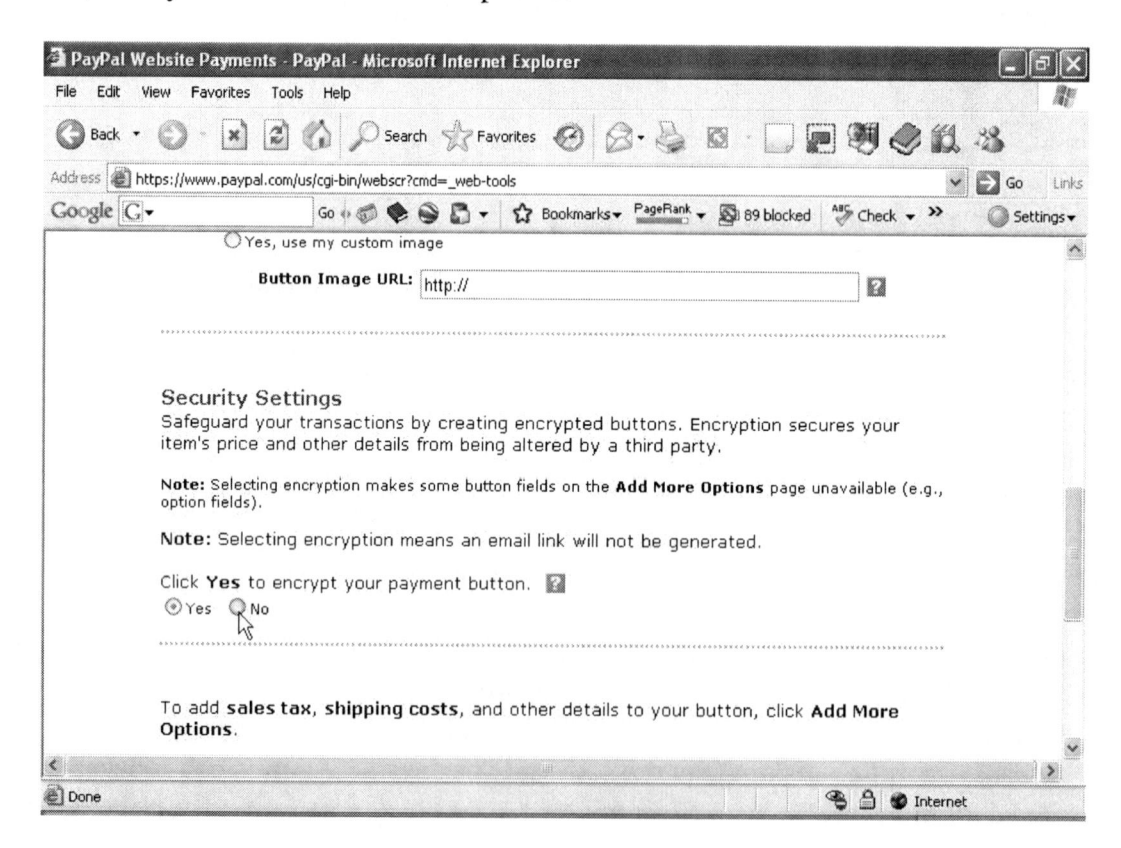

Choosing to not encrypt your button does not make it less safe; it just lets you add more options for your customers, giving them the ability, if you choose, to leave a note or comments with their payment.

Basically, it allows customer interaction. We never encrypt our buttons because we add in Payment Successful and Payment Cancelled pages, as well as the option for customers to leave a comment with their purchase.

Then all you have to do is copy the code PayPal gives you onto your site or into your email campaign.

Chapter Ten
Meta Tags (keywords) Explained.

Now that you know the basics about site building and adding inventory, we think it's time to teach you how to optimize your site so that you have a chance of ranking well in the search engines.

First, we're going to teach you how to find proper, targeted, keywords for every page in your site. Second, at the end of this chapter, you'll find step-by-step instructions for actually implementing the process.

Optimization takes a great deal of work and "thinking outside the box," so take your time, absorb the information as best you can, and follow the steps to optimize your site as we lay them out for you.

Also, keep in mind that true site optimization is a *job*. You can't just do it once and expect your site to be getting targeted visitors and sales. Every few months you need to re-evaluate your keywords to make sure they are still the *absolute best* ones for your site.

It sounds like a lot of work, yes, but remember what we said in the Intro, that only about 2% of all sites on the internet even know what they are doing…this is why.

Optimization is the one thing that can make or break your site. So, with that in mind, absorb what you can, follow our instructions, and never stop learning. If you stay up on this aspect of your site, we guarantee that you'll find success. If you don't, if you let this slide, then you'll slip out of the 2%, and you may never rank in the search engines.

META TAGS.

The best way to think about meta tags is that they are keyword phrases and variations that you think a visitor might type into the search engines to find your site with. And, the most important thing about them is that they need to be **targeted to the content of your site**, and still be broad enough to get the most visitors.

This is one of the mistakes that we made. For Shop Lizards, we used keywords like:

shopping, free shipping, etc.

These are entirely too broad and will only get us ranked in the search engine's bottom billion results.

We should have used keywords like:

diecast cars, diecast airplanes, etc.

See the difference? **Shopping** is much too broad a keyword, but we might actually get page views for the keyword **men's Ferrari Black cologne**.

Definitely take the time to find the keywords that will work the best for you. **This is the most important task that you will have in gaining visitors.**

Mainly, without huge marketing campaigns, keywords are the best way to get ranked in search engines. There's more to this, though, like the text on your pages should reflect the keywords that you choose, and even the titles of the pages need to reflect the keywords in some way, but it will all make sense soon.

Before we get into all the details of putting in the meta tags, first, we need to teach you how to find the *right* keywords for every page in your site.

WHY CHOOSING THE RIGHT KEYWORDS FOR YOUR SITE IS <u>SO</u> IMPORTANT.

Getting ranked in the search engines hinges on how well you do one thing (well several things, but we'll hit the rest later), keywords, aka meta tags. How well you estimate your site's best keywords and keyword phrases determines how well your site ranks overall.

It's been floating around that using as many keywords as possible is the key to great search engine rankings. In fact, some sites have typed in the keyword over and over and colored it the same as the site background so that visitors wouldn't be able to see, all in an attempt to "trick" the web bots.

Those sites have now been banned from the search engines because the web bots do not like such tricks. **Never attempt to hide anything from the search engines.**

Ever see those big "high-tech" sites that have flash movies before you get into the site itself? As fun as it sounds, using flash movies and images on the homepage will only *decrease* your ranking within the search engines. Why? The web bots (the search engine's crawlers) cannot "read" a flash movie or image (unless that image has optimized Alt tags).

What it cannot read, it cannot rank.

Moreover, most search engines will only scan the first three hundred words of text on your page, regarding it as the most important. So, you must get your keywords into that first few hundred words to get the best results.

Also, the more frequent (within human-readable reason) the keywords appear, and the closer they appear to the beginning of the page, the greater the chance of a higher search engine rank.

Effective keyword usage in the text of the pages on your site is called Search Engine Optimization, or SEO, and is the second most important thing in high search engine placement. The most important is the Title Tag, which we'll discuss in just a moment.

It has become something of a myth that the most important page in your site is the home page. Actually, every page can rank just as well based solely on your efforts of optimization. **But none of your pages will rank well if your keywords do not *accurately* reflect the content on that page.** Do not use keywords for travel on a page if that page does not use the exact same keywords within the text itself.

The most important thing to take from this about your meta tags is that they must *accurately* reflect the content of your site, and they must be targeted to your preferred visitors (the ones that will **buy** from you).

Also, single word keywords like "dog" are near to useless, so before you even begin, you need to think about your product in terms of its keyword phrase—like "rhinestone dog collars"—instead. Once you start thinking this way, you'll already have an advantage in terms of proper search engine optimization.

HERE'S A GEM: Targeting the *right* visitors is called "controlling the eyeballs." It takes a while to really understand what this means, but basically, you want to target your keywords to the customer that your product or service is literally intended for. Don't say everyone!

You need to take a moment and very seriously consider who it is *exactly* that is most likely to buy your product. For example, Harry, a 48 year old man who loves reading in the bathroom will not come to your site to buy cozy floor mats for his bathroom (but he might buy a more comfy toilet seat). However, his younger sister Sally might because she's been watching those home decorating shows lately and wants to improve her bathroom.

Both customers would need different marketing to get them to purchase from you. Harry would need you to play on his love for comfort, while Sally would need you to play on her need for nice esthetics. Neither would buy from you if you don't get this right.

Think about your target customer. Think hard.

Let's give you an even better example. Say you are selling an ebook on the art of Tantric sexual positions. You went through the work and picked out a decent keyword phrase, "Tantric sex positions," but you have a very immediate and serious problem, here. Perhaps fifty percent of all searches online are for porn or sexual related terms, but they are not searching for *products*, they are searching for *pictures*. Free, x-rated pictures.

With your keyword phrase, a great deal of your traffic could come in this way, but they are in no way targeted to your product, plus they are generally looking for free pictures and won't even be able to absorb your sales page. They are in no way targeted to your product, yet they use your exact search phrase to find you. That's a problem. You don't want these eyeballs.

You want the eyeballs of people interested in the *art of Tantra,* people who are searching for information, and who are much more likely to make a purchase because they are expecting to find the information they are looking for.

See the difference? While "Tantric sexual positions" could bring in thousands of visitors, they are untargeted visitors. They are the wrong eyeballs. A better way to go would be to use the search phrase "the art of Tantric positions" or "Tantra methods" which would actually bring in the right kind of eyeballs, people looking to buy your product.

In reality, this can and does happen with any keyword phrase, the untargeted traffic just has different agendas. You don't want people looking to buy skinny jeans if you only sell leather pants and you don't want people interested in information on how to find the best cancer doctors if you only sell homeopathic methods for treatment. Neither are targeted and neither will buy from you. They are looking for something specific and intend to find it—so they'll leave.

Keep in mind *every* eyeball that could be searching for what you're selling. If you bring in the right eyeballs, you'll get more sales. If you bring in the wrong eyeballs, you'll get a lot of traffic and fewer sales.

FINDING YOUR KEYWORDS.

Ready to fix your tags to get you more visitors and a higher ranking in the search engines? First, we're going to teach you how to find the best keywords for your site, and second, we'll show you how and where to put them onto your site.

Go to http://www.google.com (because it's the most extensive search engine, period), and type in a few keywords that you think will work for your site right at this moment. Note how many websites there are for each keyword.

Remember what we discussed about niche markets? A niche is a search result that equals less than a million hits, preferably closer to 100,000. The smaller the number, the greater the niche. But remember that *too* small a number equals a niche that no one wants, so choose wisely here.

Sometimes, though, if your product is new to the market—say you've manufactured a product yourself—you could create your own niche. You'll actually see this phenomena from time to time when a new product is released. Eventually, if they launched their product with enough hype and excitement, the searches will grow and the niche will begin to expand as other websites spring up to sell or promote similar items.

If you're ready to begin, go ahead and use the five things you came up with during the exercise in the last chapter, or come up with more ideas about what you'd like to sell now.

Next, we suggest using (http://www.iwebtool.com/keyword_lookup/) to really configure the keywords. You'll need to create an account (it's free) with them, but you can use their fantastic little lookup tool to see what keywords are being searched for, and how often.

More importantly, you can enter in a keyword that you think will work for your site and it will give you other suggestions, as well as how often your word and the suggestions are being searched for. Play around with this tool and pick out the keywords that you think best work for your site.

Remember to go back and forth.

If iwebtool suggests a fantastic keyword or phrase that you had never thought of, go back to Google and try it as a search.

Choosing the right keyword is perhaps even more important that naming your company (though when naming your company, take your keywords into account), so take the time to get it right.

For example:

In Google, we tried the keyword "dog collars."

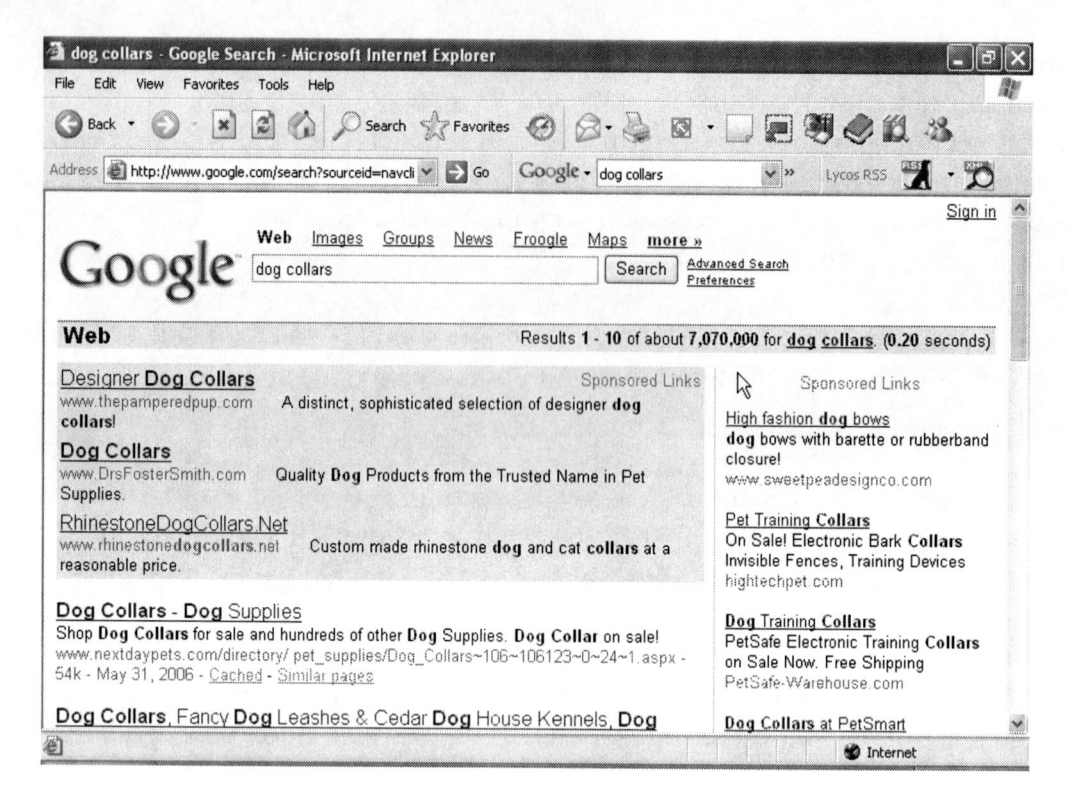

Note that on the top right of the page Google reveals that the results are "1-10 of about 7,070,000 for dog collars."

This means that there are over **seven million** other sites that use the keyword "dog collars" on their site. And, it also means that there are about seven million competitors for this keyword.

Let's go to iwebtool and see how "dog collars" ranks.

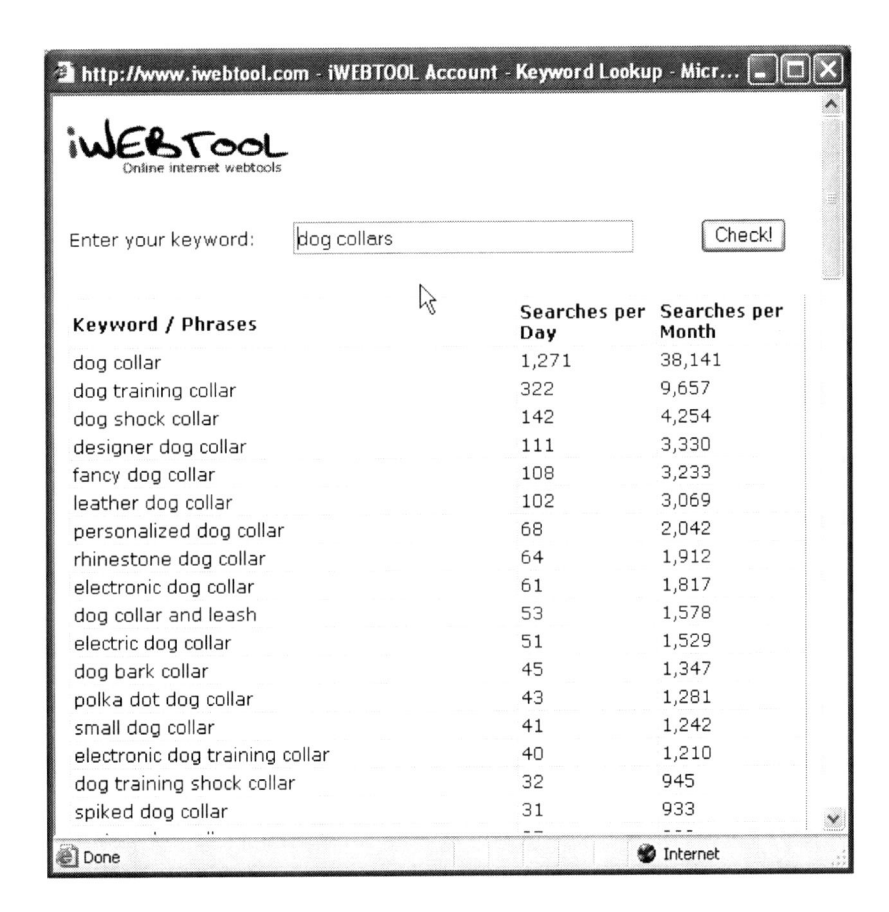

> | Keyword / Phrases | Searches per Day | Searches per Month |
> |---|---|---|
> | dog collar | 1,271 | 38,141 |
> | dog training collar | 322 | 9,657 |
> | dog shock collar | 142 | 4,254 |
> | designer dog collar | 111 | 3,330 |
> | fancy dog collar | 108 | 3,233 |
> | leather dog collar | 102 | 3,069 |
> | personalized dog collar | 68 | 2,042 |
> | rhinestone dog collar | 64 | 1,912 |
> | electronic dog collar | 61 | 1,817 |
> | dog collar and leash | 53 | 1,578 |
> | electric dog collar | 51 | 1,529 |
> | dog bark collar | 45 | 1,347 |
> | polka dot dog collar | 43 | 1,281 |
> | small dog collar | 41 | 1,242 |
> | electronic dog training collar | 40 | 1,210 |
> | dog training shock collar | 32 | 945 |
> | spiked dog collar | 31 | 933 |

See how iwebtool breaks down the searches? Dog collar (without the "s"—this isn't important, it's just how things get recorded) gets 1,271 searches per day and 38,141 searches a month. Not bad.

But in a market of over seven million? The odds aren't *that* great.

We need to be a bit more targeted to get sales right away (or ever). So, say we sell *rhinestone* dog collars.

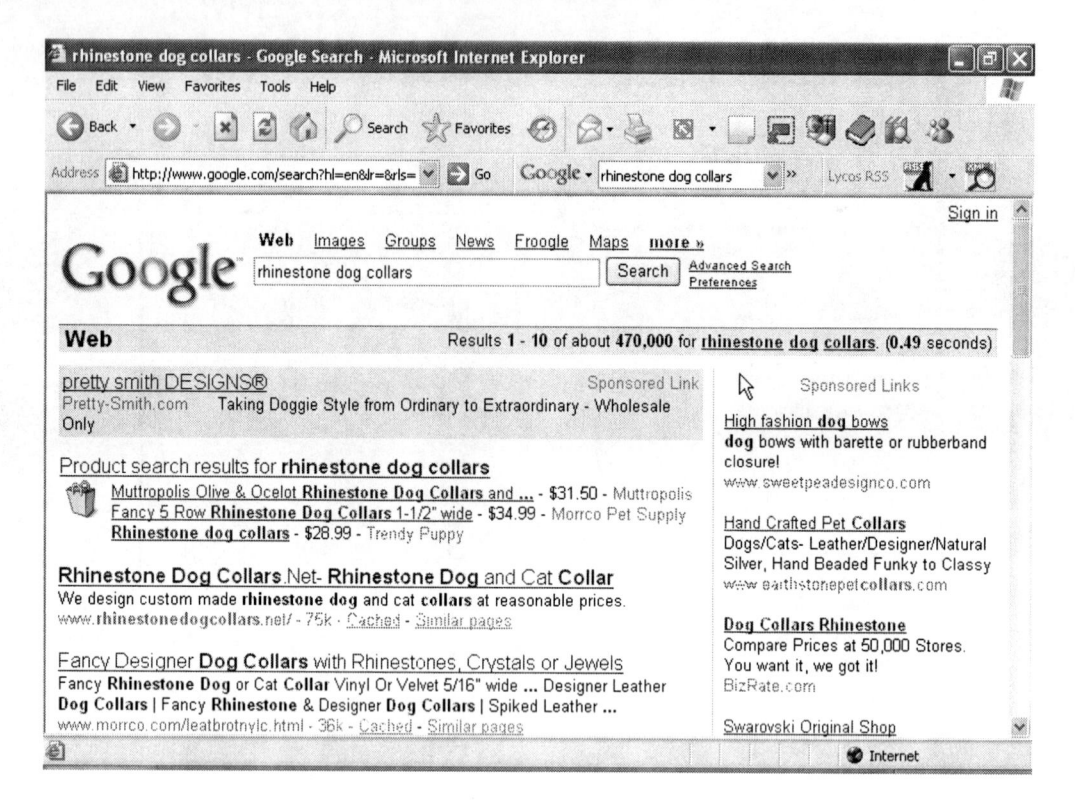

The new search in Google for our more targeted keyword "rhinestone dog collars" reveals that there are only 470,000 other competitors. That's a niche and it'll work. Plus, it targets a very specific audience, those that want rhinestone dog collars.

So, now let's check iwebtool and see how rhinestone dog collars does.

iWEBTOOL Keyword Lookup

Enter your keyword: rhinestone dog collars

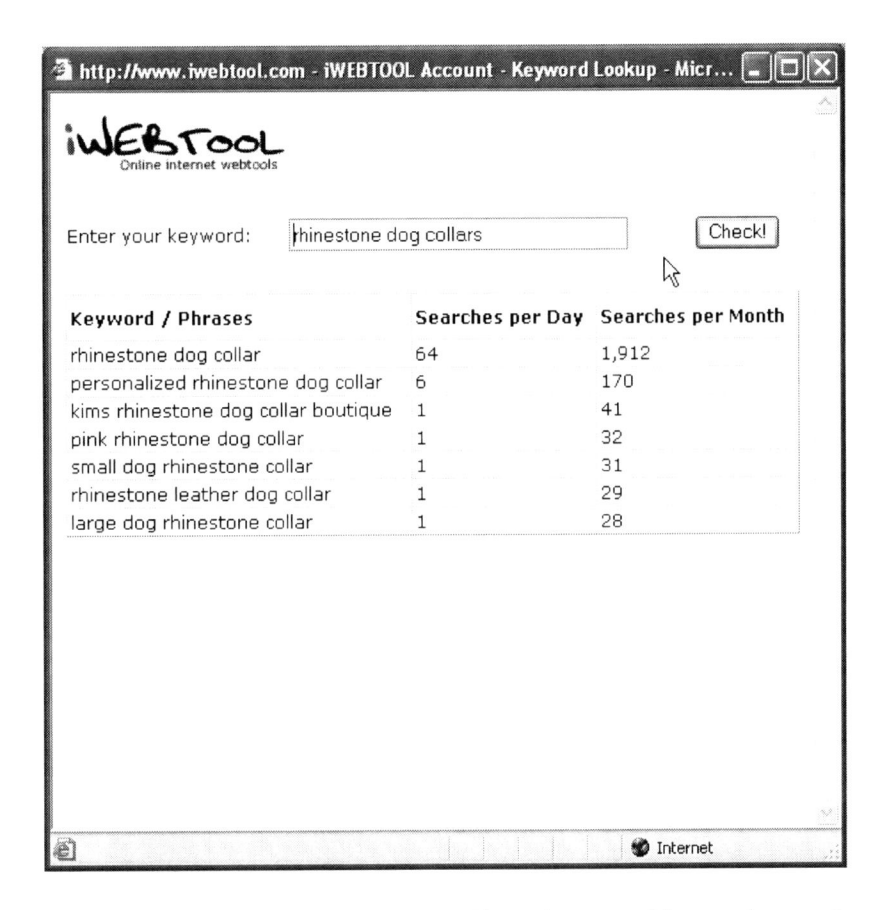

Keyword / Phrases	Searches per Day	Searches per Month
rhinestone dog collar	64	1,912
personalized rhinestone dog collar	6	170
kims rhinestone dog collar boutique	1	41
pink rhinestone dog collar	1	32
small dog rhinestone collar	1	31
rhinestone leather dog collar	1	29
large dog rhinestone collar	1	28

Rhinestone dog collar (again without the "s") only gets 64 searches a day, and 1,912 searches a month, and in a market of 470,000 other competitors, that may not be the traffic that we need for this kind of business. But we could give it a try and see how things go, feeling good with the fact that in just a short time, because we have our keywords right, we'll rank on the first page.

But now you should see how important this research is to the future of your business. The right keyword will literally make or break you, so spend the time (lots and lots of time, even) and get it right.

Now, to select the right keywords for use as your meta tags, you need to take a close look at the numbers. "Rhinestone dog collars" may be what we are fictionally selling, but "dog collars" gets more people looking per month.

But who are we targeting here?

Anyone who has a dog and needs a dog collar? Or people who are specifically looking for a rhinestone dog collar? How about the people who can't remember the word "rhinestone" and just search for "dog collars," or a different version…Do you see how difficult this can be? But, more importantly, are you beginning to see why it is so important?

If we were to simply target everyone searching for "dog collars," then they may come to our site, but they might leave immediately because we only sell fancy dog collars, and maybe they just wanted information on how to buy the right size dog collar.

When people come to our site, we want them to stay awhile and buy something; we don't want them to be disappointed because they didn't find what they were originally searching for. And surfers have notoriously fast click through rates. If a visitor doesn't see what they were expecting to find on your site within five seconds, they'll just leave without even checking your site out further. That's why targeting is so crucial. You want the right visitors.

Moreover, when choosing keywords, you need to select the ones that you think you can optimize your site for, but they must have enough traffic for you to have a chance at doing well in the search engines, and they must be targeted with a *specific* customer in mind.

This may seem confusing because in the last chapter we told you how important niche markets are. And yes, if you have a niche, you need to find the best keywords for that niche, using the numbers iwebtool provides. If you don't have a niche, you need to select the best keyword based on sheer numbers alone.

If you do everything right, you'll see that you can rank as well as anyone else, because as we mentioned in the Intro, only 2% of all sites on the internet even have their act together when it comes to proper keyword usage and optimization.

HOW TO FIND KEYWORD STEMS.

Keyword stems are a greatly overlooked way to increase your traffic because they rarely get as many hits as your main keywords and can seem like a waste of time to bother with—you've probably even seen quite a few when you went through the process of selecting the best keywords. However, by including these variations, they can often double your amount of effective keywords, and thus double your amount of targeted traffic.

Even if a variation is getting five visitors a day, that is still five highly targeted people who are more likely to purchase from you. And targeted visitors are much more likely to purchase from you than untargeted visitors.

So what exactly is a keyword stem? It's basically a variation of your main keyword phrase. It can include literal stems from a word, like plan and planning, but often includes words that have nothing to do with the stem, like house and floor. Both examples, though, are stems in terms of search options.

Because this is how your visitors think, you need to think this way as well to get as much targeted traffic to your site as possible.

We actually found a fantastic free tool to help you in this process, http://www.gorank.com/seotools/ontology . To use this tool, you type in your first keyword, and it returns a list of all possible variations for that word. Let's look at an example:

Our keyword phrase is "house plan" so we typed "plan" into the tool. And it returned a list:

plan
planning
plans
strategy
planner
carte
plane
planes
plano
plan's
planning's
planner's

Now, the list seems a bit weird at first and some of the terms might turn out to be useless for our keyword, but it helps us to see that perhaps "strategy" might be a great keyword variation. And, although some of the terms like "plane" seemed useless at first, we realized that they very well could be common misspellings for our keyword, so they might be worth including as well. We weren't even sure how "carte" was related but we looked it up and found it can refer to a map or chart.

"House" returned this list:

house
home
housing
floor
houses
home's

All of them actually work well for our keywords, and, the addition of "floor" could add a great deal of targeted traffic that we might have overlooked otherwise.

When looking into keyword stems, you'll find that this might happen to you as well. You might even find keywords that will work better for you than the ones you had selected before. Be flexible in your options here and keep in mind that if you can't find a place for your new keywords in your main tags, they can always be used in your other less important tags, or simply added into your content.

HOW TO USE YOUR KEYWORDS PROPERLY.

Once you've found the most targeted keywords for your site, you need to consider how you'll use them in your meta tags and site content. It's very important to note that exact matches are best. You'll rank higher for "cat clothing" than "cat and dog clothing" if "cat clothing" is your main keyword. If both are equally important to you, then you'll be best served by either using both "cat clothing and dog clothing" or creating a separate page for each—each page devoted to one keyword phrase or the other.

We'd choose the second option to get the most power out of our keyword and create a separate page for each one, writing the title tags like so:

Title Tag: Cat Clothing, Cat Costumes, and Unique Cat Clothes
Title Tag: Dog Clothing, Dog Costumes, and Unique Dog Clothes

This not only doubles our content, but gives each keyword the most power available, as well as giving an opportunity to put full use to keyword variations. This is your ultimate goal.

PLACING YOUR KEYWORDS.

Keywords and keyword phrases must occur in five main places on your site (in order of importance): the Title Tag, the content of your web pages, the Description Meta Tag, the Keywords Meta Tag, and the image Alt Tags.

More frequent keyword use means a greater search engine rank. But overuse equals a bad rank, and even removal from the search engines altogether.

So what to do?

Optimize each page for one main keyword or phrase (no more than two keyword phrases), and make it count by doing it right.

We'll give the HTML headings for each tag, just so you know what they are when you look up your source code, but Tripod does the work for you in the **Site Organizer** under **Page Properties**. You'll have to go through each page and optimize them separately, but it's an easy enough process once you get going.

Also, it's best to find your main keyword and use it (and all variations of it) up to three times per page, as you'll see in our examples. We'll get to the step by step process for adding your tags to your site after a bit more exposition.

HOW TO VIEW YOUR WEB PAGE SOURCE CODE:

We use Internet Explorer (and instructed you to use it for Tripod as well) and will tell you how to find the source code for this browser. If you use a different browser, you'll still be able to find the source code for your site (or any site) by searching through your options. When you get into SEO and get good enough at it that you offer to do it for others (hey, dream big!), you'll need to use the source code to find out what all of their meta tags are.

Open up your site and on the very top bar of the browser click on:
View→Source

You don't actually need to know how to do this, but it's a good thing to be aware of if you choose to learn more about HTML in the future.

USING KEYWORDS AS TEXT LINKS.

You know how important the proper keywords are to your success. Well, you can also use them as the links to, within, and away from your site.

This goes right along with external linking. If you get someone to put a link to your site on their site, it had better say "Personalized Rhinestone Dog Collars," or just "Designer Dog Collars." Otherwise, you're just wasting your time. Why?

Because the web bots can *read*, and if they read a link to "Joe's Page," it has nowhere near the same rank weight as "Dog Collars," unless of course, you want to rank well for the keywords "Joe's Page."

In a strange way, that reciprocal link counts as a meta tag for your site if it has the same keywords in it that you use on your pages. So, if you're going to put in the work to get the links, make sure they'll benefit you by using your keywords.

You'll find, and this may shock you, that this is actually the most important aspect of your site's search engine optimization. But don't worry, you'll learn all about this strategy in Chapter 11.

HOW TO OPTIMIZE YOUR SITE.

There are five main areas where all search engine optimization (SEO) professionals make changes to get the most optimized site possible. What we are about to reveal, you could pay as much as a couple grand to find out…so get ready and, if you can read this (that's how easy this is), keeping in mind everything we just told you about choosing the right keywords, you too can optimize your site *as well as* any SEO professional out there. Trust us!

You'll find, as we have, that proper search engine optimization is a trial and error process. But, once you know the process and how to use the tools, you really have no where to go with your site than up in your search ranking.

THE TITLE TAG.

The Title Tag is your most important tag because it alone can land your website among the top search results.

The Title Tag, or, in Tripod, the **Browser Page Title**, can be found under **Site Organizer→Page Properties**.

Browser Page Title
60 character limit. HTML tags are not allowed. Some search engines use the title tag as the link to access your web page. This title can be different from the page title shown on your web page.

`RHINESTONE DOG COLLARS, DESIGNER`

HTML Example: <TITLE>RHINESTONE DOG COLLARS, DESIGNER DOG COLLARS, DOG COLLARS</TITLE>

What we'd type into the Browser Page Title: RHINESTONE DOG COLLARS, DESIGNER DOG COLLARS, DOG COLLARS

Tripod only allows 60 characters, including spaces, but as long as you get in your main keyword two to three times, and the most targeted variations in as well, you'll have created the best possible tag that you can.

We've capitalized the tag in our example, but we've found recently that it neither helps nor hurts your ranking. The most important thing to keep in mind here is that this is your "sales" moment. This is what shows up in the search results. As you'll rarely see capitalization in the search results, capitalizing looks different enough to get visitors to click through. Play around with your options here, maybe capitalizing just a few of the words for greater effect, or just the first letter of each word like a headline. This is your moment to get people to click, so make the most of it.

We could do the same tag quite a few different ways. Here are a few examples:

Title Tag: RHINESTONE DOG COLLARS, DESIGNER DOG COLLARS, DOG COLLARS

Title Tag: RHINESTONE DOG COLLARS, Designer Dog Collars, & Dog Collars

Title Tag: Rhinestone Dog Collars, Designer Dog Collars, & Dog Collars

Since we determined that "rhinestone dog collars" was our most targeted keyword, we made sure to get it in first. "Cat Clothing & Unique Cat Clothes" has much more power and ability to rank well than "Krazy Ken's Cat Clothing & Unique Cat Clothes." It's basically the same thing, but Google reads the first three words as most important. For that reason alone, you must get your most important keyword at the very beginning of your Title Tag.

We suggest opening up a Word document and typing up your sentences. That way, you can count the characters (highlight the words you want to count, then select Tools→Word Count), and check for spelling mistakes at the same time.

If you only have the chance to do one tag on your entire site, get the Title Tag done. It is the most important tag of them all. It should begin with the most commonly used search phrase that you determined would target the most visitors for your site, and it should list your most important keyword as many as two or three times.

Again, play with variations of this. Working in your keyword twice is better than cramming your keyword in three times. Often your keyword phrase might be a bit long, and you'll only have room to use it once. Space is at a premium, so use it well. Getting your targeted keyword phrase in once at the front of the tag can often work better than a lesser targeted keyword worked in three times.

Most importantly, it should *not* list your company name or slogan unless you've determined that your company name is the most commonly searched term.

Now, before you optimize your Title Tag, you need to think about this as your opportunity to sell your potential visitors into clicking on your site in the search results. At the very least, you should make your Title Tag somewhat compelling to your visitors. For example:

So-So title: Cat Clothing, Cat Clothes, Cat Costumes
Better title: Cat Clothing, Cat Clothes, & Unique Cat Costumes for All Occasions

Also, every page needs a Title Tag, but every page should also have a *different* Title Tag. Let's look at a few variations so you can see how this works:

Home page: Rhinestone Dog Collars, Designer Dog Collars, & Unique Collars
Contact Us page: Contact us about Rhinestone Dog Collars & Unique Collars
Site Map: Browse our Information on Rhinestone Dog Collars

Vary each a bit for best results. This makes your site look more authoritative to Google and puts your keyword on all of your pages as well

DESCRIPTION META TAG.

The Description Meta Tag functions like your mini sales page. It should be human-readable, but include your keywords as well as all important keyword variations in a few sentences. Keep in mind that these sentences should be crafted to make people want to click through to your website

The Description Meta Tag can be found under **Page Properties** in the **Site Organizer**.

Description Meta Tag
200 character limit. HTML tags are not allowed. Some search engines use the description in the search engine results.

```
We sell rhinestone dog collars, matching
rhinestone leashes, designer dog collars, and
collars that are fancy, unique, and inexpensive
```

HTML Example: <META NAME="description" CONTENT=" We sell rhinestone dog collars, matching rhinestone leashes, designer dog collars, and collars that are fancy, unique, and inexpensive for small, medium, or large dogs, all with free shipping.">

What we'd type into the Description Meta Tag box: We sell rhinestone dog collars, matching rhinestone leashes, designer dog collars, and collars that are fancy, unique, and inexpensive for small, medium, or large dogs, all with free shipping.

Tripod only allows 200 characters (each letter and space equals a character), so use them well. In the example above, we only use 192 characters and we repeat our keywords as many times as human-readably possible.

We suggest opening up a Word document and typing up your sentences. That way, you can count the characters (highlight the words you want to count, then select Tools→Word Count), and check for spelling mistakes at the same time.

Search engines will often use your description meta tag when they display search results. If you don't have a description meta tag, or the search engines choose not to use them, then they will compile one for you based on the content of your pages.

Most often though, if you crafted your description meta tag correctly, they will display it in the search results because it makes their job a whole lot easier. This is a very good thing—the best case scenario, actually—because it looks a lot better in results than random words pulled from your page that happen to match a search result.

That's why getting the content right is so important. A description meta tag like "products shopping free" will mean nothing to potential visitors. Write the description meta tag for *your visitors*, using the keywords that you so carefully selected for best results and the search engines will reward you.

Most importantly, do not just stuff in a bunch of keywords without attempting to create a complete sentence. Search engines will view this as "keyword stuffing" and will rank you lower in the rankings, at best, or at worst, will label you as spam. This is your opportunity to get more clicks, so don't waste it by being clever.

KEYWORD META TAG.

The Keyword Meta Tag has changed over the last year in search engines. Now, it is looked at as a way of adding your website to the search results, but they are no longer used to determine relevancy for a particular keyword. Basically, this is a good tag to fill in, but now you have the opportunity to add in common misspellings, synonyms, and lesser searched for variations of your keywords that you had no room to place elsewhere.

The Keyword Meta Tag can be found under **Page Properties** in the **Site Organizer**.

Keyword Meta Tag
200 character limit. HTML tags are not allowed. Separate keywords by a comma. Example: web design, animation, design, create. Some search engines augment the text that they index on a page with the contents of this field.

```
rhinestone dog collars, rhinestone, rhinestones
dog collars, designer collars, dogs, designer,
unique, cool, fancy, personalized, pink, polka
```
[Done]

HTML Example: <META NAME="keywords" CONTENT=" rhinestone dog collars, rhinestone, rhinestones dog collars, designer collars, dogs, designer, unique, cool, fancy, personalized, pink, polka dot, spiked, small, medium, large">

What we'd type into the Keyword Meta Tag box: rhinestone dog collars, rhinestone, rhinestones dog collars, designer collars, dogs, designer, unique, cool, fancy, personalized, pink, polka dot, spiked, small, medium, large

Try to get in all of the important keywords and keyword phrases, knowing that you can use them up to three times each.

Tripod only allows 200 characters (each letter and space equals a character), so use them well. In the example above, we only use 175 characters and we repeat our keywords as many times as we have room.

Again, we suggest opening up a Word document and typing up your keywords. That way, you can count the characters (highlight the words you want to count, then select Tools→Word Count), and check for spelling mistakes at the same time.

The thing about the keyword meta tag is that you need to be as specific as possible, yet repeating is discouraged. Repeating keywords *more than* three times in the meta tag is called spamming the search engines.

If you do this, you could be banned forever. **But for best results, you should use that main keyword three times.** It's a tricky line to walk, but this is how we accomplish it:

A slight variation of each word counts as that same word (unless you use the stem of that word for variations), so you need to have a purpose in mind. So, "dog" can be used three times, or we can add in a close variation of that word and use "dog" two times and "dogs" once.

We decided that "rhinestone" was our most targeted keyword, so we get it in three times like this: "rhinestone dog collars, "rhinestone," and "rhinestones."

"Collars" is also important to us, so we get it in three times: "rhinestone dog collars," "dog collars," and "designer collars."

IMAGE ALT TAG.

The Image Alt Tag is the most often overlooked tag when doing search engine optimization. It takes a bit more effort to actually add it to your website than the other tags, but over the last year, it has grown in its importance as a tag so it should definitely be a priority. Also, keep in mind that if you link your image to something, even if it is only linking back to itself in a larger size, it has more weight in the search engines. At the very least, your site logo can be linked back to your homepage. Combined with Alt tags, this creates a much more powerful presence for your website than Alt tags alone.

The Image Alt Tag can be found on all of the **Photo Edit** screens by selecting either **Edit Picture**, **Add Picture**, or **Edit Site Title** (since you're using an image as your Site Title).

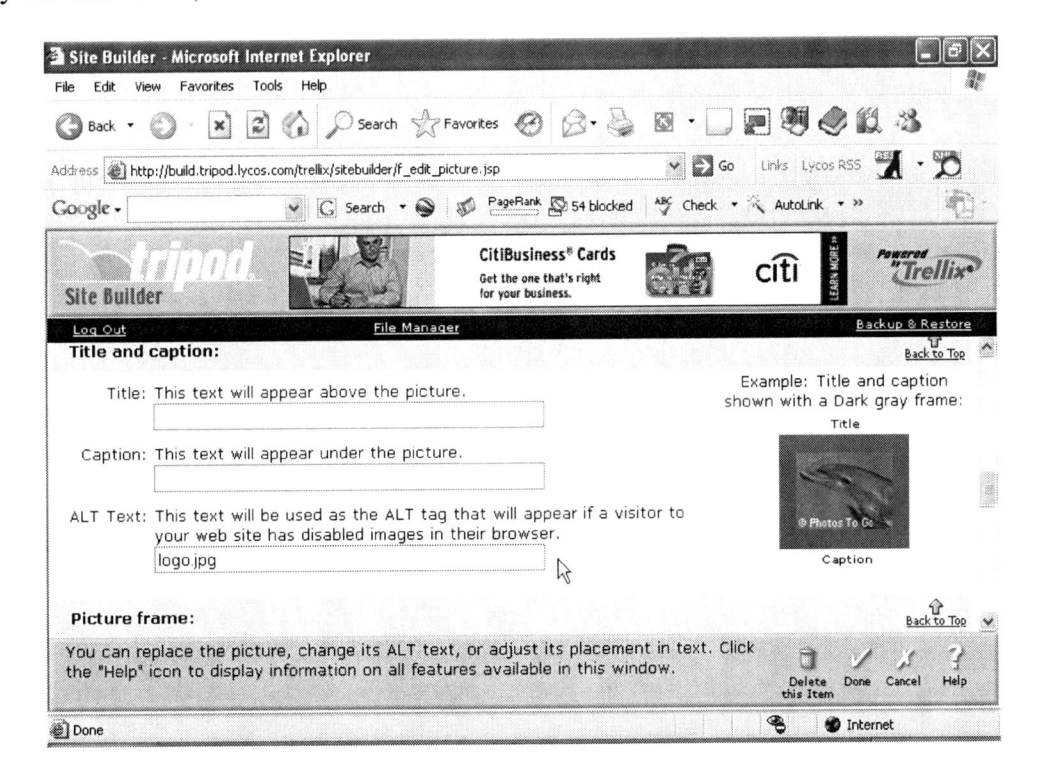

HTML Example: <IMG SRC="logo.jpg" WIDTH="200" HEIGHT="50" ALT=" rhinestone dog collars, designer, dog collars">

What we'd type into the ALT Text box: rhinestone dog collars, designer, dog collars

Tripod allows about six to seven words (or about 47 characters) in the Alt tag, depending on the length of the words chosen. Fill in the tag for *every* picture that you place on your site, being careful to avoid misspellings.

You can tell which pictures have Alt tags by hovering over them with your mouse. If they don't, it'll say "logo.jpg" (or whatever the original name of your picture). If you've done the Alt tag, it'll read as what you typed in.

Now, the Alt tag needs to actually refer to the content of that picture. We had a ghillie suit page, and had about thirty different ghillie suit pictures, so to save time and avoid typing the same Alt tag in over and over again, we just copied a few variations into a Word document and pasted the variations into each picture's Alt tag. Simple, yet effective.

But our ghillie suit Alt tag wouldn't have worked for any of our leather jacket pictures. Each picture must have a relevant Alt tag.

In regards of importance to the search engines, the Alt tag is the lowest; however, if you don't have them you run the chance of being ranked lower than you would've had you put them in. So, spend the time and treat them as you would any other tag.

Recently, search engines like Google have begun "image searches," in which a person can type in a keyword and find a particular image based on that keyword. We have even brought in a great deal of traffic for our own sites this way, simply because we did the work on our Alt tags. So, if you get your Alt text targeted enough, your images will begin showing up in Google's image search for the keywords that you target them for.

Isn't that great?

Now, not only can you get ranked in the search engines, but your images can get searched for and found too!

Moreover, since you might have more than one picture that you need the same Alt tags for, like we often do, you can use the same tags, or use variations of the tags to cover more keywords at a time (keeping in mind that you can use the same word or variations of that word up to three times).

For example, say we have five pictures of rhinestone dog collars, but we'd like to vary things a bit (without actually using any real keyword stems or variations), so we'd do this.

Picture one: rhinestone dog collars, designer, dog collars
Picture two: designer dog collars, rhinestone, dog collars
Picture three: personalized rhinestone dog collars, rhinestone
Picture four: unique rhinestone dog collars, dog collars
Picture five: dog collars, unique, rhinestone, personalized

They are all less than 47 characters (which is the maximum), and they all say basically the same thing, but they are just different enough that each image has a chance to show up in the image search for the particular keywords that it has in its Alt text.

You can do this too, coming up with variations for your keywords based on what you gather from the iwebtool and the gorank ontology tool.

STEP BY STEP OPTIMIZATION.

Ready to use what you've just learned to optimize your site? The good news is that you've done the hardest part already, simply by reading this chapter. The bad news is that you now need to sit down and dedicate another day or so to actually getting things done right, and optimize *every* page and *every* image on your site. Be patient, this is where it gets exciting—seeing it all come together.

And, don't worry, it's very simple and we'll go over it step by step. Plus, at the end of this chapter you'll find a checklist to ensure you don't miss any important steps.

NOTE: Do not optimize pages that you don't want visitors to be able to find in the search engines, like your Payment Successful page, etc. Instead, make sure you put them in your Robots.txt file.

STEP ONE: First you need to use the iwebtool, Google, and the gorank ontology tool to determine the most important, most targeted keywords and variations for all of your products like we discussed moments ago. If you only have one product right now, you have an easy job because you can use the same keywords on your homepage that you'll use on your inventory page, using variations to get the most out of your keywords.

If you have more than one product and many pages of inventory (like we do), then the job is a bit more difficult, and optimizing the homepage gets dicey because you'll need to select your "main" product to optimize for. Also, you can use your lesser variations and actually end up ranking in the top results for those keywords. This has happened to us on numerous occasions, so it is definitely something you need to keep in mind.

Also, keep in mind that in most cases, your inventory pages will actually be the ones that show up in the search results for your main keywords rather than your homepage simply because they'll have more related content on them. If these pages are well made, you should be able to convert many visitors into sales.

Now, open up a Word document so you can count your characters and check for spelling errors and **write out** your Title Tag, Description Meta Tag, Keyword Meta Tag, and Alt tag, for every page, taking everything we mentioned earlier into account.

Oh, and you can use **&** instead of **and** to save characters in all of these tags, but you'll notice if you come back to that page's Page Properties later, that Tripod has changed the **&** into:

&

It's not a big deal, but you'll need to change every **&** back to **&** before you leave the Page Properties. It's just one of those things...

So, before moving on to Step Two, for *every* page, you must have:

- 60 character or less Title Tag
- 200 character or less Description Meta Tag
- 200 character or less Keyword Meta Tag
- 47 character or less Alt Tag

STEP TWO: When you're ready to get started, click on **Site Organizer**, and then select the first page that you'd like to work on, like the page that you just found keywords for, and then select **Page Properties**.

For every page that you optimize, you must get your most important keyword for that page into the **Web Page File Name**, often referred to as the page file extension.

Chapter Ten: Meta Tags (Keywords) Explained 281

Change the page file name.

Web page file name: [id23.html]   *Do not change the .html extension or your web page may become inaccessible.

In the picture above, our current file extension is **id23.html**. If we are selling rhinestone dog collars on this page, and since we decided that it was our most important keyword, we'd need to get it into the web page file name.

So, we'd change it to: **rhinestonedogcollars.html**. Keep in mind that while every page needs to have a keyword in the web page file name, none of them can be the same. So, you cannot have two **rhinestonedogcollars.html** pages. Instead, you can do something like this:

rhinestonedogcollars.html
rhinestonedogcollars2.html
rhinestonedogcollars3.html

or even,

rhinestonedogcollars.html
rhinestonedogcollar.html
rhinestonecollars.html

Variations are good here and will help you get your main keywords into the file extensions of your domain name—which is the most powerful optimization tool of all.

Once you get all of your web page file names optimized, you'll be coming back for the exact file name, or file extension, which you'll be able to see from the **Site Organizer**, when it comes time to create your Site Map in Step Four.

NEXT, we'd move on to the **Browser Page Tile**, or the Title Tag.

Browser Page Title
60 character limit. HTML tags are not allowed. Some search engines use the title tag as the link to access your web page. This title can be different from the page title shown on your web page.

Fill in the box with the keywords you wrote up, remembering that this is your moment to sell your potential visitors into clicking on your website in the search results. So don't waste it. Get your main keyword phrase in first, then fill in with a variation or two as well.

THEN, we'd do the **Description Meta Tag**.

> **Description Meta Tag**
> 200 character limit. HTML tags are not allowed. Some search engines use the description in the search engine results.

Fill in the box with the keyword-rich sentences you've crafted, remembering that complete sentences are important, here, because this will be what many search engines use when your page comes up for a search result. Sometimes they won't, but if your keywords are in it when a customer searches for that keyword, usually your description will be the focus.

THEN, we'd do the **Keyword Meta Tag.**

> **Keyword Meta Tag**
> 200 character limit. HTML tags are not allowed. Separate keywords by a comma. Example: web design, animation, design, create. Some search engines augment the text that they index on a page with the contents of this field.

Fill in the box using the keywords and keyword variations that you came up with, keeping in mind that you can also list misspellings, synonyms, and all variations you've come up with here.

FINALLY, when we had all of these tags done for *all* of our pages, then we'd start with the images, getting the Alt tags in, filling in an Alt tag for *every* image on the site.

To enter an Alt tag, click on **Edit Picture** for one of your pictures currently on your site that you've come up with keywords for. Or, if you've just started adding pictures, when you first **Add Picture**, you can do the Alt text at that time, on the **Edit the Picture Settings** screen.

> ALT Text: This text will be used as the ALT tag that will appear if a visitor to your web site has disabled images in their browser.

As we mentioned in the Alt tag section, you can use variations of your 47 characters, using the same keywords a bit differently for each picture. This is also a good place for your keyword stem variations that you haven't been able to use in your other tags.

STEP THREE: Now, it's time to write up keyword-rich content for every page, getting in the keywords as much as possible. We go over content more thoroughly in the next chapter, but it is the third step to properly optimizing your site, so you'll do it once you have all of your keywords figured out.

STEP FOUR: You must have a Site Map and Privacy Policy on your site like we discussed in Chapter 8. You can customize the Privacy Policy that we provided for you, and the Site Map is easy enough, however, you shouldn't create the Site Map until after Step Two has been accomplished because the web page file names, or file extensions, will have changed from a number, **id23.html**, to your most important keyword, **rhinestonedogcollars.html**, for every page.

Follow the instructions in Chapter 8 for creating your Site Map and the Site Map text file that you'll submit to Google.

STEP FIVE: Once you've published your site and have been online for a while, you can check to see if you rank yet for any of your keywords. Since you'll have submitted your Site Map to Google, you should have some idea of when they finally crawl and index your site.

If you're anxious, you can check and see how many of your pages have been indexed by Google (and every other search engine), by going to google.com and typing:

site: shoplizards.com

You'll substitute your domain name instead of ours, without the **www** part. Google will then return a list of all pages that they have indexed of your site. If none of your pages show up, then Google has yet to index your site properly and you just need to wait a bit longer. It may take some time, of course, but Google will get to you.

We found a great little rank checker to check and see how we rank for each keyword, called Google Rankings, http://www.googlerankings.com

Simply input a keyword and your web address and in a few moments, you'll be shown where you rank for that keyword, and if you do, which page you're ranked on in the results.

Now, one of two things will happen. First, if your site isn't optimized for the keyword you chose, you probably won't show up in the top thousand results.

And, if this is the case, it's time for you to get to work at optimizing your site for more specific, and relevant keywords.

Second, you may show up in just a few of the search engines listed, or not at all. For example, if you don't show up in Google, it's probably because your site isn't optimized properly, you haven't submitted a Site Map to Google, or Google just hasn't had time to get around to spidering (indexing) your site. Redouble your efforts, re-optimize your site and submit a Site Map to Google and you should be able to see your results by trying Google Rankings again in a month or so.

Whatever your results, work on your site's content and meta tags and come back to check your results again. You should be able to see improvement! Talk about exciting!

Now, because Google no longer uses an API key, you can't use Google Rankings to perform this check. Since we are feeling generous and because we value this tool so much for our own site SEO, we're going to share our API key with you. Unfortunately, we can't print it directly in this text because there are stipulations that must be followed, so you'll need to go to our site, http://www.wordpartnersink.com and click on Cyber Gold Resources.

If you don't show up in the search results after some time, go back over your keywords with the iwebtool to make sure they are still the **best**, most targeted ones for your pages. Then, in a few months, check yourself on Google Rankings again to see if you've improved.

Remember, time and learning are part of the process. We spent a year working with Shop Lizards before we figured out just which keywords work best for our products. And, getting ranked well simply takes time. The SEO experts will never admit this, but it takes them *just* as long and *just* as much time to optimize your site as it would you. Plus, they have other clients and don't have the intimate knowledge that you do of your site, so they might actually do worse!

So, don't feel discouraged if you have to keep changing your keywords or it takes a while before you show up in the rankings. We have many times, learning more each time what our potential customers are actually searching for. Each time, though, we've improved our ranking and have gotten more visitors and more sales.

So, keep on it, stay positive, and never give up. Getting ranked well in the search engines is as much about persistence as it is anything else!

STEP SIX: At some point, you'll need to think about your site's Page Rank. We go over this in the next chapter…and it has nothing to do with your site itself.

Page Rank can only be manipulated and improved by getting other people to *link* to your site. And, this can mainly be accomplished by having a quality site and content that is keyword relevant and updates often.

HOW TO GET RANKED IN THE SEARCH ENGINES IN 24 HOURS!

You've undoubtedly seen the ads that claim they can get your site ranked in the search engines for your keywords in as little as 24 hours. Most are run by scammers, but there is, surprisingly, some truth and a simple method found at the root of this madness.

Want to know the secret? Authority links. Want to know the method? Quality content on authority websites and article directories, forums, and blogs.

Okay, it's a bit more complicated than that. But it is how you accomplish this feat. Write an article about your website or product and submit it the moment you publish your website to an article directory. This counts as an authority link to your site. Because Google crawls most article directories every few hours looking for new links, your link back to your website from your article will be crawled—within mere hours of your publish! Poof, you just got listed in the search engines, for your keyword, within 24 hours.

This works with popular forums and blogs as well. Now, we never encourage spamming of any sort—so the article can't be mish-mash or crap, it has to be quality content with the proper usage of your keywords and keyword variations, in the proper percentage. However, if you spend the time and do this right, providing quality content in both your article and on your website, you'll have immediate, targeted traffic and be able to convert more visitors into paying customers.

This is the new wave of search engine optimization, and we have to say that it is a little known secret that most gurus would never disclose. Because we've had success with it in the past, and it is becoming such a fascinating and powerful way to gain traffic, we're giving you the ultimate secret to your success. Do it right and that's exactly what you'll find.

We could actually spend an entire book on this strategy, but we did compile a list of about 500 article directories that you can use to begin submitting articles to. You can download it for free on our website, http://www.wordpartnersink.com and click on Cyber Gold Resources.

SEARCH ENGINE OPTIMIZATION CHECKLIST

This checklist is fairly comprehensive and contains elements from several chapters. If you follow each step, you'll be ahead of the search engine optimization pack and have the knowledge to rank for whatever keyword phrase you choose.

- Select the best, most targeted keywords for your website using iwebtool and gorank for possible stem variations, synonyms, and misspellings. Create a list of all possible keywords that you will use.
- Every page should have a creative, well thought-out Title Tag. Each Title Tag should be less than 60 characters and should have your most targeted keyword first. Also, every page Title Tag should contain one of your keywords or keyword variations and should be unique.
- Every page should have a well-written and keyword dense Description Meta Tag. The Description Meta Tag should be less than 200 characters and serve as a mini sales paragraph for your most important keywords and variations.
- Every page should have a complete Keyword Meta Tag. The Keyword Meta Tag should be 200 characters or less and can contain all keyword phrases, variations, stems, misspellings, and synonyms.
- Every picture on every page should do two things: it should link to itself (perhaps in a larger size), or something else (another page in your site), and it should have highly targeted Alt tags. The Alt tags should be 47 characters or less and should differ, getting in your best keyword phrases and variations as often as possible.
- Every page needs an optimized page file extension. For example, id25.html should be renamed to your most targeted keyword for that page, rhinestonedogcollars.html .
- Create a Site Map and a Site Map text file and follow the process in Chapter 8 to submit it to Google.
- You have the required pages needed to please Google as outlined in Chapter 8.
- Publish your website early and submit to DMOZ.org to begin getting crawled.

- Create content rich pages. Each page requires at least 200 words of keyword-rich information.
- Begin building online presence. Submit articles about your products to article directories. Join relevant forums. And, work on finding other websites that will link to you or affiliates that you can use to augment your own information.
- Monitor your traffic daily to make changes as necessary. Watch for keywords that bring visitors in to your website. If your main keyword isn't bringing traffic in, you'll need to review your optimization to ensure it is still the best, most targeted main keyword for your website.

Chapter Eleven
Search Engines Explained.

Unfortunately, getting into the search engines requires more than just optimized keywords. We're going to give you a few secrets here, to show you how to really get their attention.

CONTENT.

Most search engines will only scan the first three hundred words of text of your pages, regarding it as the most important. So, you must get your keywords into that first few hundred words to get the best results.

Also, the more frequent (within human-readable reason) the keywords appear, and the closer they appear to the beginning of the page, the greater the chance of a high search engine rank.

As you've learned, quality content can not only help you rank better and turn more visitors into customers, but can also help get authority sites to link back to you—thus creating even more power for you and your keywords in the search engines. We could actually write an entire book on how to write and structure the content for your website and get your keywords in properly, but we happened upon a great resource that goes over the methods for writing content, strategies, and more. Go to our website, http://www.wordpartnersink.com and click on Cyber Gold Resources to find out more.

5 MISTAKES TO AVOID WHEN IT COMES TO SEARCH ENGINES.

Many newbie webmasters make mistakes. Actually, we all do. It's just part of the biz. But using those mistakes to do better the next time around is what separates the pack. As you probably already know (if not, listen up), most surfers will *only* look at search results on the first two pages. Some won't even click past page one.

Usually, if they don't see what they want in the top ten results, they'll move on. What does that mean for you? Your site must get on the first page to survive on the web.

Most sites show up in the bottom hundred thousand results because of several mistakes that could have been avoided along the way.

So how do you know what mistakes you've made? Well, when it comes to search engines, there are five major mistakes that can spell your success or failure as a new site on the web (and if you're doing these, we suggest you get your act together).

Being visible on the web is the key to being found on the web. And while you'll still need to optimize your pages, avoiding the mistakes below will save you a great deal of pain when you discover you're ranked in the bottom million results.

1. INSUFFICIENT / UNRELATED CONTENT

Every page of your website needs to have about 200-300 words of keyword dense (about 8% is dense) text to rank well. That's like one paragraph. If you sell leather jackets, write a paragraph (you can do it) on the quality of the leather and the hand-sewn lining that makes your jackets so special. Why else would someone buy from you? If they don't understand your product, the search engines won't either.

2. INSUFFICIENT LINK POPULARITY

We've all noticed that Google (among other search engine giants) ranks pages based on what other sites think of your site. In the Google world, this is called Page Rank, and it's hard to figure out and properly fix. Actually, of all the mistakes, this is the hardest one to do anything about because it takes some serious effort on your part.

So what do you do? Go to sites that are related to yours, or that would complement yours in some way and offer to do a link exchange. Spend the time and sign up on every (reputable) search directory that relates to you. Also, write up a few keyword-dense articles about your product or website and submit to article directories. Join relevant forums and use your web address in your signature, and even start a blog that you can use to write about your website and begin a sense of community for your product.

The more often your site is updated with content (good, quality stuff—not gibberish) the more often people will come to you. And if they see what they like, they might *link* to you. Poof! Problem solved.

Ok, it's not that easy. But you can see why this is a hard one.

3. FLASH MOVIES AND IMAGES

Oh, those flash movies are great, aren't they? And how great is it to have that *huge* logo that you handcrafted yourself, and the pic of your cat when he caught a bird...

Unfortunately, web bots cannot read images or flash movies because they contain no actual text. Images, luckily, can be fixed with a little insertion of Alt tags, but flash movies, sadly, have no hope.

If you must have that flash movie that details the entire inception of the Ford Mustang on your site (because you sell Mustangs, of course), put the movie *anywhere else* than the homepage (or make it a download available on the homepage, and not a movie that runs on its own). And make sure that you get those 200-300 words of text to describe the thing.

4. DYNAMIC CONTENT

Ok, there are about a thousand websites out there that will create a "cookie-cutter" site for you to get you going with their inventory (but we won't name names here). It sounds great, yes. Who would turn down a fantastic little site that only costs $39? Or those sites that are completely FREE…

The problem is that those "cookie-cutter" sites are dubbed so for a reason. They were dynamically created. What is dynamically created, you ask? It means that the site was copied from an exact original, and only your name and information has been changed. That's why it's only $39.

But the site looks so great? Here's something else. You can always tell a dynamically created site because it has a ? in the address bar. And a site that has that little ? will get completely ignored by the search engines because the web bots cannot read the ?, let alone get to your "cookie-cutter" content.

5. USING FRAMES

Frames used to be cool because you could get all the content you wanted to float around your site, and your visitor could see everything all at once. Some webmasters still use frames to ensure a uniform appearance to the site.

Unfortunately, the web bots get lost when going through a site with frames. They just get tired of having to work so hard that they'll leave before any of your content has been satisfactorily crawled.

And, if they do happen to crawl some of your content, and you do get listed, that content, when clicked upon, will *not* include your frames. Because web bots only crawl *content*. Your visitor will come to you with no frames to help navigate them along the way. They'll be stuck on the page they came in on and probably leave because they can't figure your site out. That's bad.

So, what do you do? Don't frame your pages.

GETTING THE WEB BOTS TO CRAWL YOUR SITE.

Search engine optimization means that you optimize *all* of your pages, and not just your home page. Many webmasters make the mistake of failing to optimize the internal pages as well.

However, optimizing the homepage for too many keywords is also a mistake.

Every search engine, especially the big guys like Google, Yahoo, and MSN, rank pages, *not* sites. This means that every page has the chance to rank as well as your home page. And, more importantly, other pages can often rank *better* for your keywords and keyword variations than your homepage because of their relevant content.

Basically, every page needs to be treated as if it is your only chance to get into the search engines.

So how do you get every page crawled? You have to make them accessible to the search engines by placing them on your navigation bar. Or, if space is an issue, they'd be fine in the site footer. At the very least, they'd better be on your Site Map.

Most often, the web bot will enter your site from the home page and have a brief look around. But it won't explore much if it finds this task too difficult. Dealing with frames and pages that cannot be accessed from the home page is just too much work for the bots and they'll simply leave. Yep.

They'll leave your site without crawling a thing because it was *too hard*. Lazy little things.

The key is to rank well for each page with a maximum your main keyword phrases and variations. The magic number? The web bots like to read about 200 words (or even 300 words) of text, 8% of that being optimized, meaning 8%, or about 16 words out of the 200 need to directly relate to your keywords.

Those 16 little words had better have their act together though. Remember when we discussed choosing the right keywords and phrases in Chapter 10?

That 8% can spell your fate or your doom in the search engines. Why? Because web bots (however lazy they might seem) are actually quite smart and will read through your text as they scan for appropriate pages to display in a result.

Your page will only come up in a search result if you have tailored your text *to* the search result. No matter how sparkling your meta tags. Again, you scream why…

Ah, because the web bots are smart.

They know that webmasters know the deal on meta tags, because they've been trying to break the rules with them for years. If your meta tags say "dog leashes, dog collars," etc, and your text on that page discusses the value of timeshares in Alaska, then the web bot knows something is up.

So how do you get that 8%?

A little time and a little effort. And you absolutely *must* know your product. You'll need to write up about 200 words about your product anyway, and that's nothing, it's like a medium sized paragraph. So why not talk about the quality of your product and why others simply cannot compete? Why is yours so special?

If you can't answer that question, then you need to ask yourself something else— why should people shop on your site if you don't know your product well enough to talk about it for a paragraph?

See how that works?

By knowing enough about your product, you can write enough about it to please the search engines, and if you can do that, you'll definitely improve your ranking, and probably impress your customers because you seem like an expert on your product (always a plus!).

We even found a free tool that can calculate your keyword percentage as you write it, http://www.live-keyword-analysis.com . You can tweak your content with your keyword stems and variations as well (up to three can be analyzed at once) to truly make your content work for you. And really, that's what this is all about.

Don't spend twenty minutes on two paragraphs of crap that you just threw together. Spend the time to get this right and you'll not only have the process down, but you'll never have to worry about it. Your content can make or break your sales, can encourage authority sites to link to you, and can even get you ranking well in the search engines. Don't waste this valuable opportunity by rushing. Instead, take your time, get your keywords in while providing something worthwhile about your product, and your content will work for you instead of against you.

WRITING CONTENT FOR YOUR WEBSITE.

When writing your content, it's easiest to think in terms of what your customers might like to know about your product or services. You need to understand how people are searching for what you are selling, be it cups, cat food, or car tires. What are they looking for? What questions are they asking before they make a purchase?

These are just a few of those internal questions you must ask yourself before writing your content.

You can begin with how you would search for your product. Would you just type in "rhinestone dog collars?" Or would you search for "dog collars with sparkly things," or even "fancy dog collars?" It's always going to be a bit hit and miss on this, but if you understand that people think like *people* when they search for things, then you'll have a better shot at singling out your best keywords for your content.

You should already have a fairly good idea about your best keywords if you've spent time with the iwebtool and the gorank ontology tool, but even with that research under your belt, you might find that you come up with more specific or more detailed keywords by thinking like your potential customer.

Also, people, and web bots, also like to see new content when they search through websites. Finding what seems like a great site, only to find out that the content hasn't been updated since March of 1998 is like a blow to the head.

How can you trust them if they haven't added anything new to their site in more than nine years? Are they even still online? Are they still in business?

Would you even buy from them knowing that they probably haven't checked their email in nine years either? No. Definitely not. Ok, so this is a bit extreme. But it doesn't look good if new content *never* shows itself on your site.

The answer? Start a little blog about your product. Tripod has the easiest blog builder around, and even Google isn't a slouch, (http://www.blogger.com) and blogs of all sorts can be easily linked to your site.

So, you get a blog. What do you do with it?

Well, for this to improve your ranking, you need to update your blog, article, webpage (whatever), with 200 words of new information. Yes, there's that magic 200 again. 200 words is equal to about 1000 characters, which is about 1KB (or 1000 bytes) of information. The web bots find this much information to be legitimate "Fresh Content."

You see, web bots actually have a lot of work to do. They have to crawl the web day in and day out, obediently retrieving millions of search results a second. But they know their job is difficult and thus have two types of crawls that they make: a **quick crawl**, and a **deep crawl**.

The quick crawl happens about every 11-28 days (depending on the search engine) and takes a super fast inventory of your home page, and if on the navigation bar or the site map, the other content rich pages.

A deep crawl is much more extensive and means that the web bot will hang around for a while, reading your text, checking out your products, and looking for new things. As you can imagine, with easily several billion websites out there, this deep crawl takes some time and will only happen once every few months or so.

In the time between the quick crawl and the deep crawl, the search engines will list a "cached" version of your page.

> This is G o o g l e's cache of http://www.shoplizards.com/ as retrieved on Nov 22, 2007 15:47:43 GMT.
> G o o g l e's cache is the snapshot that we took of the page as we crawled the web.
> The page may have changed since that time. Click here for the current page without highlighting.
> This cached page may reference images which are no longer available. Click here for the cached text only.
> To link to or bookmark this page, use the following url: http://www.google.com/search?
> q=cache:voPB1CE0WEIJ:www.shoplizards.com/+site:shoplizards.com&hl=en&ct=clnk&cd=1&gl=us
>
> *Google is neither affiliated with the authors of this page nor responsible for its content.*

We found our own cached page, simply by typing our domain name (without the www part) and selecting "cached" below our site in the search results, and the above Google disclaimer was at the top. Note too, that Google avoids any responsibility for changes that have been made to the site since, including pictures that may have been removed.

Luckily, Google has updated its cache of our site quite recently (it's December 2007 at the time of writing this second edition). If it said something like October 2005, we'd know that there was a problem and that we haven't attracted Google's deep crawl, let alone a frequent quick crawl.

Remember that web bots, as well as people, like fresh content.

If your page has not been updated since the last "cached" version, the deep crawl will not take place because the web bot sees no reason to return and update its cache. Why check you out if you have nothing new to offer?

So, fresh content is essential to your success as a new site. If the web bots see that you update fairly frequently (say, once a month, nothing excessive here), they'll get excited and return often to see if you have updated again.

Customers are the same way. Would you return to your favorite site (we all have a favorite site) if they never updated their content? No. Would you if they updated their content all the time? Yes.

Even if you sell fishing lures, find a reason to add fresh content to your site. The more you grow as a site, the more the web bots will return, and with them—customers.

And, face it; customers are the only reason that you made a site in the first place, right? Again, we know this can be tricky to master, but we have found a solution for you that we actually use ourselves and it can be found on our website, http://www.wordpartnersink.com and click on Cyber Gold Resources.

PUTTING OTHER PEOPLE'S CONTENT ONTO YOUR SITE.

Okay, so you've tried your best but you just can't write 200 words a month about your product. That's fine. There's a little world on the web known as "sites with free content for webmasters." Some are junk, but many have little RSS (Real Simple Syndication) links that you can place on your site and poof! Content that updates on its own, all the time. You can even select quality articles from article directories or find affiliate content relating to your products.

You'll find that there are hundreds of websites with free content for webmasters, including articles, games, and even fresh daily content. The free content can be tailored to your site easily.

The moral of the story: whatever you have to do to get new content on your site, do it. The more often the better.

If a web bot has no reason to return to your site to check on new content, neither will your visitors.

GETTING PEOPLE TO LINK TO YOUR SITE.

Our sites have been around forever and we are still learning what needs to be done to maximize our listing in the search engines and obtain that oh-so coveted Page Rank of 5 or more.

The trick? Quality links to your site from other quality sites. This is called "external linking." This technique goes back to the good old days of "we'll put a link on your site if you put a link on yours!"

Things are not so simple now, but if you can get quality links to your site, your Page Rank will go up. The more links, the higher the Page Rank, and the higher your listing in the search engines.

Google is the biggest stickler for Page Rank, though the other giants are catching up fast. You can even download a handy Google Toolbar that tells you the Page Rank of every site you visit while you peruse their pages.

The toolbar can be found at: http://toolbar.google.com

Page Rank is generally defined as not only the amount of other sites that link to your site, but also the quality of the sites linking to your site.

The more sites, and the higher the quality, the higher your Page Rank score. You'll get a score between 0-10, 10 being the highest. Many of the major sites like MSN and eBay only have a Page Rank score of 8. And, that 10, that ultimate Page Rank of 10, is actually so rarely found that of all the sites we searched, only Google itself had a 10 (ha ha!).

So, what does this mean for you?

Well, Page Rank is essential to your site's success on the web. As a fledgling site, and even for those busier sites, a Page Rank of 2-5 is primo. A 3 is great and Google will reward you for your efforts.

Anything above a 5 and you'll be barking with the biggest dogs on the web. As great as that sounds, anything above a 5 is for the big dogs for a very simple reason. MSN has an 8 because millions of people have hotmail and have it in the "Favorites," and probably hundreds of thousands of those people probably link to MSN for a variety of reasons, for their news, their pictures, their shopping, etc.

But don't let that discourage you. You can achieve a Page Rank of 2-6 by getting less than ten (the exact number here is debatable) reputable sites to link to your website. Keep in mind, here, that ten different articles on ten different article directories can accomplish this for you with little hassle. That's how important this strategy is.

Now, reputable means that they too have a good Page Rank, that they don't have a link farm, and that they do well themselves in the search engines. Reputable also extends to mean that they relate to your site in some way. Getting a porn site to link to your fly fishing site will not increase your Page Rank.

Basically, the more reputable sites that link to you, the better your Page Rank.

AVOIDING THE STINKY LINK FARM.

Often, getting people to link to your site means that they require a reciprocal link to their site. A reciprocal link is a link that you place on your site to their site once that site places a link to you on theirs. Now, this can be fine. To an extent.

A **link farm** is basically a Page Rank attempt that went horribly wrong. It's a page, or site, dedicated to many, many, many links that are unrelated and clearly only placed, and marketed, for blatant self-promotion.

Putting more than 10 links on a page is bad. Especially if those links have nothing to do with each other. Why is it bad? Well, the web bots already have a lot of work to do, and if they come to your site and see a clump of weird sites, not only will they panic, but they might just list you as spam. That's right. Spam.

You'll become one of the internet's hated and you will probably get black listed from the search engines until you fix your wild ways.

Let's digress a moment while we share with you a terrible secret from our past. Shop Lizards was once a link farm (gasp!). Yes. We joined the Link Share (http://www.linkshare.com) affiliate program and got a bit *enthusiastic* when signing up with the companies.

Actually, we got so enthusiastic that we signed up with over three hundred companies and put *all* of their banners on one page (alphabetically and by category, of course).

Little did we know that those seventy hours were so wasted that we might as well have been out partying. But once we learned of our huge and very detrimental problem, we took down the page and everything returned to normal.

This isn't to say that affiliates are a bad thing! Not at all. But use them in moderation. Maybe just put an Office Max and a Staples together on one page. But no more than ten per page. Ever.

And never, ever, link to affiliates that are your competition. Nothing is worse than giving qualified visitors over to your competition.

HOW SEARCH ENGINES AND DIRECTORIES WORK.

Search engines were designed to seek out websites on their own. That is their whole purpose, their job. The big ones, like Google, Yahoo, and MSN, are no longer run by the people who created them. Search engines are self-sustaining and do their own work all by themselves.

That means that they are constantly finding and adding new sites to their listings, because that is their job.

"Submitting" your site does not mean that you are adding it to their listing. All submitting does is add you to their list of new sites to crawl, of which yours would already be on the list because you have published your site.

If you are an older site, you may not be in the search engine listings yet, because you are not targeted to any specific (or the right) term. Or, you may still be part of the Google "sandbox." The sandbox is the place where Google puts all of the new sites, before they crawl them.

There is a set time period for these sites in the sandbox, because Google is giving them the chance to get things right before they throw them out in the big world. If you have everything right, you may only stay in the sandbox for a few weeks (or less) instead of several months…because Google rewards the sites that do well—even less if you've followed our strategies.

To be found in the search engines, by typing in a search term, you have to do a few things to your site that will help the web bots to better categorize you. That's the problem. Not that you haven't been submitted. So, don't let all of the ads and emails get you confused.

A study was done about a year ago that said that Google will crawl over four hundred billion sites by the year 2007. There are only six billion people on the planet…so you do the math and consider how many sites that is.

The search engines are very busy, but they also want to do the best job possible so that they can be the best search engine possible. They aren't going to skip your site out of spite, or forgetfulness. They are designed to crawl every site ever made, and it just takes time to get to them all. But know that just publishing your site will get you on the list to crawl.

If the bots can't decide which search terms you want to be your "keywords," then how can they possibly rank you for the keywords that you thought you'd get ranked for? They can't, so they wont rank you…not until you get your act figured out.

Once you decide which keywords your site was designed for, then you can SEO your site, and the search engines will soon crawl you again, and rank you for the keywords that you have now targeted your site for. It's not rocket science; it just takes a little research, which you should now know how to do.

THE TRUTH ABOUT SEARCH ENGINE SUBMISSION.

There are tons of companies out there that say they'll submit your site to 500 (or more) search engines and directories. By now, you should know that line is absolute crap. Please don't waste your time and money doing so. You already know that the only real search engines that even matter are the top three: Google, Yahoo, and MSN. And all of the other search engines get their "searches" from the top three.

We'll be bold and just say it: we know how to get you ranked in Google, Yahoo, and MSN, and we're going to tell you how to do it too, right now…**Each page on your site must have content that is targeted to a *specific* keyword phrase, or you just won't rank.** It's that simple.

Once you get your keyword phrases and variations figured out and optimize your site, you will be listed in the search engines. Period. It's how they work.

And it isn't all that hard to do; it just takes time and detailed research, which, by now, you should know how to do. And, once you get listed in the search engines, you stay there. Over time, your ranking only improves—especially when you're doing things right.

Did you know that it takes more than a month (sometimes up to a year) for the search engines to find you and crawl your site on their own? Even if you resubmit every single day…it would still take a month (or more) for them to crawl you. **They crawl you when they decide to crawl you, and they index you into their listing only when you've gotten things right.** You will have wasted all that time (and money) resubmitting to search engines that will be ignoring you until you get things right. Scary, huh?

But you now know how to get your website crawled much faster. Not only that, but you now know how to keep them coming back and re-crawling your site. Amazing, isn't it?

You have to understand that we've spent years learning these techniques and gathering information. It's hard to digest it all in one take, but you have just been given a very special gift. Millions of websites are published every day, probably even millions by the hour. But, and we can almost guarantee this, probably less than one percent of them were published with any idea of how to rank, how to select the best keyword phrases and variations, how to craft their content properly, or how to get quick and continual traffic by providing that content to article directories.

You now know everything you need to not only properly optimize your website for the search engines, but also to get traffic and authority sites linking to yours without hassle. You can bypass the Google sandbox, the hype, and the drama and stress by doing things right, taking your time, and most importantly, thinking like your customer.

SEARCH ENGINE SUBMISSION.

Okay, there is one directory (not a search engine) that you do physically need to submit your website to called the Open Directory Project, aka, DMOZ (Directory Mozilla), http://www.dmoz.org . They're free and will only take two minutes of your time. The reason we suggest submission with DMOZ is because they, as you'll read a bit later, provide the content for all of the major search engines, Google included.

Your site would eventually get listed with DMOZ, but it's something that could take up to a year and we are giving you the accelerated way to get into the search engines and ranking for your keyword—as fast as possible. And completing this step is just one more thing that can help you rank all that much faster.

When you're ready to submit with them—some point between initial publish and completed website will work—you'll need your perfected Title Tag, Description, and potential category for your website (you'll choose this by searching through DMOZ before you submit your site for a category). They're very straight-forward, so just follow the instructions to submit your website.

THE TOP SEARCH ENGINES.

These are the top search engines in alphabetical order (we only list one directory on this list, because all of the others get their search results from it):

ASK (responsible for almost all of their own search results, they also feed other smaller engines with their results like MyWay, Lycos, Excite, and HotBot)

AOL (gets all of its results from Google...though it manipulates the results so it looks like they do the work)

DOGPILE (gets all of its results from Google, Yahoo, MSN, and Ask)

DMOZ (No one searches on DMOZ, but DMOZ is responsible for feeding their results to Google, Yahoo, MSN, and anyone who feeds off of them like other directories)

EARTHLINK (gets all of its results from Google)

GOOGLE (responsible for almost all of their own search results, though they use DMOZ a bit)

IWON (gets all of its results from Ask)

MSN (responsible for nearly all of their own search results, though they rely on DMOZ a bit)

MYWAY (gets all of its results from Ask...though it manipulates the results so it looks like they do the work)

NETSCAPE (gets all of its results from Google and DMOZ...though it manipulates the results so it looks like they do the work)

YAHOO (responsible for nearly all of their own search results, though they rely on DMOZ a bit)

So...really the only search engines and directories that matter (in order of importance, this time) are:

- Google
- Yahoo
- MSN
- DMOZ
- Ask

That's it. **There are no other search engines that matter because all of the others get their results from these top five.**

Do your own research if you don't believe us. Seriously, if five hundred (or a thousand!) search engines sprang up out of nowhere and actually got more visitors or results than Google, wouldn't more people use them?

Without people to search the search engines, the search engines literally don't exist. And you want your site to be found. If you get in the top four search engines and the top directory, don't you think your site will be found?

Yes.

So, get your keywords figured out, get them into the content on your site, make sure you have the required pages on your site, update your content on a regular basis, follow the strategies we've given you, and then sit back and relax. That's all you have to do to do well in the search engines.

Chapter Twelve
HTML Primer.

Ready for a little course on HTML? Well here goes…

HTML is not as difficult as it may sound, or even look. **The basic rule of thumb to keep in mind is that all things must match.**

Oh, and because it would be a pain to type all of these codes out yourself, we've added them to our site at http://www.wordpartnersink.com and click on HTML Codes.

THE BASICS.

HTML is really quite easy once you get the hang of things. Here are a few of the most common codes you'd need, with their explanations **bolded** to the right:

Code	Explanation
<b> </b>	**bold**
<i> </i>	**italics**
<u> </u>	**underline**
<p>	**new paragraph**
 	carriage return (same as a new paragraph)
<hr>	**draws a line across the screen to separate things, like you'll see when we write out bits of code for you**

To insert a link, you'd use this (where "Click here" is your link):

<A HREF="http://www.mysite.com">Click here</A>

TO GET THIS: USE THIS:

Animal   <b>Animal</b>
Animal   <i>Animal</i>
<u>Animal</u>   <u>Animal</u>

For example, if you want to bold something,

animal

it will need a beginning bold, **** and an ending bold, **** so animal bolded looks like this in HTML…

animal

In regular text,

animal

Notice that the **b** is within two brackets?

and

That's how HTML works. **Make sure that you get all of the brackets right and your code will work.** If it doesn't, check your brackets and make sure that every bit of code always has a beginning, **<>** and an ending, **</>**

Most often, the brackets are to blame.

Every aspect of HTML works this way, though to varying degrees of difficulty.

LINK TAGS.

External links work by linking another website to your own (like with reciprocal linking). Internal links will jump to a page within your own website. Anchor tags will link to another spot within the same page, or within a different page, on your site. And, email links will link directly to your email address.

We use anchor tags almost religiously, you'll see them on all of our Shop Lizards pages because they work so well to display a lot of information, and provide a handy link to it all.

Now, in HTML, quotes are just as important as the brackets in regards to your code actually working.

For every

<A HREF>

or

<A NAME>

you'll need to make sure that you have an ending

</A>

to make the code work. And, notice where the quotes are in the examples below, because they are needed for the computer to recognize that you are making a link.

TO GET THIS: USE THIS:

External Link	<A HREF="http://www.msn.com">Go to MSN</A>
Internal Link	<A HREF="#cube">Nintendo Game Cube Games</A>
Anchor Tag	<A NAME="parttwo">Go To Part Two</A>
Email Link	<A HREF="mailto:shoplizards@yahoo.com">Email Us</A>

INSERT AN IMAGE.

Because Tripod is so helpful, adding in most all HTML for you, you may never actually need to insert an image with HTML; but we have, so it's worth a mention here. In fact, you may want to insert an image on your blog or even on the more advanced pages of eBay, for example. To do so, you'll need a bit of HTML:

<IMG SRC="http://www.tripod.com/image.jpg"/>

With the insert image tag, you do not have an ending tag and it is the only HTML code like this, so it makes things a bit confusing. The most important thing to keep track of, then, is the / and quotes that surround your image location.

How this code works: if we wanted to link to our Shop Lizards logo from our Google blog, we'd need to have the picture stored somewhere online where it could be accessed directly by a web address. Luckily, the Tripod Picture Gallery works just this way. So, we upload our logo to Tripod, get the exact file extension (the hardest part) and insert it into our blog using HTML. Very easy.

Now, Tripod actually just updated their homepage, so getting the image file extension from the Picture Gallery is even easier than it was before. Log in to your account and click on **File Manager** on the top, light blue, toolbar. You'll be taken to your website directory.

To find the exact image location, the easiest thing to do is to scroll down through the file list and click:

Sitebuildercontent→Sitebuilderpictures→click on the name of your image

Because the purpose of this is to get the exact file location, you can either copy the web address from the window that pops up or, follow the directory path as you go:

Directory: http://shoplizards.tripod.com/sitebuildercontent/sitebuilderpictures/

So, this is how we'd link to our Shop Lizards logo:

<IMG SRC="http://shoplizards.tripod.com/sitebuildercontent/sitebuilderpictures/shoplizardslogonew.gif"/>

sitebuildercontent is where the information is stored in our directory
sitebuilderpictures is where all of our images are kept
shoplizardslogonew.gif is the name of our image

You can also specify **size**, **alignment**, and add **alt tags** like this:

<IMG SRC="http://shoplizards.tripod.com/sitebuildercontent/sitebuilderpictures/shoplizardslogonew.gif" width="753" height="269" alt="shopping, shop online" align="center"/>

For image width and height, we used the exact pixels of our logo. To do this, you'll need to open up your picture in your photoshop program and click on Image Properties to get this number. You can play around with the numbers in the code a bit to change the size of your image, but it's best to stick with the image's actual size, and if it needs to be changed, change the image itself in your photoshop program, then upload to Tripod's Picture Gallery and start again.

Alt tags (utterly important, as you know) are best kept at under 47 characters, and, as always, try to make them as targeted to the image as possible. Ours (shopping, shop online) are extremely poor examples.

Finally, the image alignment can be either "center," "left," or "right." If you don't enter in this value, most often the internet will center it for you, but there's no guarantee.

To make this code work without problems, the only thing to keep in mind is the placement of your quotes. If one quote is off the image will either display crazy or not display at all. Other than that, this code is simple as can be.

ANCHOR TAGS.

You won't find a code for an anchor tag that links to an item on a different page on the internet, so we re-wrote the anchor code a bit so that it works. Say that you need a page of text links that will link to items on a different page. This is how you would do it:

On the list page, for example, on your Xbox page where you'll list all the items, but won't actually have the items, you'll need to place an anchor into the title of the item, for example,

for Turok Evolution:

<A HREF="http://www.shoplizards.com/xboxgames.html#turokevolution">Turok Evolution</A>

The file extension, **xboxgames.html** comes from the page that all the items are listed on. Since we had optimized this page first, you know we changed the file extension to an important keyword. So, make sure that you get the file extension right.

Then, on the page where the items will be, **xboxgames.html**, you'd do this:

<A NAME="turokevolution">Turok Evolution</A>

Notice the placement of the:

#

The number sign makes sure the computer knows to go to **#turokevolution** and not some other website that sells Turok Evolution.

Note that you'll do all of this under the **Add Text** box in Tripod, clicking the **Edit HTML** button to actually add in the HTML. Then, you'd click the **Hide HTML** button to see what that HTML looks like. It should now look like regular text, but your new link should now appear as underlined, if you've done it right.

But, this is just for one link. If you want a bunch of anchor links on one page, that go to another page, like we wanted, without a list format, you'll need to do it as a **Site Add-On** and select **Add HTML**.

Now, if you want to create a box full of anchor tags, that link to another page, here is the code that we rewrote:

```
<FORM>
<SELECT WIDTH="20" onChange="JumpToIt(this)">
<OPTION VALUE="None"> Game Gallery
<OPTION VALUE="http://www.shoplizards.com/gamecubegames.html"> Nintendo Game Cube
<OPTION VALUE="http://www.shoplizards.com/playstation2games.html"> Playstation 2
<OPTION VALUE="http://www.shoplizards.com/xboxgames.html"> XBOX

</SELECT>
<SCRIPT LANGUAGE="JavaScript" TYPE="text/javascript">
<!--
function JumpToIt(list)
{
var selection = list.options[list.selectedIndex].value
if (selection != "None")
location.href = selection
}
//-->
</SCRIPT>
</FORM>
```

Use the entire code, from **<FORM>** to **</FORM>** and note the spacing and strange characters. As with all HTML code, copy it *exactly* as shown, then make your changes as necessary.

This is how the Anchor code looks on the page:

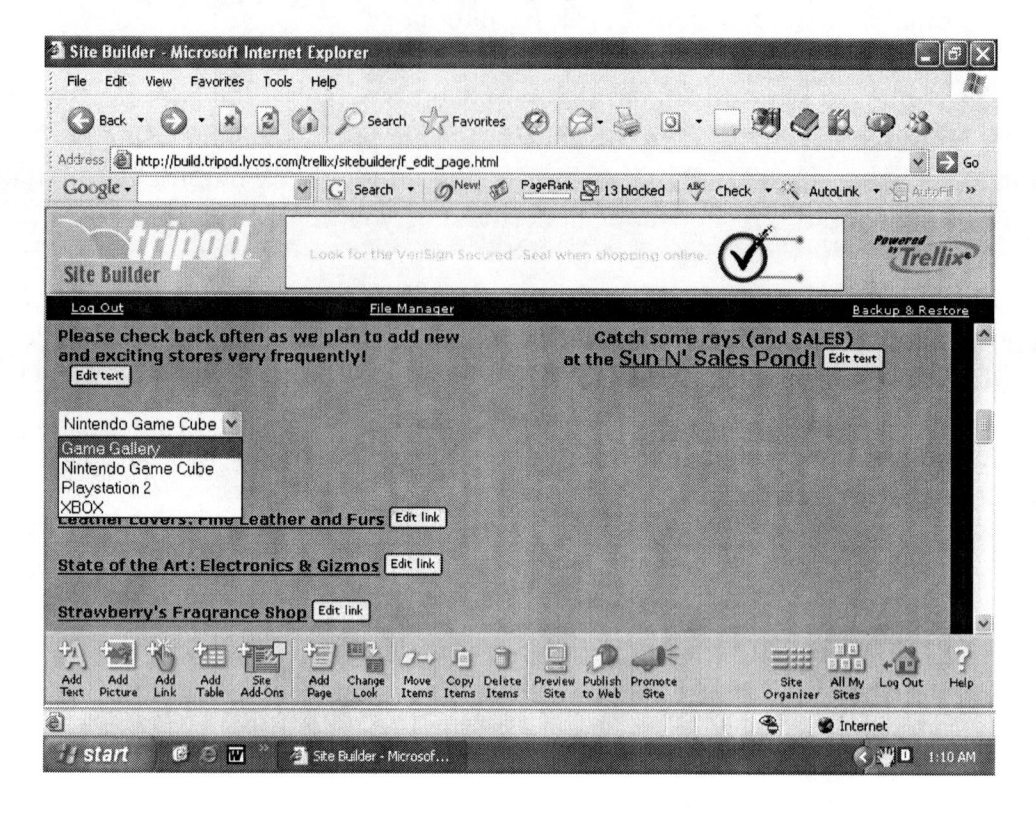

[Screenshot of Site Builder in Microsoft Internet Explorer showing the Tripod Site Builder interface with a dropdown menu open displaying "Game Gallery, Nintendo Game Cube, Playstation 2, XBOX" options]

Notice the white box open in the picture above. It can be as long or short as you need, and expands automatically depending on how many links you add inside.

This code will work without a corresponding anchor tag as long as you get your **file extensions** spelled right. Make sure that you double-check the extension in the Site Organizer.

A WORD OF CAUTION...

in the Site Builder, you *cannot* test this anchor tag box until you publish. If you do, Tripod goes a little crazy. So, to test this anchor box, you'll need to first publish the site. Then it works great. When you're done checking all your links, you can get right back to editing your site again by clicking **Edit Your Site**.

For every bit of code like this that you create, you should always take the time and go through each, checking every link to make sure they work. If just one is wrong, and it's the one a visitor clicks on, they may never return to your site because you had that one mistake and they got lost.

So, as in everything, check your work!

ANCHOR TAGS THAT LINK TO SOMETHING ON THE SAME PAGE.

We tend to do this sometimes, and surely you've seen it on the web before. Basically, it's a tag that links to another part of the same page. For example, say you have a longish essay on your site and you want readers to be able to link to other sections (like a Table of Contents) without scrolling through the whole thing to get to the section they want to read.

In the top, where you're giving readers the option to skip down like a Table of Contents, you'd do this (in the Add Text editor of Tripod, and click Edit HTML):

<A HREF="#partone">Go to Part One</A>

When you click back to regular text view, the **Go to Part One** text will appear as underlined, like this:

Go to Part One

The **#partone** in the code automatically sets the anchor to what you will be adding next…

Then, where Part One actually begins (put it in the text), you'd do this:

<A NAME="partone">Part One</A>

It's a very simple way to create links for your visitors, and is perhaps the easiest code to implement and check. Note that the most important part of this code is the "name" that you choose to make as the link. If we were going to have a Part Two link and a Part Three, and so on, that name would need to change for each one. So, Part Two's "name" would be #parttwo

And Part Three's "name" would be #partthree

And so on…Just make sure that you get them in the right order as you create the section where it will link to.

And, as always, check your links to make sure they all work, and make sure they all link to where you intended once you publish.

BACK TO TOP LINK.

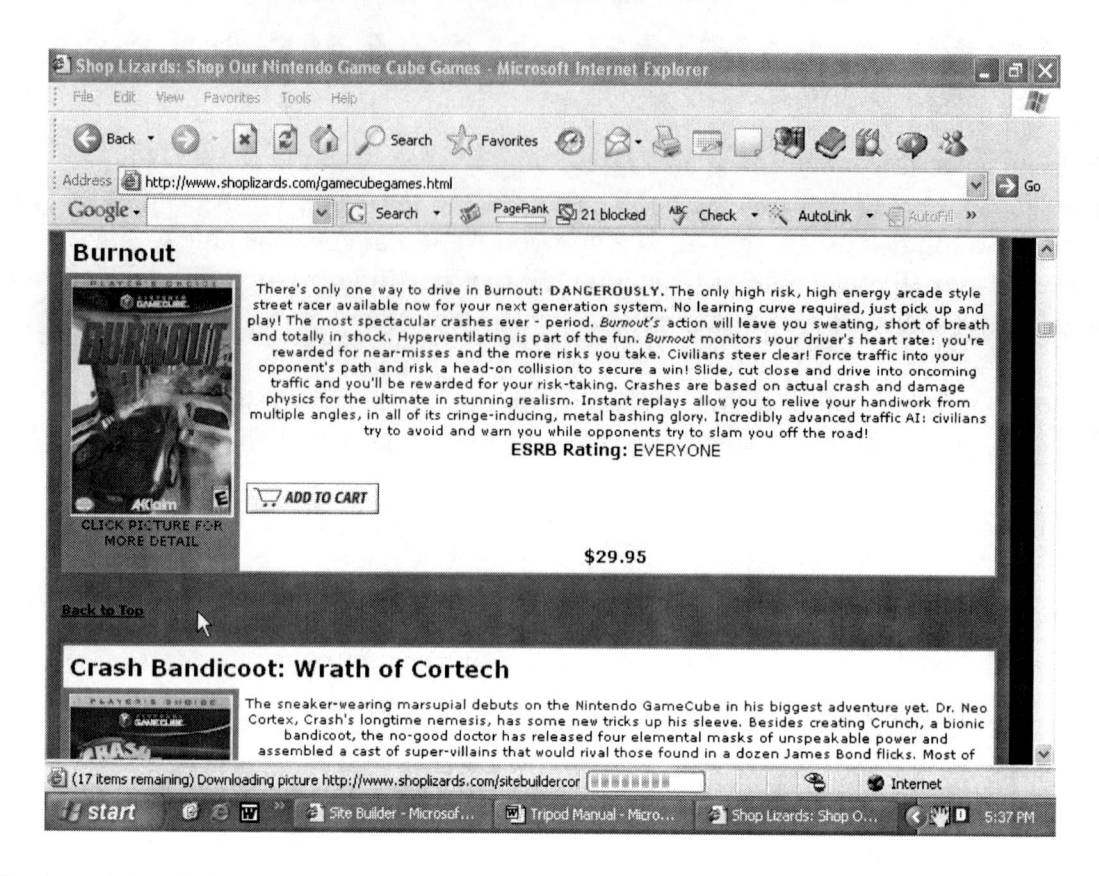

Back to Top links are great because if you have a long page, your visitor can click the link and be taken right back up to the top without scrolling. In the picture above, you can see our Back To Top links between each item we have for sale, simply because it helps visitors get around our long pages faster.

The easiest way to create a Back To Top link is to **Add Text** in Tripod, and click on **Edit HTML**, to get the code right.

Your text should look like this in the Edit HTML view:
<A HREF="#top">Back To Top</A>

When you click back to regular text view, the Back To Top text will appear as underlined, like this:

Back To Top

Basically, a Back To Top link is just an anchor tag. The **#top** in the code automatically sets the anchor at the top of every page.

We've found that when making really long pages, using these Back To Top links really helps to keep us on track, and provides that little something extra to make surfing our site easier for customers.

Actually, on all of our long pages, you'll find Back To Top links, spaced between every item. To make more, just use the copy function in Tripod. And, Back To Top links can be used while you edit, so you don't have to keep scrolling back up to the top of the page!

DROP-DOWN LIST ON THE SAME PAGE.

This works just like the previous code, except that it only functions on the *same* page. We use this code on literally every Shop Lizards page.

Here's the code we used for a bit on our affiliates page:

ANCHOR TAG CODE / SAME PAGE:

```
<FORM>
<SELECT WIDTH="20" onChange="JumpToIt(this)">
<OPTION VALUE="None"> Select a Store
<OPTION VALUE="#favoritesuperstores">FAVORITE SUPERSTORES
<OPTION VALUE="#applestore9">Apple Store
<OPTION VALUE="#asseenontv">As Seen On Tv
<OPTION VALUE="#thrifty2">Thrifty Car Rental
<OPTION VALUE="#veteransadvantage">Veteran's Advantage

</SELECT>
<SCRIPT LANGUAGE="JavaScript" TYPE="text/javascript">
<!--
function JumpToIt(list)
{
var selection = list.options[list.selectedIndex].value
if (selection != "None")
location.href = selection
}
//-->
```

</SCRIPT>

</FORM>

The entire code is needed, from **<FORM>** to **</FORM>** but you can add more **OPTION VALUE** lines to make it as long as you need. To use this code, notice what we put in each **<OPTION VALUE="">**

For example,

<OPTION VALUE="#asseenontv">As Seen On Tv

where As Seen On Tv is the name of our store and #asseenontv is the anchor tag.

In the

<OPTION VALUE="None">Select A Store

it says **none** because people cannot actually click on Select A Store. All of the others work, if they have the # in front.

Now, to actually make this code work, though, there's a second step. Since we have:

<OPTION VALUE="#favoritesuperstores">FAVORITE SUPERSTORES

we'll need to add an anchor tag where FAVORITE SUPERSTORES will link to. And it will look exactly like this in HTML (from the Add Text screen, Edit HTML):

<A NAME="favoritesuperstores">Favorite Superstores</A>

Make sure that you put this HTML where you want the anchor link to jump to.

Chapter Twelve: HTML Primer 315

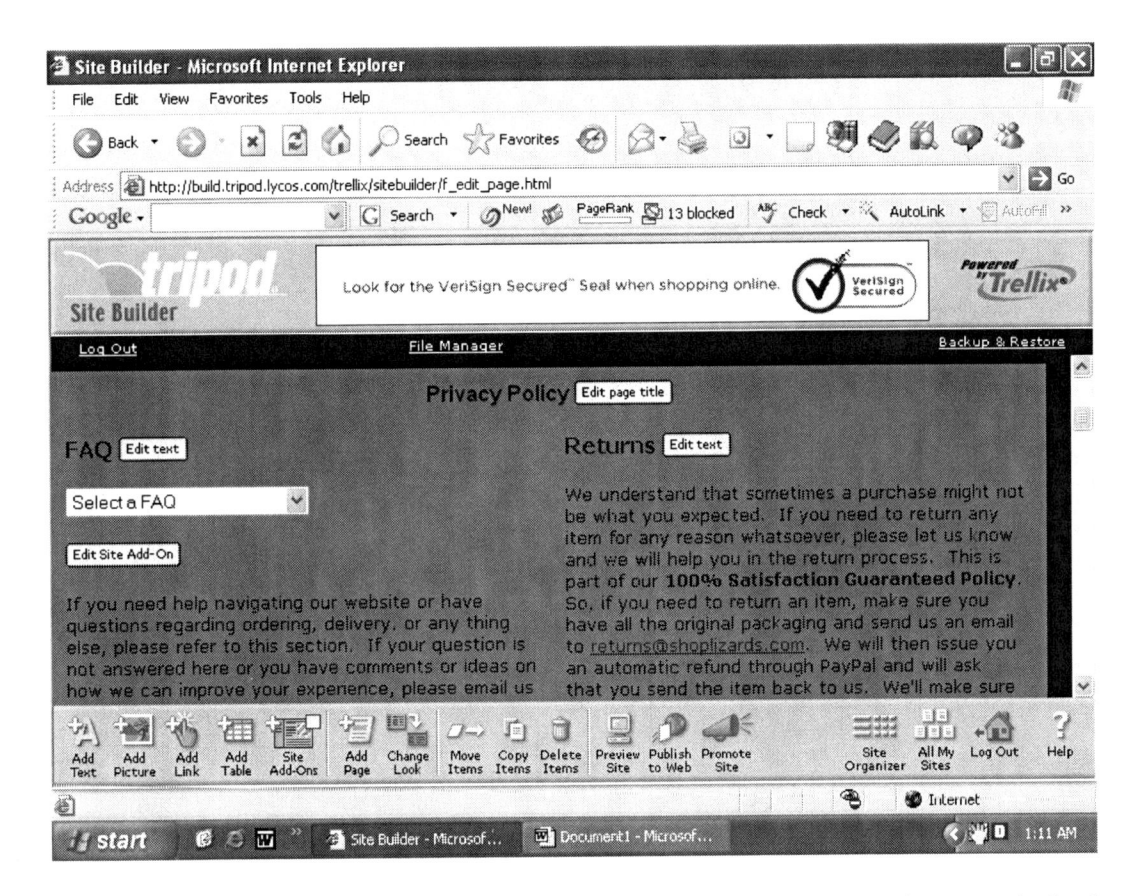

In the picture above, the white box below FAQ is what this drop-down code looks like on the page. The text, **Returns**, on the right hand side of the page is an anchor from that drop-down list.

Make sure that there are no spaces in the code, and that you spell it exactly the same way in both tags. If your code doesn't work, this would be the problem, or the <> parts may be wrong or missing.

Also make sure that you add the corresponding link for every anchor you place in the code, then publish to check all of the links to make sure they work.

CALENDAR CODE.

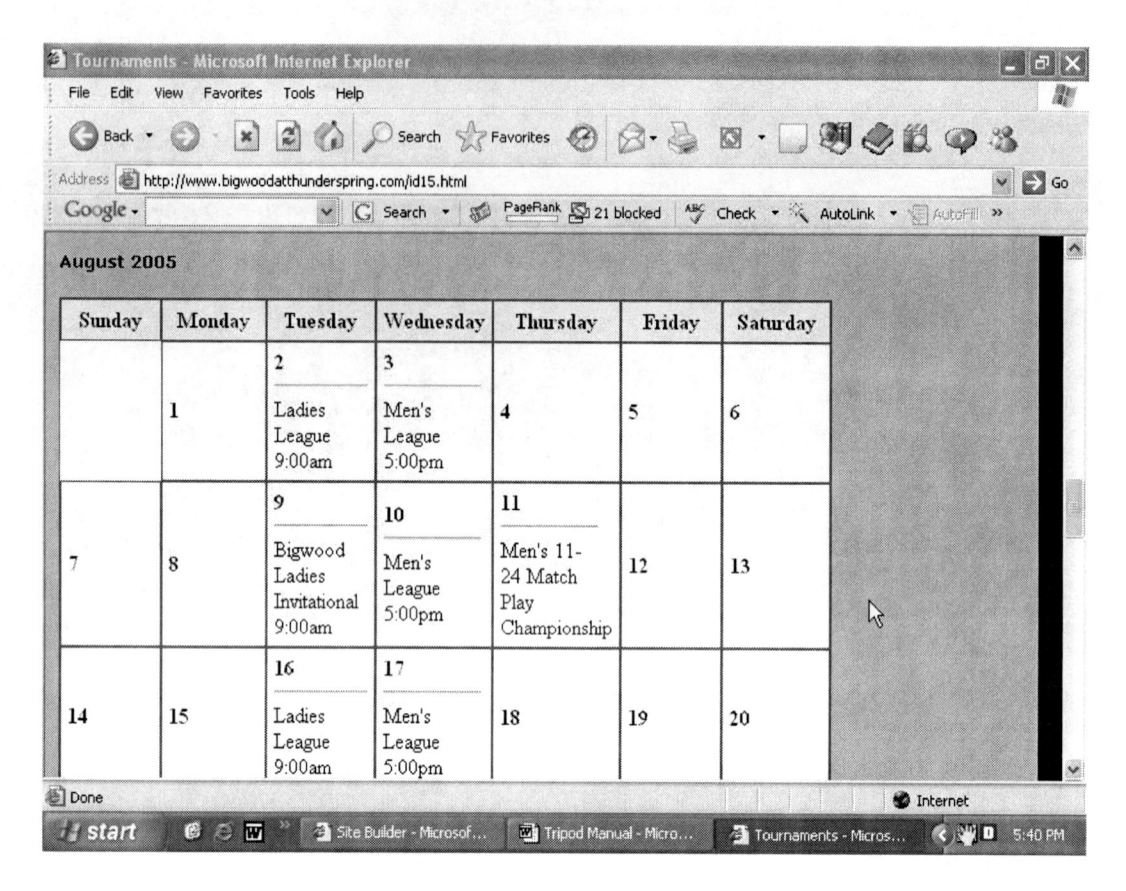

We also found a great code for making a calendar, which we used on Bigwood at Thunder Spring's website (http://bigwoodgolfcourse.tripod.com), under the Tournament section. Notice the column form of the HTML, this makes it easier to read and easier to find mistakes in.

This is the calendar code:

```
<table bgcolor="#ffffff" width="80%" border="1" cellspacing="0"
cellpadding="5" bordercolor="#006600">
<tr><td bgcolor="#ccffcc" align="center">
<b>Sunday</b></td>
<td bgcolor="#ccffcc" align="center">
<b>Monday</b></td>
<td bgcolor="#ccffcc" align="center">
<b>Tuesday</b></td>
<td bgcolor="#ccffcc" align="center">
<b>Wednesday</b></td>
<td bgcolor="#ccffcc" align="center">
```

```html
<b>Thursday</b></td>
<td bgcolor="#ccffcc" align="center">
<b>Friday</b></td>
<td bgcolor="#ccffcc" align="center">
<b>Saturday</b></td>
</tr><tr>
<td width="75" height="60">
<b></b></td>
<td width="75" height="60">
<b></b></td>
<td width="75" height="60">
<b></b></td>
<td width="75" height="60">
<b></b></td>
<td width="75" height="60">
<b></b></td>
<td width="75" height="60">
<b>1</b></td>
<td width="75" height="60">
<b>2</b></td>
</tr><tr>
<td width="75" height="60">
<b>3</b></td>
<td width="75" height="60">
<b>4</b></td>
<td width="75" height="60">
<b>5</b><hr>Ladies League 9:00am</td>
<td width="75" height="60">
<b>6</b><hr>Men's League 5:00pm</td>
<td width="75" height="60">
<b>7</b></td>
<td width="75" height="60">
<b>8</b></td>
<td width="75" height="60">
<b>9</b></td>
</tr><tr>
<td width="75" height="60">
<b>10</b></td>
<td width="75" height="60">
<b>11</b></td>
<td width="75" height="60">
<b>12</b><hr>Ladies League 9:00am</td>
<td width="75" height="60">
```

```
            <b>13</b><hr>Men's League 5:00pm</td>
            <td width="75" height="60">
            <b>14</b></td>
            <td width="75" height="60">
            <b>15</b></td>
            <td width="75" height="60">
            <b>16</b></td>
            </tr><tr>
            <td width="75" height="60">
            <b>17</b></td>
            <td width="75" height="60">
            <b>18</b></td>
            <td width="75" height="60">
            <b>19</b><hr>Ladies League 9:00am</td>
            <td width="75" height="60">
            <b>20</b><hr>Men's League 5:00pm</td>
            <td width="75" height="60">
            <b>21</b></td>
            <td width="75" height="60">
            <b>22</b></td>
            <td width="75" height="60">
            <b>23</b><hr>Wine Auction Picnic</td>
            </tr><tr>
            <td width="75" height="60">
            <b>24</b></td>
            <td width="75" height="60">
            <b>25</b><hr>Potluck 4:00pm</td>
            <td width="75" height="60">
            <b>26</b><hr>Ladies League 9:00am</td>
            <td width="75" height="60">
            <b>27</b><hr>Men's League 5:00pm</td>
            <td width="75" height="60">
            <b>28</b></td>
            <td width="75" height="60">
            <b>29</b></td>
            <td width="75" height="60">
            <b>30</b></td>
            </tr><tr>
            <td width="75" height="60">
            <b>31</b><hr>Season Pass</td>

            </tr></table>
```

You can change the size and color of the calendar to suit your needs, but that is how it appears in HTML. Make sure to copy and paste the entire code into a Word document so that you can do some editing, and then you'll need to copy and paste it into the **Add HTML** section in Tripod, under **Site Add-Ons**.

To use this code, you'll need to do some editing, but it's not as difficult as it looks.

Notice where the names of the days are? Sunday, Monday, etc? Sunday starts the first column of the calendar, just like a regular calendar would.

Then, after Saturday, there is this bit of code:

```
<td bgcolor="#ccffcc" align="center">
<b>Saturday</b></td>
</tr><tr>
<td width="75" height="60">
<b></b></td>
<td width="75" height="60">
<b></b></td>
<td width="75" height="60">
<b></b></td>
<td width="75" height="60">
<b></b></td>
<td width="75" height="60">
<b></b></td>
<td width="75" height="60">
<b>1</b></td>
<td width="75" height="60">
```

Each **<b></b>** section before the **<b>1</b>** is a blank space on the calendar because the Sunday of this month wasn't the 1st of the month. If it was, you would put the **1** in between the *first* **<b></b>**.

So, the best way to do this is to have a calendar in front of you, count how many blank spaces there are before the 1st of the month, and fill in the HTML accordingly.

You'll also notice:

```
<b>1</b></td>
<td width="75" height="60">
```

```
<b>2</b></td>
</tr><tr>
```

The **</tr><tr>** is the edge of that week on the calendar, so every seven days, or seven **<b></b>**, you will see a **</tr><tr>** to start a new line of the calendar.

If you've been following along, you'll notice that the **</tr>** comes before the **<tr>** That's because it *is* actually ending the column and beginning a new one.

So, when you add a new column break, like on an actual calendar, make sure that you get them in the correct, if backwards, order. When you are changing the days to fit your calendar, you'll find that you might need a new line, so just cut and paste it into the right spot.

After a few tries, you'll see how this works.

You can also change the colors of the calendar and change the starting day of the week, if you want. Just some advice, though, do not delete any part of this code unless you save the master copy. It's exceptionally hard to replicate if the code gets messed up or lost.

Honestly, you'll get an idea of how this code works once you play around with it for a bit. We learned from scratch, all on our own—so trust us, you'll be able to learn it too.

Now, if you want to add an event for certain days, the code will look like this:

```
<td width="75" height="60">
<b>5</b><hr>Ladies League 9:00am</td>
```

Notice that the event, **Ladies League 9:00am**, is placed between the **<hr>** and the **</td>**

Now, to use this code, you'll need to take out all of the events that we've added. You can just leave the space blank where they were, or add new events. We only left them in so that you could see how the code works.

But, notice that you'll also need to remove the <hr> codes. This is the carriage return, or straight line, that separates the event from the date of that event on the calendar. Also, when you add in new events on different days, make sure to add in the **<hr>** to keep the calendar looking right.

A FINAL NOTE ON HTML.

That's all of the basic HTML that we have to offer, and most of which, you'll probably find use for in the building process of your site.

Keep in mind that there are tons of sites on the web that offer bits of code for free. If you go this route, make sure to copy a page and use that page as the "tester" for the code to make sure nothing goes wrong.

With HTML, if something is wrong, it has the potential to mess up that whole page, or your whole site, to the point where you'll have to rebuild it—like we did...

To digress, we actually had this problem with a bit of code that we put into the site footer of Shop Lizards. As you'll remember, the footer is part of every page on the site and, because the code was screwed up it ruined every page on our entire site because we didn't test it first.

Needless to say, the Shop Lizards you see today is the second version, because we made a mistake with HTML, a mistake that we actually knew better than to make.

But as they say, shit happens.

We moved on, grieved a bit, and then rebuilt Shop Lizards. Actually, we like it better now because we truly know the price of making mistakes and we've grown from it.

Hopefully, you'll learn from our mistakes and be cautious but creative in your site building.

Extras.

When someone asks you, 'A penny for your thoughts,' and you put your two cents in, what happens to the other penny?

--George Carlin

In this part...

This is your basic catch-all section where the reference points we felt must be included found a home as well as some great extras and resources.

In this part you'll learn:

How to Upgrade Your Computer: RAM & Video Card, 325-337

Final Checklist, 338

E-Commerce Resources, 339-341

Word University Online Course Information, 342-348
- Testimonials, 345
- Course Certificate, 347

Appendix, 349-353
- Web Address Quick Reference, 349-350
- File Types, 351
- Checklists/Mistakes, 352
- How to Exercises, 353

Index, 354-366

About the Authors, 367

How to Upgrade Your Computer.

It sounds intimidating at first, but upgrading your own computer can save you quite a bit of money and isn't as hard as it sounds. To be honest, the hardest part is often getting the casing off of your computer tower.

Recently we decided to upgrade one of our computers instead of buying a new one because we want to give Vista a bit more time on the market before we switch from XP, and while we made the upgrade, we noticed a few details that weren't included in our installation guides (and they probably aren't in yours either) that will make your life a lot easier.

First, we did a little research. Our computer is a Dell 2400 2.6Ghz with 256MB of RAM and an internal Intel video card (we wanted to upgrade the video card as well because we'll be playing some of the newest games on this computer, but if you aren't concerned about games, just upgrading RAM will vastly improve your computer's overall performance making programs and online videos run faster). You can find out what your computer is by **right** clicking on **My Computer** and selecting **Properties**. The **General** tab will display your current statistics.

To find out what sort of video card you have installed, click the **Hardware** tab, then **Device Manager**. This will take you to a new screen that displays everything installed on your computer. Click on the **Plus** sign next to **Display Adapters** to see the video card you have installed. Go ahead and Disable it now before you take the tower apart by right clicking on it and selecting **Disable**.

The instructions that came with your new video card might say that you have to **uninstall** your old card before continuing. Don't do this, just **disable**, because if the card is part of your motherboard, or is still currently installed on your hard drive, it will just reinstall itself.

So, to make this upgrade, we purchased 2GB of DDR RAM (our computer is only compatible with the DDR and not the newer DDR2—which can be discovered if you look up your computer online) for about $100. Now, you probably have two slots for available RAM, but some computers might have four.

We purchased two 1GB sticks of RAM because we had found in our research online that our computer was expandable to 2GB total, so make sure to look this up online (or call your computer manufacturer or even OfficeMax) before you buy six sticks of memory when you can only use two.

Then we bought a 3D Fusion NVIDIA 256MB DDR video card for around $80. We also purchased a can of Static Guard for $4—because if anything can go wrong, it's the presence of static near a computer! The danger, here, is not that you'll get shocked, but that static electricity can zap your computer and you'll be looking at a dead motherboard. Liberal static management will keep your computer safe.

Then, just to be on the safe side, we wanted to be sure to back up our hard drive. This is an easy enough task with the website MediaMax, http://www.mediamax.com where you can save up to 25GB of files for free. You can create as many accounts as you need, saving up to 25GB of files in each account (or you can upgrade to the paid versions to get more available storage). Once your account is established, all you have to do is select **Go To My Account→click the Go To My Account green button→Upload** to begin uploading files. It takes a little time but the screen will refresh with an upload box.

SINGLE FILE UPLOAD   MULTI-FILE UPLOAD

Download MediaMax XL software for faster uploads, downloads and more!

Drag and Drop files from your computer into the box below.

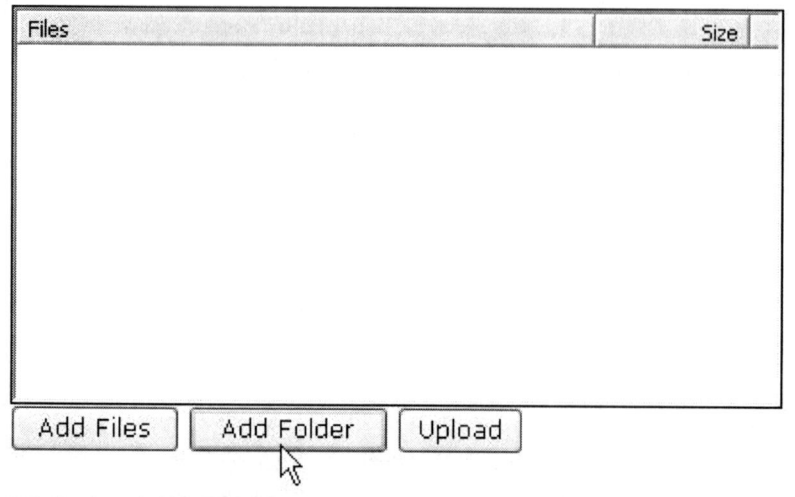

Files	Size

[Add Files]   [Add Folder]   [Upload]

Click the **Add Folder** button or the **Add Files** button to begin. Either option will take you to the files on your computer where you can browse and select the ones you want to save online. When you've selected everything you want to save, click the **Upload** button to continue. MediaMax will add all of your files to your secure online account where you can then access them at any time. Normally, installing RAM or a video card is just about as safe as it can get and will do nothing to harm your computer. However, we've become fans of backing up since our laptop's hard drive died after a plane trip.

To be on the safe side, just back up your important files. Trust us, the one time that you don't will be the one time where something bad or unexpected goes wrong. And, to be honest, backing up your work is always a good habit to get into.

HOW TO ADD RAM TO YOUR COMPUTER.

Tool List:
1. Vacuum with nozzle attachment
2. Can of Static Guard
3. Rubber or latex gloves
4. Phillips screw driver or ¼ in. socket, if needed

Okay, first things first. Get a vacuum ready because when you open up your computer you'll definitely find a lot of dust. Turn off your computer and unplug your power cord (it's okay to leave all other cords plugged in as long as you have room to work—if not, unplug your cords so you can lay your computer on its side).

Then, get your computer to an area where you'll be able to lay it down on its side and liberally spray yourself down with the static guard.

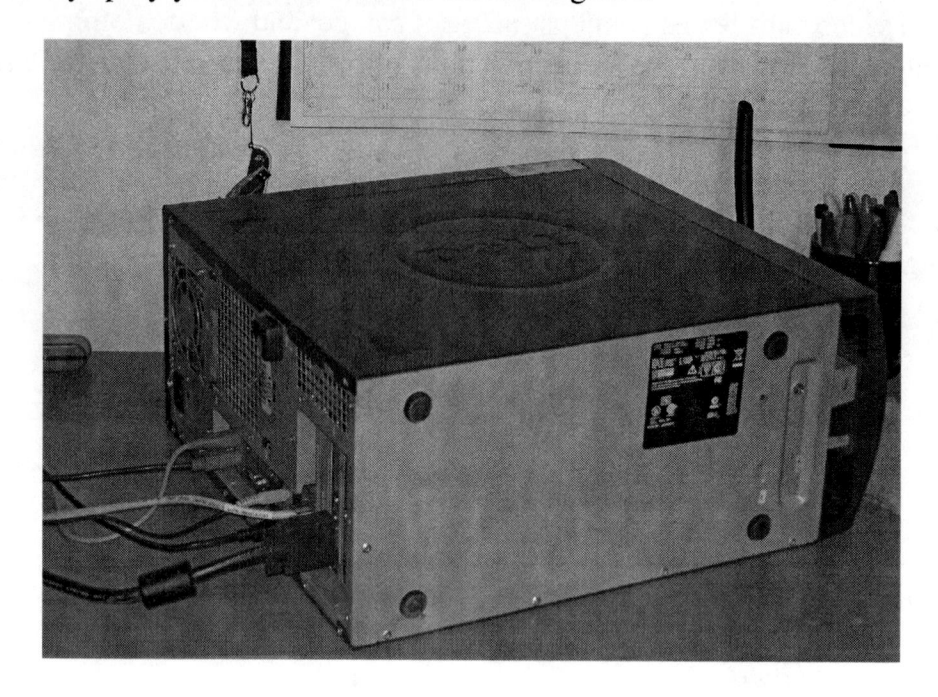

Now, comes the part that requires patience. You have to get your computer tower's casing off. Most times, it comes off on the left side (looking at it from the front) and will slide to the rear. With our Dell, there was actually a huge lever on the back that we had to push to get it to slide properly.

With our older HP, there were a few tiny screws that had to be removed before the casing was able to pull out sideways. Most, however, will slide to the rear, and will have a latch of some sort to make this happen.

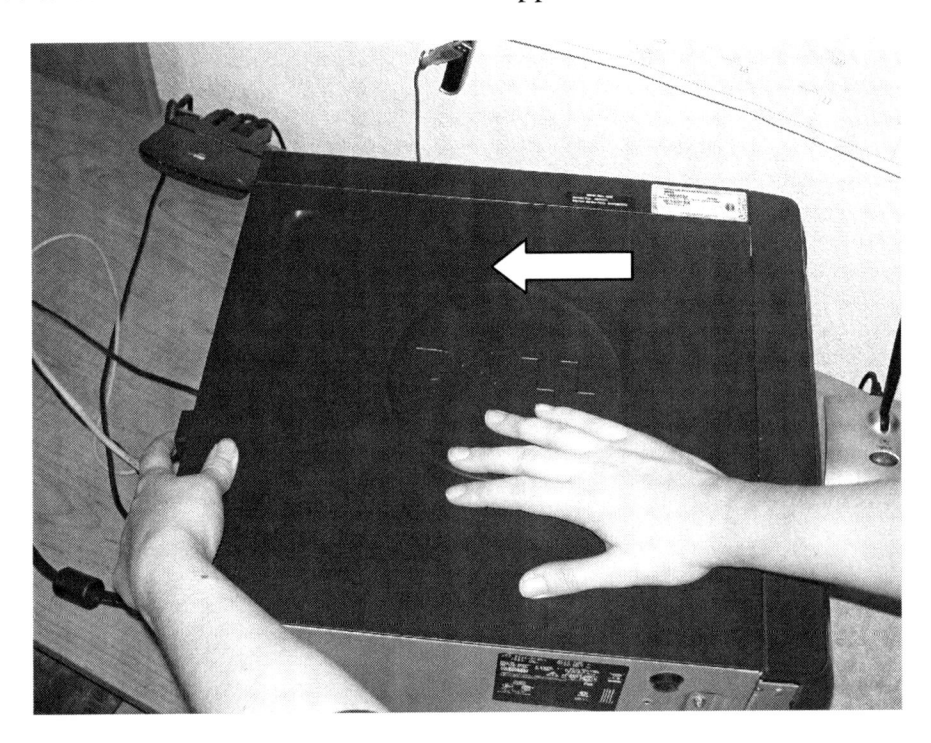

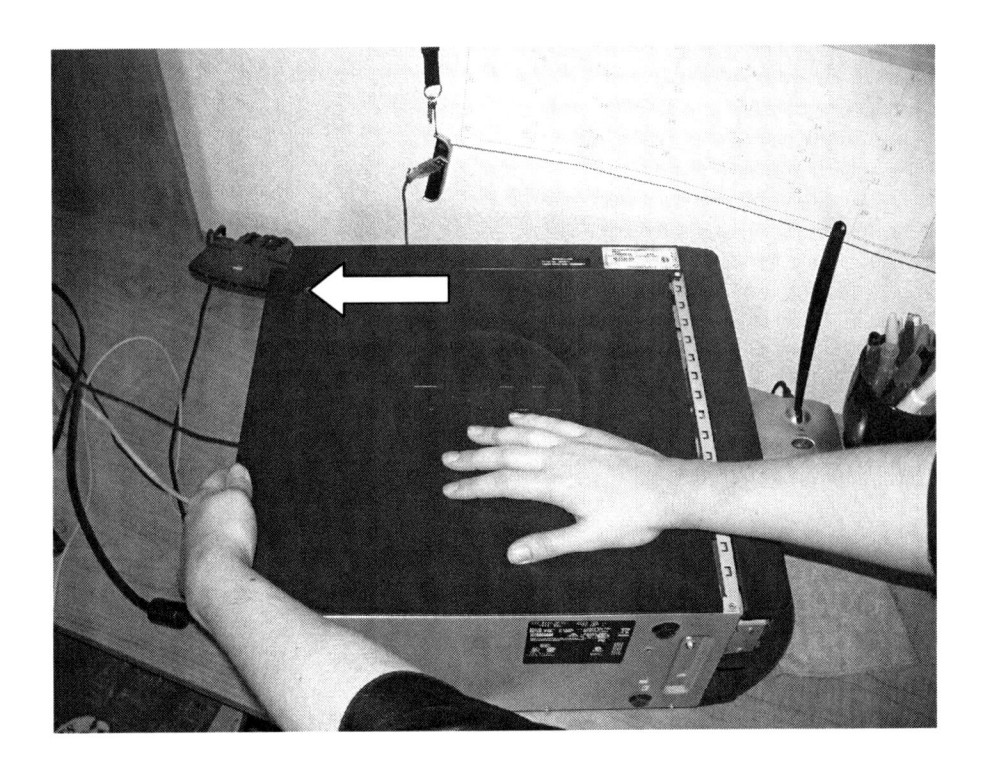

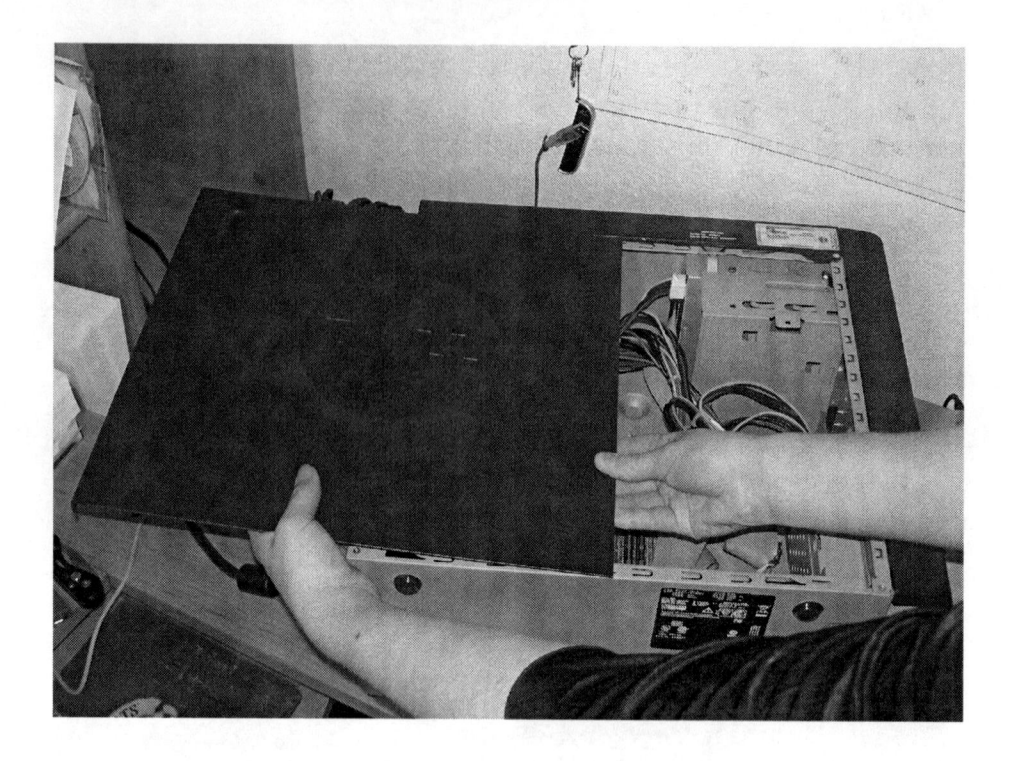

NOTE: This is the hardest part of the installation and requires the most patience because it's often not always easily identifiable as to how the casing comes off—but it will! The thing to keep in mind, here, is to go slowly and try not to use force. You do, after all, want to be able to put the casing back on.

Once you get the casing off, get the vacuum ready. Carefully remove any dust from inside your computer (you'll probably find big globs of it everywhere), then re-spray yourself with the static guard and put on your rubber gloves. Safety first!

Now, you need to take stock of your situation. You'll usually find the RAM near the middle of your computer.

You might have all of your slots full or just one.

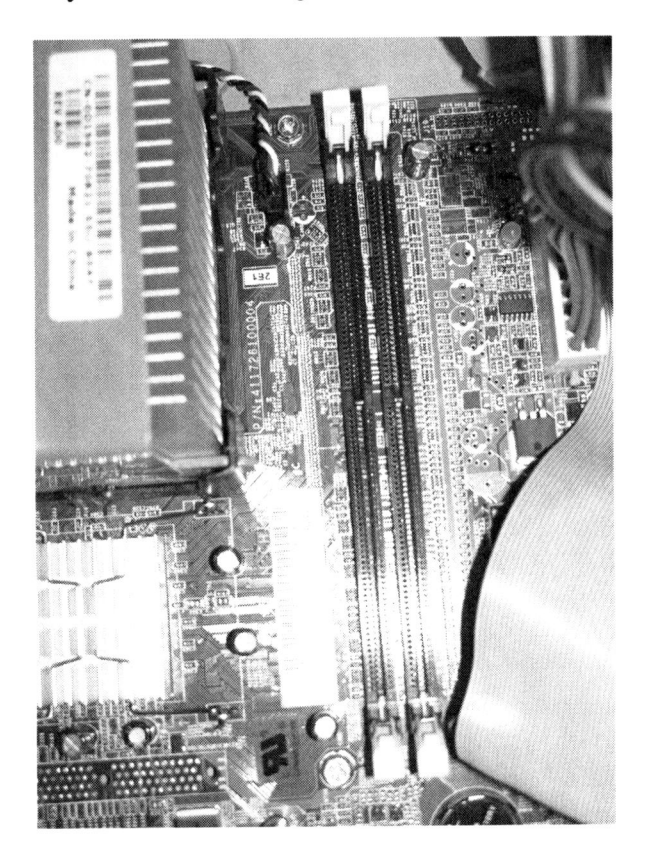

The picture above shows two slots with memory sticks removed.

To remove your old RAM, push the white latch backwards to release it.

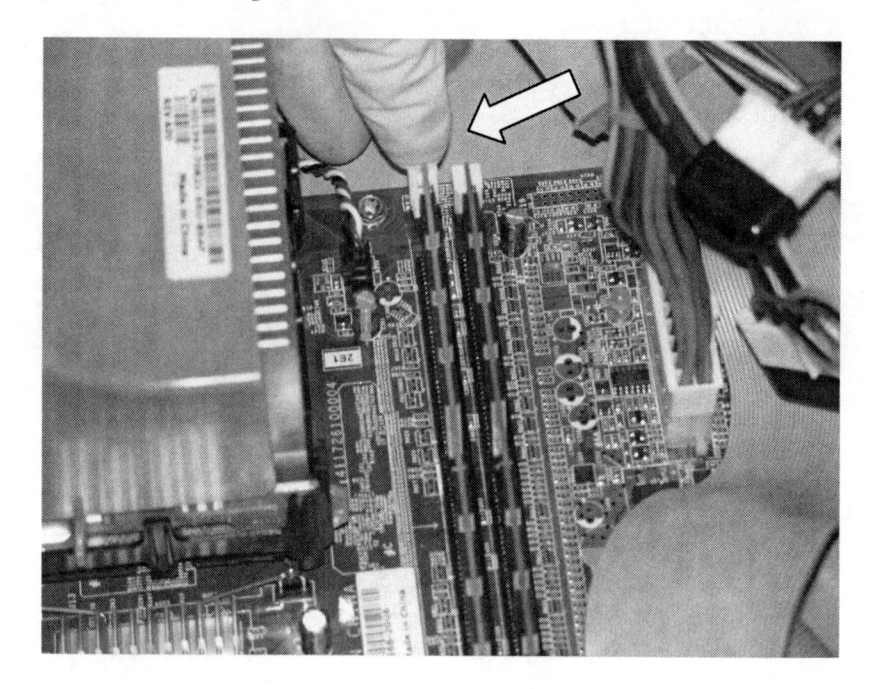

To insert new RAM, carefully slide the sticks into place and re-latch (as you push the sticks in, the latches will snap back on their own, but you may have to re-latch them with your fingers).

We took out our 256MB stick and placed both 1GB sticks into the open slots. Note that most sticks only fit in one way because of the way the slots are made (one may be longer than the other), so line them up and don't try to force them in any other way. Make sure everything is in securely…and that's all you have to do to install RAM!

HOW TO INSTALL YOUR VIDEO CARD.

We found out after we opened our computer tower that the Intel video card didn't occupy any slots and was instead part of the motherboard itself. This means there was nothing for us to remove. This also meant that to install a new card, we'd have to **Disable** the Intel video card instead of **Uninstalling** it once we turned the computer back on (but you can do this before you even shut down your computer). If this is your situation as well, when you follow the instructions for installing a new video card, it may say that you must uninstall any current video cards before continuing, but you computer won't be able to uninstall something that is a permanent fixture! So, come back to the screen in the **Hardware** tab (**right** click on **My Computer→Properties**), click on the **Plus** sign next to **Display Adapters** and **right** click on your video card where you'll be able to select **Disable**. A red "x" will appear next to that video card.

Now, to install a video card, you need to find an open slot near the back of the computer. We have four slots total, one currently has the DSL modem installed (the picture shows us pointing to the new video card installed and the arrow points to our last two open slots with the DSL card in the middle).

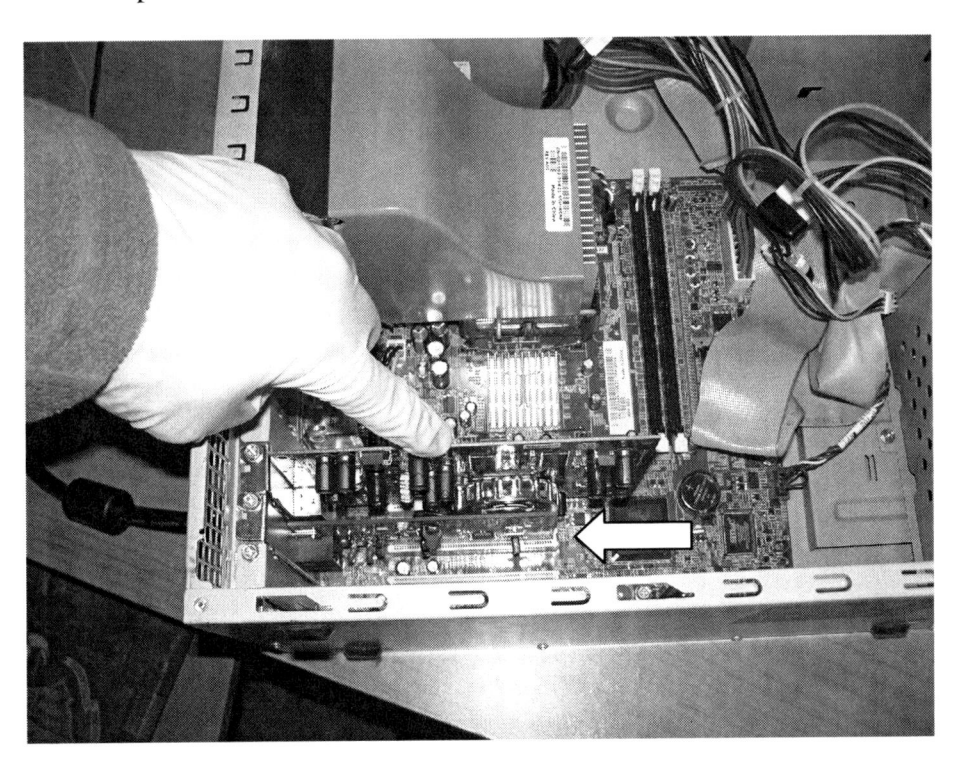

Spray yourself down again with the static guard and then pick any available slot and use a screw driver to remove the screw and the metal dummy plate to make room for your video card. We placed our video card right next to the DSL card.

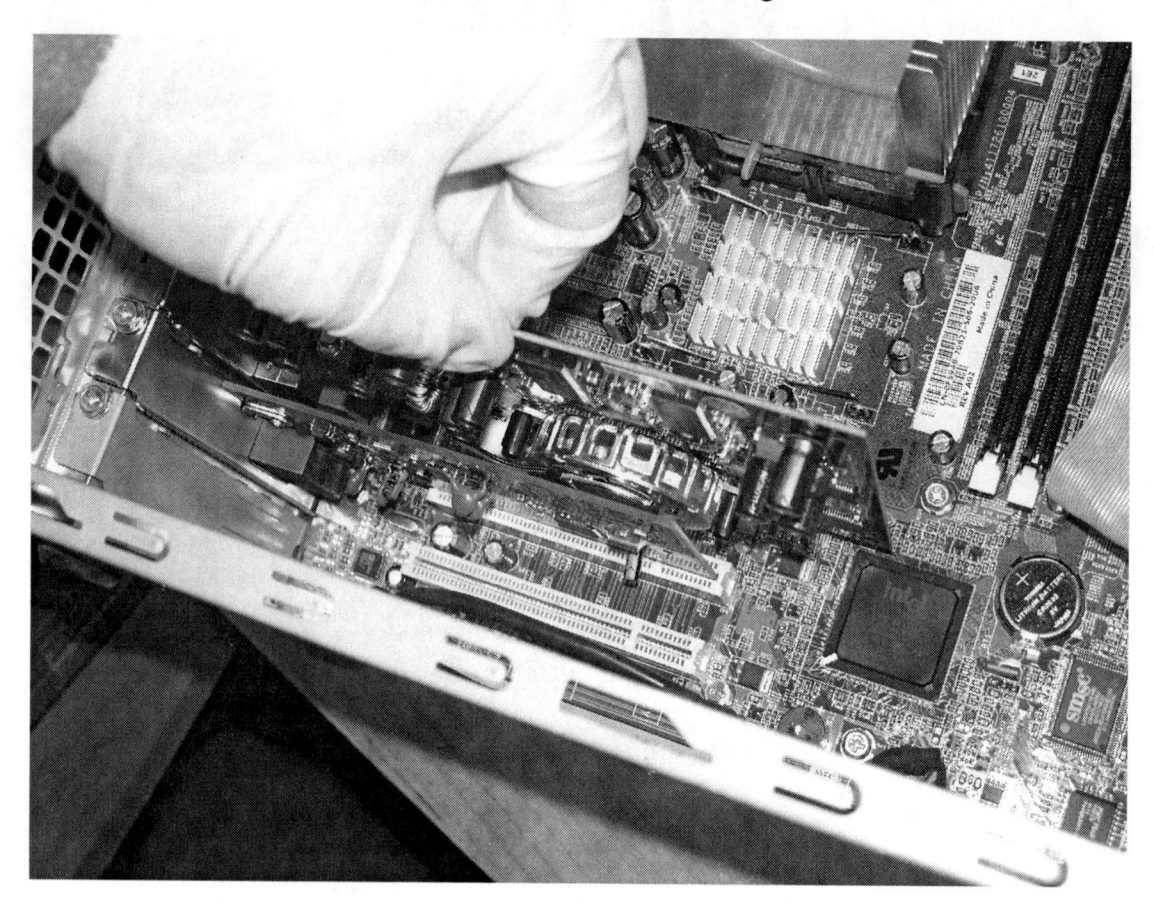

Carefully slide your video card into place, making sure it goes in securely, then replace the screw.

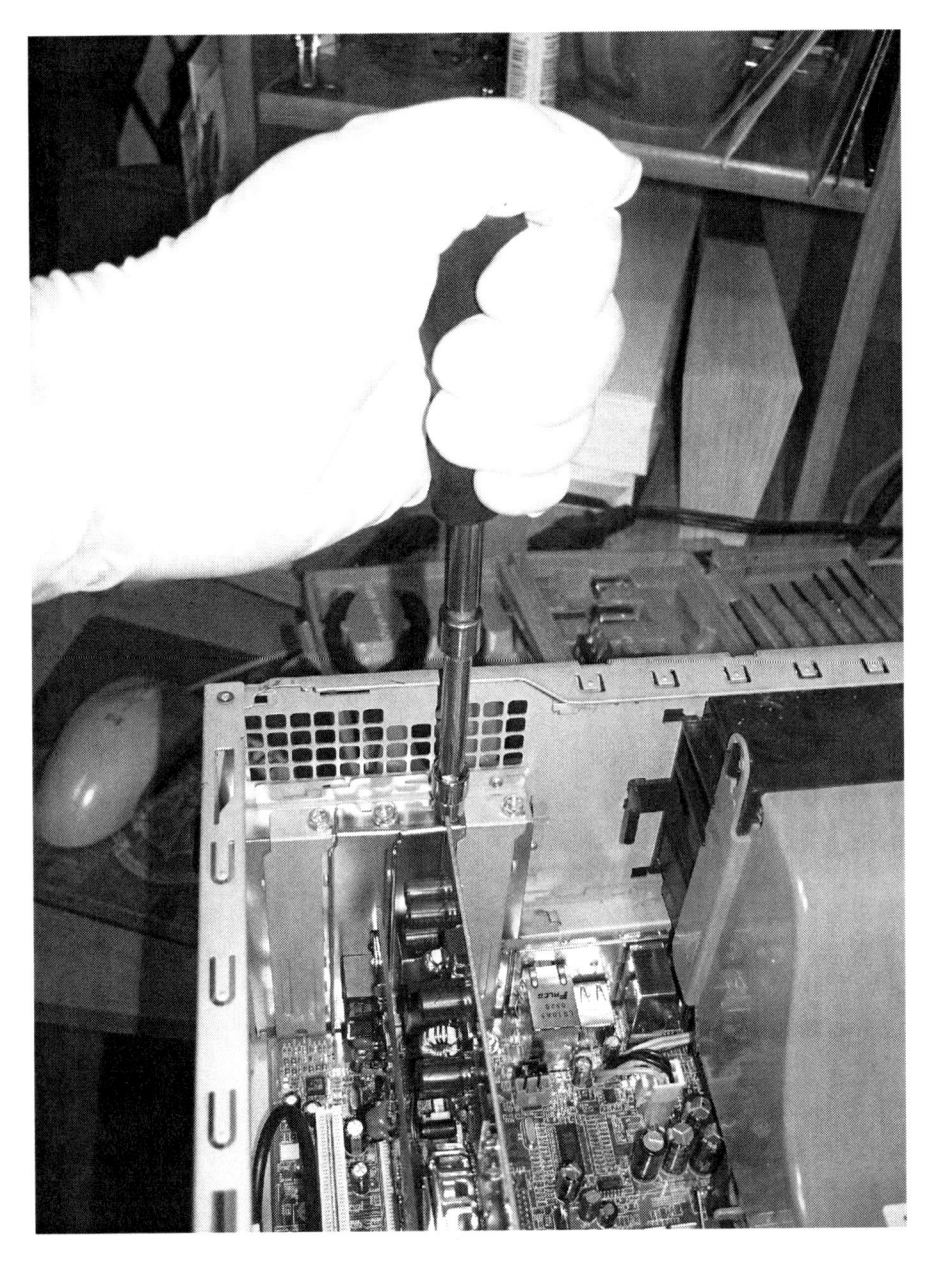

Ours sticks out the back of the computer tower (which is why we needed to remove the dummy plate) and needs to have the monitor plugged in to it once we put the tower casing back on—yours might have this feature as well.

336   *Cyber Gold: Extras*

Once you're done, put your computer's casing back on, plug your monitor cord into your new video card (if yours has a plug on it, shown in the picture below, instead of the old monitor plug), plug your computer back in, and turn it on.

Once your computer comes on, follow the instructions that came with your video card to complete the installation. Again, if you were in the same situation as us, with no video card to remove, then you'll need to make sure you **disable** it before completing the installation for your new card.

Then, go back to **My Computer**, **right** click and select **Properties**. Your new RAM should be displayed on the **General** tab. Click on the **Hardware** tab, click **Device Manager** and click on the **Plus** sign next to **Display Adapters**.

Make sure your old video card has a red "x" next to it and your new one is enabled. It should look something like this:

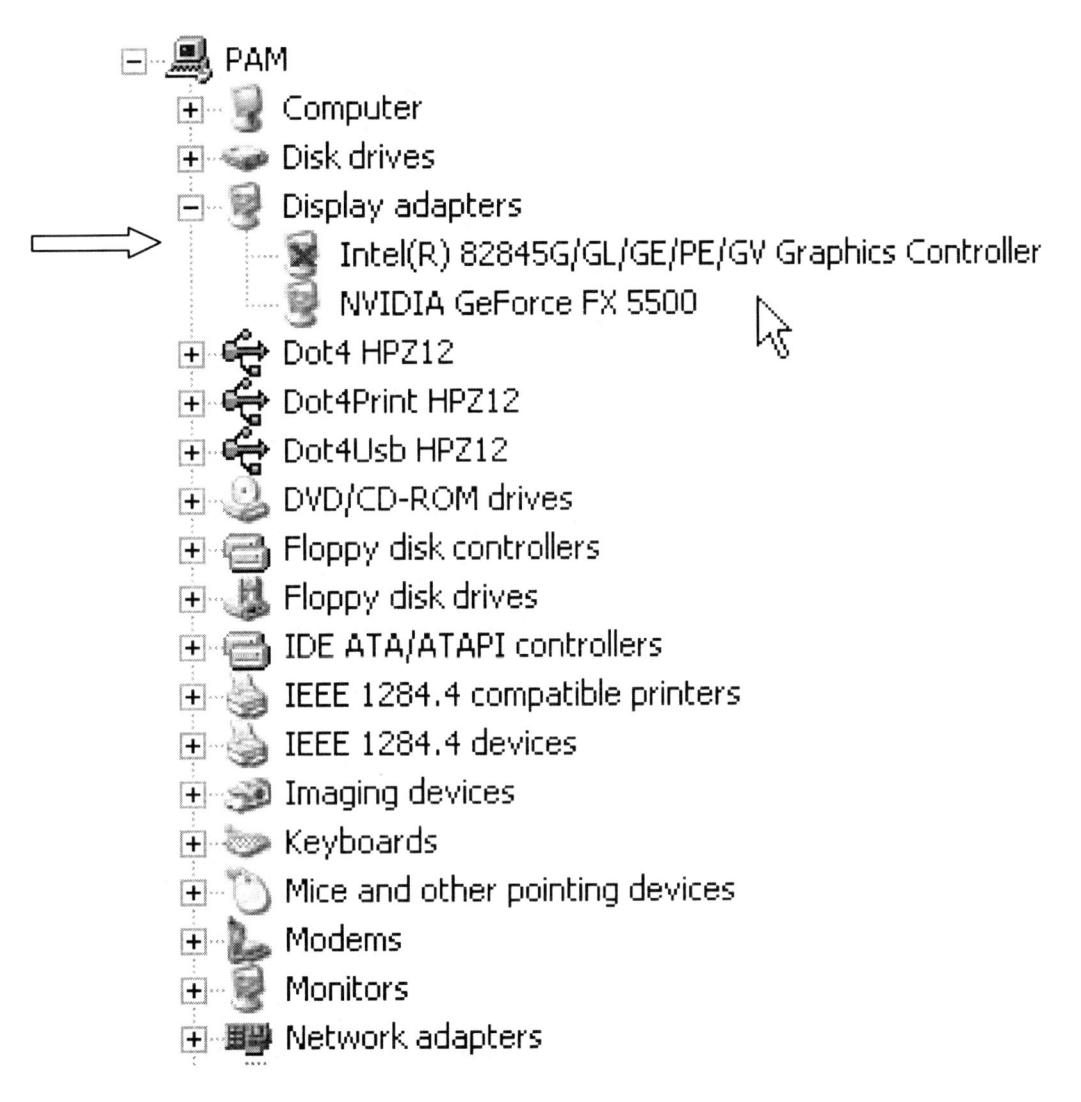

```
PAM
├── Computer
├── Disk drives
├── Display adapters
│   ├── ✗ Intel(R) 82845G/GL/GE/PE/GV Graphics Controller
│   └── NVIDIA GeForce FX 5500
├── Dot4 HPZ12
├── Dot4Print HPZ12
├── Dot4Usb HPZ12
├── DVD/CD-ROM drives
├── Floppy disk controllers
├── Floppy disk drives
├── IDE ATA/ATAPI controllers
├── IEEE 1284.4 compatible printers
├── IEEE 1284.4 devices
├── Imaging devices
├── Keyboards
├── Mice and other pointing devices
├── Modems
├── Monitors
└── Network adapters
```

And that's all you have to do.

Final Checklist.

You should now know how to start a business and build a website that you can be proud of. So, just because we like them, we thought we'd make a final checklist for you, so that you can track your progress.

- ☐ Business name reflective of what you plan to sell
- ☐ Business identity, complete with colors and logo
- ☐ All business licenses required for your state
- ☐ Membership with Tripod and PayPal (Business Account)
- ☐ PO Box
- ☐ Site shell created on Tripod
- ☐ Something to sell on your site (drop shipping, services, etc)
- ☐ List of inventory with prices, shipping costs, and fees known
- ☐ Process for taking orders, including contacting drop shippers, packing items yourself, etc
- ☐ Prepare inventory by gathering pictures and item descriptions
- ☐ Create and build site; with uniform appearance and business colors
- ☐ Publish site and upgrade to Tripod Pro (or upgrade to the Plus plan if you already own a domain name)
- ☐ Fill site with keyword related content to "please" the search engines
- ☐ Site is easy to navigate, and easy to purchase on
- ☐ All meta tags completed, with targeted and researched keywords placed
- ☐ Have required pages, including the Site Map and Privacy Policy
- ☐ Site Map submitted to Google
- ☐ Check site thoroughly for errors, bad links, and typos
- ☐ Have fresh-content generating plan to keep customers coming back
- ☐ Begin writing articles and submitting to article directories
- ☐ Join relevant forums, and create a blog
- ☐ Keep learning!

E-Commerce Resources.

This is our list of resources. A few were not discussed in this guide, but we thought them important enough to make the list—and, you'll find a complete listing of all the web addresses used throughout in the Appendix.

HELPFUL WEBSITES:

Backgrounds Archive. http://www.backgroundsarchive.com Free tileable and full page backgrounds for your website or computer.

CafePress. http://www.cafepress.com Sell your own custom t-shirts and unique gifts, or link it to your new website.

ClickBank. http://www.clickbank.com If you plan on using affiliates, ClickBank has more than 10,000 to choose from and each pay more than 40% commission on sales.

Copyright Services. http://www.copyright.gov/register Copyright your logo.

Entrepreneur Magazine. http://www.entrepreneur.com Informative articles and business plan information.

Employer Identification Number. http://www.irs.gov Get your free EIN number.

Google Sandbox. https://adwords.google.com/select/KeywordToolExternal Offers keyword and meta tag suggestions.

Google Zeitgeist. http://www.google.com/press/zeitgeist.html Check out search trends around the world.

Iwebtool Keyword Lookup. http://www.iwebtool.com/keyword_lookup Free keyword lookup tool.

Iwebtool forum. http://talk.iwebtool.com Free online forum where you can learn and discuss website and design issues.

Keyword Discovery. http://www.keyworddiscovery.com Free keyword lookup tool.

MediaMax. http://www.mediamax.com Store up to 25GB of your files free online.

Network Solutions. http://www.networksolutions.com Use to look up domain names to see which are available before you buy a Pro Account on Tripod.

PDF 995. http://www.pdf995.com Create PDF files (ebooks) from your documents for free.

Rip Off Report. http://www.ripoffreport.com Check for potential scammers.

Small Business Administration. http://www.sba.gov Informative articles and tax information.

PHOTO/DESIGN PROGRAMS:

There are tons of photo and design programs out there, some cost more than others, and some are just plain useless. We've found our favorites, all worth the cost, and all able to perform for specific needs.

- Art Explosion Publisher Pro (for brochures, business cards, and PDF creation)
- Logo Creator (create your logo quickly and easily)
- Photo Impact 12 (best overall for enhancing images and pixel work)

VIRUS & SPYWARE PROTECTION:

If your computer begins acting up, especially while editing on Tripod, most often spyware is the culprit. To deal with this, follow the steps for computer maintenance in Chapter 1. These are the programs that we use:

- Ad-Aware. http://www.adawareresource.com (free)
- Avast Virus Protection. http://www.avast.com/eng/avast_4_home.html (free)
- Defender Pro & Defender Pro Anti Spy ($19 bucks at Wal-Mart)
- PC-Tools Virus Protection. http://www.pctools.com (free)
- Spybot Search and Destroy. http://www.spybot.com/en/download/index.html (free)

PAY PER CLICK (PPC) / ADVERTISING:

Pay Per Click can seem confusing and daunting, at first. The main thing to keep in mind, here, is that your money will only be well spent if you advertise on the search engines themselves—like on Google AdWords or Yahoo Search Marketing.

Google AdWords. https://adwords.google.com (Your source for PPC sponsored listings on Google, minimum bid of .5 cents per click)

Yahoo Search Marketing (used to be owned by Overture). http://searchmarketing.yahoo.com/ (Bid a top 3 position and get sponsored listing in Google, Yahoo, and MSN. Minimum Bid of .10 cents per click)

BOOKS WE RECOMMEND:

Harroch, Richard D. Small Business Kit for Dummies. New Jersey: Wiley Publishing, 1998.

Holden, Greg. Starting an Online Business for Dummies. 4th Ed. New Jersey: Wiley Publishing, 2005.

TRIPOD:

Tripod Extras, 85-86

Tripod Membership Plans, 81-85

Word Partners Ink University

Online Course Information.

The best time to plant a tree is ten years ago, the second best time is now.

--Ancient Chinese Proverb

Welcome Reader!

This past year, we've had an exciting time writing the 2nd Edition of *Cyber Gold,* developing this new online course, and teaching live classes to local students. With all of this newfound experience and overwhelming requests, we decided to produce an online course with detailed videos and instruction that includes solutions to all the little hang-ups and questions of our previous students.

The e-class we have developed is exactly what you need to ensure you are heading in the right direction and will get you the best results in the shortest amount of time. Rest assured, the e-class at Word Partners Ink University is not a long and boring course comprised of hundreds of pages of confusing manuals and fifteen-CD sets that you'll likely never get through. This course is a straight to the point, step by step, actionable program for anyone who wants to implement cutting edge search engine optimization methods to increase their current traffic and income.

You'll have full access to videos for every how to exercise, live personal instruction, as well as a syllabus that you can follow to build your website and business step by step.

We've structured this course in a way that anyone can easily understand and implement with minimal effort and minimal funds. Our course will be delivered on our website via Camtasia videos and downloadable pdf files so that you will be able to watch from the convenience of your own home or office.

You're not alone. Building a website isn't scary, it isn't hard, and you can do it with our online community.

I have had the opportunity to take the "Cyber Gold" course instructed by Pam Mosbrucker and Tobin Alder. It was an excellent course! The instructors were very informative and the textbook is well organized and easy to follow. I started the course almost computer illiterate and had a whole new world opened to me. It was a great experience. I have been able to launch a wonderful website. It was so much fun to learn how to create a website and I look forward to creating more. I am more than satisfied with the "Cyber Gold" program. Thank you.

Website address is: http://www.customrusticmirrorsandfurniture.com.

Thanks so much.

Holly Gerdes

Course Highlights.

- ✓ Detailed, step by step instructional how to videos on:

  - How to find targeted keywords
  - How to find a niche market
  - How to add inventory to your website
  - How to get ranked in the search engines in 24 hours
  - How to optimize your website, complete search engine optimization
  - How to select the perfect domain name
  - How to upload pictures and videos to your website
  - And lots more!

Custom modules tailored to authors, photographers, professionals, church and spiritual groups, and entrepreneurs allowing you to choose the module syllabus best suited for your goals.

- ✓ Forum access to other classmates and instructors
- ✓ Extensive graphic design instruction, including Photoshop and logo design

Weekly search engine optimization and marketing strategy updates.

Fred
"Pam and Tobin were very knowledgeable about the internet and setting up websites, were clear and relevant with their answers and obviously knew what they were talking about. I wish I could attend the class they are getting ready to teach in Idaho. I did get one of the few available copies of their book, though, so that's nice." My website: http://www.dothecarribean.com

Kay Carlson
"Excellent, timely information. Knowledgeable speakers."

Celeste
"Although I'm not quite ready to create my own webpage yet, I have to say I was so impressed with the info presented by Pam and Tobin. Their book *Cyber Gold* would be a wonderful reference to anyone building their site and I plan to recommend it to a few people I know just starting out. Glad I attended."

Catherine D
"Very stimulating speakers and group! Best Friday night I have spent in a long time...."

Toni
"Very informative"

(Live panel discussion in Raleigh, North Carolina, September 2007)

Hi Pam & Tobin,

I met you guys in front of the Walden Bookstore in the mall with my little girl. Just wanted to say I love the book! Wish I would've had it when I started my business a year and a half ago. It's filled with tons of things I need to go back and do, especially on the business side. I was always clueless about the entire dropshipping business. I never knew there were lists of wholesale products out there. That's awesome! (That's something I've always wanted to know!)

BengalDens.com, the local Pocatello Rental Classifieds, is going really well. I've learned a ton about SEO and after a year we are one of the most visited real estate sites in Pocatello. So after designing, debugging and running BengalDens.com I realized I had learned .php and mysql databases.

The combo works really well with Realtors and Property Managers for their home/rental listings. So I realized I had something to offer, now I'm starting an all-in-one Web Design business called MySitesRock.com. I'm also going nation-wide next year with an online rental classifieds, Rentology.com. We'll see how it goes!

Congratulations on your book! If I can help with ANYTHING just let me know. Sorry I can't make it to your class this semester. I'm a stay @ home dad with a wife that travels a ton (it's hard for me to find babysitters, at least during volleyball season)... maybe I can buy you both lunch sometime and pick your brain even more :)

Thanks,
CJ Robinson
BengalDens.com
MySitesRock.com

Word Partners Ink UNIVERSITY

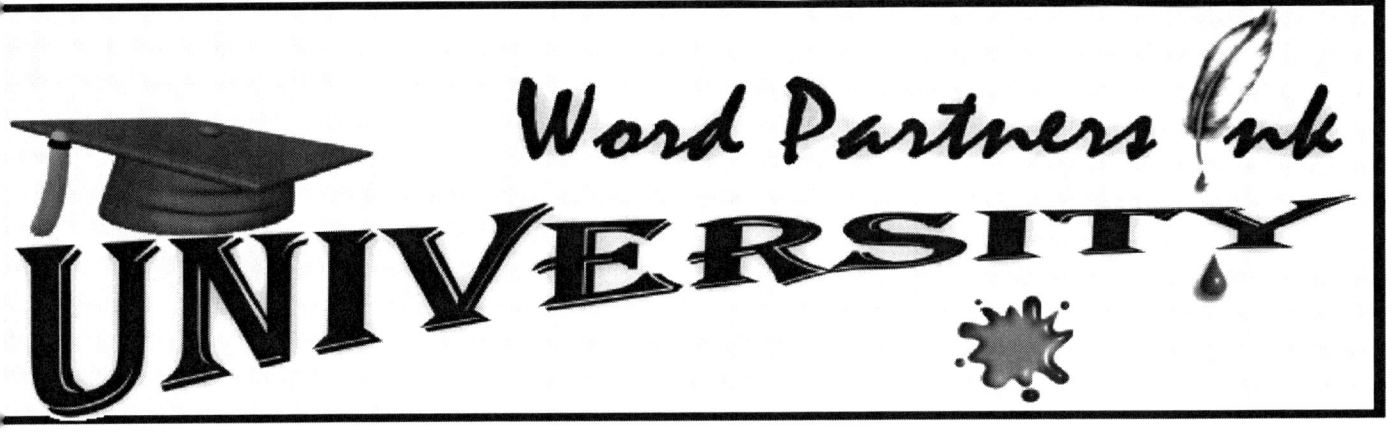

Exclusive Online Course Reservation Form

Thank you so much for purchasing Cyber Gold, 2nd Edition. We are confident, if your desire is to develop a professional and successful online presence, your enrollment will change your life and more easily kick start a successful internet business. Due to our gratitude, we are offering all of our book buyers an exclusive reduced rate for our online course which gives you Member's Only access to detailed, step by step downloadable videos and personal instruction. Plus, you get guaranteed enrollment and 10% off the current online admission fee. Once again, thank you. Pam & Tobin.

Tear off the portion below to make your reservation.

Members Reservation

☐ Yes, Pam and Tobin, count me in. I can't wait to get started with Word Partners Ink University's e-commerce online course giving me access to the exclusive Member's Only area for personal and instantly downloadable video instruction. I want to take advantage of your member's reduced offer because I purchased *Cyber Gold*, 2nd Edition and see for myself how I can produce a fully operational e-commerce business. I'm making a one-time special member's reduced payment. That's 10% off the current online admission fee (see website for pricing details, http://www.smallbusinessonlinecollege.org/freedom.html).

Full Name:_____

Email Address:_____

Mailing Address:_____
(To ensure you receive your password and username if we can't reach you via email)

City:_____ State:_____ Zip:_____

We respect your privacy and we hate spam. We will not sell or share your email address or mailing address with anyone for any reason at any time.

☐ I am enclosing a money order **payable to Word Partners Ink**

To enroll by mail please send this completed form to: Word Partners Ink, PO Box 91, Pocatello, ID 83204

*NOTE: If you would prefer to pay online via PayPal, credit card or debit card, please go to: http://www.smallbusinessonlinecollege.org/freedom.html

Appendix.

WEB ADDRESS QUICK REFERENCE

Ad-Aware, http://www.adawareresource.com 39
Backgrounds Archive, http://www.backgroundsarchive.com see E-Commerce Resources
Big Wood Golf Course, http://bigwooodgolfcourse.tripod.com 73, 148, 316
Blogger, http://www.blogger.com 294
CafePress, http://www.cafepress.com see E-Commerce Resources
Certificate of Assumed Business Name, http://www.idsos.state.id.us/corp/corindex.htm 46
ClickBank, http://www.clickbank.com 44
Copyright, http://www.copyright.gov/register 47, 187
DMOZ, Open Directory Project, http://www.dmoz.org 286, 301
eBay, http://www.ebay.com 33
Employer Identification Number (EIN), http://www.irs.gov 47
Entrepreneur, http://www.entrepreneur.com 75
Google, http://www.google.com 262
Google AdSense, http://www.google.com/adsense 44
Google AdWords, http://adwords.google.com see E-Commerce Resources
Google Rankings, http://www.googlerankings.com 283
Google Robot File Checker, http://www.google.com/webmasters/tools 212
Google Sandbox, https://adwords.google.com/select/KeywordToolExternal see E-Commerce Resources
Google Site Maps, http://www.google.com/webmasters/sitemaps 195, 204, 207
Google Toolbar, http://www.toolbar.google.com 297
Google Zeitgeist, http://www.google.com/press/zeitgeist.html see E-Commerce Resources
Gorank Ontology Tool, http://www.gorank.com/seotools/ontology 269
Internet Explorer updates, http://windowsupdate.microsoft.com and http://www.microsoft.com/windows/ie/downloads/default.mspx 24
Iwebtool Keyword Lookup, (http://www.iwebtool.com/keyword_lookup), 214, 263
Iwebtool Forum, http://talk.iwebtool.com see E-Commerce Resources
Keyword Discovery, http://www.keyworddiscovery.com see E-Commerce Resources
Link Share, http://www.linkshare.com 44, 298
Live Keyword Analysis, http://www.live-keyword-analysis.com 293

Logo Creator, http://www.logocreator.com 73
MediaMax, http://www.mediamax.com see E-Commerce Resources
Network Solutions, http://www.networksolutions.com 45, 70
Open Directory Project, DMOZ, http://www.dmoz.org 286, 301
PayPal, http://www.paypal.com 27, 46, 191, 236
Patents & Trademarks, http://www.uspto.gov/main/trademarks.htm 48, 187
PDF995, http://www.pdf995.com see E-Commerce Resources
Rip Off Report, http://www.ripoffreport.com 55, 62, 218
SEO Book, keyword research, http://tools.seobook.com/keyword-tools/seobook
Shop Lizards, http://www.shoplizards.com 74, 163, 174-176, 196, 199, 205, 238
Small Business Administration, http://www.sba.gov see E-Commerce Resources
Small Business Online College, http://www.smallbusinessonlinecollege.org 74
Spybot Search & Destroy, http://www.spybot.com/en/download/index.html 39
StatCounter, http://www.statcounter.com 150, 167
Trademarks & Patents, http://www.uspto.gov/main/trademarks.htm 48, 187
Tripod, http://www.tripod.com or http://www.tripod.lycos.com 79, 103, 164
Tripod Email, http://webmail.domains.lycos.com 175
Windows updates, http://windowsupdate.microsoft.com and
    http://www.microsoft.com/windows/ie/downloads/default.mspx 24
Word Partners Ink, http://www.wordpartnersink.com 12, 43, 73, 75, 200, 204-
    205, 211, 218, 238, 284, 286, 288, 295, 304
Word Partners Ink University, http://www.smallbusinessonlinecollege.org 74
Yahoo, http://www.yahoo.com 175-176
Yahoo Search Marketing, http://searchmarketing.yahoo.com see E-Commerce
    Resources

SEARCH ENGINES & DIRECTORIES

Ask, http://www.ask.com 302
AOL, http://www.aol.com 302
DogPile, http://www.dogpile.com 302
DMOZ, http://www.dmoz.org 302
EarthLink, http://www.earthlink.net 302
Google, http://www.google.com 302
IWon, http://www.iwon.com 302
MSN, http://www.msn.com 302
MyWay, http://www.myway.com 302
Netscape, http://www.netscape.com 302
Yahoo, http://www.yahoo.com 303

PICTURE FILES

.bmp, 32, 38, 111
.gif, 32, 111, 173, 225
.jpeg, 32, 111, 173
.jpg, 32, 111, 173, 225
.tiff, 32, 38, 111
.zip, 32, 111

SOUND FILE TYPES

.av, 151
.mid, 151
.midi, 151
.mp3, 151
.ra, 151
.rm, 151
.wav, 151

VIDEO FILE TYPES

.avi, 151
.mov, 151
.mpeg, 151
.mpg, 151

FLASH FILE TYPES

Flash, 151, 290
Shockwave, 151

Checklists/Mistakes.

We compiled a list of every checklist that can be found in the book as well as lists of mistakes to avoid, in alphabetical order for easy reference.

CHECKLISTS:

Character allowance (for meta tags, SEO), 280, 286
Drop shipper product/inventory checklist, 227
Final Checklist, 338
Inventory checklist for PayPal buttons, 238-239
Search Engine Optimization Checklist, 286-287
Ten steps to success, 43-52

MISTAKES:

Mistakes for your business & website, 52-60
Mistakes to avoid with search engines, 288-291

How to Exercises.

We compiled a list of every how to exercise that can be found in the book, in alphabetical order for easy reference.

How To:
- Add a Site Map, 204-209
- Add inventory to your site, 225-257
- Add/edit your PayPal button, 236-257
- Add/edit your PayPal button drop-down choices, 253-256
- Add sales tax to your PayPal button, 240, 243
- Add shipping preferences to your PayPal button, 240, 243
- Create a robots.txt file to protect your pages, 210-212
- Find a niche market, 213-217
- Find targeted keywords, 262-270
- Find keyword stems and variations, 268-270
- Gather item (inventory) information, 226-227
- Get the right content on your site, 293-296
- Get ranked in the search engines in 24 hours, 285-286
- Get Verified by Google, 206-210
- Get web bots to crawl your site, 291-293
- Optimize your website (SEO), 272-287
- Place your keywords, 270-272
- Purchase a new computer, 20-23
- Select a domain name, 69-70
- Set your inventory prices, 220-222
- Solve a customer's problem/find your core marketing message, 65-68
- Upgrade your computer: RAM and video card, 325-337
- Upload a picture/photo, 106, 111-120
- Use your keywords, 270-272

Index.

All websites have a full listing with their web addresses in the Appendix. Search engines and directories, file types, checklists, mistakes, and how to exercises can be found there with page numbers as well.

•A•

&Amp;, 280
.av, 151
.avi, 151
Accent:
    Image, 126-128
    Stripe, 129
Account, Tripod, 164-181
Ad-Aware, 39, see Appendix
Add:
    Buttons, 138
    File download, 150-151
    Flash, 150-151
    HTML, 150, 248-249, 251, 309, 319
    Inventory, 225-234
    It here, 139-140, 227
    Link, 138, 145-146
    More Options, 256
    Option fields, 244-245
    Page, 138, 155, 207
    Picture frame, 144
    Picture, 138, 143-145, 231-234, 282
    Sales tax, 240, 243
    Shipping preferences, 240, 243
    Site Map, 204-206
    Sound, 150-151
    Table, 146-148, 225-234

Add:
    Text, 138, 140-143, 309-310
    To Cart, 241-249
    Video, 150-151
Adding more than one picture, 233-234
Adding PayPal buttons, 236-249
Add-Ons, Site, 138, 149-155, 202
Adobe, 24
AdSense, 44
AdWords, see Appendix
Advanced Options, 177-179
Affiliates, 44, 56-58, 298
Alignment of:
    Navigation links, 131-132
    Picture, 143
Alt tags (text), 260, 270-271, 277-282
American Express gift card, 88
Anchor tags, 308-315
ANSI Encoding, 211
AOL (America Online), 302
API key, 284
Apple keyboard, 31
Art Explosion Publisher Pro, see Appendix
Ask, 302-303
AutoTrader.com, 89
Authority links, 285
Avast Virus Protection, 40, Appendix
Avoiding link farms, 298

•B•

.bmp, 32, 38, 111
Back to top link, 312-313
Background color, 123, 128
Bandwidth, 85, 165
Bigwood Golf Course, 73, 148, 316
Blog, 64, 174, 185, 294
Books we recommend, see Appendix
Bottom Area, 134-135
Bottom Area (Runner/Footer):
    Background color, 134
    Background image, 134
    Color for accent stripe, 134
    Height for accent stripe, 134
    Text color, 134
Browse button, 203
Browser page title, 272-274, 280-281, 286
Browsers:
    FireFox, 25, 28-29
    Internet Explorer, 24-25, 28-29, 239
    Netscape, 25, 28-29
    Security settings, 25
Build and edit menu, 176-177, 212
Build your own table, 146-148, 225-234
Building your site, 90-101
Business:
    Account, PayPal, 46, 236
    Colors, 70-72
    Identity, 63-75
    Image, 137
    Logo, 72-74, 115-120
Business:
    Name, 45, 68-69, 87
    Plan, 75
    Tools, 151-155
Buttons:
    Add It Here, 140, 143-147, 149, 227
    Add More Options, 244

Buttons:
    Buy Now, 256-257
    Delete Items, 160
    Done, gray, 112-113
    Drop Down, 244, 253-256, 313-315
    Edit HTML, 309-311
    Edit page, 155
    Edit table, 228
    Edit text, 225, 229-231
    Encryption, 257
    Move Items, 156-158
    Move It Here, 156-158
    PayPal, 238-257
    Rename, 156
    Select a view, 108-110, 113
    Shopping cart, 238-257
    Upload, 203
    View Cart, 245, 248-249

•C•

Caching, 194-195, 294-295
Calendar code, 316-320
Call tag, UPS, 222-223
Caption, 232-234
Census Bureau, 14
Certificate of Assumed Business Name, 46, see Appendix
Change:
    Layout, look, 121-122, 138
    Picture size, 143
Character allowance, 280, 286
Checklist:
    Drop shippers, 227
    Final, 338
    Inventory, PayPal buttons, 238-239
    Search Engine Optimization, 286-287
    Ten steps to success, 43-52

Choose:
    Add to cart button style, 243, 245
    A new design, 121-122
    Your email address, 175-176, 247-248
    View cart button style, 245
Christmas shoppers, 218-219
Click picture for more detail, 232
ClickBank, 44, see Appendix
Clipart and Photo Gallery, 106-115
Colors, 70-72
Confirmation code, 89
Constant Contact, 180
Contact information, 186-187
Content, 49, 58-59, 283, 288-289, 293-296
Content:
    Cool, 150
    Dynamic, 290
    Insufficient/unrelated, 289
    Fresh, 293-296
    Other people's, 296
Cookie-cutter site, 290
Copy:
    Add to Cart button, 248
    Items, 138, 158-160, 235-236
    Page, 155-156
    Site, 178
    Table, 235-236
Copyright, 47-48, 187, see Appendix
Core marketing message, 64-65
Creating inventory table, 225-239
Custom report, view, 167-173
Customer:
    Changes mind, 223-224
    Information, 188-191
    Notes & special instructions, 247

Customizing:
    Buyer's experience, 246
    Payment pages, 185-186, 195, 198, 210-212, 237-238, 245-246, 256-257, 279
    Template, 99-100
Cyber Gold Resources, 75, 284, 286, 288, 295

•D•

Daily Summary, 168-170
Damaged goods, 222-223
Dashboard, 212
Debit MasterCard, 46, 50, 236
Deep crawl, 294
Defender Pro, 25, 38-40
Defender Pro Anti Spy, 40-41
Defragment, 40-41
Delete:
    A photo, 114
    Items, 138, 160
Deluxe Account/plan, 85
Description meta tag, 270, 274-275, 279-282, 286
Desktop Computer, 20-23
Desktop, 35-38, 201, 203
DHL, 219
Directory Report, 169, 173
Disallow, 211
Disk Space, 86, 114, 166, 177, 179
Display:
    An image, 105
    Size, 143
DMOZ, 286, 301-303
DogPile, 302
Domain:
    Email, 167, 175-176
    Forwarding, 83, 200
    Info, 167-174
    Masking, 175
    Report, 168, 170-171
Domain name, 45-46, 69-70, 174

Domestic sales tax, 240, 243
Domestic shipping, 240, 243, 246-247
Donald Trump, 61
Done button, gray, 112, 119
Downloads (security), 24
DreamWeaver, 90
Drop down lists, 253-256, 313-315
Drop ship, 43, 217-225
Drop shippers, 50-51, 56, 217-225, 227
Drop shipper:
    Fees, 220-222
    How to find, 217-219
    Setting prices, 220-222
Drop Ship Source Directory, 43
DSL, 20, 23-24, 110, 172
Duplicates, 114
Dynamic content, 290

•E•

EarthLink, 302
Ebay, 33
Ebooks, 43, 67
E-Commerce resources, 339-341
Edit:
    Design, 96-100
    Navigation, 98-100
    PayPal button, 236-257
    Picture, 143-145, 231-234, 277-279, 282
    Site Add-Ons, 139, 249
    Site title, 105-120
    Table, 146-148, 225-236
    Text, 140-143, 229-231
    Your current design, 96-100
EIN (employer identification number), 47, 54, 217-218, see Appendix
Email address, 175-176, 247-248
Emotions, 67-68
Entrepreneur, 75, see Appendix

Event Gear, 152, 154
Examples (see Appendix, How to Exercises)
Excel, 48
Extensions, 32, 111, 162-163, 280-281
External link, 146, 271-272, 306

•F•

Factory Warranty, 222-223
FAQ info page, 185, 192-193, 222-223
Feedback Gear, 152-154
FedEx, 219
File type, 32, 38, 111, 151, 173, 225, 290
File types:
    Flash, 151, 290
    Sound, 151
    Video, 151
    Word, 31, 230, 273-276, 280
File:
    Download (security), 24
    Extensions, 32, 111, 162-163, 280-281
    Manager, 114, 195, 202-203, 307
    Size Report, 168, 172
    Type Report, 168, 173
Final checklist, see Appendix
FireFox, 25, 28-29
Flash, 151, 290
Font and font size, 131
Footer, 47, 95, 134-135, 187
Frames, 291
Free online games, 64
Free Account/plan, 81-82, 87, 200

•G•

.gif, 32, 111, 173, 225
Gathering item information, 226-227
GB (gigabyte), 21-23
Gear pricing, 152-155
Gear, 152-155
General Summary, 168-169
Getting the right content, 293-296
Getting verified, 206-210
Google, 44, 53, 57, 195-212, 258-303
Google:
    AdSense, 44
    API Key, 284
    Blogger, 294
    Dashboard, 212
    Image search, 278
    Rank checker, 284
    Sandbox, 197, 299
    Site Map text file, 198-204
    Toolbar, 296-297
    Verified, 206-210
Gorank Ontology Tool, 269-270, 279, 281, 286, 289
Gray done button, 112, 119
Guest Gear, 152, 154

•H•

Header, 105-120
Headline Gear, 152, 154
Help, 139, 181
Home Occupation Certificate, 46
Home page, 185
Hosting, 79-80
Hourly Summary, 168, 170
How directories work, 299-303
How search engines work, 299-303
How to:
    Add a Site Map, 204-209
    Add inventory to your site, 225-257

How to:
    Add/Edit PayPal button, 236-257
    Add/Edit PayPal button drop down choices, 253-256
    Add sales tax, 240, 243
    Add shipping preferences, 240, 243
    Create Robots.txt file, 210-212
    Find keyword stems, 268-270
    Find a niche market, 213-217
    Find targeted keywords, 262-270
    Gather item information, 226-227
    Get the right content, 293-296
    Get ranked in 24 hours, 285-286
    Get Verified by Google, 206-210
    Get web bots to crawl, 291-293
    Optimize your website (SEO), 272-287
    Place your keywords, 270-272
    Purchase a new computer, 20-23
    Select a domain name, 69-70
    Set inventory prices, 220-222
    Upgrade your computer, 325-337
    Upload a picture, 111-120
    Use your keywords, 270-272
Horizontal navigation, 98-100
HTML, 150, 251-256, 271, 304-321
HTML:
    Add, 150, 251-256, 271, 304-321
    Basics, 304
    Color value, 125, 129, 133

HTML codes:
    Anchor tag, 308-315
    Back to top link, 312-313
    Bold, 304-305
    Calendar code, 316-320
    Carriage return, 304
    Drop down list, 313-315
    Email link, 306
    External link, 306
    Insert an image, 306-308
    Insert link, 305-315
    Internal link, 142, 306
    Italics, 304
    Line, 304
    Link tags, 305-306
    New paragraph, 304
    Underline, 304

•I•

IBM, 21, 171
IRS, 54
Image:
    Alignment, 143
    Alt Tags, 277-279
    File extensions, 32, 111
    Properties, 117
Indexing of site, 285-286
Info/FAQ page, 185, 192-193
Information (item), 238-239
Input:
    Item ID/number, 238, 241-242
    Item price, 238, 242
    Item weight, 238, 242
    Product name/service, 238, 241
Insert picture, 306-308
Intel Core 2 Duo, 22-23
Interactive features, 150
Internal link, 142, 306
International sales tax, 240, 243
International shipping, 14, 240, 243
Internet Explorer, 19, 24-32, 239, 271

Internet Explorer:
    Options, 25, 29
    Printing, 31
    Privacy, 24-28
    Security, 24-28, 67
    Tab feature, 29-30
Inventory, 217-236
Inventory table, 225-236
Item:
    Description, 230
    Information, 226-227
    Number, 241-242
    Picture, 231-234
    Price, 231
    Title, 229
Iwebtool, 214-217, 263-268, see Appendix
iWon, 302

•J•

.jpeg, 32, 111, 173
.jpg, 32, 111, 173, 225

•K•

Keyboard shortcuts, 31
Keyword:
    Lookup exercise, 262-270
    Placing, 270-272
    Stems/Variations, 268-270
    Targeted, 262-270
    Using, 270-272
Keyword Discovery, 214
Keywords:
    As text links, 271-272
    Meta Tag, 275-277, 280, 282, 286
Kinko's, 73

•L•

Laptop, 22-23, 26
Layout, 102-135
Link:
    External, 142, 146, 271, 306
    Farm, 298
    Gear, 152, 154
    Internal, 142, 306
    Popularity, 289-290
    Reciprocal, 271-272, 298
    Tags, 305-306
Linking pictures, 118-119, 144-146, 231-234
Links, 118-119, 144-146, 231-234, 305-306
Link Share affiliate program, 44, 298
Link to:
    Another web page, 146
    Mail message, 146
    Another page in site, 146
Live, 101
Lock status, 26, 175
Logout, 177, 180-181
Logo, 72-74, 105-120
Logo as Site Title, 105-120
Logo Creator, 73

•M•

.mid, 151
.midi, 151
.mov, 151
.mp3, 151
.mpeg, 151
.mpg, 151
Mac (Apple), 20-21, 31, 171
Macromedia DreamWeaver, 90
Mail message, 146
Main area, 132-133
Main area options:
    Font, 132
    Page title color, 132
    Page title font, 132
    Page title size, 132
    Text color, 132
    Background color, 132
    Background image, 132
Manufacturer's customer service, 222
Mark up percent, 220-223
MasterCard, PayPal, 46, 50, 236
McAfee, 38
Membership Account/plan, 81-85
Memory:
    Active, 21
    Storage, 21
Merchant:
    Account, 46, 236
    Tools, 237
Meta Tags, 58-60, 213-217, 262-286
Microsoft, 24
    Excel, 48
    FrontPage, 81, 90
    Word, 31, 230, 273-276, 280
Mimic (pages), 119
Mistakes, 52-60, 288-291
Mistakes to avoid with search engines, 288-291
Monthly Report, 168-170
Move:
    It here, 156-158
    Items, 156-158
MSN, 291, 299, 302-303
Multi:
    Media, 150-151
    Page template, 93
My Account:
    Bandwidth, 165
    Disk Space, 166
    Domain Email, 175-176
    Domain Info, 174

My Account:
    Membership Info, 173-174
    Traffic Report, 165-174
    Page Views, 166-167
    Website Details, 167
My:
    Account, 165-176
    Computer, 35
    Pictures, 106-114
MyWay, 302

•N•

NASA, 21
Navigation, 98-100, 130-132
Navigation:
    Alignment, 130-132
    Area, 130-131
    Background color, 130-132
    Bar options, 157, 159, 163
    Bar, 98-100, 129, 146, 157, 159, 163
    Font, 130-131
    Height, 130-131
    Horizontal, 98-100
    Links, 130-132
    Size, 130-131
    Vertical, 98-100
Netscape, 25, 28-29, 302
Network Solutions, 45, 70
New content, 293-296
New folder, 36-38
Newsletters, 180
Niche Market, 44-45, 60, 213-217, 262-270
Norton Anti Virus, 24, 38
Notepad program, 198

•O•

OfficeMax, 298
Online:
    Games, 64
    Payments, 236
    Privacy, 25-26
    Security, 24-28, 237
    Success, 52
Operating System Report, 168, 171-172
Optimization (SEO), 272-285
Optimizing:
    Site Map, 195-198
    Website, 272-285
Option fields, 244, 253-256
Organization Report, 168, 171
Other people's content, 293-296
Overwrite, 112, 114
Overwriting duplicates, 114

•P•

Page Rank (PR), 16, 296-297
Page:
    Background, 124-129
    File extensions, 162-163, 280-281
    Properties, 156-160, 163, 272-276, 280
    Views, 165-166
Paint can, 99, 141
Payment Cancelled, 185-186, 210-212, 237-238, 246
Payment Successful, 185-186, 195, 210-212, 237-238, 246, 279
Payments online, 236
PayPal, 27-28, 46-47, 189-191, 236-257

PayPal:
    Add to Cart button, 238-257
    Business Account, 46, 236
    Buy Now button, 256-257
    Buttons, 238-257
    Debit MasterCard, 46, 50, 236
    Fees, 46, 50, 221
    HTML code, 251-256
    Merchant Tools, 237
    Sales tax, 240, 243
    Shipping preferences, 240, 243, 246-247
    View cart button, 245, 248-249
Pay Per Click (PPC), 49, 53, 57, see Appendix
Patents/Trademarks, 48, 187
PC Tools Virus Protection, 40
PDF file, 24, 151
Picture/Photo:
    Add, 143-145, 231-234, 277-279, 282
    Alignment, 143
    Edit, 143-145, 231-234, 277-279, 282
    Frame, 144
    Gallery, 105-115, 143, 145, 177, 180, 202, 227, 231-234, 307
    Link, 118-119, 145-146, 231-234
    Name, 144
    Options, 115-116
    Rename, 114
    Save, 32-38
    Size, 143
    Title/caption, 143-144
Pixels, 116-118, 128
Placing your keywords, 270-272
Planning & Development Services Office, 46
Plus Account/plan, 82-83, 87, 174, 200, 238

PO Box, 46, 186, 224
Poll Gear, 152, 155
Preview, 123
Preview site, 138, 160
Pricing, 55-56, 220-222
Privacy Policy, 188-192
Privacy Policy template, 191-192
Pro Account/plan, 70, 83-84, 87, 108, 153, 165-166, 174, 200, 238
Product descriptions, 226-227, 230
Promote your site, 138, 161
Promotion button, 138, 161
Publish, 101, 138, 160-162, 203, 212
Publish to web:
    Edit your site, 162
    Promote your site, 138, 161
    Rate your Site Builder experience, 162
    View your site, 162
Purchasing computer, 20-23

•Q•

Quick:
    Crawl, 294
    Summary, 168-169
QuickBooks, 222

•R•

.ra, 151
.rm, 151
RAM (random access memory), 21-23, see Appendix
Rank checker, 283-284
Rate your experience, 162
Reciprocal link, 298
Rename picture, 114
Report:
    Directory, 169, 173
    Domain, 168, 170-171
    File Size, 168, 172

Report:
    File Type, 168, 173
    Monthly, 168-170
    Operating System, 168, 171-172
    Organization, 168, 171
    Request, 169, 173
    Search Word, 168, 171
    Status Code, 168, 172
Reset design, 123
Request Report, 169, 173
Required:
    Pages, 185-212
    Site elements, 185-212
Research, niche market, 213-217, 262-270
Restocking fee, 222-224
Return policy, 185, 192-193, 222-223
Returns & Info page, 185, 192-193, 222-223
Rip Off Report, 55, 62, 218-219
RMA (return merchandise authorization), 222-224
Robots.txt file, 210-212, 279
RSS, 296
Runner area, 134-135

•S•

Sales tax, 240, 243
Sandbox, 197, 299
Save picture, 32-38
Scammers, 60-62
SD-RAM, 21
Search engine:
    Breakdown, 302-303
    Rank, 260-262, 285-286
    Submission, 53, 161, 285-286, 301
    Search engines, 288-303
Search Word Report, 168, 171

Security:
    Lock, 24-28, 88
    Settings, 24-28
Select a View Cart button, 245, 248-249
SEO (search engine optimization), 58-59, 258-287
SEO Book (keyword research), 350
Server requests, 169
Setting prices, 220-222
Shipping and handling costs, 219
Shipping and returns, 192-193
Shipping:
    Address (requiring), 246
    Calculator, 240, 243
    Charges, 219, 240
    Companies, 219
    Method, 243
    Preferences, 240, 243, 246-247
Shockwave, 151
Shop Lizards, 74, 163, 174-176, 196, 199, 205, 238
Shopping Cart button, 238-257
Shortcuts, 31
Signature, personal, 136-137
Site Add-Ons:
    Business Tools, 151
    Cool Content, 150
    Flash, 151
    HTML, 150-151
    Interactive Features, 150
    Multimedia, 150-151
    Sound, 151
    Video, 151
Site:
    Add-Ons, 149-151, 180, 202, 309
    Design, 96-100
    Footer, 47, 95, 134-135, 187
    Header, 105-120
    Name, 95
    Promotion, 177, 180

Site:
    Shell, 102-135
    Title position, 126-129, 272-274, 280-281, 286
    Title, 105-120
Site Builder, 103, 177-181
Site Builder:
    Advanced Options, 177-179
    Disk Space, 177, 179
    Help, 177, 181
    Logout, 177, 180-181
    Picture Gallery, 177, 180
    Site Promotion, 177, 180
    Website Tools, 177
Site Map, 193-210
Site Map:
    Adding, 204-206
    Account, 195
    Optimizing, 195-196
    Template, 194
    Text file, 198-204
Site Organizer, 139, 146, 155-160, 162-163, 179, 196, 196, 207-209
Site Organizer:
    File Name, 162-163, 280-281
    Page Properties, 156-160, 163, 272, 274, 276, 280
Small Business Administration, 47
Sound file, 151
Source code, 271
Spam, 55, 60-62, 218, 298
Special offers, 89
Spidering, 285-286
Spreadsheet, 48
Spybot, 39
Spyware, 38-41
StatCounter, 51, 150, 167
Staples, 298
Status Bar, 26, 88
Status Code Report, 168, 172
Step by step optimization, 272-285
Storage space, 21

Subdomain forwarding, 83-86, 175
Subdomains, 83-86, 175
Summary:
    Daily, 168, 170
    Hourly, 168, 170
    Quick, 168-169

•T•

.tiff, 32, 38, 111
Tab bar (Internet Explorer), 29-30
Table:
    Building, 146-148, 225-234
    Copying, 235-236
    Examples, 148
    Gallery, 147, 228
Tab feature (Internet Explorer), 29-30
Targeting visitors, 260-262
Taxes, 47, 54
Template:
    Choices, 97-100, 122
    Designs, 96-100
    Express site, 92
    Multi-page, 92-94
    Thumbnail, 100
Templates, 91-100
Text:
    Add, 140-143, 229-231
    Edit, 140-143, 229-231
    Gear, 152, 155
    View, 108-110
This week only (sales), 231
Thumbnail View, 108-110, 113, 232
Tile image, 127
Title and caption, 143-144
Title:
    Accent image, 126, 128
    Area, 126-128
    Area Background Color, 128-129
    Area Size, 127

Title Tag, 272-274, 280-281, 286
Tools, Site Add-Ons:
    Event Gear, 152, 154
    Feedback Gear, 152, 154
    Guest Gear, 152, 154
    Headline Gear, 152, 154
    Link Gear, 152, 154
    Poll Gear, 152, 155
    Text Gear, 152, 155
Top:
    Accent stripe, 129
    Search engines, 302-303
Tray, 239
Trademarks/Patents, 48, 187
Tripod, 73-74, 79-321
Tripod:
    Blog builder, 294
    Buttons, 103-104, 138-139
    Character allowance, 280, 286
    Deluxe Account/plan, 85
    Domain Name, 174-175
    Extras, 85-86
    Free Account/plan, 81-82, 87, 200
    Gear pricing, 152-155
    Gear, 152-155
    Membership plan, 81-85
    Plus Account/plan, 82-83, 87, 174, 200, 238
    Pro Account/plan, 70, 83-84, 87, 108, 153, 165-166, 174, 200, 238
    RSS, 152-155
    Save feature, 101, 160-161
    Toolbar, 103-104, 138-139
    Upgrade plan, 81-86, 165-166, 174
    Webmaster Account/plan, 84

•U•

Unpublish, 178
Updates (security), 24
Upgrading, 81-86, 165-166, 174
Upload:
    Button, 203, 208
    Images, 106, 111-120
    Pictures, 106, 111-120
    Site Map, 204-209
UPS call tag, 222-224
URL, 146
User statistics (Census Bureau), 14
User agent, 211
Using:
    Frames, 291
    Windows tray, 239
USPS, 219
UTF-8 Encoding, 201

•V•

Vehix.com, 89
Verified by Google, 206-210
Verified by Google:
    Manage site, 210
    Site Map account, 207
    Summary Page, 210
    Upload HTML file option, 208
    Upload Via Button, 203
    Verified button, 210
Verisign, 191
Vertical navigation, 98-100
Video file types, 151
View:
    Cart button, 245, 248-249
    Source code, 271
    Traffic Reports, 165-168
    View Custom Report, 165-173

View Custom Report:
    Daily Summary, 168, 170
    Directory Report, 169, 173
    Domain Report, 168, 170-171
    File Size Report, 168, 172
    File Type Report, 168, 173
    General Summary, 168-169
    Hourly Summary, 168, 170
    Monthly Report, 168-170
    Operating System Report, 168, 171-172
    Organization Report, 168, 171
    Quick Summary, 168-169
    Request Report, 169, 173
    Search Word Report, 168, 171
    Status Code Report, 168, 172
Virus protection, 25, 38-41, see Appendix

•W•

.wav, 151
Wal-Mart, 40, 56, 60, 64
Web:
    Bots, 188, 193-196, 260, 291-300
    Monkey Toolbelt, 176
    Page file name, 196, 199, 237-238, 280-283
Webmaster Account/plan, 84
Website:
    Details, 165, 167
    Encryption, 27
    Host, 79
    Tools, 177

Wholesale price, 55-56, 217-222
Windows, 21-24, 30-31, 171
Windows:
    Tray, 239
    Update, 24
    Vista, 22, 40
    XP, 40
Word:
    Count, 273, 275-276
    Document/file, 31, 230, 273-276, 280
WordPad, 198
Word Partners Ink, 12, 43, 73-75, 200, 204-205, 211, 218, 238, 284, 286, 288, 295, 304
WYSIWYG, 28

•Y•

Yahoo, 175-176, 302-303

•Z•

Zion's Bank, 88
.zip, 32, 111

About the Authors.

Pam Mosbrucker graduated from Idaho State University with a Bachelor of Arts in Creative Writing. She is currently in the process of publishing her first fantasy novel as well as instructing at her alma mater with her co-author Tobin. She is published in the Journal of Geoscience Education and several online magazines. She served in the United States Army until an injury brought her back to Idaho where she found herself the Internet Manager at a prestigious local business. There, she met Tobin and a remarkable friendship and partnership in business emerged.

Tobin Alder graduated from Idaho State University with a degree in Aviation Maintenance Technology and is an FAA A&P aircraft mechanic and former Marine. He is also a licensed pilot, ski instructor, scuba diver, and avid photographer and loves nothing more than an excuse to spend his day in the sky. He's always had the mind for entrepreneurship and decided that since the internet was around to stay that he'd put the computer to good use. Willing to look outside the confines of "that's what everyone does," his ideas transformed a simple information website into three businesses, and thus *Cyber Gold* was born.

Best Wishes,

Pam Mosbrucker & Tobin Alder
Word Partners Ink
wordpartnersink@yahoo.com

P.S. Don't forget to sign up for our FREE monthly SEO e-zine and be sure to check out Word Partners Ink University.

http://www.wordpartnersink.com

http://www.smallbusinessonlinecollege.org

Thoughts & Notes.

Thoughts & Notes.

Thoughts & Notes.

Thoughts & Notes.